Secularity and Science

What Scientists Around the World Really Think About Religion

ELAINE HOWARD ECKLUND
DAVID R. JOHNSON
BRANDON VAIDYANATHAN
KIRSTIN R. W. MATTHEWS
STEVEN W. LEWIS
ROBERT A. THOMSON JR.
DI DI

OXFORD
UNIVERSITY PRESS

OXFORD
UNIVERSITY PRESS

Oxford University Press is a department of the University of Oxford. It furthers the University's objective of excellence in research, scholarship, and education by publishing worldwide. Oxford is a registered trade mark of Oxford University Press in the UK and certain other countries.

Published in the United States of America by Oxford University Press
198 Madison Avenue, New York, NY 10016, United States of America.

Library of Congress Cataloging-in-Publication Data
Data Names: Ecklund, Elaine Howard, author.
Title: Secularity and science : what scientists around the world really think about religion / Elaine Howard Ecklund, David R. Johnson, Brandon Vaidyanathan, Kirstin R. W. Matthews, Steven W. Lewis, Robert A. Thomson Jr., and Di Di.
Description: New York : Oxford University Press, 2019. |
Includes bibliographical references and index.
Identifiers: LCCN 2018040399 (print) | LCCN 2018054937 (ebook) |
ISBN 9780190926762 (updf) | ISBN 9780190926779 (epub) |
ISBN 9780190926755 (hardcover) | ISBN 9780190926786 (online content)
Subjects: LCSH: Religion and science.
Classification: LCC BL240.3 (ebook) | LCC BL240.3 .S43 2019 (print) |
DDC 201/.65—dc23
LC record available at https://lccn.loc.gov/2018040399

9 8 7 6 5 4 3 2 1

Printed by Sheridan Books, Inc., United States of America

Secularity and Science

CONTENTS

Acknowledgments vii

CHAPTER 1 Introduction—Science and Religion Around the World 1

CHAPTER 2 Cases and Concepts 11

CHAPTER 3 United States—The "Problem" of the Public 25

CHAPTER 4 United Kingdom—"New Atheists" and "Dangerous Muslims" 54

CHAPTER 5 France—Assertive Secularism in Science 79

CHAPTER 6 Italy—A Distinctively Catholic Religion and Science 104

CHAPTER 7 Turkey—The Politics of Secular Muslims 125

CHAPTER 8 India—Science and Religion as Intimately Intertwined 145

CHAPTER 9 Hong Kong and Taiwan—A Science-Friendly Christianity and Folk Religion 169

CHAPTER 10 An Integrated Global Science and Religion 194

Appendix A: Detailed Tables 207
Appendix B: Survey and Interview Sampling Procedures and Response Rates 219
Appendix C: Survey Instrument 243
Appendix D: Main Sample Interview Guide 275
Notes 281
References 319
Index 333

ACKNOWLEDGMENTS

We are thankful to the graduate students, postbaccalaureate fellows, postdoctoral fellows, research staff, subcontractors, and others who collected data and contributed in other ways to the Religion among Scientists in International Context study. Special thanks to Nihal Celik, Esther Chan, Jared Peifer, and Eva Shih. In addition, we would like to thank Laura Achenbaum, Bora Akgun, Julie Aldrich, Shelby Allen, Anne Baubert, Dan Bolger, Nikita Desai, Adriana Garcia, Simranjit Khalsa, Elizabeth Korver-Glenn, Samuel Kye, Jing Li, Ard Louis, Jing Luo, Rose Medeiros, Sharan Kaur Mehta, Matteo Pasquali, Pamela Prickett, Esmeralda Sánchez Salazar, Christopher P. Scheitle, Brad Smith, Alexa Solazzo, Ceylan Sonmez, Katherine Sorrell, Courtney Stefancyk, Heather Willrich Stern, Ken Sun, Morena Tartari, Renny Thomas, Cleve V. Tinsley IV, Christian Turquat, Virginia White, and Elisabetta Zaffaroni. We are grateful for Sarah Hamshari's assistance with project management and for Hayley Hemstreet's and Heather Wax's assistance with manuscript editing.

Thank you to the undergraduate students who assisted with the analysis of data: Peter Abraham, Kaitlin Barnes, Gabriela Barrios, Mini Bhattacharya, Lauren Castiglioni, Bonnie Chan, Timothy Chang, Selina Chen, Daniel Cortez, Colton Cox, Jericho Du, Kristian Edosomwan, Parker Eudy, Naomi Fa-Kaji, Emily Flood, Kristin Foringer, Colleen Fugate, Cara Fullerton, Kristin Gagalis, Molly Goldstein, Rachel Gowen, Henry Hancock, John Heo, Jacob Hernandez, Juan Hernandez, Rebecca Hsu, Steve Hu, Sally Huang, Tracy Huynh, Sarah James, Max Katner, Shirin Lakhani, David Liou, Rebecca Loftis, Jena Lopez, Thomas Loughlin, Dylan Mendelson, Martin Miller, Neethi Nayak, Sherry Ning, Anna Ng, Kelsey Pederson, Emily Remirez, Brianne Rodgers, Clara Roberts, Emily Robinson, Sahar Sawani, Jane Su,

Adi Sirkes, Hannah Thalenberg, Madeleine Tibaldi, Amber Tong, Nesibe Tiryakioglu, Sabrina Toppa, Leah Topper, Amol Utrankar, Ruth Wang, Wendy Wu, Jennifer Xiao, Charie Xiong, Vicky Yang, Abraham Younes, Lilly Yu, Catherine Yuh, Yue Zhang, and Melanie Zook.

Portions of the book were reviewed as part of Rice University's Religion and Public Life Program Books in Public Scholarship workshop. We are grateful to Alper Bilgili, Greg Cootsona, Helen Rose Ebaugh, Mahmoud El-Gamal, John H. Evans, Salman Hameed, Jared Peifer, Chantal Saint-Blancat, David Voas, and Fenggang Yang for taking the time to carefully review this work. We thank our editor Cynthia Read for the opportunity to publish this work.

There were two advisory boards convened to advise on matters related to the research. We are grateful for the advice and expertise provided by all members. The Social Sciences Advisory Board included Pierre Bréchon, Helen Rose Ebaugh, Mahmoud El-Gamal, John H. Evans, Prema Kurien, Elizabeth Long, Ipek Martinez, Chantal Saint-Blancat, Laurel Smith-Doerr, David Voas, and Fenggang Yang. The Natural Sciences Advisory Board included Ugo I. Amaldi, Yildiz Bayazitoglu, Gianpaolo Bellini, Francesco Bertola, Paul C. W. Chu, Robert Curl, Cemil Celik, Dipshikha Chakravortty, Dipankar Chatterji, S. Semahat Demir, Aldo Fasolo, Mario Guzzi, Alice S. Huang, Neal Lane, G. Balakrish Nair, Tayfun Ozcelik, Meral Ozguc, Giuliano Francesco Panza, Andrea Pession, Alberto Pimpinelli, C. N. R. Rao, M. R. S. Rao, Lucio Rossi, Bernhard Schrefler, Ajay K. Sood, Annick Suzor-Weiner, Asli Tolun, Paolo Tortora, Fiona Watt, George Wei-Shu Hou, and, informally, Karl M. Ecklund. Their generous service on our advisory boards does not mean that each member of the board has read the book in its entirety or endorses all specific analyses or opinions represented in the book.

Finally, our gratitude to the Templeton World Charity Foundation for funding this research, Grant #TWCF0033/AB14. Special thanks to Andrew Briggs, Dawid Potgieter, Betty Roberts, Marie Souder, Bonnie Poon Zahl, and Andrew Serazin. We received additional support from Rice University and from the Faraday Institute for Science and Religion. We are particularly thankful to Denis Alexander for his initial encouragement of this research. We are also thankful to the Templeton Religion Trust (Grant #TRT0157), for funding related to analysis and writing. Our deepest personal thanks go to our families, specifically Karl and Anika Ecklund; Laura Johnson; Claire Vaidyanathan; Rob, Kaitlin, and Daniel Matthews and Danielle Toussaint; Jillian, Zander, and Aubrey Thomson; and Zhiying Li, Qi'an Di, Peiyu Chen, Li Sun, and Jiasheng Chen, who supported extended periods of travel and work that were necessary to carry out this project. And finally, we thank the many scientists who gave generously of their time to be part of this study.

CHAPTER 1

Introduction

Science and Religion Around the World

ELAINE HOWARD ECKLUND MET ravi, a scientist in a US physics lab, a few years back. Ravi lived his early life in India, where he received much of his formative scientific training. When Ecklund asked him how he thought scientists ought to respond to religious individuals showing up at school board hearings to oppose the exclusive teaching of evolution in public school science classrooms, he paused for a moment, then asked, "Why do you Americans talk so much about conflict between religion and science? We Hindus never talk in these terms. Our religion only makes us think more deeply about the ways that science allows us to see the world of the gods."[1] When we read that interview several years later, we started to wonder what scientists outside the United States think about religion and the relationship between science and religion, and how they might differ from US scientists in their views and attitudes. We have spent the past eight years trying to answer that question.

We know how Richard Dawkins, one of the most famous scientists in the world and the former Professor for the Public Understanding of Science at the University of Oxford, feels about religion. He believes religion and science are never compatible. Millions of people—not just in the United Kingdom, his native land but also around the world—have read his book *The God Delusion*, which asserts belief in God is irrational and religion is harmful. We also know how Francis Collins, director of the US National Institutes of Health, feels about religion. In *The Language of God* he argues that science is completely compatible with his Christian faith and people do not need to choose between science and God. But what about scientists who aren't famous and don't have the same public platform as Dawkins and

Collins? How do different ranks of scientists in different countries and different disciplines really think about religion and the relationships among science, faith, and God? Until now, the answer to this question has been: We do not know.

Why should we care what scientists in different national contexts think about the religion–science interface? In most countries, religion influences the transmission and public acceptance of science. In the United States, we see debates between science and religion over issues such as the teaching of evolution in public schools, climate change, and human embryonic stem cell research. Battles over how evolution is taught have also emerged in Asia, and there has been public controversy in India over the proposed introduction of astrology into the science curriculum. The European Union has witnessed a resurgence in religious opposition to scientific research, and public leaders in the United Kingdom worry that a recent influx of Muslim immigrants may pose unique religiously based challenges to science. Debates about the proper relationship between science and religion are under the glare of a global spotlight—and scientists are often at the center of these debates.[2]

As Ecklund and our colleague Elizabeth Long explain in an article they wrote for *Sociology of Religion*:[3]

> Scholars and public intellectuals almost uniformly perceive scientists as the carriers of a secularist impulse, a group responsible for building the modern research university and undermining religious authority by their success in deciphering the mysteries of the natural order without recourse to supernatural aid or guidance.[4]

Scientists have long been viewed as strong carriers of the process of secularization,[5] and building on the social thinker Max Weber's ideas, scholars have assumed a linear relationship between science and secularization regardless of differences in national culture and science infrastructure.[6] But research looking only for secularization (or lack thereof) among scientists has major blind spots. It ignores the religious life histories of scientists and the various ways they might use religion or spirituality, whether or not they are religious in a conventional sense.

There is good reason to believe that the relationship scientists have with religion is more complex than a linear version of secularism would predict. Ecklund's previous work[7] surveying US natural and social scientists revealed that nearly 50 percent of scientists in the United States who work at top research universities have some form of a religious identity, though it is often very different in character from the religious identities found among the general public. In addition, she found that more than 20 percent of *atheist* scientists consider themselves spiritual to some extent. (She calls this group "spiritual atheists.") There have been other studies of what scientists think about religion. Like Ecklund's earlier work, these studies have largely been based in the West, conducted mainly among US and UK scientists. The psychologist James Leuba, for example, conducted surveys in 1916 and 1934[8] on the attitudes of American scientists toward Christian belief—defined as participation in Christian worship and acceptance of the Christian theology of life after death. He discovered that these scientists were less likely than the general US public to believe in God, and the most successful scientists were the least likely to be religiously involved. But those studies and others like them were conducted years ago.[9] We wanted to look at what modern-day, multicountry research could tell us about the religious beliefs, practices, and attitudes of scientists in different national contexts.

Before we conducted our research, it was unknown, for example, how the religious character of a nation—such as whether or not the population is highly religious, the presence or absence of state religions, or varying levels of secularity—influences the country's scientific enterprise.[10] There was also little knowledge of the factors that influence how scientists think about religion or how their religious views are changing the character of the sciences. Without such analyses, we can only claim that scientists are relatively nonreligious and assume that science made them so. We cannot accurately understand the social variables that influence religiosity and how these differ among scientific disciplines and national contexts.

From a scholarly perspective, we reasoned that our research examining the beliefs of scientists would provide insight into the major theoretical issues related to religious change and the impact of science on religion—and religion on science—in different national contexts. Our goal was to understand how science is related to ideas about secularization, or the decline of religion's vitality and influence, among scientists and societies. For policy makers and the general public, our research would reveal how national ideologies and policies related to religion affect scientists' work, and how this in turn might affect the way science is presented and implemented in their nations. We also wanted our research to increase understanding of how the personal religious views of scientists can shape their practice, dissemination, and interpretation of science, as well as how their scientific work can shape their religious views. Ultimately, where there is conflict between science and religion, we wanted our research to illuminate the root of this conflict. Does science destroy religious belief and authority? Does increased commitment to science really lead to decreased commitment to religion? How do views on religion affect how scientists approach research, teaching, and interactions with their colleagues, students, and the public? How many scientists see conflict between science and faith? Are there ways that scientists and religious communities can work together for the common good?

To answer these questions, we took a distinctively sociological approach. We completed the most comprehensive cross-national study of scientists' attitudes toward religion ever undertaken. We surveyed more than 20,000 scientists in countries representing both Western and Eastern scientific and religious contexts.[11] We traveled to France, Hong Kong, India, Italy, Taiwan, Turkey, and the United Kingdom to study junior and senior biologists and physicists at universities and research institutes. Then we came back to the United States, where we studied U.S. scientists again.

Examining what scientists in different national contexts think about religion is vitally important because it helps us understand both the local and global nature of the relationship between science and religion, and the globalization of science more generally. Do scientists, regardless of where they live and work, all think that science and rationalism will dispel and replace the truth claims of religion and lead to secularism? Or do their ideas about the science and religion relationship depend heavily on their local environment? When it comes to their views on religion, do scientists think like scientists in other countries, or are they more likely to share the beliefs of the general population around them? How does the local religious climate affect how they view the relationship between science and religion? Does science have a personally secularizing effect on scientists? Which background, identity, and cultural factors (things like gender, race, ethnicity, and immigrant status, for example) shape the attitudes scientists have toward religion? What are the conditions under which scientists—even those who consider themselves secular—encounter, respond to, and use religion in the context of their daily lives and work?

Our survey gave us a broad view of how scientists think about religion. Then, to dive more deeply into the beliefs and attitudes of these scientists in their own terms, we conducted in-depth interviews with more than 600 of them. A detailed discussion of how we went about collecting the data is included at the back of the book in a methodological appendix. There, you will also find our survey guide and a version of the in-depth interview guide we used. In addition you will find an appendix of supplementary statistical tables, which correspond to each chapter.

In Chapter 2, we provide a rationale for why we examine scientists in the particular disciplines of biology and physics, as well as why we chose to study what scientists think about religion in the particular national contexts we selected. We also provide a more thorough treatment of how we measure religion. In particular, we see ourselves as studying three aspects of religion: (1) belief and identity, (2) religion in the workplace, and (3) religion in lifestyles and private lives (where we find religion affecting even some atheist scientists). Differences in religion and science infrastructure in each region motivated comparison of these cases. Some countries have established national religions, some have pluralistic contexts that include traditions emphasizing literalism, and some have long-standing histories of conflict between religion and science. Simultaneously, some countries are at the core of the global science infrastructure and attract religious minorities from around the world (in the United States and the United Kingdom, for example, nearly half of the scientists originate from other countries, often bringing their religious traditions with them), while other countries have less developed infrastructures and science workforces that are more or less culturally and religiously homogeneous. The contours of the relationship between science and religion, and how scientists view it, should vary from region to region in distinctive ways. International comparison anticipates such variation and helps us identify *how*, and in some instances *why*, such variation occurs. It is important that we stress the *narrowness* of our comparisons in this work: We see these eight nations and regions as merely a starting point for studying scientists' religious beliefs and attitudes in a global and more complete way. Our study does not examine how scientists from all the world's countries and religions think about science. Rather, the goal of our study was to examine nations and regions that would allow us—in a scholarly space where little international comparative work exists—to begin to expand our understanding of how scientists in different contexts see religion.

In the West, we chose to study scientists in the United States, the United Kingdom, France, and Italy. Europe, on the whole, is more secular than the United States across several measures, including public religion and personal religious beliefs and identities,[12] and many prominent European scholars are quite outspoken when it comes to their views on the conflict between science and religion.[13] Few other studies (and no recent ones) have examined the religious beliefs, identities, and practices of scientists across different European national contexts. In the United States, a nation marked by "freedom of religion," scientists are more personally religious than scientists in other Western nations tend to be. Yet, as might be expected, they are significantly less religious than the general US population. We also find that the makeup of the scientific community in the United States is different from other nations we studied in that religious minorities, such as Jews, Muslims, and Hindus, are considerably overrepresented relative to their share of the general US population. Among scientists in the United States, we find what we might call "soft secularism": For the most part, scientists believe science and religion should be kept separate and government should be secular, but they are not actively hostile to religion. Thus, we were surprised to see more conflict between scientists and religious believers in the United States than we see in other countries. This is likely because the United States has a large religious population—in particular, a large conservative, politically involved, Christian population—and many scientists (whether or not this perspective is completely accurate) see these religious individuals as hostile to science, particularly evolution.

In the United Kingdom, changing demographics have influenced how many scientists talk about the relationship between science and religion. Immigrants, in particular, are changing the religious landscape with their faith traditions. While the United Kingdom is one of the most secular countries we studied, 52 percent of people in the United Kingdom are worried about rising Islamic extremism, according to a 2015 Pew Research Center survey.[14] We found more "outsider" antagonism in the United Kingdom than in countries that are more religiously homogeneous. Yet we also found more atheist scientists who identify with a religion than we did in the other nations we studied, and that a majority of scientists in the United Kingdom think there are basic truths in many religions. Scientists in the United Kingdom seem remarkably friendly to the value of religion—or at least *certain* religions—in society.

The constitution of France defines the country as secular, but the French approach to secularism is different from what we observe in the United Kingdom. Secularism in France is based on the concept of *laïcité*, or freedom from religion. Political scientist Ahmet Kuru describes France's ideology as "assertive secularism,"[15] in which the state plays an active role in excluding religion from the public sphere, thereby confining it to the private domain. The assertive secularism of France is omnipresent among French scientists, which has a particular impact on how French scientists view religious believers (specifically Muslims). Nearly 76 percent of these scientists consider themselves either agnostic or atheist, and only 33 percent identify with a religion, one of the lowest proportions among the national samples of scientists we studied.

Italy, on the other hand, appears to be an exception to the idea that Western Europe exemplifies the classical model of secularization. Religious affiliation and belief are still strong and widespread in the country, the home of the Roman Catholic Church. According to sociologist Franco Garelli, Italy exhibits a distinctive "version of religious modernity" that is for the most part a "flexible, easygoing, selective, 'made to measure'" Catholicism.[16] While being Italian is generally synonymous with being Catholic, it is, for most Italians, a cultural identity; they do not actively practice their faith and adherence is only nominal. As we heard over and over in different variations: "Everyone's Catholic. And nobody cares." There doesn't seem to be a religious public that antagonizes segments of the scientific community, nor is there a large immigrant population that creates challenges or tensions within the religious sphere or between science and religion. Evolution, which the Church supports, is not a highly controversial issue in Italy.[17] Generally speaking, religion does not seem to be an issue for Italian scientists—religion is even pervasive inside the scientific community—though, interestingly, a number of Italian scientists told us they believe scientists in Italy who are part of certain Catholic groups can more easily gain access to funding, jobs, and other opportunities because of their religious network.

We then moved to Turkey, a nation that hangs between Europe and the Middle East. Turkish scientists are more likely to identify as religious than are scientists in most of the other nations we studied, and by several measures they are nearly as religious as the general Turkish population, yet they may not personally consider themselves religious. Turkey was established as a secular republic modeled after France, but in light of recent developments, including the ascendency of a religiously conservative government that is trying to insert religious values into education and suppress traditional academic freedoms, scientists in Turkey are deeply concerned about the impact of a certain form of politicized Islam on their developing science infrastructure.

In the Asian countries and regions of India, Hong Kong, and Taiwan, we found a grassroots religiosity and a renewed commitment by scholars to study religion in the midst of a developing—and, in some cases, burgeoning— science infrastructure. India is unique among the nations we studied in that the country's scientists are more religiously affiliated than the general Indian population: 79 percent of Indian scientists identify as Hindu, compared with 72 percent of the general public, and most of the remaining scientists are committed to another religious tradition, such as Islam or Christianity. Even some atheist Indian scientists consider themselves religious. Yet, the Indian scientists we interviewed were hesitant to make claims about religion or even define religion as a concept, and they had a difficult time articulating their thoughts on religion. We believe this is because religion is so pervasive that it almost goes unnoticed. In fact, Indian scientists often connect religion to their scientific work without seeming to notice. To many Indian scientists, the idea of inherent conflict between science and religion is a Western invention.

In both Taiwan and Hong Kong, we also found scientists are more religious than the general population, though nonaffiliation is relatively high in Hong Kong, where nearly 70 percent of both scientists and the general population are religiously unaffiliated. (In Taiwan, only 43 percent of scientists are religiously unaffiliated, compared with 22 percent of the general population.) Both regions also have a residual history of Christianity in their education system. In Hong Kong, many scientists talked about attending schools founded by Christians, and several scholars said they believe Christians still control the school boards, science education, and research funding. Scientists we interviewed in Hong Kong also mentioned that in attending Christian churches, they are likely to meet faculty and administrators in the sciences.[18]

We chose to study scientists in the United States, the United Kingdom, France, Italy, Turkey, India, Hong Kong, and Taiwan because each of these countries and regions exhibits distinctive religious characteristics and thus contributes a unique outlook on the relationship between science and religion. From the stories of scientists in these nations, it is apparent that a variety of conditions and conceptions influence how they view religion and its relationship to their work and field. Based on our findings, *Secularity and Science* makes four big claims:

1. *Around the world, there are more religious scientists than we might think.* The scientific community is more religious than many people believe. When we examine the religious characteristics of the scientific community on a global scale, we find that a significant proportion of scientists can be characterized as having religious identities, practices, or beliefs. In India, Italy, Taiwan, and Turkey, a majority of scientists identify with some religious affiliation. In all the other regions we studied, approximately one-third of scientists are religiously affiliated. Of course, religious belonging does not necessarily translate into believing and practicing; in some contexts and under certain conditions, scientists who are religiously affiliated can be seen as simply following a cultural tradition without personal meaning or carrying the residue of religious socialization during adolescence. In India, Italy, Taiwan, and Turkey—the same places where a majority of scientists say they belong to a religion—more than half of scientists identify as at least "slightly religious." Religious scientists are in the minority in France, Hong Kong, the United States, and the United Kingdom. While religious affiliation tends to be higher than levels of belief and practice, nontrivial proportions of scientists around the world practice their religion and believe in God or a

god. About 10 percent of scientists in the United States and United Kingdom, one-quarter of scientists in India, and two-thirds of scientists in Turkey have "no doubt" that God exists. A substantial minority of scientists across these national contexts pray and attend religious services regularly. Religious affiliation and belief can seem much less prevalent in the scientific community than they are because few scientists discuss their religious or spiritual views with colleagues. Scientists we met in the eight regions we studied frequently noted they were not aware of any religious colleagues, and when we asked scientists who took our survey to estimate the proportion of scientists in their department or institution who were personally religious, they consistently underestimated.

2. *Scientists—even some atheist scientists—see spirituality in science.* Especially in Western contexts, we found segments of nonreligious or atheist scientists who see spirituality in science. These scientists sometimes describe a "science-consistent spirituality" that they use to approach questions of meaning and purpose. Furthermore, substantial minorities of atheists and agnostics identified as spiritual but not religious in most regions. And nearly one in ten atheist scientists in the United States, India, and France identified this way. This spirituality—sometimes described in their own terms through notions like awe, beauty, and wonder, found in the experience of discovery in science—is seen as wholly different from conventional religion (of course having a sense of awe and wonder does not always equal spirituality for atheist scientists).

3. *The conflict perspective on science and religion is an invention of the West.* We find that the idea that science and religion are inherently in conflict is mainly a Western paradigm. When we talk with scientists around the world, we see most have a different view of the relationship between science and religion that has an impact on how religion interacts with their scientific work. The United States, the United Kingdom, and France are the only nations in our study in which support for the conflict perspective approaches one-third of scientists. In the eight regions we examined, the prevailing view of the relationship between science and religion among scientists is one of independence—the notion that science and religion refer to different aspects of reality. In most regions, approximately half of the scientists we surveyed adhere to the independence perspective. We also found that in each national context, a strong minority of both biologists and physicists think religion and science can collaborate. A substantial majority of scientists in the regions we studied also do not believe there is inherent conflict between being religious and being a scientist. One of the most common justifications we heard for this perspective was having

worked with a religious scientist who has developed a successful career. Respected religious scientists seem to act as *global boundary pioneers*,[19] by bridging the realms of science and religion while maintaining integrity and legitimacy in both domains. Having a religious graduate student can often have a similar effect, despite the fact that a graduate student might not yet have achieved career success.

4. *Religion is not kept out of the scientific workplace.* In some ways, Stephen Jay Gould's ideas about nonoverlapping magisteria, which we discuss in greater detail in the next chapter, may be tenable in abstract matters of belief and ideology, but do *not* gain traction in actual social life. When we follow scientists into their offices, laboratories, and homes, we find that religion often does enter the scientific workplace, sometimes in unexpected ways. In this book, you'll meet scientists who talk about religion, accommodate religion, make arguments in support of religion and its collaboration with science, or strongly and resolutely call for the separation of science and religion. Our interviews reveal numerous ways in which religion comes up in the workplace, both for religious scientists—some of whom try to compartmentalize their faith—and for nonreligious and atheist scientists.

How science and religion interface with one another is undoubtedly tied to epistemologies, cultural traditions, and histories as well as political agendas. But science and religion are also *social* realms, inhabited by scientists you will read about in these pages. It is thus vitally important that we take a social scientific approach to studying the nature of the relationship between science and religion, looking at how scientists themselves experience and navigate the two domains. In our research, we systematically examine the views and stories of scientists in different national contexts, scientific disciplines, and career stages to see how science has an impact on their religious attitudes and how religion influences their scientific work. Together, the eight contexts examined in this book offer a new perspective on the science–religion interface that could not be revealed by studying any one country or region alone. From our data emerges the real story of how scientists approach religion and religious issues, and the true relationship between science and religion in the lived experiences of scientists around the world.

CHAPTER 2 | Cases and Concepts

THIS BOOK IS ABOUT what scientists around the world think about religion. But which scientists? And what do we mean by religion? The question of how to define religion remains the subject of ongoing debate. Some scholars offer substantive definitions that make claims about what religion *is*; others focus on functional definitions, which emphasize what religion *does*. Others adopt approaches that combine the two. When we asked the scientists we interviewed how they would define the concept of religion, we found their responses reflected the many versions offered by scholars.

Substantive definitions tend to define religion as a system of beliefs about God, higher powers, or other supernatural or superhuman entities. Anthropologist Edward Tylor, for example, defined religion as "belief in spiritual beings."[1] Sociologist and philosopher Herbert Spencer defined religion as "one or other modification of the doctrine that all things are manifestations of a Power that transcends our knowledge."[2] Sociologist Edward Ross understood religion as having to do with "man's beliefs as to the Unseen."[3] Such views were frequently echoed among our scientist respondents, who often associated religion with a belief in God or higher powers. This conception is remarkably similar across the diverse national contexts we examined. One UK scientist,[4] for example, told us, "[R]eligion is the belief in something that's not manifested or proven to exist . . . and that entity could be a god or several gods or something like that," while an Indian scientist[5] stated religion "is always linked to some supernatural power, like God."

In addition to identifying religion with God or supernatural entities, many of our respondents also see religion as an organized belief system taught and shared by a specific community. As one UK scientist[6] explained, religion is "a somewhat coherent set of ideas that formulate a consistent ideology that explains the world to a community." An Indian scientist[7] described it this way: "Religion is an organized social structure where the members are connected by a certain way of belief in a supernatural being guiding them and helping them and sort of who is behind all the activities of this universe."

Other respondents emphasized the centrality of rules and rituals to religious systems, stating, for example, that religion "sets up rules in lives"[8] or offers a "common set of rules or values or moral codes to follow."[9] As one Indian scientist[10] said, religion is "a proper, distinct way of living a life with following certain rules." Others, like this Taiwanese scientist,[11] also emphasized the communal and structural dimensions of religion: "Believing in a religion requires a community. . . . And then there are usually hierarchies. The top level will have a pope or a master, something like that. I have never seen a religion that does not fit this criterion."

Functional definitions of religion, by contrast, emphasize the social and psychological functions religion serves, such as providing meaning, social order, and other ways of living and being in community. Sociologist Emile Durkheim, for instance, defined religion as "a unified system of beliefs and practices relative to sacred things, that is to say, things set apart and forbidden—beliefs and practices *which unite* [emphasis added] into one single moral community called a Church, all those who adhere to them."[12] Sociologist Charles Cooley saw religion as a response to the fundamental human need "to make life seem rational and good,"[13] with this fundamental need reflected in very specific actions.

Several of our respondents offered functional definitions of religion, highlighting the consequences of religious belief and practice. For example, one Indian scientist[14] said:

> Religion is a belief, and I think it gives strength, because if you believe in something and you have confidence, then you think that things will be all right if we follow certain rules and pray to some unknown natural, supernatural thing.

Another Indian scientist[15] said, "[F]or me, religion is something that gives you solace, that gives you peace of mind." Others described religion as answering questions of meaning that people are otherwise unable to satisfy, while we also heard respondents talk about religion as having a problem-solving function for adherents. "They treat it as something that will answer to every wish," one Taiwanese scientist[16] told us.

Not all functional definitions offered by our respondents were positive. Some saw religion as primarily a tool of social control and a source of violence. For instance, one Turkish scientist[17] said he sees religion as "a bunch of, I would say, man-made laws or rules or arguments to try to control large populations." Others argued that religion is mainly a means to "manipulate people"[18] and, as one scientist[19] put it, that religions "make a virtue of doing atrocities in the name of God."

One weakness of substantive definitions of religion is that their specific content—particularly if the definition posits belief in a god or higher power—can exclude from consideration traditions such as Theravada Buddhism and Confucianism; scholars ask whether either fits the definition of a religion. Functional definitions, on the other hand, might be so broad as to include things like sporting events and communism, which can fulfill the same social functions of providing meaning, identity, and social cohesion as does traditional religion. As a result, many scholars have tried to integrate substantive and functionalist elements in ways that overcome their respective deficiencies. For instance, sociologists Martin Riesebrodt and Christian Smith have put forth a practice-centered definition of religion: religion as a complex set of shared practices, premised on beliefs about superhuman entities, and with the goal of securing blessings or avoiding misfortune.[20] This definition emphasizes aspects of religion that can be accessed by the tools of social science, namely things about religion that we as scholars can see. Again, we find such considerations present in some of our respondents' definitions of religion. For one Taiwanese scientist,[21] religion is:

> to believe there are super beings beyond human being[s] who can intervene [in] our physics or maybe change the course of history, for example. And also maybe give us some advice in some obscure way maybe, to help people, help human beings, to help human beings' development.

Some scholars contend that because the concept of religion is a relatively recent invention of Western scholars, and has been used to justify Western imperialism and colonialism, it ought to be jettisoned altogether.[22] We agree with philosopher of religion Kevin Schilbrack, however, that none of our concepts are free of political baggage, and we believe it is still sociologically useful to retain the concept of religion.[23] Our goal here, in any case, is not to resolve debates in the field of religion scholarship, nor to develop any new theory of religion. In trying to understand the role of religion in the lives of the scientists we study, we want to understand and take seriously the definitions offered by these scientists, an approach that we think brings the best tools of social science to the table.

At the same time, we also rely on standardized survey questions across national contexts, and our interviews and observations allow us to identify religious elements that some participants may not interpret as such. For instance, in India it is common in scientific institutions, as well as elsewhere in the country, to celebrate festivals honoring various Hindu deities. While some nonreligious scientists who participate in such events consider them to be purely cultural celebrations, we would argue that, sociologically, they still ought to be understood as religious events. Here, we follow scholars such as Riesebrodt, Schilbrack, and Smith in understanding religion as any set of shared practices that are premised on the existence of superhuman entities. Surveying and interviewing scientists, more often than not in their own contexts, which also brought an element of ethnography to our study, was an important part of our methodological process. We were able to reveal how scientists understand the concepts and practices of religion in their own terms and how important or relevant these concepts and practices are in their lives.

We also asked our respondents how they understand the concept of spirituality. In contrast to the concept of religion, which tended to have more theistic (or at least superhuman), organized, communal, and ritualistic connotations, respondents' definitions of spirituality identified a phenomenon at the individual (rather than organized or communal) level, which involves deeper questions of meaning. Their responses reflect the definitional criteria for spirituality developed by psychologists of religion, such as Peter Hill and colleagues:

> The feelings, thoughts, experiences, and behaviors that arise from a search for the sacred. The term "search" refers to attempts to identify, articulate, maintain, or transform. The term "sacred" refers to a divine being, divine object, Ultimate Reality, or Ultimate Truth as perceived by the individual.[24]

We found considerably more variation in respondents' definitions of spirituality than in their definitions of religion. For some, the term "spirituality" didn't mean anything at all. Others found the term hard to define. For instance, one UK scientist[25] told us:

> Well, it's hard to tell in words because I don't think of [spirituality as] concerning reason or concerning something practical. So it's hard to tell. It's another sphere, it's another—it's kind of another dimension and it's something that you have to trust.

For some respondents, spirituality denotes something beyond, or greater than, the realms of science and logic. As another UK scientist[26] explained,

"I'd say maybe spirituality believes that there is something . . . greater than things that . . . facts and logic can reason." Another respondent[27] understood spirituality as believing in ghosts and the afterlife.

For some respondents, spirituality is unrelated to religion. An Indian scientist,[28] for instance, said spirituality is "just self-conscious or understanding self, and again, I feel it has nothing to do with God." A UK scientist[29] told us:

> I tend to think you only live once and the bit that makes life worth living is not the day to day and the practicality, but it's how much you enjoy life and what you put into it, in your relationships with other people. And I suppose spirituality comes into that bit for me, that there's an essence in people and that's what you're interacting with.

Others, however, see spirituality and religion as connected, like the Taiwanese scientist[30] who stated, "They are related . . . but they are not equivalent. They are not the same thing. I think more or less religion is a man-made subject based on their spiritual experience or their beliefs from their past [or] current experience." For some, spirituality means following the ethical implications of a religion. "To my understanding, what [spirituality] means is being ethical based on religious principles," said an Indian scientist.[31] He continued:

> So the religion says do not kill or do not do this or do not do that. So a spiritual person is somebody who tries to live his/her life on an ethical and moral plane, which is dictated by the religious [teachings].

Often, respondents would talk about religion as a more institutionalized form of spirituality. We heard things like, "Religion is when it [faith/spirituality] becomes corporate or communal,"[32] and "[R]eligion is organized spirituality."[33] While some thus see spirituality as more "fundamental" than religion, others view spirituality as a "higher" or more advanced aspect of religion. "I feel that the so-called 'spirituality' refers to the messages God gives you in life after the conversation with God through prayers," one Taiwanese scientist[34] told us. Similarly, we heard from a Turkish scientist[35] that "spirituality is above everything else, religion should be evaluated as a means to get to it." According to an Indian scientist,[36] "spirituality is probably a step higher than religion . . . [being spiritual is] to be really a hard-core believer." During interviews we also measured religion in ways it is commonly understood while also allowing scientists to put it in their own words.

Why We Studied Religion Among Biologists and Physicists

Why did we decide to study physicists and biologists for our cross-national study of what scientists around the world think about religion? For one, physics and biology are classic natural-science disciplines. In addition, many philosophers and sociologists of science postulate a hierarchy of science in which physics and biology occupy top positions (characterized by high levels of empiricism and generality), while disciplines such as psychology and anthropology occupy lower rungs (characterized by varied standards of empiricism).[37] The prestige of physics and biology is reflected in public perception; people are more likely to recognize the names Copernicus, Einstein, Newton, Darwin, Pasteur, and Watson than the name of a sociologist, anthropologist, or psychologist. Case in point: During the time of this writing, the great physicist Stephen Hawking passed away at age seventy-six; his death garnered three full pages in the *New York Times*, and he was interred in Westminster Abbey, alongside Isaac Newton and Charles Darwin.[38]

While controversial, the idea of a hierarchy of science also manifests itself in organizational features of science: Because of the perceived importance of the two disciplines, most major research universities have departments of physics and biological sciences.[39] As a result, it is, as a practical matter, much easier to study the relationship between religion and physics or religion and biology on a global scale than it would be to study the relationship between religion and anthropology, for example.[40]

Gender differences in religiosity also motivated our decision to study scientists in physics and biology. We find a significantly greater representation of women in biology than physics, though female biologists are still underrepresented at higher ranks and more elite schools. The female representation in each discipline may have an impact on how religion is perceived within the discipline, since research shows women generally tend to be more religious than men. Because of the difference in the representation of women between the two disciplines, together they provide the opportunity to examine how religiosity and perceptions of the science–religion relationship among scientists may be influenced by gender and gender representation. Looking at the impact of gender on scientists' views of religion has not yet been examined sufficiently at a broad range of institutions or beyond the United States.[41]

Perhaps most importantly, we chose to study scientists in physics and biology because religion routinely intersects with these two disciplines in meaningful and public ways, more so than other disciplines, in part because of the claims they make for how we should understand the natural and physical world.

In both biology and physics, we see a foundational idea conflicting with religious views of creation and rejected by some religious believers. These conflicts remind us that the science–faith interface is not simply an abstract epistemological issue but also a social issue that is situated in groups. In a number of countries, there have been public debates over the theory of biological evolution, which shows that humans and other living things have evolved over time through natural processes. Based on the specific form of their belief in God as creator and the specialness of humans in creation, some religious individuals and groups reject the scientific explanation for the origin and development of human life in favor of alternative explanations drawn from their faith traditions.[42] In physics, the big bang theory, the prevailing scientific explanation for the origin of the universe, conflicts with certain religious views. Some religious believers (most notably, conservative Protestants) see this model as being at odds with their belief that there is a creator of the universe.[43] (We should point out, of course, that entire groups of religious believers have no concerns about evolution or the big bang.) Sociologist John H. Evans examines the commitment that some groups of conservative Protestants may have to an implicit view of science that stresses fact claims based on the observable. According to Evans, this view of science would assert, "Since the Big Bang and human evolution are abstractions that cannot be observed, they are not properly scientific questions, but are religious questions."

We also see religiously based moral opposition to certain research and technologies in the biological sciences, such as human embryonic stem cell research, cloning, genetic modification, and reproductive technologies, especially in the United States and the United Kingdom.[44] The opposition is often centered on a belief in the uniqueness and sacredness of human life. Some religious individuals are concerned that particular biotechnologies, especially reproductive genetic technologies, undermine the idea that humans are created by God, in the image of God. In other cases, religious believers feel scientists and other individuals using these biotechnologies are "playing God." Physics, on the other hand, has historically had less tension with religious morality, yet has fostered discussions about the ethical dilemmas and moral implications of science, such as nuclear power and the risk of nuclear proliferation.[45]

Selecting the National Contexts for Our Study

Until now, social scientific research on religion among scientists has been conducted almost exclusively in the United States. With this body of research, we have made considerable progress in understanding how scientists view religion and the science–religion relationship more generally, yet it nevertheless provides a narrow perspective: that of a pluralist but predominately Christian country at the core of the global science infrastructure. So it is necessary to go beyond the United States, to look at the relationship between science and religion in a more expansive way. But how does one decide in which regions to carry out such a study?

Both practical and theoretical factors motivated our case selection of France, Hong Kong, India, Italy, Taiwan, Turkey, the United Kingdom, and the United States. We needed to conduct the study in contexts in which our team had language proficiency and regional expertise. Members of our research team have lived or traveled extensively in each of the regions of the study. Additional practical considerations included safety and logistics. Safety concerns applied not only to our ability to conduct fieldwork but also to respondents in the study. When we had conducted earlier research with scientists in mainland China, for example, some had refused to be recorded because of the distinctive social and cultural norms operating in mainland China. Logistically, we needed to be able to conduct nationally representative surveys and spend weeks in each region conducting interviews at a reasonable cost. We therefore chose to conduct research in Taiwan and Hong Kong to approximate the broader Chinese society. The political climate in Hong Kong and Taiwan enabled us to gain access to their scientific communities. Of course, we are aware of the differences between Hong Kong and Taiwan, as well as their distinctiveness from mainland China. For our purposes, however, Taiwan, Hong Kong, and China share a similar ethnic culture, broadly defined. With globalization, the economic relationships among the three contexts have become increasingly closer. Some scholars even label the three regions as "the Chinese circle."[46] Politically speaking, we note two things: that the status of Taiwan as a country is contested, and that Hong Kong is a Special Administrative Region of the People's Republic of China.[47] Hence, throughout the book, we refer to these societies as "regional" contexts. As we explain in Appendix B, we encountered other logistical difficulties in conducting the study. Political unrest in both Turkey and Hong Kong, for example, delayed our survey of scientists in both regions.[48]

Theoretical considerations more heavily influenced how we selected the locales for our study. Overall, we sought a design that included both most-different and most-similar national and regional cases on different axes of analysis. In short, we wanted to maximize variation in order to capture nation-level factors that may influence how scientists view religion and perceive the science–religion relationship, such as religious characteristics of the population, the state–church relationship, and the level of science infrastructure.

There are at least two critical ways in which religious characteristics of the population matter. The first concerns the overall level of religiosity. Generally speaking, we can rank our cases on a "religiosity scale," with India, Italy, the United States, and Turkey as the most religious (albeit in very different ways), France and the United Kingdom as the most secular, and Taiwan and Hong Kong somewhere in between. Debates related to religion and science are more likely to emerge in the public sphere and shape how scientists view religion in a context like the United States, where the population is highly religious, than in a very secular context, such as France. Individual exposure to religion also varies in this respect and can similarly influence how scientists view religion, as well as the proportion of scientists who identify as religious. Scientists in Turkey and India are more likely than scientists in Taiwan, for example, to have been exposed to or participated in religion as children. In the chapters that follow, we examine the religiosity of the population in each national context in greater detail.

In some regions, identifying with a particular religious tradition is decoupled from maintaining faith beliefs and practices. (We see this, for example, among Anglicans in the United Kingdom, Hindus in India, Jews in the United States, and Catholics in Italy.) Thus, in addition to religiosity, it is important to consider religious tradition and affiliation within a region. Religious tradition and affiliation matter in part due to doctrinal positions that can impact how scientific issues and ideas are perceived, and thus how both adherents and nonadherents view the relationship between religion and science. For example, in a 2014 speech to the Pontifical Academy of Sciences, Pope Francis reaffirmed the Catholic Church's support for acceptance of evolutionary theory and the big bang theory, by positing that a divine creator was the initial cause of the evolutionary process and birth of the universe. Pope Francis's statement might be viewed as an attempt to reduce tension between scientific theories and religious beliefs, thereby rejecting—and helping others to reject—the conflict perspective on science and religion.[49] In 2010, members of the Church of England voted for a motion that rejects the idea that science and Christian belief are incompatible.[50]

The state–church relationship in each region matters because it can officially structure the region's approach to religion or secularity. We wanted to choose contexts that included both religious states and secular states. France and Turkey are characterized by assertive secularity, wherein governments impose stringent policies that separate religious symbolism and influence from governmental organizations and the public sphere (though, as we mentioned in the previous chapter, Turkey is seeing a rise in religious influence under the current politically Islamist government).[51] Other regions in our sample have official state churches. Italy, while not formally governed by the Catholic Church, is influenced by the Vatican, which is seated in Rome. Though not applicable to all of the United Kingdom, the Church of England, the mother church of the transnational Anglican Communion, is the official state church of England. The United States represents a middle ground between state religion and secularity. While the United States exercises a more passive form of secularism than France and Turkey, it is committed to the separation of church and state; yet, this separation is not strict: the government recognizes God, integrates religious symbolism into its practices, and makes accommodations for religious groups. And religion certainly plays a role in public life.

The science infrastructure in each region matters because of its effect on immigration and consequently the religious makeup of the region. National contexts with the most globally competitive science infrastructures—which we determine by research and development funding, scientific workforce, and numbers of publications and patents (Table 2.1)—are most likely to attract students and scientists from other countries, and thus religious diversity. There are three important dynamics to consider here. First, given the patterns of immigration among scientists, we can expect that nonnative scientists increase the overall religiosity of the scientific workforce in a region. Second, we can expect that religious pluralism increases in the scientific community in countries like the United States and the United Kingdom as non-Western scientists move there for their careers. Finally, in countries with a less competitive science infrastructure, such as Italy and Turkey, we can expect higher levels of religious homogeneity in the scientific community. Each of these dynamics has implications for how scientists encounter and view religion, its relationship to science, and its place in the scientific workplace.

Religion in the Scientific Workplace

Studying religion in the scientific workplace provides a new way of thinking about independence, conflict, and collaboration between science and religion. Consider the independence perspective, which posits that science and religion refer to different aspects of reality and represent different areas of knowledge. We typically think of this view in its epistemological sense, that is, what types of questions science and religion ask and answer. Paleontologist

TABLE 2.1. Dimensions of comparison for national/regional cases.

COUNTRY	STATE/CHURCH RELATIONSHIP	DOMINANT RELIGION	RELIGIOUS DIVERSITY[a]	% R&D (2015)[b]
United States	Separation of church and state	Protestant and Catholic Christianity	Yes	2.74
United Kingdom	Official state church in Church of England	Nonaffiliation and Anglicanism	Yes	1.70
France	State-sponsored secularity	Catholicism	Yes	2.22
Italy	Seat of Roman Catholic Church	Catholicism	No	1.33
Turkey	State-sponsored secularity	Islam	No	0.88
Hong Kong[c]	Freedom of religion	None	No	0.76
Taiwan	Freedom of religion	Folk Religion	Yes	3.05
India	State-sponsored secularity	Hinduism	No	0.63

[a] We define a nation as having religious diversity when more than 30 percent of the nation identifies with a nondominant religion.
[b] Funding as percent of GDP. National Science Board. 2018. "Cross-National Comparisons of R&D Performance." Retrieved from https://www.nsf.gov/statistics/2018/nsb20181/report/sections/research-and-development-u-s-trends-and-international-comparisons/cross-national-comparisons-of-r-d-performance.
[c] Hong Kong data retrieved from https://www.censtatd.gov.hk/hkstat/sub/sp120.jsp?tableID=207&ID=0&productType=8.

Stephen Jay Gould famously called science and religion "non-overlapping magisteria"—separate and limited spheres of inquiry and authority—with science dealing in empirical facts and theories, while religion deals with meaning and moral values.[52] For most scientists, science is clearly the more legitimate realm for evaluating truth and evidence.

Yet examining religion in the scientific workplace complicates the notion that science and religion are easily kept separate. As sociologist José Casanova has argued, even as modern societies secularize, private religion makes its way into various public spheres.[53] This includes the highly secular context of science. Religious practice and discourse can permeate scientific research laboratories, university offices, undergraduate classes, and doctoral training, even if an individual scientist believes, in the abstract, theoretical sense, that science and religion are completely separate domains. Religion can influence which topics a scientist studies. Scientists may use religiously based ethical frameworks. Religion can even affect how nonreligious scientists engage with the public. Some scientists accommodate the religious practices of colleagues and students in the workplace. In other cases, the emergence of religion in the workplace can be met with derogation and prejudice. Religious scientists may view science and religion as independent, and even compartmentalize their personal faith from their scientific work, but the two spheres may cease to be independent if, for example, they experience discrimination based on their religious beliefs. Nonreligious scientists may see the two spheres as conflicting and take the side of science, but nevertheless accommodate the religious needs of a graduate student. Thus, we also examine the conditions under which religion comes up in the scientific workplace to gain a better understanding of the possibilities for conflict and collaboration between scientific and religious identities.

Comparing Scientists with the General Public

Even if scientists do not engage with religion in the workplace, they are still situated in nations with populations that have diverse attitudes toward religion and its relationship with science. At the same time, scientists represent their own transnational community. Professional socialization, international associations, conferences, collaborations, and publications all encourage a collective identity that transcends geography, such that scientists from different regions exhibit similar beliefs and dispositions. Accordingly, we might expect that scientists retain some of the religious and spiritual character of their home nation, while exhibiting collective differences from their home nations. Scientists in Turkey, for example, may generally be more religiously liberal than the general population in the country, while also expressing more religiosity than scientists in a less religious nation, such as France.

Thus, it is important to compare not only the different scientific and religious characteristics of different countries, and scientists from one country to another, but also how scientists in each country compare with the general public in their region when it comes to views on religion and the science and religion relationship. If you are a scientist who seeks to enhance public understanding of science, your task is infinitely more difficult if you lack an understanding of the religious contours of your audience, especially if the scientific ideas you wish to communicate may be in tension with certain religious beliefs held by members of that audience. The task is equally challenging for those who seek to create dialogue between scientists and the public in a region but do not empirically understand how these two groups differ in their religiosity and approach to religion.

It is also important to compare scientists with the public to better assess the popular idea that scientific education erodes religious belief. The basic assumption here is one of individual-level secularization, in which scientific training, scientific knowledge, and the rational and analytical thinking of science lead to a decline in religiosity. Thus, we should expect scientists to be less religious than individuals who have had less exposure to scientific thought. According to this logic, scientists in all regions should be less religious than the general population. And yet, we also want to point out that comparing scientists and the public (alone) cannot entirely help us address this idea specifically. *And* it is really only by talking with scientists (through our in-depth interviews with them, rather than through our survey) that we can more fully assess—by listening to their stories in their own terms—how much their scientific training influenced their religiosity or religious views.

The empirical evidence for this claim, however, is mixed. In many national contexts, scientists are significantly less religious than the general population. Yet scientists are not less religious than the general population in Turkey, Taiwan, or Hong Kong, according to several measures. Ecklund's decade-old work on the religiosity of natural and social scientists at top US universities did reveal that nearly 50 percent of scientists have some form of a religious identity, though it is often very different in character from the religious identities found among the general public. At the same time, a separate study of US students by sociologist Christopher Scheitle shows that evangelical Christians take more college-level science classes than nonreligious students and that the erosion of religious belief among students who take numerous natural science classes is no different from students who take fewer science courses.[54] While, as we mentioned in the previous chapter, James Leuba's surveys found that American scientists were less likely than the general public to believe in God and that the most successful scientists were least likely to be involved in religion,[55] other scholars argue that rather than discovering conflict between scientific and religious ways of knowing, these studies simply assumed the conflict.[56] These scholars have offered additional empirical findings and theories that counter those of Leuba's studies. They found that scientists did not view religion as being in opposition to their work, and that individuals with an active religious faith were no less likely to pursue academic careers than those without an active religious faith.[57] Religious studies scholar C. Mackenzie Brown also contends that Leuba, and later scholars who supported Leuba's work, used a narrow conception of religion that is no longer relevant for much of the American public[58] (and, we would add, is especially irrelevant for a global public).

Assumptions about individual-level secularization, it should be noted, rarely consider other dimensions of religiosity besides belief, such as religious rituals and practices, nor do they tend to consider non-Western religious traditions. It is possible, for example, that religious adherence persists even if faith beliefs erode. We could imagine this scenario in nations like India and Italy, where the importance of cultural religious traditions could outlive a loss of religious belief. Furthermore, research shows that while science and religion may represent different ways of knowing, conflict between science and religion is mostly limited to a handful of scientific issues, and that when we look beyond a specific tradition within the Christian faith, we find that other forms of Christian religious traditions, as well as forms of Judaism, Islam, and Hinduism, all have within their traditions ways of emphasizing religion and science as supportive of one another.[59]

CHAPTER 3

United States

The "Problem" of the Public

All that stuff I was taught about evolution, embryology, big bang theory, all that is lies straight from the pit of hell. It's lies to try to keep me and all the folks who are taught that from understanding that they need a savior. . . . I believe that the Earth is about 9,000 years old. I believe that it was created in six days as we know them. That's what the Bible says. And what I've come to learn is that it's the manufacturer's handbook, is what I call it.

THIS IS WHAT FORMER Republican congressman Paul Broun, a physician on the House of Representatives Science, Space, and Technology Committee, notoriously told a Baptist church in a 2012 speech while running unopposed for reelection as a Georgia representative. In response to his views, when the election came, nearly 4,000 people wrote in Charles Darwin in a protest vote. In the United States, where Protestant Christianity, and evangelical Protestantism in particular, is still the dominant public religious tradition, there often appears to be *public* conflict between science and religion. According to a recent Pew Research Center survey, 59 percent of the American public say science and religion often conflict, up from 55 percent in 2009. Yet, only 30 percent say their personal religious beliefs conflict with science. According to the report:

> There are only a handful of areas where people's religious beliefs and practices have a strong connection to their views about a range of science-related issues. Statistical modeling shows religious differences in affiliation and worship service attendance come to the fore when the issue is related to human evolution or the creation of the universe.

The United States appears to be behind other developed nations in terms of acceptance of core scientific theories, in particular those that seem to have implications for biblical interpretations of who God is and how special humans are. For example, when compared with Canada and thirty-two European countries, the United States has the second lowest overall rate of public acceptance of evolution[1] (even though 98 percent of scientists connected to the American Association for the Advancement of Science believe humans evolved over time). While today virtually all scientists accept evolution, the Americans who do not accept the theory seem to have concerns because they see the scientific explanation as conflicting with their religious beliefs about God's role in the world and the uniqueness of humans.

Related to these concerns, many religious Americans also take issue with the use of human reproductive genetic technologies (also known as hRGTs), which include various techniques related to the genetic screening, selection, and treatment of embryos, as sociologist John Evans has argued in his book, *Playing God: Human Genetic Engineering and the Rationalization of Public Bioethical Debate*.[2] These technologies can be separated into two categories: disease-focused hRGTs and selection-focused hRGTs. The latter refer to technologies allowing the selection of preferred characteristics in an otherwise healthy embryo, while disease-focused hRGTs attempt to treat diseased embryos.[3] Recent research shows that almost two-thirds of US adults say that *selection-focused* hRGTs are morally wrong, but only 13 percent of US adults view *disease-focused* hRGTs as morally wrong. The moral consideration of these issues is not exclusively religious. More than half of religiously unaffiliated Americans, for example, are opposed to selection-focused hRGTs. Nevertheless, evangelicals are significantly more likely than the general population to oppose both selection-focused and disease-focused hRGTs.[4]

While there are often debates in the United States over the appropriateness of human embryonic stem cell research, hRGTs, and the use of vaccines, evolution remains the most common source of conflict between the scientific community and religious believers from certain faith traditions. In many states and local school boards, there have been debates over the teaching of evolution in public schools; and from 2000 to 2012, legislators in 26 states introduced 110 "antievolution" curriculum reform bills in state government.[5]

We interviewed scientists across the United States at public and private universities in each region of the country. We found that scientists in the United States, a nation marked by "freedom of religion," are more personally religious than scientists in other Western nations tend to be. There are still a number of secular scientists in the United States, and a number of atheist and agnostic scientists are spiritual. While many nonreligious scientists accept their religious peers without question, there is also a pervasive cynicism about religion in the scientific workplace, driven in part by how scientists view the religious public. More than in any other nation we studied, we found that the religious public looms large in the minds of scientists—most frequently in the form of a large, conservative, politically involved, Christian population that many scientists characterize as hostile to science. They tend to view conservative evangelical Protestants, in particular, as representative of all Christians, and believe evangelical Protestants are universally skeptical of science and scientists. These views are often reinforced by religious undergraduates and, in some contexts, can produce a climate of hostility and even discrimination toward religious scientists.

Cultural Context of Science and Religion in the United States

The United States is one of the most religious contexts in our study. Among the Western countries we examined, it is the most Protestant Christian nation. As sociologist Robert Wuthnow explains, even as Muslims, Hindus, and other non-Western religious adherents increase in the United States, most Americans still regard the United States as a chiefly Christian society.[6] Indeed, according to the Pew Religious Landscape Study, 70 percent of Americans identify as Christian—with conservative Protestant traditions, such as evangelicals, accounting for more than one-third of the population. Yet, the share of Christian Americans is decreasing overall, mainly due to declines among Catholics and mainline Protestants. Non-Christian faiths, especially Islam and Hinduism, are on the rise, and the percentage of religiously unaffiliated Americans, called the "nones," is also clearly growing—rising from 16 percent of the US population in 2007 to 23 percent in 2014. Growth was also in the number of Americans who identify as evangelical Protestants and the proportion of evangelical Protestants and Catholics who are not white. We also see that many Americans have switched to evangelical Protestantism from other religious traditions—from 2007 to 2015, it was the only major Christian group that gained more adherents than it lost through religious switching.[7]

The religious culture of the United States is characterized by what political scientist Ahmet Kuru refers to as passive secularism.[8] Passive secularism as a policy regime involves official church–state separation alongside considerable tolerance for the exercise and visibility of religion. In the United States, pledges that invoke God are recited in public schools, "In God We Trust" appears on all currency, and official oaths for federal and state offices include the statement "so help me God." We also find accommodation of religion, such as school voucher systems that allow government subsidies for expenses at religious schools.

While some religious Americans believe US social institutions are hostile to religious beliefs and values, religious groups wield considerable power in the political sphere. Although not a monolithic movement and certainly not representative of all of American evangelicalism, the "Christian Right" consists of a broad social network of US religious and political organizations that attempt to shape policies by electing candidates with conservative political platforms that expand religious freedom and protect so-called family values.[9] At times, these conservative political platforms have implications for scientific issues, such as the teaching of evolution or human embryonic stem cell research.

Of the eight regions where we studied scientists, the United States has one of the most well developed science infrastructures in terms of the number of scientists, science funding, and universities and institutes devoted to scientific research. Today, the United States has more than 6.7 million scientists and engineers out of a population of 326 million. The United States spends more than any other country on research and development—$497 billion in 2015, which was 2.74 percent of its GDP.[10] The United States is at the core of the global science infrastructure. Its research universities dominate the rankings of the highly regarded Shanghai Jiao Tong University measurement of scientific achievement, and the massive volume of scientists these universities produce makes competition for research positions in academia intense. While there is considerable interest in recruiting more women and underrepresented minorities to STEM fields, women are still underrepresented in science (though less so than in the past in some areas), and black and Latino/a Americans remain vastly underrepresented. We should note too that women and racial minorities are more likely than men and whites to be religious.

Religion and Science in the Public Sphere

The United States has played a central role in the emergence and incubation of the conflict perspective on science and religion in the West. As historian Ronald Numbers explains, the notion of conflict between science and religion became popular in the United States with the publication of books by New York University Professor John William Draper and Cornell University

President Andrew Dickson White in the late nineteenth century. These widely read books—which explored the relationship between science and religion and sought to identify sources of disagreement and division—helped perpetuate the public perception that science and religion were in conflict with each other (even as Christian theologians rejected such an idea).[11] Two decades later, conflicts between science and religion began to play out on the public stage when a Christian farmer and Tennessee representative lobbied the state legislature to ban the teaching of evolution in public schools, leading to the famous Scopes trial. The trial did little to change the sense that science and religion were at odds.

As the conflict view of science and religion gained popularity, the psychologist James Leuba conducted surveys of scientists in the United States, asking them about their views on Christian belief, which Leuba defined as participation in Christian worship and a Christian theology of life after death. In 1916 and 1934, he found that US scientists were less likely than the US public to believe in a personal God and the most successful scientists were the least likely to participate in religious practices.[12] Other scholars repeated Leuba's 1916 survey in the late 1990s and found little change from Leuba's earlier work, with 60.7 percent of the scientists they surveyed "expressing disbelief or doubt."[13] Work by Ecklund and her colleagues also demonstrated an overall decline in religiosity among scientists who work at *elite* academic institutions. Religious affiliation was lower among these scientists in 2005 than in 1969, and regular attendance at religious services among these scientists decreased from 24 percent to 19 percent during this time, although the proportion of Catholics increased.[14] It is important to note that existing comparisons of elite and nonelite scientists seem to imply a correlation between success in science and disbelief in God, but only recently has research been able to look more closely at how scientists at different types of institutions compare in terms of their religiosity.

While historians have done a nice job of documenting cases of conflict between science and religion in the public sphere, social scientists have just started to produce a detailed view of what Americans think about science and religion. In 2012, Ecklund conducted the *Religious Understandings of Science* survey, a nationally representative general population survey of more than 10,000 Americans. The research resulting from this survey found that while there is indeed a segment of the American public that holds the conflict perspective on science and religion, the proportion that takes the side of religion is considerably smaller than the proportion of the US public that is religious. It is also smaller than the proportion of the US public that identifies as conservative Protestant. Only about 14 percent of the US public said their personal understanding of the science-and-religion relationship would be described as one of conflict and they are on the side of religion. By comparison, 13 percent of the US public said they view science and religion as having a relationship of conflict and take the side of science. It is much more common for Americans to view the science-and-religion relationship as one of collaboration (39 percent) or independence (34 percent). That said, religious Americans do still have some reservations about science and the scientific career. For example, Catholics, evangelical and mainline Protestants, Jews, and other religious groups are more hesitant than the religiously unaffiliated to recommend that their children pursue careers in physics, biology, and engineering.[15]

Religion and Spirituality Among US Scientists

Among the nations we studied, the US scientific community does not stand out in terms of its patterns of religious affiliation. About two-thirds of US scientists do not belong to a religious tradition (Table 3.1). Scientists in the United States are approximately twice as likely as the US public to be religiously unaffiliated—60 percent of scientists say they don't belong to a religion compared with 34 percent of the general population.

As we see when we compare their share of the scientific community with their proportion of the general population, Catholics and Protestants are underrepresented in science, while Orthodox Christians, Jews, Muslims,

TABLE 3.1. Religious affiliation in the United States.

RELIGIOUS TRADITION	POPULATION (%)	SCIENTISTS (%)
Roman Catholic	22.0	10.0
Protestant	24.8	11.4
Orthodox	0.3	1.3
Judaism	1.9	3.4
Islam	0.3	2.0
Hinduism	0.4	4.6
Buddhism	0.6	2.0
Other	16.1	4.9
None	33.7	60.5
Total Respondents	2,185	1,890

NOTES: Based on weighted data. Values exclude nonresponse.
SOURCE: World Values Survey United States 2011; RASIC United States Survey 2015.

Hindus, and Buddhists are overrepresented. The overrepresentation of non-Western religious traditions in science is likely because the United States is at the core of the global science infrastructure: 42 percent of US scientists were born outside of the country. It is particularly noteworthy that 5 percent of US scientists identify as Hindu because, outside of India, Hindus have no comparable presence in science.

When we dive deeper into our survey data, we find that, for the most part, we do not see major differences in religious affiliation among scientists by gender, discipline, university status, or career stage. There are some exceptions, however, found among minority traditions. Muslim and Hindu scientists, for example, are more likely to work in nonelite universities than in elite universities, and they are more likely to be enrolled in doctoral study than to possess a doctorate, meaning that in the years to come we may see more US Muslim and Hindu science professors. Jewish scientists are more likely to work in elite universities and to already be professors rather than students working on their degrees.

US scientists do stand out from scientists in other countries in a number of ways with regard to belief in God (Table 3.2). The level of disbelief in God among US scientists is striking, largely because belief in God is so high among the general US population: 92 percent of the US public believes in a personal God or a higher power, compared with 36 percent of US scientists. While only 3 percent of the US public identifies as atheist, nearly 35 percent

TABLE 3.2. Belief in God in the United States.

BELIEF ABOUT GOD	POPULATION (%)	SCIENTISTS (%)
I don't believe in God.	2.8	34.6
I don't know whether there is a God, and I don't believe there is any way to find out.	5.0	29.4
I don't believe in a personal God, but I do believe in a Higher Power of some kind.	10.3	12.2
I find myself believing in God some of the time, but not at others.	3.5	3.2
While I have doubts, I feel that I do believe in God.	16.9	9.9
I know God really exists and I have no doubts about it.	61.3	10.7
Total Respondents	1,353	1,844

NOTES: Based on weighted data. Values exclude nonresponse.
SOURCE: International Social Survey Programme 2008: Religion III (United States); RASIC United States Survey 2015.

of scientists say they don't believe in God. While other regions we studied also have many more atheists in the scientific community than in the general population, the difference in the United States is larger than in any of these other regions.[16]

We see a similar pattern when we look at agnosticism among US scientists and the US general population. While only 5 percent of the public identifies as agnostic, 29 percent of US scientists say they don't know whether there is a God and don't think there is a way to find out.

We did find that 12 percent of US scientists don't believe in God but believe in a higher power of some kind, a proportion slightly higher than in the US public and similar to the share of scientists in other Western regions who hold this belief. Scientists we interviewed described the higher power they envision in various ways. A professor of biology,[17] for example, said her view of God is: "The emergent property of humanity. . . . It's impossible for any single one of us to understand what the being is that we're a part of. But there's definitely something. There is a being." Other scientists described an abstract creative force in the universe. A graduate student in physics, who identifies as slightly religious,[18] said, "There are too many things that are too beautifully done and too elegantly created to believe in an accidental universe. But as far as what form that takes, I don't know." From other scientists who described their belief in a higher power we heard language such as a "reality that's bigger than me," "a greater essence," and "a spiritual mass that connects everything"—while sometimes expressing discomfort with even defining the higher power as "God."[19]

Eleven percent of US scientists say they believe in God without doubt, making it the second most common way of expressing belief in God among them—though still significantly lower than the 61 percent of the general US population who believe in God without doubt. In contrast to the abstract descriptions we heard from scientists describing a higher power, scientists who talked about their belief in God sometimes described a figure that was real, personal, and prominent in their lives. It is worth noting that scientists who held this devout view of God did not feel it required biblical literalism. A conservative Protestant professor of biology at an elite university,[20] for example, explained that while she believes God came to Earth in the form of Jesus, she places heavier emphasis on some aspects of scripture that for her are the "meat of what it means to be Christian."

The conceptions of God that scientists described were tied to doctrines of their religious traditions. For example, we spoke with a Baptist graduate student in physics[21] who, when discussing her conception of God, explained,

"We're a lot like Him. . . . He's not like a series of physical laws that hold the universe in place. He has emotions and as such you can have a relationship." A Mormon graduate student in biophysics[22] told us:

> I hold the traditional Mormon conceptualization of God as a man who has a form that is similar to humans and that really exists in an embodied form. . . . I believe in God and in Jesus as a separate entity who is also embodied, also real. Yeah, they're very real beings.

We find that 8 percent of scientists at elite institutions believe in God with no doubts, compared with 13 percent of scientists at nonelite institutions.[23] When it comes to disbelief in God, we find the opposite pattern: 40 percent of scientists at elite institutions don't believe in God compared with 31 percent of scientists at nonelite institutions.[24] These patterns hold even when we take into account a host of other factors—academic discipline, career stage, religious affiliation, gender, age, having children at home, and immigration status.

US scientists are twice as likely as members of the US public to never attend religious services (Table 3.3), a finding that is not surprising given that US scientists are twice as likely as the US public to be religiously unaffiliated.

Only 11 percent of US scientists say they attend religious services once a week or more, compared with nearly 34 percent of the US population. Overall, scientists in the United States have the third lowest level of religious service attendance among the countries we studied, after scientists in France and the United Kingdom.

TABLE 3.3. Religious service attendance in the United States.

FREQUENCY	POPULATION (%)	SCIENTISTS (%)
More than once a week	11.5	2.4
Once a week	22.3	9.0
Once a month	9.8	5.7
Only on special holy days	8.9	10.5
Once a year	5.2	6.0
Less often	11.8	7.5
Never, practically never	30.6	58.8
Total Respondents	2,202	1,885

NOTES: Based on weighted data. Values exclude nonresponse.
SOURCE: World Values Survey United States 2011; RASIC United States Survey 2015.

One very interesting feature of religious service attendance among US scientists is that there is a small subset of nonreligious scientists who attend religious services relatively frequently. For example, a professor of biology[25] who characterizes himself as "very strongly agnostic" told us religion is a major component of his family life and he attends a Methodist church almost weekly. An associate professor of physics identifying as nonreligious[26] told us she does not know if she believes in God but she and her family attend a Catholic church weekly. Envisioning her future self, a graduate student in physics,[27] who plans on converting to Catholicism to please her fiancé's parents, said she would be "just an atheist sitting in a Catholic church."

Relationship Between Science and Religion for US Scientists

Given the long and enduring history of public tension between science and religion in the United States, it is not surprising that we find the conflict view of science and religion to be more popular among scientists here than in all the other countries we studied, except the United Kingdom. (We explore the possible reasons the conflict view is more prevalent there in our chapter on the United Kingdom.) We found that 29 percent of US scientists view the relationship between science and religion as one of conflict (Table 3.4). Supplementary analysis of our data also revealed that a significantly larger proportion of male scientists (33 percent) than female scientists (19 percent) embrace the conflict view of science and religion.[28]

Most US scientists who see the relationship between science and religion as one of conflict see this conflict as something that's created by certain

TABLE 3.4. Perceived relationship of science and religion among scientists in the United States.

RELATIONSHIP	%
Conflict; I consider myself to be on the side of religion	0.4
Conflict; I consider myself to be on the side of science	28.6
Conflict; I am unsure which side I am on	0.2
Independence; they refer to different aspects of reality	50.9
Collaboration; each can be used to help support the other	12.1
Don't know	7.9
Total Respondents	1,830

NOTES: Based on weighted data. Values exclude nonresponse.
SOURCE: RASIC United States Survey 2015.

religious groups or beliefs rather than originating in the scientific community or inherent to the relationship between the two realms. A postdoctoral researcher in biology[29] who identifies as slightly religious said, "I don't think there's any inherent conflict between science and religion. I think there are only ones that are invented by a few very highly publicized groups. . . . It is particularly strong in our country." The majority of the churches this researcher is familiar with are focused on social justice issues and have no tension with science, she said, but "they're just not the ones that get most of the media attention in our country." A nonreligious graduate student in physics[30] told us he believes conflict between science and religion exists for "very, very far-right-wing Christians in this country or very conservative Muslims in other parts of the world."

It is very interesting to note that most US scientists who believe there is conflict between religion and science see that conflict originating from biblical literalism or beliefs about the age of the Earth or human origins among members of the US religious public—but not among religious scientists. In other words, they do not think these religious beliefs are an issue for their colleagues. A nonreligious professor of physics,[31] for example, told us, "I certainly know many scientists who are also religious, and I would say they tend to have more abstract religious worldviews" than strict interpretation of religious texts. A graduate student in physics[32] shared a similar view, saying a biblical literalist view of the origin of the universe could "affect you as a scientist, but I think, for the most part, the religious scientists that are around are not affected, their religion doesn't affect their science." A slim majority of US scientists—51 percent—view the relationship between science and religion as one of independence. There is nothing special about how US scientists express this view. Similar to what we observed in other regions, the narratives of independence that US scientists employed included references to the notion of nonoverlapping magisteria, distinctions between what is measurable and nonmeasurable, and the idea that science and religion address different questions. A nonreligious postdoctoral physicist[33] explained her view of science and religion as independent this way:

> The old saying, "Render under Caesar those that are Caesar's and under God those that are God's"—I believe that was a wise statement. You live in the world of Caesar, which is the physical world, and then you can turn around and go into the church and live in the world of religion, which is faith-based, and to me there's no overlap between the two. Here in the lab, you're applying the scientific method. If you're in church, you're applying faith.

When we look at the gender breakdown of US scientists holding the independence view of science and religion, we see the reverse of what we observe in analyzing the conflict view: A significantly larger proportion of female scientists (63 percent) than male scientists (45 percent) embrace the independence perspective.[34]

Only 12 percent of scientists in the United States believe science and religion can be used to help support each other. This collaboration view is more prevalent in non-Western regions. While Muslim and Hindu scientists in other regions often referenced religious texts when discussing how science and religion can support one another, the narratives of collaboration we heard from Christians in the United States were relatively general. Consider, for example, the religious graduate student in biology[35] who told us, "For me personally, I don't experience a conflict. My religious side guides my hopes for my professional work, and my professional work guides my openness to my religion." When we analyzed the data on US scientists who hold the collaboration view, we found that there were differences by academic discipline (see Appendix A, Tables A.1 and A.2 on the United States): A larger proportion of physicists (17 percent) than biologists (10 percent) are likely to view the relationship between science and religion as one of collaboration.[36] It could be that the prevalence of public debates on evolution and religion makes it especially difficult for biologists to see how science and religion could support one another—or discourages individuals who see science and religion as collaborative from entering the field of biology. We see a lack of major public disputes between physics and religion, which may make physicists more amenable to the collaboration view or the field more open to those who see science and religion working together.

Religion can discourage science "when you make it compete with science and with everyday experience," said Susan, a religious graduate student completing her doctorate in physics,[37] whom we met during our fieldwork in the "Bible Belt." Susan was homeschooled in an evangelical Christian community, where she was taught creationism and there was distrust of mainstream science, especially evolutionary theory. Science, she said, was seen as potentially dangerous to religion. For a time, Susan avoided studying astronomy and astrophysics because she was afraid to learn more about disciplines of inquiry she thought could threaten her faith. Then she learned about Dutch theologian Abraham Kuyper's idea of vocation and was inspired. Kuyper believed that people must make the best use of their skills, gifts, and talents for the glory of God—and this idea motivated Susan to go further into science than she was raised to believe she could, to learn more about science so she could better integrate it with her faith.

She doesn't know if any of the scientists she works with are also religious, she said. Though Susan still considers herself a person of faith, like many US scientists who were raised in a conservative religious tradition, she has lost her "certainty of belief" over time, and some of her beliefs have changed. "Christianity isn't better than any other belief system," she told us. Today, though she doesn't think science will completely replace religion, she does believe science is a way humans can make the world better, and she sees less tension between science and religion than when she was younger. In her view, whether you view science and religion as in conflict depends on "how fragile you formulate your faith to be."

Religion in the US Scientific Workplace

Luis, a graduate student in biology at a large public university in the Mid-Atlantic,[38] is now an atheist but grew up in a highly religious Catholic community in Puerto Rico that he says would ostracize people for going into science or medicine. "It's very complicated for Caribbean peoples," he said. He described their distrust of scientists as rooted in a "mishmash" of Roman Catholicism, African spiritual religions, and an intense adherence to the Bible that makes individuals more likely to look to their neighborhood botanica than to scientific discoveries to cure their illnesses. Early in life, he was kicked out of his Roman Catholic class for "questioning everything," and said he "never really took to" religion. Critical of religion for much of his adolescence, he "became a lot softer on the comfort it gives people," he said. Luis is fascinated with arachnids and their beautiful changes, and while he does not consider himself spiritual, as a scientist, "You need a sense of wonder—'holy crap that's an amazing thing!' If you don't have that you can't be a great scientist." He told us about a religious colleague who also sees evolution in the changes of arachnids, yet embraces a deist view that God created the universe but does not intervene in the world. He has encountered religious students who are confrontational with professors in class or who write caveats on their exams so that their answers do not conflict with their religious beliefs.

Separation

Some religious scientists in the United States, as in most of the regions we examined, compartmentalize their faith at work because they view their scientific work and religious faith as unrelated. For this group, separation is not an active cognitive or social strategy to draw boundaries between their two identities; in their minds, there is simply no overlap between science and religion and thus nothing to have to separate. As one religious associate professor of physics[39] explained, exemplifying this approach:

> I personally am a religious person and I don't think it really influences what I do in the lab, those are sort of separate parts of my life. . . . In terms of the day-to-day operation of my lab, I don't think it has any real impact in terms of what science we do. . . . [Nor do I] think it really influences my research goals.

Some scientists who shared this view with us did note that while they see no relationship between their faith and their scientific practices—the technical dimensions of their work—they do see how their religious beliefs shape the interpersonal aspects of their work, such as how they treat colleagues and students. Apart from this distinction, religious scientists who separate religion from work see no overlap between being a scientist and being religious.

Among the religious scientists for whom separation is an active sociocognitive strategy, there are three rationales for compartmentalizing their religious identity at work. One is tied to the view of public universities as secular. A professor of biology who identifies as slightly religious[40] explained to us, for example, "I'm at a state public university and we really shy away from any intersection of religion and public school education. . . . I make it a strict policy not to talk about religion or politics in my professional life." In some respects, such a rationale is surprising, since religious expression permeates other secular arenas of public life, such as the government and primary and secondary schools.

A culture of professionalism is another factor that motivates separation between science and religion among US religious scientists. From this perspective, even if research goals or experience of work is shaped by their religious identity, scientists may avoid any aspect of religious expression in the workplace to limit their interactions with colleagues to strictly scientific issues or because of a sense of disinterest among their peers. A religious graduate student in biology[41] depicted this view when he explained:

> I think there's kind of a "don't ask, don't tell" policy within science, unless you really wanna get into the hotly debated arenas of evolution and creation and all that. . . . There's just kind of a: "OK, you can believe what you want, that's fine."

Most commonly, however, compartmentalizing faith at work for US religious scientists was motivated by the perception of hostility toward religion (55 percent of the US scientists we surveyed agree or strongly agree that their colleagues have a negative attitude toward religion). This stands in contrast to the sense that colleagues do not care about religious belief and is instead driven by a desire to avoid mockery, discrimination, and stigma. Scientists whose narratives of separation fell into this category discussed outspoken colleagues, general concerns about how they would be judged, and a desire to avoid representing the religious public to nonreligious scientists. These scientists seek to avoid both inaccurate views of their religious beliefs and evaluation of their work as scientists based on their religious identity rather than merit. A religious postdoctoral researcher in biology,[42] for example, described a devout Christian colleague who joined her lab: "[My colleague] was very surprised coming to America and having people say, 'Oh, you're Christian, well that must mean that you're against gay marriage and you don't like abortion.'" Another postdoctoral researcher in biology[43] explained to us, "I don't want to be the representative Christian in the whole lab. . . . There's very little exposure . . . to that in the scientific environment and I don't really want to be the envoy for my whole religion." On why he compartmentalizes his faith at work, one graduate student in biology[44] simply said: "Maybe they will question my ability to look at the data . . . and not be able to make my own critical decisions."

Overlap

When religion does enter the scientific workplace, we see dimensions that are unique to the United States. Although US scientists seem to rarely interact with the broader public to share and discuss science—save for specific instances of outreach—scientists nevertheless construct in their minds the notion of a religious public that rejects science. Encounters with religious undergraduates often reinforce or contribute to this view of religious individuals, and the negative attitude that accompanies this way of thinking can manifest itself in discrimination and mockery, mainly toward conservative Christians (likely because Christians make up the largest share of the religious population and conservative Christians are the most vocal participants in public debates between science and religion in the United States). For religious scientists, we see that religion influences the pathways they pursue and ethical frameworks they use in science, although not in the manner that most nonreligious scientists would expect.

The US Public

When religion comes up in the scientific workplace in the United States, it is most often tied to how scientists view public attitudes toward science. This theme predominately emerged in the accounts of nonreligious scientists, but it was not limited to this group. While some scientists interface with the public through their research or science outreach, in most instances public attitudes toward science do not materialize in the day-to-day work of scientists. Nevertheless, the public looms large in how scientists conceptualize their "social contract" with society. How scientists perceive the public approach to science has implications for how they disseminate knowledge in the public sphere, generate support, and recruit future scientists to the profession. Scientists often see the religious public as monolithic—a group hostile to science that rejects evolution, climate change, and other scientific truths. They see religious individuals bringing religion into science—while at the same time creating conflict between the two realms. One graduate student in physics[45] described "religious people in other parts of the country" who question climate change and the big bang: "It's usually sort of all of us thinking those people are idiots, which is not the most charitable thing, but it reflects the frustration." A postdoctoral scientist in biology,[46] raised Presbyterian but now agnostic, explained:

> We're sometimes confronted with this mentality in America that's religiously driven . . . the need to deny the veracity of evolution. . . . We'll get bizarre phone messages on our lab answering machine [and emails] having to do with denying evolution or climate change . . . when we have a paper come out with a fair amount of media attention.

Some scientists do see some religious groups as more hostile to religion than others, and there's a clear tendency to aim their ire and critiques at evangelical Christians and other politically conservative religious communities. Yet for a few scientists, "progressive" religious groups may also be objects of frustration. A postdoctoral researcher in biology who attends a Unitarian church in a liberal college town[47] spoke of "suspicion of science from the left" in her church community. In her view, many individuals in her religious community possess inaccurate views of genetically modified organisms (GMOs), and consequently, she tries:

> to convince people that GMOs are not inherently evil. You can take a stance against industrialized agriculture and that there are valid reasons to be concerned about that. But scientists moving genes between plants is essentially a technology driven version of the plant breeding that has gone on for centuries.

While religion plays a key role in influencing attitudes on only a handful of scientific ideas or research topics—namely, those that cause epistemological or moral conflict with religion—public conflicts have left many scientists with the false impression that religious individuals wholly reject science in favor of their faith. For many scientists, this results in little motivation to attempt to create productive dialogue that could alter misunderstandings and biases—both in terms of how religious individuals see science and how scientists view religious people. Instead, we find frustration or indifference. Overall, we find US scientists have little interest in engaging in dialogue with religious groups about science. Such disengagement exists despite evidence that, according to sociologist Christopher P. Scheitle and coauthors, religious groups are willing to seek out both religious and scientific sources of information when questions about science emerge.[48]

That said, some scientists do try to engage religious individuals whom they see as skeptical of science. For some of these scientists, the approach is to communicate reservedly so as not to stoke conflict. Luis, whom we met earlier,[49] said the policy of a nonprofit organization where he volunteers generally informs his own approach:

> We have to choose our words carefully. . . . Their official policy . . . is to say, "These are the views of the [organization]. I am not qualified to speak to you about it." And I think that's kind of how people treat the topic as a whole when communicating to the public.

Some US scientists believe there is a need for a more engaged approach. If religious individuals are placing religion above science, the answer is not to isolate them further from the world of science or to leave them to their own false conclusions. A religious postdoctoral researcher in biology[50] spoke of the religious public's distrust of scientists and noted:

> Socially, we don't do enough to sort of promote our cause. . . . If I have a question about disease or health, I would listen to doctors. . . . [But] with things like climate change and evolution . . . it's a popularity contest. You listen to people that think like you [instead of] listening to experts.

In contrast to promoting the cause, so to speak, other scientists stress the importance of sensitivity. A professor of biology whose research is tied to genetically modified organisms,[51] for example, told us:

> I've had personal experience. For example, if I am talking to someone who is very religious and they ask me what I do, I'm a little cautious at saying certain

words. [A religious friend asked about recombinant DNA.] I wanted to give her my viewpoint, but I also wanted to be sensitive to whatever she might be thinking . . . because [she might think] "you're 'playing God.'"

We also found concern among some US scientists that religious views of science could also have consequences for research funding. They worry that religious individuals in government will use religious doctrine to form their positions on scientific issues. A postdoctoral researcher in physics[52] explained, "The people who control funding for science, for example, have their own view of Christianity and what it means and what you can and can't fund or how old the Earth is and whether or not we're affecting it." Some nonreligious scientists also discussed their belief that individuals raised in a religious home—especially if it's a conservative Christian home—would be discouraged from participating in science. In the opinion of one graduate student in biology:[53]

> Religious people are [often] homeschooled or they're taught in schools that have textbooks that purposely misconstrue scientific information. . . . If you have a child that is brought up with that as the understanding of the world . . . they will not be gravitating toward a scientific career in a way.

Some of the religious scientists we spoke with did share experiences of their religious communities creating religiously based conflict with science. Luis,[54] for instance, told us:

> I come from a Latino community. You're immediately ostracized if you do go into the sciences. . . . Intense Christianity that tells people, you should not deviate from what the Bible says, and when you try to toss in that, "Well, no, because science works this way," it becomes very difficult. . . . What ends up happening is in the Latino community, people hate scientists, doctors, things like that.

While we cannot generalize to all Latino Christian communities based on this example, Latinos are underrepresented in science and overrepresented in theologically conservative Christian traditions. There is also some research that underscores the possibility that there is skepticism toward scientists in minority communities with fewer resources for science education.[55]

Undergraduate and Graduate Students

One of the primary places religion comes up in the workplace for scientists is in teaching undergraduate and graduate courses where they can encounter religious individuals, sometimes of other faith traditions. For nonreligious scientists, religious students are at times seen as representative of the religious public at large. References to religious students came up more frequently in our interviews in the United States than in other regions we studied, most commonly citing students perceived to be evangelical Christians.

In undergraduate education, it is typically students who bring religion into the instructional context of scientific work. This typically does not happen in a public manner. For example, a graduate student in biology[56] who served as a teaching assistant for a "quietly religious" Muslim professor told us:

> One of the students we had last semester was a fanatic Christian, and she wrote on one of her tests that [her Muslim professor] needed to be baptized, and so he took that as a threat and wanted to file it as a threat, but he ended up just saying, "This is inappropriate." . . . [The student] said he's going to hell if he doesn't get baptized.

While religion sometimes enters the workplace through interpersonal student–teacher issues related to religious identity, other scientists offered examples tied to epistemological issues. Luis[57] told us about students responding with religion when evolution was a topic in the classroom, explaining:

> A student was intentionally trying to be confrontational with the professor who was teaching a lecture. . . . I've [also] heard of other people who have actually had students like this in the past, and they, for example, on an exam would write, "Common scientific knowledge says . . . " before every statement, so as not to conflict with their own beliefs.

The scientists we talked with generally avoided engaging with the religious views or beliefs of students, even when confronted publicly. Some religious scientists suggested they are comfortable discussing science and religion in one-on-one private meetings with students, but they would be reluctant to engage in conversation about religion were the topic to come up in the classroom.

In some instances, however, scientists may reference religious ideas in the classroom to the extent it is necessary to teach scientific explanations to religious students and achieve their pedagogical objectives. A professor of physics,[58] for example, said religion rarely comes up in his work, but told us:

> Twice in my basic physics classes . . . I would sort of begin talking about the big bang theory and cosmology . . . and I realized I was talking to people who

perhaps had other beliefs altogether. I took a poll twice. I said, "How many of you think the world was created about 7,000 years ago?" And I got a majority in both cases.

As a result, this physicist said, he introduced new content in the introduction of the course that explained how the understanding of motion had evolved over time from assuming a deity's active role to an understanding based on Newtonian physics. A religious biologist who teaches a course on evolution[59] explained that in her course:

I have a slide, "What are the misconceptions and misuses of evolution?" . . . But [that's] pretty much the only extent I go into when it comes to my teaching. If a student has more in-depth questions and that student comes to my office . . . I usually give them a little paper on teaching evolution from a Christian perspective—if a student is Christian.

While most professors have complete autonomy over the content they include in their courses, graduate students who teach classes may have little or no control over course content. A nonreligious graduate student in physics[60] described teaching a course on physics and having to include lecture materials explaining that science and religion do not conflict with one another. When asked why the course included such content, she responded:

Arguably for the same reason that I actually had to teach a lesson on human evolution [in an astronomy class]. . . . Science education in this country is not in a good state, to put it mildly. It's a bad sign when textbook makers have to put [religious] disclaimers in the [high school] science textbooks. . . . If you have students in college who went to high schools that taught out of those books, how solid of a science education do you think they got? So, a lot of what I was doing was arguably remedial. . . . It was at . . . a major institution. But yes, we had to emphasize the fact that religion and science are in fact not in conflict, they are very different things, but there are some people . . . who do not appreciate that fact and feel threatened by it for whatever reason.

Even if agitated in some contexts, scientists do not appear to respond negatively to religious undergraduates and instead do their best to approach course content in a way that keeps religion from interfering in the science.

Religion also surfaces in graduate training. Again, most of the narratives we heard referenced evangelical students, perhaps because most religious graduate students in science are Christian or perhaps because, as we have seen in their accounts of the religious public and undergraduate students, US scientists see evangelicals as the face of religion. One nonreligious professor of biology[61] told us stories about a religious doctoral student she described as a "white evangelical farm girl":

> On the day of her thesis defense, when she got to the point where she had to say the word evolution, she kind of choked and she never said that word and modified her talk because in the audience was her future in-laws, who are ultra religious. . . . The rest of her talk, she was kind of stumbling because I think she felt bad that she didn't actually, to the scientists in the room, explain her work in the way it should have been explained. [Also,] we participate in a science fair . . . and she was invited because she was very active with the society that was putting on a booth. But when she saw the activities that would be presented, she said, "I can't do this. I'm sorry." And she explained because they were going to be giving some demonstrations or explanations having to do with Darwin, and she said that it was against her religion.

Another professor of biology[62] described a graduate student who rejected major aspects of evolutionary theory. When asked, "How do you feel about awarding a Ph.D. to an individual who, in your words, rejects a core organizing principle of your field," she responded:

> That was the dilemma. But the fact is the guy had done a good job on his research, and so you have to separate the two. . . . Our understanding was that he was going to go and teach at one of the Christian schools, you know, colleges, and he was going to deliver an anti-evolution message. So, that was something that I was concerned about, sure, because we have a problem in this country.

While US scientists do not necessarily confront religious students about the ways in which their religious beliefs might interfere with their scientific education or future scientific work—especially if they are executing quality work in the specific area of their research—there is ire for evangelicals or others whose faith traditions sometimes do not accept core principles within a field. Scientists expressed concern if, beyond a student's particular research, the student rejected foundational scientific principles or undermined the integrity of the scientific enterprise.

Discrimination and Mockery

After work one night, a group of graduate students went out to dinner, and a religious graduate student in physics[63] described some of the conversation that took place:

> One of the other students was like "OK. Who here believes in God and who here doesn't? And who here feels persecuted for that?" And it was interesting because those that were essentially atheist, they were like, "Oh yeah, I feel like I'm a minority" and those who were basically Christian, they were like, "Oh no, we feel like we're a minority," and so basically everyone feels uncomfortable.

Atheists are a minority in the general US public, leading to feelings of social discrimination. In science, however, religious groups are a minority, which leaves them more open to discrimination in the scientific workplace, even though they may wield considerable power in the public sphere. Given the negative way US scientists tend to view the religious public, it is not surprising to find some discrimination of religious scientists. This discrimination can take many forms, such as denying access to opportunities like jobs or using derogatory and abusive language. Science is considered a secular institution, and to maintain its authority and power, religion can be derogated and religious expression suppressed—and religious scientists who deviate from these norms can be stigmatized. To some extent, mockery and discrimination may filter out religious groups from science.

In our survey, less than 10 percent of US scientists reported overt conflicts about religion in their department. Yet, 29 percent of religious scientists in the United States indicated they have experienced some level of religious discrimination in the workplace. Among the countries we studied, it struck us that it was only in Turkey where a greater number of scientists reported experiencing discrimination (34 percent). Among US scientists, reports of discrimination were highest among Muslims (57 percent) and Protestants (40 percent), including evangelical Christians. Discrimination against Protestants in the US scientific community is noteworthy given that they are the largest religious group in science and in the US public.

Fifty-four percent of US scientists we surveyed agreed that scholars in their discipline had a negative attitude toward religion. "I've definitely heard colleagues make offhand comments that didn't portray religion or religious people in a positive light. . . . If I was religious, I would've felt a little bit uncomfortable," a nonreligious graduate student in physics[64] responded when we asked about discrimination. Religious scientists in the United States also noted occurrences of "unnecessarily vocal Christian bashing"[65] and stated that religious scientists "have to have a thick skin in order to be in the science realm."[66] Our survey revealed that 24 percent of US scientists are uncomfortable letting people in their academic department know their views on religion, including 35 percent of religious scientists. A female graduate student in physics[67] explained to us that being religious "opens you up to be not taken seriously because of the mocking comments you get . . . along the general lines of the stereotypical 'religion is a crutch, you must not be able to function well.'"

A religious associate professor of physics[68] described a faculty social he attended for new members of his university where he encountered another scientist who had attended a religious university in the southern United States:

> [The school was part of] a denomination I hadn't heard of before. So I was curious. I asked him about that and he said, "Oh, well, don't worry. It's nothing nearly as crazy as the Mormons for example." [*Laughs*] He hadn't realized that I was Mormon. So I kind of stared at him and he said, "Oh, let me guess." And I said, "Yup, I am Mormon." [*Laughs*]

Perhaps because they expect some level of ridicule, some religious scientists take jokes and mockery of religion as good-natured ribbing without hostility. However, the "baseline" of a hostile climate for religion in the scientific workplace begins with mockery that may be intended as lighthearted humor by the nonreligious, but feels contemptuous to religious individuals, which then influences religious expression in the workplace. Both religious and nonreligious scientists agree this is the case. When delivered by nonreligious scientists, jokes about religion may produce discomfort among religious scientists because, when such jokes occur within the scientific workplace, they are understood in relation to professional identity.

Mockery and jokes can be a way of constructing boundaries of group membership. In the context of the scientific workplace, nonreligious scientists use mockery to classify themselves as legitimate members of the scientific community while religious scientists are not. A religious professor of biology,[69] who noted that there is "absolutely" discrimination toward the religious in science, described the legitimacy of group membership among biologists as predicated on "a culture of acceptance of those who are atheist in their inclination."

Such group boundaries form the basis of subtle or explicit discrimination. While no US scientists admitted discouraging a religious scientist from joining their group or lab, religious scientists did assume discrimination among their colleagues on the basis of perceived epistemological conflict. Consider the account of a religious professor of biology[70] who believes religious individuals in science experience discrimination:

> I think it's probably subtle. My guess would be that it's: "How could he believe that stuff? What's wrong with him? Why is she? Why would they need that?" And I think that that just comes from . . . close-mindedness and ignorance of the [fact that] people are able to disconnect. . . . They can study natural phenomena and still believe in God, right?

Assumptions that nonreligious scientists make about religious scientists may factor into judgments made about applicants for doctoral programs or faculty positions. While the application process often does not reveal whether a scientist is religious, this can become obvious if an applicant completed undergraduate, doctoral, or postdoctoral training at a religious college or university. While our sample of US scientists includes alumni of these institutions who successfully attained doctoral degrees or faculty positions at a range of institutions, our interview data illustrate ways in which having trained at a religious institution may invite discrimination against a scientist. A religious professor of biology[71] described what has happened at her elite institution with doctoral applicants: "We have had students apply from universities, like Liberty University [a conservative Protestant university in Virginia], and my colleagues when they're going through the admission process will say, 'Well we can't pick them, look where they went to school.'" This biologist, who holds an endowed chair, also described how she is able to advocate for such applicants, who are otherwise qualified candidates. In other circumstances, religious scientists with less power may not feel capable of intervention. It might also be the case that while religious scientists who compartmentalize their beliefs sympathize with religious applicants, they do not take action because they are unsure if the applicant similarly separates religion and science or, perhaps even more likely, because they worry about having their own identity and approach to science and religion questioned by others.

It is also important to note that discrimination against scientists by religious communities can also work to keep religious individuals out of science. Earlier, we met Susan,[72] who grew up being homeschooled in a community that was very traditional and "very distrustful of modern science," she said. Once she began her scientific training, she realized that some of the assumptions about scientists she had been exposed to were incorrect:

I grew up being scared of other scientific ideas and to be somewhat distrustful of different sciences. Especially in biology and evolution, and actually, the same for astronomy because of the suggestions that the universe was a lot older. But meeting the people and seeing their work, and seeing the integrity that they had, made me realize that my distrust was misplaced.

Many religious scientists encountered similar stereotypes of scientists during their adolescence. Other graduate students, for example, discussed their first religious communities and described distrust of scientists and concerns about scientists "playing God." They also shared prior fears about how they would be perceived by their fellow adherents after pursuing their scientific careers. In much the same way that interreligious contact can reduce erroneous stereotypes of believers, exposure to what scientists actually think and do can help reduce erroneous stereotypes of scientists among religious believers.

Religious Pathways and Ethical Frameworks in Science

When you ask nonreligious scientists in the United States how they think religion influences the work of religious scientists, many answer that religious individuals may avoid epistemologically contentious areas of scientific research (such as evolutionary biology) or morally contentious topics (such as hereditary genetics). Some US scientists, particularly those who perceive antiscientific sentiment among conservative Protestants, believe individuals from certain religious communities would—and should—avoid careers in science altogether. In our interviews, we did hear about how religion influenced career pathways for religious scientists, but it was not in the manner nonreligious scientists assume.

For the religious scientists we spoke with in the United States, religious beliefs were often what motivated their pursuit of a life in science. A Catholic physicist,[73] for example, had this to say when asked how religion influences her work:

> My spiritual seeking, which started when I was quite young, certainly did influence my choice of careers. I mean, I really believed I experienced the presence of something far greater than myself in the natural world and I was interested in pursuing it.

She noted explicitly that it was her spirituality—and not organized religion— that pushed her toward a scientific career. From this account and others like it, we saw that personal spiritual beliefs could motivate religious scientists to pursue a career in science, even if they may have been exposed to skepticism toward science within their religious community.

Scientists in the United States have developed a vast rhetoric of what spirituality entails. During our interviews, we discovered that scientists who self-identify as spiritual but not religious have creative and individualistic ways of constructing, understanding, and interpreting their spirituality. A professor of biology[74] who was raised as a Catholic but "was always suspicious about the idea of God" described her approach to being spiritual but not religious. While she has "practiced Buddhism for years and years," she does not have "strong beliefs, at least not in this typical religious way that people have," she said. She often goes into the university chapel "just to meditate or have really quiet moments." An associate professor of biology[75] reflecting on her spirituality said, "I go outside. That's where I find spirituality; it's by being outside." Other scientists experience their spirituality through everyday exploration in science, such as a physicist[76] who told us:

> As a scientist, the more things that you learn and the more things that you're exposed to, it almost gets harder to imagine that there wasn't some sort of grand plan. Or, at least, you have to sort of step back and marvel at the beauty of it. However that came about. So I think that could feed your belief as well.

We did find that religion influenced the topics that religious scientists selected to work on, as some nonreligious scientists believe—but not because they were consciously or purposefully trying to avoid epistemologically or morally contentious areas of research. While we did encounter stories of undergraduate students who abstained from particular laboratory experiments due to their religious beliefs, we did not encounter working scientists who said religion led them away from any particular topic. Rather, most scientists discussed how religion influenced their research goals by leading them to consider the societal impact of their work. A religious graduate student in biology[77] explained: "I don't think you can be a very devout Catholic, Protestant, whatever you are, and do work that means nothing to you or that you don't believe is going to improve anyone's life." There is a range of ways in which scientists construct concrete societal impacts, but in the narratives we heard, scientists primarily referred to areas of science associated with applications.[78] Religious scientists told us that religion motivated their desire to conduct research that, in the words of one scientist, "is not just interesting, but useful to people."[79] For example, when we asked religious scientists about the influence of religion on their goals as a researcher, one postdoctoral researcher in physics[80] responded, "I am trying to work on a field which I hope will have a beneficial impact for the world in terms of clean energy." A graduate student in biology[81] answered that religion:

> influences me to go toward medically relevant research. . . . It's an important religious value for me to do things that help people who need a lot of help rather than do something that might just make a few people a lot of money.

We also heard religious scientists discuss how religious belief can have an impact on the ethical frameworks they bring to the production of knowledge. Values prominent in these narratives included transparency, integrity, balance, and accountability. Religious scientists often invoked these ideals when talking about how their religious beliefs and values shape their response to the competitive pressures inherent in science. A graduate student in biology[82] described the struggle between her moral character and the competitive nature of science:

> People do underhanded things to get their research out there. . . . It's made me feel like science is a lost cause. . . . It makes me feel like I want to give up. . . . I'm not cutthroat enough, I'm not this, I'm not that. . . . Religion has influenced the way I look at science now and I definitely have more scrutiny for science than I did before.

While some religious scientists find their religious identity at odds with the competitive work environment, raising doubts about continuing a career in science, others find religion acts as a resource for responding to such pressures. "My spirituality tells me . . . I'd rather be poor, not famous, but have to be ethical. I cannot create data and follow the gold rush or whatever," an associate professor of biology[83] explained. "I just follow my conscience. . . . Everybody says that I don't sell myself enough, but that's just me." Other religious scientists talked about religion as a resource for coping with the pressures of science by helping them expand their perspective and priorities. An associate professor of physics[84] described "single-minded scientists" and then stated, "[T]here are other aspects in my life that are more important than my scientific research. For example, my home and family and church. Pursuing scientific research takes a backseat to other responsibilities that I have."

There is a subset of highly religious scientists for whom commitment to their religious organization is as central to their self-identity as their professional identity as a scientist. Within this group, we find scientists who serve as lay ministers or Sunday school teachers, or whose practices include daily devotionals at home with family members. An associate professor of physics[85] shared with us:

> One of the focuses of my church is social justice and I am involved in several activities through my church where we interact with the community. My children are involved and that's been an important community for them. . . . It's an important part of our social life and an important part of our identity as a family because it is something that we try to do on a weekly basis.

Religious scientists discussed how ethical frameworks and values based on their religion informed not only how they navigated their own careers but also how they interacted with colleagues. We saw this best exemplified in the case of a Catholic physicist[86] who told us she has received "pushback" because of her need for transparency, integrity, and high ethical standards. In her words:

> Behavior that comes out of my faith . . . has definitely had an impact and not necessarily a positive one. . . . [For example], if I feel that there's a group that really has an extraordinary amount of political clout which is not necessarily based on good science, I've been known to publicly challenge people on that. I feel an obligation to do so. Most of my colleagues will not do that, I can assure you.

Conclusions

How US scientists perceive the US religious public highly influences the relationship between science and religion in the United States. When many US scientists think of religious Americans, they picture evangelical biblical literalists who are antiscience. The US religious public is not so monolithic, of course— though there are religious communities that are skeptical of science, and religious Americans often have trouble accepting scientific research or findings that contradict their religious beliefs. The best social scientific data available though reveals gross inaccuracy in how many scientists imagine the US religious public approaches science. In general, as Ecklund and co-author Christopher P. Scheitle argue in their book *Religion vs. Science: What Religious People Really Think*, the American public (including the American religious public) thinks scientists and science have a high degree of authority.[87] Take the issue of human origins and evolution. Since the 1980s, Gallup polls that ask Americans about the origin and development of human beings have consistently found that 40 to 45 percent of the US public embraces the young-Earth creationist view that "God created human beings pretty much in their present form at one time within the last 10,000 years or so."[88] A problem with these polls, however, is that they offer only three limited answer choices and do not capture how convinced respondents are of their answer or how much their answer informs their attitudes toward science more generally. A nationally representative survey by sociologist Jonathan Hill asked much more subtle questions and found that creationists who are certain of their belief—who reject human evolution and believe that God created humans—represent 29 percent of the American public.[89] This is a considerably smaller segment than other surveys have led us to believe. Hill also shows that views of human evolution are quite varied and, once certainty of these positions is taken into account, both antievolution creationists and atheistic evolutionists turn out to be very small proportions of the US public. This is just one example that suggests religious individuals may be more open to changing their mind to accept scientific findings than many scientists believe—and greater engagement between US scientists and religious believers could improve public understanding of science in the country.[90]

Discrimination against religious scientists undermines the US scientific endeavor. While some religious Americans may reject science in favor of religious teachings and beliefs, most US religious scientists compartmentalize their work and their faith. The hostility that nonreligious scientists in the United States have toward religious scientists seems to be driven by an erroneous view of how religious groups think about science that is promulgated in the public sphere. Almost half of all scientists who are Protestant—the largest religious group in the US scientific community—feel they have experienced discrimination. Women and minorities—key groups that the scientific community seeks to recruit and retain in scientific careers—may be especially at risk for discrimination, given that they are more likely than white males to be religious, particularly those at less elite institutions.[91] As we've seen, many religious scientists indirectly use their faith to select research that will benefit society as a whole, maintain positive relationships with colleagues, or bring religiously promoted virtues into the workplace, and thus may be an asset to a scientific enterprise that seeks to produce work that has a positive impact on society.

CHAPTER 4 | United Kingdom
"New Atheists" and "Dangerous Muslims"

ARIYA,[1] A MUSLIM BIOLOGIST in the United Kingdom, believes her religion obligates her to be ethical, to do her work well and in the right ways. She has rejected certain research projects for religious reasons, she told us, and yet, she does not think there is any conflict between being religious and being a scientist. As she sees it, as a Muslim she has "religiously . . . been asked to go out and get the knowledge," and "wherever you have to go for it, you should be prepared to do that." Religion, she said, "did not stop me to become a scientist." Ariya was raised in Pakistan, moved to the United Kingdom for her job, and has chosen not to wear the hijab; she said that the anti-Islamic sentiment she has faced since she's been working in England has made her faith grow even stronger.

Immigrants like Ariya are changing the religious landscape of the United Kingdom and, as a result, are influencing how many UK scientists talk about the relationship between science and religion. The United Kingdom—here we primarily include Wales, Scotland, and England, but not Northern Ireland (because of its religiously different context) in our analyses—is one of the most secular countries we studied; participation in religious practices has been in decline since the 1950s. And yet a 2015 Pew Research Center survey found that 52 percent of people in the United Kingdom are worried about rising Islamic extremism. We also found more "outsider" antagonism in the United Kingdom than in countries that are more religiously homogeneous. One scientist[2] we met at a conference told us that Muslim immigrants coming to the United Kingdom might be similar to evangelical Christians "you see in the US—they may be a problem for science."

The United Kingdom is also home to prominent scientists and academics with *very* different perspectives on the relationship between science and religion. On the one hand, for example, there is famous atheist biologist Richard Dawkins, who is hostile to religion and sees science and religion as intrinsically incompatible and conflicting.[3] On the other hand, there are scientist-theologians—like John Polkinghorne, a theoretical physicist, and Alister McGrath, with a doctorate in molecular biophysics—who argue that science and Christian faith are completely compatible.[4] Sociologist Tom Kaden and colleagues argue that there are differences between lay and thought leader perspectives on science and religion; vocal leaders like Dawkins and Polkinghorne may have very different views then the average scientist.[5]

"First of all, I guess the best thing for me to say outright is that I'm an atheist," said Simon,[6] one of the youngest scientists appointed as a lecturer at his university in central England. Simon looks like the Royal Navy officer he wanted to be as a child: aviator watch, closely cropped hair, and meticulously organized office. While he did not grow up in a religious home, Simon did receive religious education as a youth, but he frustrated his teachers by asking what he calls "the awkward questions"—such as why religious texts claimed the Earth is around 6,000 years old when in other classes he was learning the Earth is billions of years older. He couldn't bring science and religion "together in any rational sense," he said. "I've never truly had any spirituality or any faith in any religious context from the beginning," he told us, and thus could "throw off the shackles of religion."

Today, he is an avid reader of Dawkins and other "New Atheists" like Christopher Hitchens, Sam Harris, and Daniel Dennett, and though he shares their concerns about the role of religion in society, and is in "complete disagreement" with religion, he would not characterize himself as "militant" the way they are. Simon is what we might call a religiously affiliated atheist. He was married in a church and his children were christened. When his son recently asked about God, heaven, and hell, Simon said, "I'll tell you what I think," but said he tries to avoid imposing his "scientist atheist views" on his children or his wife's religious friends, though on occasion he has offended them.

At the university, Simon's academic department is "a melting pot of cultures" and immigrant religions, he said, yet he believes the scientists who are Muslim, Hindu, Sikh, Christian, and Jewish probably only maintain cultural elements of their religious traditions. "I wouldn't say they've continued true religious beliefs," he said. "I find it very difficult," he explained, "for somebody to be a full, proper scientist to also harbor true core religious beliefs." He rejects the idea that science and religion overlap or occupy separate spheres. In his view, religion and science are incompatible. "If you're a scientist and you use evidence to support your ideas and work . . . but then on a Sunday morning you get up and go to church and take that completely out, you're living two lives, in my opinion," he said. "There's a Jekyll-Hyde about it."

Like Simon, a majority of UK scientists are nonreligious. They do not believe in God, belong to a religious tradition, or attend services. Yet our survey did find that 37 percent of UK scientists do belong to a religious tradition,[7] with those from minority religious traditions (Muslims and Hindus, for example) appearing to practice their traditions most seriously. UK physicists and biologists born outside the United Kingdom are more likely than those born within the United Kingdom to belong to a religion. When thinking about the relationship between science and religion, 47 percent of UK scientists believe the two realms are independent, referring to different aspects of reality. Like Simon, 35 percent think that science and religion are in conflict, taking the side of science—and yet they too do not tend to see themselves as being as militant as Dawkins or other public New Atheists.

Immigrant scientists have also had an impact on the religious ecology of UK science. While native-born UK scientists are most likely to be nonreligious or nonpracticing Protestants, immigrant UK scientists are most commonly Muslim and Hindu. Many of the immigrant scientists come from a former British colony and are trained in schools modeled on the UK system. Their highest goal is to go to a UK university to practice science, and yet they maintain cultural and religious ties to the places from where they come. The changing demographics of the United Kingdom—including UK science—have influenced how many scientists think about the relationship between religion and science.

Cultural Context of Science and Religion in the United Kingdom

The history of the relationship between science and religion in the United Kingdom is complex.[8] Christianity has played an important role in shaping the United Kingdom's social, cultural, and political institutions. Although Anglicanism and Catholicism, in particular, have had a lasting influence on UK society, actual participation in these religious traditions has dropped considerably over time. In England, the official state religion is the Church of

England, part of the broader Anglican Communion. According to one UK scientist[9] we talked with,

> You grow up in a society, and obviously that shapes your viewpoint to a certain extent. And this country has an established religion, and I'm old enough that when I was in school, every day had to start with an act of Christian worship. . . . And growing up, it's just understood that that's the setup.

In the other UK nations outside of England—Scotland, Wales, and Northern Ireland—the Anglican Communion exerts significant social influence. The Catholic Church, the second biggest church in the United Kingdom, is also a prominent religious and social force (in Scotland, the Church of Scotland is the national church).[10] And yet, membership in these institutions has long been on the decline in the United Kingdom where many believe without belonging, as coined by the sociologist Grace Davie.[11]

At many points in the history of the United Kingdom, religion has influenced the development of scientific thought. As sociologist Robert K. Merton[12] details in his work, the emergence of science in seventeenth-century England was considerably driven by the correlation between Puritan theologies and the philosophies and values of science. As he argues, the nascent institution of science found legitimacy in the values of Puritanism, and Puritans found in the pursuit of science activities consistent with the teachings of their faith, such as the glorification of God through work, the regularity and predictability of the natural world, and the ability to enlarge control over nature. The universities of Oxford and Cambridge, today recognized as two of the most advanced scientific research institutions in the world, stem from a tradition of theological inquiry rooted in Christianity.[13] While religious influence in both public and private spheres has decreased over time in England, in particular, the Church of England's status as a state church and the country's compulsory religious education symbolically suggest that even if citizens are not personally religious, they are expected to have a baseline knowledge of religion.[14]

Today, the relationship between science and religion in the United Kingdom faces new challenges and opportunities due to transformations in the country's religious landscape. On the whole, UK religion appears to be in decline. Key indicators, such as religious affiliation, belief, and attendance, reveal that younger Britons are less religious than older Britons. While it is believed by some that individuals in the United States still tend to become more religious as they grow older, similar age effects have *not* been observed in the United Kingdom.[15] Instead, changes in religiosity are more likely to be seen *between* generations, rather than *within* a generation over the life course.[16] Longitudinal data from the British Social Attitudes survey (which covers Great Britain but not Northern Ireland), indicate that Britons in the same age cohort experience little variation in their religiosity as they grow older.[17] Since younger Britons today are less religious than earlier generations, we can expect religiosity to continue on a downward trend.[18]

More specifically, the United Kingdom is experiencing greater religious diversity—a decrease in the Christian population and an increase in the proportion of individuals who belong to non-Christian religious traditions, the result of a migration trend.[19] According to the 2011 Census of England and Wales, only 59 percent of residents identify as Christian, down from 72 percent in 2001.[20] Alternatively, results from the British Social Attitudes Survey (which includes England, Scotland, and Wales) suggest that Christians are already a minority of the population. In 1983, Christians accounted for 67 percent of the population, yet by 2012 only 46 percent of the British public affiliated with a Christian tradition: 20 percent as Anglican (down from 40 percent in 1983), 9 percent as Catholic, and 17 percent as part of another Christian tradition.[21] (Christian immigrants, particularly from Africa, tend to go to independent, often minority-led, evangelical churches, leading to what actually appears to be an increase in those attending independent churches.[22]) Although Christianity in all its varied forms is still the dominant UK religion, Christians tend to be older and whiter than the average Briton, and thus we might expect the country to continue on a path to becoming a Christian minority nation.[23]

Between 2001 and 2011, 70 percent of the United Kingdom's population growth was a result of immigration. Although a high proportion of immigration to the United Kingdom over the past 15 years has been from eastern Europe, immigrants are also likely to be non-Christians from countries like India and Pakistan. The proportion of the UK population that belongs to non-Christian religions has grown from 2 percent in 1983 to 6 percent in 2012.[24] Perhaps more impressive, from 2004 to 2010, both Hinduism and Islam grew around 40 percent, which has led to rapid growth in their share of the United Kingdom's population. The influx of Muslims, in particular, has also led to heightened public awareness of the intersection of religion and science in public life, and new religious narratives and practices that have an impact on the relationship between religion and science in public discourse and the scientific workplace.[25] For example, in 2011, professors at the University College London expressed concern over increasing numbers of Muslim biology students boycotting biology lectures on evolution because they felt the information presented in the lectures conflicted with ideas in the Qur'an.[26] Incidents like this present a challenge for scientific institutions, which are accustomed to working with individuals from predominantly white, Christian backgrounds and don't have much experience with groups outside this demographic.

Religion and Science in the Public Sphere

Debates regarding the proper relationship between science and religion feature prominently in UK public life. So-called New Atheists and religious fundamentalists, who actually represent a small portion of the UK population, receive a disproportionate share of media attention. The push for secularism in the United Kingdom is not a new phenomenon, but in recent years, outspoken New Atheists have made significant attempts to secularize society, criticizing religion and arguing that it is incompatible with science and has no place in the public sphere.[27] In no other national context where we studied scientists did we observe such vocal hard-line opinions on the relationship between science and religion. How much, we wondered, do these individuals and the media coverage they get have an impact on the view scientists have of the relationship between science and religion? We wondered the same about so-called religious fundamentalists, who are often also at the center of debates regarding religion and science in UK public life. Have vocal religious minorities, such as strict Muslims and evangelical Christians, also exerted considerable influence over the perception of the science–religion relationship?

The tensions between New Atheists and those they call religious fundamentalists have come to a head many times. The 2002 Emmanuel creationism controversy is one example. The Vardy Foundation, sponsor of Emmanuel College, a school that received funding from the state,[28] sought to build additional schools to expand its educational network in different UK cities. Controversy emerged when *The Guardian* reported that evangelical Christian teachers at Emmanuel undermined biology courses at the school by rejecting evolution.[29] Soon after, there was an organized backlash against the foundation, alleging that its mission was to promote creationist thought. In a public statement, Dawkins condemned the Vardy Foundation for engaging in what he called "educational debauchery."[30] One of the first major public scandals involving creationism in the United Kingdom, it sparked debate over including creationism as part of biology curricula.

Before the Emmanuel creationism controversy, legislation did little to ban the teaching of creationism.[31] But since then, UK education policy has changed significantly to reflect growing concerns about religious challenges to science. In 2011, the British Humanist Society spearheaded the "Teach Evolution, Not Creationism!" campaign, which received widespread support from New Atheist leaders. Ultimately, the push succeeded. In 2014, the UK government banned the teaching of creationism as science from free schools—which are funded by the government but do not have to follow the national curriculum[32]—and also revised the national curriculum to include a primary school module on evolution. Nonetheless, it is unlikely that battles over creationism will dissipate any time soon.[33] Social scientists Amy Unsworth and David Voas point out that attitudes toward evolution are still mixed among certain religious communities, particularly certain Christian groups and Muslims.[34]

Other science–faith controversies have emerged around reproductive issues. In 1978, after the first birth via in vitro fertilization, the UK public grew concerned about the speed at which scientific advances in human reproduction were occurring. Throughout the early 1980s, the UK government initiated a series of investigations to determine a course of action, concluding with the seminal 1984 Warnock report, named after British philosopher Dame Mary Warnock, who led the UK commission. These efforts led to parliament passing the Human Fertilisation and Embryology Act of 1990, requiring all IVF and human embryo research to be licensed by a new agency, the Human Embryology and Fertilisation Authority.[35] Over the past three decades, however, the act has been updated periodically to adapt to and include licensing for new areas of research including research on human embryonic stem cells, somatic cell nuclear programming for "therapeutic cloning," as well as animal-human hybrids and "three-parent" embryos. Many of the updates were controversial, including the 2008 revision to allow scientists to create animal-human hybrid embryos—which was supported by a number of medical groups and widely criticized by religious organizations, such as the Catholic Church and the Church of Scotland. *The Guardian* described the new act as "among the most emotive and divisive bills [to come] to parliament since its decision to enter the Iraq War."[36]

Transformations in UK society, like the decline in religiosity and increasing diversity, all have an effect on the scientific workplace. Moreover, given the role of academic scientists as thought leaders and teachers, they are in a unique position to shape future discussions on religion and science. As a result, it is important to examine how UK scientists understand religion and perceive the relationship between religion and science. It is to this effort that we now turn.

The United Kingdom scientific infrastructure also seems to be on the decline more recently.[37] It spent $46 billion on research and development in

2015, behind Germany and France. This total accounted for only 1.70 percent GDP, below the European Union average (1.96 percent) and has been declining since 1981 (when it was 2.24 percent).

Religion and Spirituality Among UK Scientists

We found that scientists in the United Kingdom tend to associate "religion" with certain rituals or institutions. Their definitions of religion generally encompassed three major themes: religion is belief in a personal god, religion is a system of beliefs, and religion is a source of meaning. "Spirituality," on the other hand, was more related to personal revelation.[38] The UK scientists we interviewed defined spirituality as a source of ethics or morality related to the individual or inner self and not necessarily to religion. While UK scientists often distinguished between religion and spirituality, most emphasized some degree of overlap between the two concepts and tended not to hold spirituality in as high esteem as did some US scientists. Some UK scientists even derided the concept of spirituality as being too individualistic and even "too American."

UK scientists are significantly less likely than the UK general public to belong to a religion (Table 4.1). Sixty-three percent of UK scientists are religiously unaffiliated compared with 47 percent of the general UK population.

TABLE 4.1. Religious affiliation in the United Kingdom.

RELIGIOUS TRADITION	POPULATION (%)	SCIENTISTS (%)
Roman Catholic	10.9	11.6
Protestant	28.1	14.0
Orthodox	0.3	3.4
Jew	0.3	0.6
Muslim	4.1	2.2
Hindu	0.9	2.0
Buddhist	0.4	0.3
Other[a]	5.1	2.7
None	47.0	63.3
Total Respondents	1,041	1,531

NOTES: Based on weighted data. Values for scientists exclude Fellows of the Royal Society.
[a] Population value includes response options on the World Values Survey that were not available on the RASIC survey (i.e., Anglican, Christian, and Jehovah's Witness).
SOURCE: World Values Survey United Kingdom 2005; RASIC United Kingdom Survey 2013.

TABLE 4.2. Religious service attendance in the United Kingdom.

FREQUENCY	POPULATION (%)	SCIENTISTS (%)
More than once a week	7.2	2.4
Once a week	10.0	5.7
Once a month	6.3	3.2
Only on special holy days[a]	10.6	10.7
Once a year	9.1	6.4
Less often	10.0	6.0
Never, practically never	46.3	65.6
Total Respondents	1,035	1,531

NOTES: Based on weighted data. Values exclude nonresponse.
[a] Reads "Only holy days" on the World Values Survey.
SOURCE: World Values Survey United Kingdom 2005; RASIC United Kingdom Survey 2013.

And when we turn to attendance, we find that 66 percent of UK scientists never attend religious services compared with 47 percent of the general UK population (Table 4.2). Conversely, the share of the population in the United Kingdom that attends religious services once a week or more often (17 percent) is more than double that of scientists in the United Kingdom (8 percent).

When we look at the survey data, we see that Protestants (including those from an Anglican tradition), Muslims, and Buddhists are underrepresented in science, when compared to the presence of these groups in the general population, by about half. For example, Muslims represent about 4 percent of the general UK population but 2 percent of scientists in the United Kingdom. Orthodox Christians, Jews, and Hindus, on the other hand, are overrepresented among UK scientists. The largest gap is found among Orthodox Christians, who represent 3.1 percent of scientists and only 0.3 percent of the general population. We see a similar proportion of Catholics among UK scientists and the general UK public, making it the only religious tradition to be represented almost equally.

UK scientists are significantly less likely than members of the general public in the United Kingdom to believe in God (Table 4.3). Only about 14 percent of members of the population in Great Britain take the atheist position, saying they do not believe in God, compared with nearly 43 percent of scientists in the region.[39] Twenty-five percent of scientists in Great Britain take an agnostic position, saying they don't know whether there is a God and they don't believe there is any way to find out. By contrast, a larger share of the British public (15 percent) than scientists (9 percent) say they don't

TABLE 4.3. Belief in God in Great Britain.

BELIEF ABOUT GOD	POPULATION (%)	SCIENTISTS (%)
I don't believe in God.	18.3	42.9
I don't know whether there is a God, and I don't believe there is any way to find out.	18.9	24.7
I don't believe in a personal God, but I do believe in a Higher Power of some kind.	14.5	9.1
I find myself believing in God some of the time, but not at others.	13.1	4.0
While I have doubts, I feel that I do believe in God.	18.3	9.8
I know God really exists and I have no doubts about it.	17.0	9.4
Total Respondents	1,958	1,464

NOTES: Based on weighted data. Values for scientists exclude Fellows of the Royal Society.
SOURCE: International Social Survey Programme 2008: Religion III (Great Britain, omits respondents in Northern Ireland); RASIC United Kingdom Survey 2013 (omits respondents housed in Northern Ireland).

believe in a personal god but do affirm belief in a "Higher Power of some kind." This leaves about 23 percent of scientists in Great Britain—compared to nearly half (48 percent) of the general population—who adopt some form of theism, ranging from a convinced belief in God to believing in God only some of the time. We find less than 10 percent of scientists in Great Britain have a convinced belief in God.

For all their secularity, however, UK scientists do seem remarkably friendly to the value of religion—or at least *certain* religions—in society. Thirty-seven percent of UK scientists consider themselves part of a religious tradition and 53 percent think there are basic truths in many religions. It is in the United Kingdom that we find the most atheist scientists identifying with a religion, and many atheist scientists think they have benefited from being taught about religion in primary and secondary school. "It is in the UK where scientists know an awful lot about the God they are rejecting," one of us observed during our interviews.

When we asked UK scientists to reflect on whether their scientific training and knowledge has made them more or less religious, almost 59 percent stated that exposure to science has had no effect on their religiosity. Of those scientists who said their scientific training had some effect on their religiosity, the majority reported that science has made them less religious.

Analyses of the data suggest that UK physicists show higher levels of adherence to traditional religious beliefs than do UK biologists. We thought that for some measures of religiosity, the difference might be explained by slight differences in religious affiliation between scientists in the two disciplines, but when we account for religious affiliation by examining religious service attendance, for example, we find the disciplinary difference in belief remains. As a discipline, biology may experience a greater influx of individual-level secularity. We speculate that UK biologists may be more secular than UK physicists in part because many religious individuals feel the idea of human evolution conflicts with their religious beliefs about the origins and development of life. Physics does not appear to have an equally controversial core concept for religious individuals. Furthermore, a number of the most outspoken antireligious UK scientists are biologists (like Dawkins), whereas some high-profile UK physicists (like Michael Faraday) publicly expressed compatibility between their scientific work and religious identity.

We also find that UK biologists and physicists in elite universities are less likely than those in nonelite universities to attend religious services. Exact explanations for this difference are difficult to deduce; it is possible that elite universities select for irreligion in some way. And it is possible that scientists who work for nonelite universities are simply more like the general population, thus more religious.[40]

Family life also seems to play a special role in how UK scientists view religion. Among UK biologists and physicists, we found that having children at home is significantly linked to higher religious affiliation and religious service attendance.[41] We observed similar relationships in the United States, but religion and family were not as strongly linked for US scientists.[42] We can imagine different explanations for why this link exists. It could be that UK scientists with children at home are more likely to belong to a religion as a way of passing on a moral or cultural identity to their children or because their spouses are religious, though it is also possible that scientists who belong to a religion are more likely to have children, so we cannot be sure of the causality here. Quality of schooling may also play a role. Many people in the United Kingdom believe church-linked schools are superior to ordinary state schools and thus religious affiliation could be a practice motivated by a desire to gain better schooling for their children. We also find that gender is a significant predictor of religiosity among UK scientists as it is in the general population, with women more likely than men to be religious. And UK women in science are less likely than UK men in science to say they do not believe in God.

Relationship Between Science and Religion for UK Scientists

Overall, we find that UK scientists do not perceive an epistemological conflict between science and religion. We should note, however, that while only a third of UK scientists believe science and religion are in conflict (Table 4.4), scientists in the UK actually rank *first* in adherence to the conflict view when we compare scientists from the nations we studied (this shows just how *un*popular the conflict view is among the global science community). As in the United States, a little less than a majority—47 percent—of UK scientists hold the independence view of science and religion, making it the most popular choice among scientists in the United Kingdom. In other words, the largest share of UK scientists think that religion and science should be completely separate (see Appendix A, Table A.3, on the United Kingdom, for more detail). Only 12 percent of UK scientists think science and religion can be used to help support each other. "Well, in my experience, there is not a conflict and I know of many good scientists who are also very religious and they don't see any conflicts," one biology lecturer[43] told us. "And I think sometimes misunderstanding of religion or misinterpretation of some of the religious precepts or scriptures could lead to that conflict, but I don't relate to that."

Separating Science and Religion

With few exceptions, even religious scientists in the United Kingdom see science and religion as realms of thought and practice that should be kept totally separate. This does not necessarily mean that they perceive the two

TABLE 4.4. Perceived relationship between science and religion among scientists in the United Kingdom.

RELATIONSHIP	%
Conflict; I consider myself to be on the side of religion	0.2
Conflict; I consider myself to be on the side of science	34.6
Conflict; I am unsure which side I am on	0.18
Independence; they refer to different aspects of reality	46.8
Collaboration; each can be used to help support the other	11.7
Don't know	6.5
Total Respondents	1,531

NOTES: Based on weighted data. Values exclude Fellows of the Royal Society.
SOURCE: RASIC United Kingdom Survey 2013.

realms as *inherently* separate, but rather that the boundary between science and religion is actively socially constructed and maintained.[44] The solid boundary that UK scientists create between science and religion is reflected in the way they talk about the relationship between the two realms. Some scientists described science as addressing one set of questions or aspect of reality, while religion addresses another set of questions or aspect of the way the world works. As one biologist[45] put it, "religion and science are just dealing with different parts of the world we live in."

Many UK scientists take for granted the separation of science and religion, and see religion as not playing much of a role in their lives or as absent altogether. In the view of one physicist,[46] for example:

> Working in science, you actually don't have to engage with these issues [of religion] very much. If I was a social worker, let's say, I would have to engage with religion much more. . . . Being a scientist, if you like, relieves me from having to think about: Why do some people believe some things and behave in some ways? . . . Science doesn't expose you to situations like that very often.

Many religious scientists in the United Kingdom seem determined to ensure that religion does not influence the execution of their science or the questions they address in their work, at times anxious that their colleagues would think them less of a scientist for being religious.

Other UK scientists expressed their views on the separation of science and religion by expanding on the conception of science and religion as "nonoverlapping magisteria"—science in the domain of facts and religion in the domain of morals and values.[47] Yet, science is clearly the more legitimate realm for most scientists, as they tend to think religion operates with lesser standards for evaluating truth and evidence. Specifically, scientists discussed the difficulty of testing religious ideas in scientific terms.

Most UK scientists, including even some who identify as religious, questioned the rationality of certain religious viewpoints. During these discussions, scientific findings were framed as "factual," while certain beliefs, views, doctrines, or explanations that emerge from religion were framed as irrational, arbitrary, and incompatible with science. "Much of our life is based on faith. But to have faith in something, you have to think it's reasonable," said a physicist,[48] reflecting on his loss of religious belief. "I thought there were people using religion to justify some basically untenable viewpoints," said a biologist[49] who drifted away from religious belief as a teenager. For these scientists, science is rational, and rational belief is important, so when religious beliefs conflict with the rationality of science, they lose legitimacy.

While many UK scientists made it clear that they did not consider all religious teachings a problem for science, some pointed to specific religious beliefs they see as encroaching on the domain of science. They objected to any form of religious belief or doctrine attempting to explain the physical world that contradicts explanations provided by science. In their view, religion is entirely illegitimate when it competes with science in this realm. Scientists across the spectrum of religious belief and practice agreed on this point. For example, one biologist, who described religion as "mass psychosis,"[50] explained,

> My basic view is that scientific methodology—scientific philosophy—requires that the laws of physics and chemistry are constant, as we know. Which means you can't have miracles; you can't have God interfere. You can't explain anything in terms of God. . . . So, if God can make people walk on water, then [how can we have a] theory of fluids? To have a theory of fluids, it has to be that fluids always have the properties that fluids have. Not that sometimes they'll support human weight.

A physicist who serves as a warden in an Anglican parish and says religion is important in his life[51] expressed similar objections to using God as an explanation for natural phenomena, and told us he does not even believe in certain core tenets of the Christian faith. He said,

> I still get to church, but I find it hard when, say, priests or other people say: "Thank God for the creation or the beauty of nature," and things like that . . . so those people don't understand what nature is or how it can be understood in physical laws. . . . Science doesn't need religion. Science has shown that so much of what religion says is just not needed, not correct and false. And so, either religion will fall by the wayside completely as more people understand it or it needs to adapt. . . . I wouldn't want to reject religion completely . . . [but] I'm not going to stick with bits that I think won't be worth keeping.

Both religious and nonreligious scientists most often cited creationism, the belief that the universe and life were created by God over a short period of time rather than through natural processes, as scientifically problematic since it rejects scientific explanations. One devout Catholic,[52] for example, told us she feels distressed by religious people who interpret the Bible literally and thus believe in creationism. A Baptist physicist[53] explained,

> There are organizations like Answers in Genesis, who I find very frustrating. . . . [They take] a starting point: my specific interpretation of the Book of Genesis

must be correct; therefore, I'm going to interpret all of my data in view of that—and to me, that's just bad science. . . . If you decide what it means before you've looked at the data, you're not doing science.

It is important to note, however, that UK scientists often used creationism as an example of an "extreme" religious view that a number of religious individuals they know don't adhere to and that mainly emerges as a problem from Muslim and fundamentalist Christian groups specifically. They also believe that creationism is not as much of an issue in the United Kingdom as it is in the United States. This biologist's[54] response was typical:

I think that it's important to make a distinction between different camps. . . . Not all Christians, for example, are creationists. They're rather a minority view in this country. But where religion does make scientific claims—and the claim of creationists is a fundamentally scientific claim—then there is a conflict between the two, and we can bring evidence to bear on our side of the debate, but there is no evidence to bear on the other side of the debate.

"Flexible" Religion with Possibilities for Collaboration

As Cambridge neuroscientist Denis Alexander writes in *Creation or Evolution: Do We Have to Choose?* atheism is not a prerequisite for accepting evolution.[55] This notion that scientific claims and religious beliefs can both be true underscores a broader pattern in our interviews that religious tradition shapes how UK scientists reconcile science and religion. When UK scientists think about religion, it's generally the Anglican Church that they have in mind, and the Church of England is seen as adaptable to science, moderate rather than extreme, and flexible rather than dogmatic. Scientists in the United Kingdom often contrasted the Church of England with what they perceive as more fundamentalist forms of religion. For example, one atheist physicist[56] said,

I know several scientists, whom I respect, who are able to reconcile science and religion. I think it helps that in this country, we have a very forgiving Church of England, which is not dogmatic about very much at all. . . . I think there are conflicts with fundamentalist Christians, but that's a nuttier branch of religion, I would say, regretted by many of the people I know to be religious.

UK scientists also cited Quakerism and Buddhism as flexible forms of religion. Even Catholicism, which was frequently critiqued by UK scientists for its social conservatism, was perceived as somewhat adaptable to science. One biologist[57] said:

Even within the heart of the Catholic Church, [I don't think] there are views or ways of thinking that are inconsistent with this sort of scientific perspective on the physical world that I've been talking to you about. There's an acceptance now of Darwinian evolution.

"Well, some claims are just preposterous, like the world is 5,000 years old," another scientist[58] said. "I've never been in the situation of talking with someone like that because even my religious ultra-Catholic friend wouldn't claim that. . . . He wouldn't claim anything against scientifically established facts." For most of these scientists, religious expression, practice, and beliefs that are moderate rather than what they perceive as fundamentalist, flexible rather than restrictive, and adaptive to science rather than dogmatic or contradictory can be seen as valid. "I don't think it's necessarily the religions; it's the flavor of religion," an atheist physicist[59] remarked. The problem, he said, "tends to be the fundamentalist side of whatever religion it is." By distinguishing among religious beliefs and ideas in this way, scientists in the United Kingdom build strong boundaries between good and bad religion worked out according to binary oppositions. By distinguishing between legitimate and illegitimate religion, UK scientists are participating in what the sociologist Pierre Bourdieu called a "classification struggle," where binary oppositions enter to name moral categories.[60]

There were also UK scientists who cited examples of the positive influence that moderate religious voices can have on society broadly and even science narrowly. Some spoke generally of the benefits of having moderate religion address questions science does not. Others see moderate religion as a check against more extreme forms of religion. For a few, moderate religion helps legitimize the role of science in society by supporting certain policy measures and engaging in dialogue on the value and ethics of new technologies and the authority of science. Reflecting the small proportion of UK scientists who think science and religion can collaborate, one biologist[61] stated,

I think in a society where [science and religion] can cohabit without conflict . . . in terms of policy and funding and people being discriminated against, then there's no issue. Because if the religious lobby, for example, is a lobby which is able to make us think about the moral consequences of the things we do as scientists, that's a good thing. That's what they should do. They should help us to philosophize about whether what we're doing is right or wrong, and whether we should continue this or not. . . . So if it's moderate and if it's intelligent and conscious, then I think it's very beneficial. If it's irrational and hysterical and dogmatic, then I think it can be very dangerous and can block science.

A physicist[62] discussed the benefits of bringing moderate religious voices to the table in policy discussions with a specific example:

There was quite a large public debate about: What should we do about cloning? What should we do about genetic modifications? And quite wisely, we set up a panel of wise people, mostly from the House of Lords, who were sort of quite hard about this. They don't say you can do anything you want. No. They say, "We're going to talk about this," and it seems to work . . . there certainly was religious input into that discussion.

Other scientists spoke about the importance and value of dialogue between scientific communities and religious groups that want to improve their scientific understanding. "I've been invited by the Islamic Society last year to their. . . conference on Islamic medicine," said one atheist biologist.[63] The "whole Islamic Society, they were really happy that I would go," she said, adding, "I like the fact that they called me and there is an exchange with them, which is nice."

Religion in the UK Scientific Workplace

In general, UK scientists lean toward agreeing with the statement, "Scholars in my discipline have a negative attitude toward religion." Among the scientists in our sample, about 42 percent somewhat agreed with this sentiment and 13 percent strongly agreed. In other words, scientists *may* generally *perceive* that their colleagues yield to a conflict perspective on science and religion, whether or not these colleagues actually do have a conflict perspective. We want to point out, however, that about 13 percent of UK scientists stated that they "don't know" whether other scholars in their discipline have a negative attitude toward religion, and nearly 15 percent have no opinion on the question. And when we asked UK scientists whether there have been conflicts about religion in their academic departments, they overwhelmingly reported that they have not seen such conflicts. Only about one in ten scientists reported religion-based conflicts in their departments.

Avoidance

It is important to note that UK scientists claimed that religion was generally considered a private matter in the United Kingdom as a whole, not just in science, and they thought UK sociocultural norms made it especially impolite to broach the subject of religion in any workplace. The secularity of the

United Kingdom, coupled with the accepted norm that religion is mostly a private affair, seems to amplify both the awareness scientists have of their students' and their colleagues' religiosity (it just seems so unusual) as well as their own desire to avoid it. Most of the scientists we spoke with reported that they actively avoid any interaction related to religion. An associate professor of biology[64] said,

> You have to watch anything you say. . . . So we are advised not to put in any reference to religion [on our syllabus or in our courses]. That goes as far now as not to be able to talk about Easter break any more . . . or Christmas break. "Take this word out of your slides—just call it 'the break' " [Chuckle] . . . management follows obviously the directives of government.

Some scientists, both religious and nonreligious, emphasized that they explicitly avoid religion, even when others bring it up for fear that to discuss religion would necessarily mean bringing conflict into scientific work. "You immediately then have 50 percent or more friends and 50 percent enemies," said a senior lecturer of physics in Scotland,[65] explaining why he avoids talking about his religious beliefs. He goes so far as to avoid telling people which schools he attended for fear that it might be used as a method for determining his religion. If scientists are aware of their colleagues' religious beliefs, it is only because they are visible in some way (such as a Muslim woman wearing a hijab) or they are mentioned as a weekend activity (such as attending a religious event). For example, one professor of biology[66] said that he knew religion was important to some colleagues because "they've been to a church get-together somewhere, when they've talked about their holiday." When we asked a biologist who identifies as "slightly religious" and believes in "something higher than us"[67] whether she feels comfortable sharing her views on religion, she responded: "No. I've not been very comfortable in the UK. . . . I think it's in science or biological science . . . there is a climate . . . in the UK that discourage[s] it." A professor of biology[68] suggests that the reason for this is because:

> The general lay of the land is that most of my colleagues would classify themselves as atheists. Those that I know do have religious beliefs tend to keep them fairly quiet, not that they're ashamed of them of course, but they tend to keep them fairly quiet. They tend to avoid that because it becomes a little bit boring, you know, because of the repetitive discussions about atheism and evolution and so on. . . . [T]o be religious or to have religious faith, at least in my field, is kind of implicitly looked down upon, although explicitly people would rarely be so rude.

And as we saw with Ariya, religion can influence decisions scientists make about what they choose to research or topics they elect to avoid. Another biologist who is Hindu[69] told us that she does not apply for jobs that would require her to work with animals because of Hindu teaching:

> You know, I'm Hindu and it's not good to kill animals to feed yourself, and if my work involved working with animal models and it means killing animals for the purpose of my study, I would not feel comfortable with that. So in that way, yes, my religious belief definitely plays a role in my work, where I don't want to move my work further into animal models. . . . [W]hen I look for jobs, it's a lot of them are *in vivo* work, and I rejected like 50 percent of the job applications because of this.

Presence of Religion in Scientific Work

Given that there is little conversation about the relationship between religion and science in the workplace, nonreligious scientists in the United Kingdom are left to speculate about the influence of religion on religious scientists' work. A common perception is that being religious has ethical implications. Being personally religious might lead scientists to "steer clear" of research on human embryonic stem cells, embryology, and cosmology—topics that may have controversial religious implications—one postdoctoral physicist[70] told us.

When religion does come up in the scientific workplace, the conversations tend to revolve around events in the news. Most frequently, religion is discussed in the same manner that scientists talk about sports, politics, or other cultural topics in the public sphere. Only occasionally do UK scientists discuss religion in relation to science or the individual lives of scientists. "It's extremely rare actually," said Freya,[71] an accomplished professor of biology who sees science and religion as separate and independent. "The only time we discuss it is where it comes into play in terms of practicalities."

Freya is elegant and frank. Her office is crammed with books, tables holding stacks of papers, filing cabinets covered with trinkets, and a kettle and microwave that allow her to eat at her desk while she works. She has nearly three decades of experience in biology, and in her view, "I don't see why you can't be very religious and still be a scientist," she said, especially when there is much science that would not seem to intersect or interfere with religious belief. She is proud to have trained "quite a diversity" of religious postgraduate students, including Buddhists, Catholics, Protestants, and Muslims, saying that Muslims are the religious group she now encounters most frequently. "I'm not intolerant of . . . [the] Muslim faith, but . . . it does have an impact on the way in which we work because we're not adapted to that religion," she told us. These impacts can range from the mundane to the substantive. For example, she felt she had to meet privately with her three Muslim students to make sure they were comfortable having the research group Christmas dinner in a pub. (She previously had postgraduate students from Africa and the Middle East who were uncomfortable with the pub atmosphere, she said.) She also described how her department held seminars on Fridays, which Muslim students often could not attend because Friday is a prayer day, so the department arranged to have the seminars videotaped so that the students could watch them later. Some festivals and holidays can be "pretty difficult" she told us, sharing the story of a student who passed out in her lab while fasting for Ramadan. "I got very angry about it," she recalled, adding, "to be in a laboratory when you're dehydrated and suffering hypoglycemia is a hazard to yourself and to everybody around you." Then there was the graduate student from northern Africa who rejected the idea that humans are products of evolution. It was "extremely shocking" and "unsettling," said Freya. "I don't want time to be spent discussing senseless things, and it's very frustrating when you have people that don't believe in what's written in textbooks." While the student designed a "very clever" thesis that focused on microorganisms without reference to human genetics and evolution, Freya felt it was her professional obligation to raise her concerns with the scientist who would judge the thesis. Though she left it at that, Freya does think it is highly problematic for someone with a doctorate in biology to reject a core principle of its knowledge base. "Absolutely," she explained. "It means that they don't fundamentally understand biology. They don't understand evolution, and they don't understand genetics. It's core to the whole thing."

Some religious scientists draw a link between the values and goals of science and religion, feeling that they are doing their work in service to God or that their work fulfills broader duties that are part of faith. A physicist who says Christian faith is important in his life,[72] for example, believes "trying to understand how the universe works is a very long tradition in the Judeo-Christian tradition." A Catholic biologist[73] described her fellow Christian scientists as having:

> the desire to make science progress for the benefit of humanity . . . they felt it was very much part of them being Christians, that it was somehow compulsory because what they were good at was being scientists and so they had to be good scientists and that would be their way to praise the Lord.

Hostility Toward Religion

While rare, we did find that some UK scientists were hostile to certain religious beliefs in the workplace, and they often felt that such hostility was necessary to protect the legitimacy of science. Although overt religious prejudice was rare, some scientists did provide examples of students being prevented from observing their religious beliefs and practices, motivated by the goal of protecting the autonomy of science. Even though the culture of his university emphasizes neutrality toward religion, one biology professor[74] relayed a time when he deterred a student who was technically skilled for a position from joining his research group because the student was a creationist: "I said, 'Look, you know you're coming into a research environment where we all accept evolution as a fact.' . . . And she kind of took the hint . . . and went away."

Some nonreligious scientists who are concerned about the influence of religion, especially immigrant religion, on science exhibit a tendency to assume religion may compromise the scientific work of religious scientists. And while we encountered several examples of scientists who discussed accommodations for Muslim students, Muslims, in particular, represent a reference group whose religious beliefs seem to be in the minds of UK scientists when thinking about religion in the workplace. Some UK scientists think of Islamic teachings as having the potential to be dangerous to science. For example, when discussing Muslim postgraduate students she has worked with, a lecturer in biology[75] suggested, "[T]hey justify the fact that what they are studying. . . at the biological level . . . they can go back and say this was the will of Allah."

Another biologist at an elite university[76] told us,

> I had a Saudi Arabian student once. . . . He was a very, very devout [Muslim]. . . .
> But I couldn't get him to repeat experiments. . . . [I]f the experiment didn't
> work the first time, then . . . Allah was directing him in a different direction.
> We didn't ever repeat something that didn't work because that was not exactly
> blasphemy, but it was being arrogant. . . . It was going against the will of God.

It is worth noting that the UK scientists we interviewed often mentioned Muslim scientists, even though Muslim scientists are a very small proportion of biologists and physicists in the United Kingdom, about 2 percent of the scientists we surveyed.

In some cases, scientists simply reveal a lack of cultural awareness or sensitivity toward Muslim colleagues. A senior lecturer in biology,[77] for example, described a Muslim student who had been in her lab by saying "she wore the head thing" rather than referring to the student's head covering more respectfully as a hijab, veil, or headscarf. Our interviews revealed at least two factors that may explain why some UK scientists have hostility toward Muslim peers. One could be embarrassment for Muslim scientists whose beliefs are at odds with basic scientific principles. A graduate student in biology,[78] for example, characterized a Muslim peer's belief about the age of the Earth as "embarrassing for the whole team." Another reason could be inconvenience. Freya,[79] who makes a point to accommodate her own Muslim students' needs for religious expression, noted that some colleagues were uncomfortable with requests—such as being videotaped during seminars that coincided with Friday prayers. In a shocking case, inconvenience was closely tied to a seeming sense of disrespect for Muslim students and peers. A senior lecturer in biology[80] admitted to misleading Muslim students about the source of animal models for experiments, telling us: "I actually did say that it was lamb rather than pig. And that satisfied everybody, and they carried on with the experiment. That perhaps was wrong of me." His decision, he said, was motivated by a desire to carry out a course without having too many students opt out of it.

The Presence of Dawkins

"Have you spoken with Richard yet?," we all remember one scientist asking in an interview. Richard Dawkins, the evolutionary biologist and atheist who wrote the bestseller *The God Delusion*,[81] came up in 48 of our 137 interviews with UK scientists. This was a tendency unique to our study of UK scientists. Even though Dawkins's ideas are well known in the United States as well, his larger-than-life presence in the United Kingdom means that how scientists talked about and responded to Richard Dawkins deserves its own section in this chapter on what UK scientists think about religion. It is worth noting that many of the UK scientists who mentioned Dawkins share his approach to religion. That is, most self-identify as atheist, although some are agnostic.

"There have been many books I've been influenced by one way or the other, even when I was religious," a nonreligious biologist[82] said when asked about influences on her view of the relationship between science and religion. "I have to say that a book that . . . didn't make [me an atheist] but it crystallized my atheism was *The God Delusion* by Richard Dawkins." For the most part, however, Dawkins did not seem to have much impact on how nonreligious UK scientists regard religion. The majority of the nonreligious scientists we interviewed were nonreligious before their scientific education and before they read Dawkins. For most, his ideas served to affirm some views they already held. In the words of one nonreligious professor of biology[83] who has read *The God Delusion*, "I'm already on [his] side." A nonreligious postdoctoral physicist[84] similarly explained,

> I read a book on religion . . . *The God Delusion* by Dawkins and then a few others, but, yeah, I mean, at the point in my life when I read them I was already . . . an atheist so it's a bit of preaching to the choir.

Where Dawkins *did* have an impact was on how scientists view their public role and communication with religious people. For a number of scientists, Dawkins became a symbol of what they do *not* want to be like in terms of portraying the relationship between science and religion. Among the forty-eight UK scientists who mentioned Dawkins in our interviews, thirty-eight of them—some religious and some nonreligious—disagreed with how he executes his role as a celebrity scientist. One cluster of scientists in this group argued that Dawkins misrepresents what science, as a process or method, can do. Independent of their religious views, these scientists believe Dawkins does not properly convey the limits of scientific inquiry. They do not believe science can deal with certain questions of meaning, purpose, and God. A nonreligious graduate student in biology,[85] who follows Dawkins and public debates on science and religion, believes Dawkins "may be talking in ways which are bigger than science can answer." A nonreligious professor of biology,[86] who discussed the need to help students understand the limitations of science and what it can and cannot address, explained,

> Some people like Richard Dawkins. . . . He's a fundamental atheist. He feels compelled to take the evidence way beyond that which other scientists would regard as possible. . . . I want [students] to develop [science] in their own lives. And I think it's necessary to understand what science does address directly.

A second and more prevalent assertion about Dawkins is that he gives the public an inaccurate impression of scientists themselves. A number of the scientists who mentioned him emphasized what they saw as his fundamentalism and the sense that he makes scientists seem dogmatic rather than open. A Christian postdoctoral fellow in physics who expressed irritation with fundamentalist religious groups that do not accept science[87] told us,

> You can understand someone like Richard Dawkins being particularly hacked off by it and retaliating, but . . . people on both sides . . . [are] overly dogmatic . . .

[and go] beyond perhaps what the state of the agenda is. The agenda of the scientist is to ask how, but it's not because I want to prove that God doesn't exist.

According to Simon, whom we met earlier, Dawkins's vigor and tone make his commentary on religion come off as "a polemic,"[88] and as a result—given his status and public profile—scientists are seen as biased against religion or as having an agenda that is aimed at getting rid of religion. Indeed, Dawkins has come to be so closely associated with an aggressive and partisan style of argument that one scientist[89] asserted that, "it would sell more books not to adopt the Dawkinesque viewpoint." While a major segment of UK scientists are atheists, many feel Dawkins's approach to science and religion does not reflect the scientific community as a whole. As a reader in physics[90] explained,

> I haven't read any of his recent books. . . . The impression I get from the newspaper reports . . . I just kind of feel that . . . he's kind of trying to be sort of a perfect, rational person somewhere but you know he's . . . kind of portraying that that's how scientists kind of think, that's what scientists say and so on and that kind of does . . . create the wrong impression.

Conclusions

Transformations in society, such as the decline in religiosity and increasing religious diversity, have had an effect on the science–religion relationship in the United Kingdom. Greater religious diversity resulting from immigration has expanded the spectrum of voices participating in political and cultural debates in a society that is used to hearing from a predominantly Christian worldview.[91] Furthermore, these demographic changes have led to greater diversity among students pursuing science careers and thus cultural and religious challenges for faculty at UK colleges and universities. Practically, there is also likely to be a significant disconnect between older, whiter, and more Christian UK scientists and their younger, more religiously diverse and devout students.[92]

Islam seems to be a particular challenge for many UK scientists. In the United Kingdom, nearly half of scientists originate from other nations, often bringing their religious traditions to the United Kingdom with them. Although Muslim scientists represent a tiny share of the overall UK scientific population, their *felt* presence seems much larger. Biologists, for example, worry that their Muslim students will bring antievolution sentiments into the scientific community much as evangelical Christians have done in the United States. As the scientific community becomes more diverse, it will need to explore ways to promote tolerance and understanding for different religions while also protecting the credibility, authority, and legitimacy of science.

The UK public might have a false impression of how scientists view religion and the science–religion relationship. When UK scientists consider the relationship between science and religion, the prominent view, based on our survey data, is that the two realms are separate and independent. Yet, the most vocal scientists promote the conflict perspective, and the loudest voices get the most attention and are most often heard. Our research underscores the need for greater dialogue between scientists and religious communities to foster a more empirically informed understanding of how scientists actually perceive the science–faith relationship. Some UK scientists also believe it would be productive if celebrity scientists engaged with more moderate religious groups that are likely to be more open to new understandings of science and religion and points of agreement between the two realms. This perspective tends to be somewhat more prevalent among religious scientists, perhaps because they have more nuanced knowledge of the spectrum of religious beliefs. One religious professor of biology[93] told us he thought someone like Dawkins is "as idiotic as the people who say God accounts for everything" because he targets fundamentalists, who this scientist thinks represent a very small proportion of religious believers. UK scientists we interviewed emphasized the need for celebrity scientists to understand the religiosity of the UK public, which is becoming increasingly more diverse with regard to religious traditions and held beliefs.

CHAPTER 5 | France
Assertive Secularism in Science

OVERLOOKING PLACE IGOR STRAVINSKY—a square in Paris's Beaubourg District famous for its playful fountains, tourists, and the Centre Pompidou—is a gigantic mural called *Chuuuttt!*, created in 2011 by renowned French graffiti artist Jef Aérosol (see Figure 5.1).[1] The art depicts a wide-eyed man with his index finger drawn tightly against his puckered mouth, gesturing emphatically for silence. By itself, the artwork makes no obvious comment on religion.[2] Yet, it appears alongside the Église Saint-Merri, a beautiful Catholic church with flamboyant Gothic architecture built in the sixteenth century. The juxtaposition of the two evokes the state of religion in France: the history and presence of religion is unmistakable, but officially and culturally, religion must not be signified or discussed in the public sphere. Sociologist Jean Paul Williame characterized France as "a Catholic country with a secular culture."[3]

The mandate to separate religion from the public sphere is enshrined in France's concept of *laïcité*, a specifically French form of secularism. Laïcité emerged as a concept during the French Revolution, was codified in 1905 when France's Third Republic enacted a law separating church and state, and was elaborated in the constitution of 1946, which states that laïcité "assures the equality of all citizens before the law, without distinction to their origin, race, or religion. It respects all religious beliefs."[4] Arguably, the main thrust of this policy is not terribly different from secularism in the United States— in both countries, the constitutional documents sought to ensure religious freedom and pluralism. Yet unlike in the United States, where secularism is an effort to protect religious people from the state, secularism in France has its origins in protecting state institutions from the influence of established

FIGURE 5.1. *Chuuuttt!* Photo credit David R. Johnson.

religion. Consequently, what some call an "avid secularism" is deeply ingrained in the cultural and political identity of the French.

Indeed, our survey and fieldwork in France revealed the most powerful separation of religion and science among all of the regions we studied. "Challenging religion is a national sport in France," one nonreligious scientist told us.[5] Another stated, "In France, secularism has almost become a sort of religion."[6] Some scientists[7] expressed annoyance that there were even questions about religion on our survey. One of us remembers a scientist saying that if the purpose of our interview with her was to discuss religion, it would be a waste of her time and ours because "we are very secular here."

A religious scientist,[8] who elected to do our interview in English, told us religion is taboo and said, "That's why it's better to talk in English [for] this interview—so people can't hear."

French scientists are the least religious scientific community we studied, even compared to the United States and the United Kingdom, which as we have discussed are also quite secular. While this led us to expect the conflict view of science and religion to be prevalent among French scientists, it turns out that a *smaller* proportion of scientists here, when compared to the United Kingdom and the United States, actually view science and religion in conflict. Yet, France's culture of secularism is actively present in its scientific community, suppressing religious expression in the workplace. Nevertheless, we did find that religion can make its way into the scientific workplace in subtle ways, often drawing the ire of scientists—not because they are necessarily antireligious, but because the country's secularism is so entrenched.

Cultural Context of Science and Religion in France

Prior to the twentieth century, a number of eminent French scientists were religious. Seventeenth-century philosopher René Descartes, one of the most important scientific and philosophic thinkers in history, developed two proofs for the existence of God in *Meditations on First Philosophy*, investigations that he claimed allowed him "to discover the foundation of physics."[9] Blaise Pascal, a seventeenth-century mathematician, rejected the Cartesian notion that the existence of God could be proved through rational arguments, but nevertheless had faith and identified with Jansenism, a Catholic theological movement.[10] In the eighteenth century, Antoine Lavoisier, a Catholic who has been called the "father of modern chemistry," was known for defending his faith against others who used science to attack it.[11]

But today we find what political scientist Ahmet Kuru refers to as "assertive secularism," in which the state plays an active role in excluding religion from the public sphere, thereby confining it to the private domain.[12] Laïcité emphasizes freedom *from* the practice of religion—rather than *to* practice religion—and the freedom of citizens and public institutions from the influence of organized religion. In prohibiting religious expression in the public sphere, French law goes beyond the basic separation of church and state observed in other nations. Historically, secularism has been relatively uncontroversial in France because the country has been a relatively homogeneous Catholic nation and because there are exceptions for this particular religion in the law. For example, private Catholic schools in France receive public funding, students can attend institutions for religious education on school-free Wednesdays, and students in half of French public schools have access to Catholic counseling.[13]

Jean-Paul Willaime notes, "the civil religion of the French Republic manages to enlist and take advantage of the symbols of Catholicism whenever it proves convenient."[14] France has the highest number of Catholic holy places among European countries, including Lourdes—a major Catholic pilgrimage site—and the calendar of French public holidays follows the Catholic calendar.[15] While Catholicism continues to play an important role in France institutionally and culturally, identification with and participation in the Catholic Church are waning. French Catholics now account for less than 5 percent of baptized Catholics around the world.[16] Baptisms, religious weddings, religious service attendance, catechism classes, and belonging to the Catholic Church have all been on the decline.[17] For example, in the late 1950s, 90 percent of the French population reported being Catholic; by 1994, this was down to 67 percent of the overall public and only 53 percent among 18- to 24-year-olds. The numbers continue to decrease.

For most of the twentieth century, when ensuring "the liberty of conscience" in the public sphere was primarily a matter for Catholics, Protestants, Jews, and nonbelievers, assertive secularism worked relatively well. Yet, France's past as a colonial power created a new reality in the 1980s and 1990s, as Muslims immigrated from Francophone nations like Algeria, Morocco, Tunisia, Mali, and Senegal, and Islam became France's "second religion."[18] Today, France has the largest concentration of Muslims in Europe.[19] The resulting changes in the religious landscape have challenged France's concept of secularity, with new controversies emerging. In 1989 and 1990, for example, Muslim schoolgirls were expelled for refusing to remove the hijab, on the basis that wearing the head covering is a form of religious expression incompatible with secularism in public schools. An increase in similar incidents resulted in a 2004 law that banned religious symbols from public schools, including "large" Christian crosses, Jewish kippas, Sikh turbans, and the hijab.[20] In 2010, the French Senate banned the burqa, an enveloping garment that some Muslim women wear to cover the body and the face. Some speculate that as French intolerance of religious expression increases, religious groups will respond with increased visibility in public, including the workplace.[21]

Because the 2004 ban specifically concerned primary and secondary public schools, wearing the hijab is not banned on university campuses. Polls of the French public, however, reveal that 72 percent of the population would support such a ban.[22] Politicians, including former President Nicolas Sarkozy and former Prime Minister Manuel Valls, have called for a ban and other stringent measures, such as eliminating religiously oriented meal substitutes in school cafeterias.[23] Newly elected President Emmanuel Macron, however, opposed a ban in higher education, suggesting such a change is unlikely in the near future. Nevertheless, even if a legal ban on religious symbolism is not applied to universities, a de facto ban through social pressure may already exist. Many university scientists we interviewed expressed such a sentiment, viewing religious symbolism in the workplace as taboo or even unacceptable.

Much like the Catholic Church, science has important institutional and historical origins in France. Under Louis XIV, France created one of the earliest academies of science, the Académie des Sciences, in 1666. France also established one of the earliest academic journals, the *Journal des Sçavans*.[24] Today, France's spending on scientific research and development (R&D) ranks second in Europe. In 2015, the country spent approximately $61 billion on R&D from both public and private sources.[25] This figure translated to 2.22 percent of France's gross domestic product, a spending percentage that has been relatively consistent over the past three decades. Most publicly funded research in France is organized and conducted by national research agencies. With more than 11,000 full-time tenured researchers in natural, human, and social sciences, the largest and most important scientific organization in France is the Centre National de la Recherche Scientifique (CNRS).[26] The CNRS was created in 1939 to merge state research organizations into one national institution to coordinate research. Perhaps one of the most important turning points in the history of the CNRS was the 1966 creation of joint research units in which university laboratories were contractually joined with CNRS. These *unités mixtes de recherche* are financed by the CNRS and staffed by a combination of university and CNRS researchers. While this structural transformation enhanced the scientific endeavor in France, it also helped shape the relationship between science and religion in the country. As a public scientific entity, the CNRS is a decidedly secular organization in which both policy and culture strongly reject religious symbolism. CNRS laboratories that blend CNRS university staff and students are places where the application of laïcité measures can get complicated.

Likely because of France's approach to religion, which seeks to confine it to the private domain, as well as declining religious attachment among the French population, there are few conflicts between science and religion in the public sphere. There were no clear topics or controversies that came up when we asked scientists we interviewed about potential public conflicts between religion and science.

Christian evangelicals, who in other regions of the world sometimes ignite debates related to evolution and climate change, have little presence in France, representing less than 1 percent of the general population.[27] The growing Muslim community, however, has led to some public incidents involving creationism. In 2007, Turkish creationist Adnan Oktar (known as Harun Yahya) mass-mailed free copies of his *Atlas of Creation*, a book attacking evolution, to schools and libraries around the world, including many in France. The French Ministry of Education required all school authorities to seize and hide copies of the book. Two years later, the French Ministry of Education followed up by requiring biology teachers to attend presentations given by six of the most influential evolutionary biologists in France, who discussed how teachers should respond to creationist and intelligent design arguments. In 2011, followers of Oktar in France held conferences at Muslim centers in Paris, Marseille, and four other cities to discuss Qur'an-based creationist views. Because the conferences were held on private premises, the French Education Ministry was unable to exercise any influence over them.[28] It is important to note, however, that while such events have stoked the concerns of the French government, Muslim creationists in France are not a vocal group.

On the issue of climate change, the French government has engaged in what we might call proactive "spiritual activism." For example, in 2015, then president François Hollande—who once stated, "I respect all [religious] confessions. Mine consists of not having any"—hosted a "summit of conscience" that brought together faith leaders from different religious traditions with the purpose of challenging them to articulate their views on climate change and how it relates to their spiritual beliefs.[29] Hollande followed this summit by prompting heads of state attending a subsequent Paris climate change meeting to address the question of climate change "from our own individual personal consciences." While Catholics in France follow the pope's encyclical on climate change, which calls on Catholics to embrace the science of climate change and fight to protect the Earth, other groups—including the Protestant Federation of France and the French Council of the Muslim

Faith—have issued statements and taken actions in support of the United Nation's Intergovernmental Panel on Climate Change.[30]

There was some concern and criticism among secularists when Michel Deneken, a theology professor and Catholic priest, was elected president of the University of Strasbourg in 2015. The appointment of a religious figure as head of the university—a public institution—seemed to some to violate France's core principle of laïcité. Because Strasbourg is situated in the region of Alsace, which was ceded to Germany in 1870 following the Franco-Prussian War and returned to France in 1919, it has a special exemption from the 1905 law separating church and state. Still, many critics felt the election of Deneken went against the secular principles and spirit of France. "The Vatican has seized power at the University of Strasbourg," the Union of Communist Students declared, and the group questioned what effect his position would have on biomedical experiments and other issues disapproved of by the Catholic Church.[31] Six professors signed an open letter asserting that "close ties to religious authorities" would damage the reputation of the university, which has four Nobel laureates in science on its faculty. For his part, Deneken stated, "universities are places where matters of faith should never interfere with teaching or research."[32]

Religion and Spirituality Among French Scientists

Among all the nations we studied, scientists in France easily stand out as the least religious on almost every dimension of religiosity. Our survey shows that religion is much weaker within the French scientific community than in the general population in France.

Religious affiliation is largely absent among French scientists. Sixty-seven percent of scientists in France do not belong to a religious tradition (Table 5.1). Among the countries we studied, France has the second highest level of scientists who are not affiliated with a religion. (Religious affiliation among scientists is also similar in the United Kingdom, where 63 percent of scientist are religiously unaffiliated, and in the United States, where 61 percent are unaffiliated.)

Catholicism represents the most common religious tradition among French scientists by far: 23 percent of scientists in France identify as Catholic. In the general French population, 42 percent identify as Catholic. Further comparing the religious affiliation of French scientists with the general public in France, we see that Catholics, Muslims, and Buddhists are underrepresented in science, while Protestants, Orthodox Christians, Jews, and Hindus are overrepresented.

TABLE 5.1. Religious affiliation in France.

RELIGIOUS TRADITION	POPULATION (%)	SCIENTISTS (%)
Roman Catholic	41.8	22.8
Protestant	1.9	2.1
Orthodox	0.2	0.7
Judaism	0.2	0.8
Islam	4.7	2.3
Hinduism	0.0	0.2
Buddhism	0.5	0.1
Other[a]	0.9	4.0
None	49.6	67.0
Total Respondents	997	738

NOTES: Based on weighted data. Values exclude nonresponse.
[a] The proportion of the population identified as "Other" includes categories from the World Values Survey that were not offered in the RASIC study, including "Evangelical," "Pentecostal," and "Jehovah's Witness."
SOURCE: World Values Survey France 2006; RASIC France Survey 2015.

The proportion of scientists who do not believe in God is higher in France than in any other region we studied. France is also the only country in which a majority of scientists—51 percent—indicated on our survey that they do not believe in God (Table 5.2). (For comparison, 43 percent of scientists in the United Kingdom and 35 percent of scientists in the United States said the same.) We should also point out, however, that lack of belief in God is also higher among the general population in France (22 percent) than in any other country we studied. Still, French scientists are more than twice as likely as the French public to embrace this view. Another 25 percent of French scientists are agnostic, saying they don't know whether there is a God and don't feel there is a way to find out.

Given the low level of belief in God among French scientists, it is not surprising that their level of religious practice is also low. Religious service attendance is lower among scientists in France than in any other region we studied, with 81 percent of French scientists indicating that they never attend religious services (Table 5.3). Religious service attendance among the general public is also lower in France than in any other region we studied: 60 percent say they never attend services, making it the only country in which more than half of the population never attend.

TABLE 5.2. Belief in God in France.

BELIEF ABOUT GOD	POPULATION (%)	SCIENTISTS (%)
I don't believe in God.	22.1	50.6
I don't know whether there is a God, and I don't believe there is any way to find out.	16.4	25.1
I don't believe in a personal God, but I do believe in a Higher Power of some kind.	13.0	10.4
I find myself believing in God some of the time, but not at others.	11.3	2.5
While I have doubts, I feel that I do believe in God.	19.8	6.5
I know God really exists and I have no doubts about it.	17.4	4.9
Total Respondents	2,396	697

NOTES: Based on weighted data. Values exclude nonresponse.
SOURCE: International Social Survey Programme 2008: Religion III (France); RASIC France Survey 2015.

TABLE 5.3. Religious service attendance in France.

FREQUENCY	POPULATION (%)	SCIENTISTS (%)
More than once a week	1.6	0.5
Once a week	5.6	2.8
Once a month	3.8	1.6
Only on special holy days	16.4	5.7
Once a year	5.2	3.6
Less often	7.2	4.5
Never, practically never	60.0	81.3
Total Respondents	999	731

NOTES: Based on weighted data. Values exclude nonresponse.
SOURCE: World Values Survey France 2006; RASIC France Survey 2015.

Only about 3 percent of scientists in France say they attend religious services weekly, ranking them lowest among scientists in all the regions we studied. Weekly service attendance exceeds 10 percent in all of the other scientific communities we studied other than in the United Kingdom, where only 8 percent of scientists say they attend services each week.

Relationship Between Science and Religion
for French Scientists

French scientists are also unique in their rejection of the collaboration perspective on science and religion. Only 7 percent of French scientists hold this collaboration view, the lowest percentage among scientists in the nations we studied. Nearly twice as many scientists embrace this perspective in the United Kingdom and the United States, and roughly 20 to 30 percent of scientists in all other regions we studied hold this view. The difference might be partly due to the fact that Muslims, Hindus, and evangelical Protestants—groups that often draw connections between their religious traditions and scientific work—are found in greater proportions in other countries than in France. On the other hand, Catholics—who make up nearly a quarter of French scientists—are statistically no more likely than non-Catholic scientists in France to affirm a collaboration view.[33] (In Appendix A, Table A.5, we include an even more detailed table of how French scientists view religion and science.)

In our interviews, we did hear variations of a collaboration perspective from both Catholic and Muslim scientists. For example, a Catholic CNRS researcher in physics[34] told us that as she sees religion and science,

> one is helping the other. The absolute truth is God in principles. You never reach it as a human. You have to try to reach it. And you have to be rigorous. So I don't see any conflict. Pascal had no conflict.

Further, a much larger share of the Muslim scientists (about 36 percent) than non-Muslim scientists (6 percent) affirmed the collaboration view, though differences by group were only marginally significant.[35] Still, most French scientists tended to agree with the view espoused by the scientist[36] who, when asked about the possibility of science and religion relating to one another, replied: "Not in scientific research. No. No. I cannot even imagine how this would be possible in our field." This response and others like it were not all that surprising, given the isolation and privatization of religion in France.

The prevailing view of science and religion among French scientists is the independence perspective, as it is among scientists in many other nations and regions we studied. Fifty-seven percent of scientists in France view science and religion as referring to different aspects of reality. Our analyses of survey data suggest the share of scientists affirming the independence view held relatively steady across both gender and discipline (see Appendix A, Table A.5).[37] Further, both religious and nonreligious French scientists embrace this perspective. In fact, a slightly greater share of French scientists who described themselves as religious (68 percent) than those who didn't (55 percent) held this view, though group differences were only marginally significant.[38] For example, a Catholic CNRS director of research in biology[39] said of the science and religion relationship,

> I don't see it in terms of conflict. I see it as things that are side by side. My feeling is that I am working to try and understand how matter works. Matter is part of what exists—all the rest is on the sides.

A religious CNRS physics researcher[40] told us,

> Sometimes I hear people talk about quantum spirituality, about quantum therapy, namely domains where scientific words or even scientific concepts are used outside the field of use of these words and of this scientific concept. That's how conflicts may arise. But if religion remains religious, and science remains scientific, then, in my opinion, there is a harmony and not a conflict.

A nonreligious CNRS researcher in biology[41] offered a similar view of science and religion independence, saying,

> So for me, this one [the conflict perspective] is fake. It has to do with your personal life, how you deal with why you are on Earth—this is really the religious part. The other is the scientific method. I've seen people that manage to separate these two things completely and be comfortable with it.

One in four French scientists hold a conflict perspective on science and religion, siding with science (Table 5.4), with little differences by gender[42]

TABLE 5.4. Perceived relationship of science and religion among scientists in France.

RELATIONSHIP	%
Conflict; I consider myself to be on the side of religion	0.0
Conflict; I consider myself to be on the side of science	26.5
Conflict; I am unsure which side I am on	0.2
Independence; they refer to different aspects of reality	57.1
Collaboration; each can be used to help support the other	6.7
Don't know	9.5
Total Respondents	674

NOTES: Based on weighted data. Values exclude nonresponse.
SOURCE: RASIC France Survey 2015.

(see Appendix A, Table A.6). That is a nontrivial amount, but not all that different from the percentage of scientists who hold this view in the United States, for example. (The percentage of UK scientists who hold this view is considerably higher at one in three.) While scientists in France are less religious than those in the United States and the United Kingdom, France does not have the public controversies related to science and religion that are so prevalent in the United States, nor does it have vocal atheists who maintain the public visibility of the conflict perspective as in the United Kingdom, which may help explain the comparative findings. Notably—given that such conflicts tend to be more salient in biology than physics—we did find a significantly larger share of biologists (34 percent) than physicists (22 percent) in France who affirmed the conflict view.[43] These differences remained even when we took into account demographic characteristics—including gender, career stage, marital status, and immigrant status—as well as religious affiliation and disbelief in God (see Appendix A, Table A.6).

While our survey data and interviews with scientists in different regions of the world suggest that the conflict view of science and religion is primarily an invention of the West, our interviews with French scientists indicate that they borrow rationales from other Western contexts to support this perspective. One of the most prevalent themes in our interviews with French scientists holding the conflict perspective was biblical literalism. One CNRS director of research in physics[44] expressed the conflict view parsimoniously, stating:

> If being religious is saying that what is written in the Bible is true then of course there is a problem. . . . I cannot understand how you can take literally the Bible and be a physicist. For me it's clearly incompatible.

It was surprising to hear this theme come up in so many of our interviews, given that Catholicism, the most popular religion in France, and thus likely one of the prime referents for how French scientists understand religion, lacks an extensive tradition of reading the Bible as literal truth, instead emphasizing metaphor, allegory, and interpretation as essential to understanding Catholic doctrine. In other words, the chief basis for conflict these scientists point to—biblical literalism—is not characteristic of most religious adherents in France. Some scientists who emphasized literalism as the basis of the conflict they saw between science and religion did point out the lack of literalism in Catholic teaching. A CNRS director of research in biology,[45] for example, noted that conflict between being a scientist and being religious depends on the way religion is practiced. He continued:

There are not many Catholics anymore who think that the universe was created in seven days, nor who think that during the feuds between the Hebrews and their enemies, God stopped Earth, or the sun, to allow them to end and win the battle. In the Catholic religion, practicing religious people take those texts as allegories, as poetical texts that shouldn't be interpreted literally.

A second source of conflict we heard from French scientists was religious dogma, seen as antithetical to a scientific mindset and scientific scrutiny. Compared to French scientists who identify as religious, a much larger share of nonreligious scientists (30 percent vs. 4 percent) say that science conflicts with religion.[46] Another CNRS director of research in biology[47] argued that being religious meant being "free of thinking" and said that, "When you're religious . . . you should follow some dogma. And so to me, it's not compatible with the experimentation of science. In science, dogma is there to be changed, removed, or adapted." A postdoctoral researcher in physics[48] noted that a scientist could be "absolutely religious . . . and be perfectly OK with religion and science," as long as the religious scientist put "aside everything that doesn't work in the dogmas." Again, we were somewhat surprised to hear this specific source of conflict emphasized in a context where Catholicism is the most prominent religion. Most Catholic teachings are not considered infallible dogma.

Religion in the French Scientific Workplace

Michel[49] told us that he is a very religious Catholic, one of the few among the French scientists we interviewed. He practices his faith regularly— following a book of prayers for mass on a daily basis—which he knows is rare among French scientists. When asked to describe God, Michel laughs and says, "God is beyond what the human brain is able to understand, and while humans can approach God, they can't understand 'Him.' " Michel said he doesn't have a strongly developed idea of the meaning of life, but feels it must be tied to being there for others, being joyful and happy, and not being too self-focused—linking his faith to an ethics he also applies to his scientific work. He believes that as a scientist and as a person of faith, he should have respect for the truth, search for it, and see to it that the results of his research do not cause problems in society.

Michel doesn't think being religious has to discourage a scientific career. He sees science and religion as separate (with the exception of quantum mechanics and spirituality), and the relationship between the two realms as harmonious. He even has a blog where he discusses both his work as a scientist and his perspectives on theology. When we asked what his colleagues think about his blog, Michel said he believes those who know about it view it in a positive light—though he has purposefully kept it only on his personal webpage not hosted by his university. When he has discussed religion with his colleagues, Michel said they can disagree, but they also maintain respect for one another. Yet, he said, religion isn't discussed regularly in the scientific workplace. As another religious scientist[50] we spoke with noted, "You never talk about religion in France—at least in our lab—no. It's very taboo."

We did find French scientists who are antireligion, such as a graduate student in biology[51] who told us religion "is a bunch of crap, to be quite frank." Yet, the majority of French scientists we spoke with maintain a seemingly neutral attitude toward religion as long as religion and religious expression remain private. For example, when asked about his view of religion and spirituality, an atheist associate professor of physics[52] responded: "I don't have any prejudice about this. . . . There is a kind of community when you are at work, so you try to respect everyone's thinking." Another physicist,[53] discussing his comfort sharing his views about religion, explained, "I am an atheist and I am not hiding it, but this is not something I am going to shout from the rooftops with no reason."

Our survey data showed that French scientists are the least religious scientific community among the regions we studied, and French scientists noted during interviews that they were unaware of any religious colleagues. "Are you joking?" a Catholic scientist in physics[54] told us a colleague asked him after learning of his religion. "A religious scientist. Does it exist?" asked a professor of physics[55] during our interview. "Do you [actually] have in your investigation people who answer that they are a religious scientist?" And a director of research in biology said he was "amazed" when he met a scientist in the United States who is actually a practicing Christian. French scientists mainly encounter religious colleagues outside the country rather than within, and quite frequently, when asked about religious colleagues, French scientists who trained or worked in other nations discussed their experiences at universities abroad. A female biologist,[56] for example, who previously held a postdoctoral position in a US university, noted,

> What was very nice about the US is that there are people from all over the world, but all different religions all together, and France is much more different because there are a lot of French people, really. Not enough people from abroad.

A female physicist[57] told us, "I had a very Christian student in the UK I had a Muslim coworker who [*laughing*] tried to save my soul in Germany. In France, I would say religion doesn't come up at all I've noticed." For the most part, scientists take their cue from the culture in France, where separating religion from public life is deeply ingrained. Nevertheless, religion does subtly make its way into the scientific workplace in some contexts, often with ensuing conflict.

Separation

Our consideration of religion in the scientific workplace in France begins with patterns of separation. Here we consider the occupational culture of secularism, which leads to creating boundaries. Subsequently, we discuss areas of overlap.

The Occupational Culture of Secularism

Three characteristics of the French scientific community encourage the separation of science and religion in the workplace. One is the overall low level of religiosity among French scientists, as demonstrated in our survey results. In principle, the lower the level of religiosity among the general public and the scientific community in a country, the lower the probability that religion will come up in the scientific workplace.[58] A second factor fostering the separation of science and religion in France is the moderately low proportion of scientists born outside the country. About one-quarter of the scientists we surveyed in France were born in other nations.[59] In the United States and the United Kingdom, where more than 40 percent of university scientists are born elsewhere, religion often permeates the scientific workplace through the faith of scientists who come from other regions. While still significant, the effect of immigrant religions is a bit less pronounced in France. This brings us to the third, and primary, factor that leads to the separation of science and religion in the French scientific community: the country's assertive secularism, codified in law and deeply rooted in French culture.

In France, we find an occupational culture of secularism unique to the country, characterized by a taken-for-granted assumption that religion will not be publicly expressed or discussed. French scientists feel strongly about laïcité, and thus seem deeply uncomfortable when religion enters the workplace in any capacity. "In France, [we] have this concept of laïcité. So you don't discuss it [at] all," said one biologist.[60] Other scientists often gave similar answers when asked whether religion is ever a topic of conversation among scientists. Describing the "one time in four years" religion became a conversation topic, one physicist[61] said she experienced "a bit of a shock" and explained,

> I find it a bit surprising that someone would want to talk about their religion if they are a rational person. . . . [T]here is a culture that sort of frowns on faith in a scientific environment. In France . . . there's a very strong desire to separate faith and other sections of their life. So it's not a problem if people have it personally, but it's sort of a problem if they bring it up.

"I consider religion as private," said a Catholic director of research in biology[62] when discussing religion in the workplace. When we asked him why, he said, "Because I'm French. And we are used to feeling this way. We should put public things in a public place and religion in a private place." While laïcité cannot prevent religion from shaping motivations, ethics, or experiences among individual scientists who are personally religious, it *does* suppress the ability of scientists to publicly express their religious identity in any way. In suppressing outward religious expression, laïcité encourages, drives, and provides a very specific rationale for the compartmentalization of religion from scientific work. "It's a spiritual aspect which holds a significant part in my life," a professor of physics[63] told us, "but religion never ever intrudes in my professional relationships nor in the way I work." Though the compartmentalization of science and religion we observed among religious French scientists is similar to the pattern we observed in other regions, we find an element of this approach that is particular to France: Perhaps because of the nation's uniquely assertive secularism that encourages such segmentation, nonreligious scientists in France have a particularly difficult time imagining an alternative to the separation of science and religion in the lives of religious scientists. A CNRS biologist,[64] for example, said,

> My belief is that most of the scientists that would be religious, especially in France . . . if they really had an issue with the way science works, they would not have gone into this field, so I think they are pretty good at differentiat[ing] what they believe from what they are doing.

A nonreligious CNRS physicist[65] echoed this view in more detail, saying of science and religion,

> They're totally different aspects of your life, right? I think most people if they have faith, they have a faith in a God, right? But that doesn't mean that they

have the faith that the God's gonna tell them how to grow a crystal, right? They still have the hypothesis of how that grows and they can test it, and they can still believe that God has defined these rules, but that has nothing to do with how a scientist tests these rules.

In France, the occupational culture of science is secular, rooted in the country's long history of separating religion from public life.

Overlap

In most regions and laboratories where we visited scientists as part of our study, religion is more likely to be discussed privately or outside of the workplace than within it. When religion does come up as a topic of conversation at work, it is most likely to be superficial and among a few colleagues rather than a major topic of discussion. As we've seen, much of this has to do with specific cultural traditions and broader public norms related to what topics and practices are considered private or taboo. The nature of religious discussions can also depend on the nature of a scientist's research; we remember, for example, an animal epidemiologist in the United Kingdom whose work on how animals are slaughtered in Jewish and Muslim communities requires discussion of religious practices among her research team. There are other factors, of course, that can impact how religion is discussed in the scientific workplace.

In France we also see how an exogenous shock beyond professional and organizational boundaries can suspend usual norms of behavior. Six months prior to our fieldwork in France, there were a series of shootings in the area surrounding Paris, beginning at magazine *Charlie Hebdo*, perpetrated by gunmen identifying themselves as acting on behalf of al-Qaeda in Yemen. These terrorist attacks, in which seventeen died and twenty-two were injured, generated discussion of religion in places where the subject normally does not come up. Numerous scientists we interviewed said the *Charlie Hebdo* attacks provoked discussion of religion among colleagues. "The surprise and the shock were so huge that we couldn't help talking about it during lunchtime or coffee breaks" in the months after, said a professor of physics.[66] Some of the conversations referenced by scientists were simply an attempt to make sense of a horrific tragedy. Other stories we heard seemed to indicate growing unrest or tension with Muslims—even as scientists drew distinctions between "everyday Muslims" and terrorists. These stories indicate that, in response to certain circumstances in the public sphere, the religiosity of a scientist's peers can become the topic of conversation in the workplace, a context that traditionally shuns such discussions.

A CNRS director of research in biology[67] said that her lab had researchers from different religious backgrounds "all working together quite peacefully," but added:

> It may be changing with the current fears that are building on all sides. . . . We've had terrorist attacks in France and isolated gunmen in different places. . . . That keeps people on edge and it makes people very negative toward other people's beliefs, 'cause they're afraid of them. . . . Somebody who's of a different faith that came from the "wrong part of the world," quote unquote, might be discriminated against. I think that they probably face quite a bit of discrimination and I think it's getting stronger right now.

A CNRS director of research in physics[68] explained:

> A strong anti-Muslim trend is growing among the population. We had tragic attacks in last January. . . . The population is a bit afraid of the Muslims. . . . All Muslims are not terrorists of course, it's only a small minority. . . . I don't know what will happen in France, but for now there is no ostracism against Muslims in laboratories, for the time being.

Amina,[69] a biologist and Muslim from Morocco who identifies as slightly religious, told us she has experienced tension in her laboratory. She characterized the place of religion in her life as "complicated"—while she does not wear a hijab, and she rarely prays or attends services, she does believe in God, despite occasional doubts, and has "moments of spirituality." Amina's faith has "a Muslim component from my parents and a Catholic one from my school," and when asked if she had ever experienced a religious shift, she said she has "felt a conflict between the two—sometimes I wanted to be a Catholic, sometimes I preferred to be a Muslim." During her scientific studies, "I almost lost my religiousness and beliefs," she said, but today, like most other French scientists, she views science and religion as "two different things." The only conversations about religion she has at work are private talks with a Jewish colleague who also "doesn't dare" signal her religious beliefs, said Amina. "It is taboo," Amina explained. "Religion and science don't marry well and nonreligious scientists don't understand [the struggle] at all."

As the relationship between France and its Muslim community has shifted toward increased tension and scrutiny, Amina's faith has posed additional challenges for her at work. "Nowadays, it's not easy to be a Muslim," she said. "People are looking at Muslims poorly. I don't feel at ease," she described. "If I tell people, anywhere, not only in science, that I am Muslim, they are going to judge me and have presumptions without knowing me."

Given the climate in her lab, she avoids bringing up religion. Her lab director, she said, is "antireligion"—"Religion sucks!" the director said during one conversation. Her boss "wanted no signs of faith" in science, Amina said, noting the director had a problem with a Muslim intern who wore a hijab. She remembers what her boss said when she caught on that Amina is Muslim too: "How strange," the director said. "You don't look like a Muslim."

Religious Symbolism

When describing how she knew a colleague was Jewish, a director of researcher in biology[70] simply replied: "hat, hair, suit." When expressions of faith do enter the scientific workplace, they primarily do so in a rather subtle fashion, leading scientists to sometimes speculate about the faith of colleagues based on very minor cues. One physicist,[71] for example, explained that she knew which scientists are religious because Catholics "tend to have a certain lifestyle that is recognizable," "dress really neatly," and "marry in church, which in France is not very common." A CNRS researcher in biology[72] said it's "small things that allow me to see it [religion]."

A Catholic postdoctoral researcher in biology,[73] who generally avoids any form of religious expression and described herself as "discreet" when it comes to religion at work, told us the following story:

> I have a keychain that was given to me by a person that I like very much and . . . there is a Notre Dame [key fob with the Virgin Mary on it] and I put that with my pen-drive because . . . I was always feeling like I'm going to lose it. . . . I remember once that my adviser looked at the keychain and then he looked at me like he was astounded by it—but he didn't say anything else because he kept it to himself, and I didn't say anything else either.

We heard similar accounts from other religious scientists, who said nonreligious colleagues were surprised or shocked to learn of their religious identity, but gave little or no other response. We do wonder, however, whether experiences are different for Catholic scientists than for religious scientists from other traditions. From what we have seen and heard, while French laïcité applies to all faiths, it is not, in practice, applied evenly across religious traditions. Rather, it appears to disproportionately target and discriminate against Muslims.[74] A number of scientists we spoke with provided support for this hypothesis. For example, the Catholic scientist[75] who told us about her keychain also told us that the presence of female Muslims who wear a hijab "makes me as a Catholic more well accepted than the Muslims—I have to admit that." Another scientist[76] stated directly, "What we don't like, actually, are mainly signs of Islam. Even if we say or make believe that it's about all religious symbols, in fact, it is the Muslim religion that is targeted. It scares people." We should note, however, that French scientists who mentioned a concern about Islam mostly did so not because of Islamic doctrine but because they feared that overt religious symbols in the workplace would violate the norm that religion should not be expressed publicly.

Overwhelmingly, it is specifically immigrant female Muslim scientists wearing the hijab who are sanctioned for their religious expression, meaning that laïcité can have a specific religious, racial, and gendered implementation. When discussing the presence of women wearing the hijab in the laboratory, a French physicist[77] explained:

Some people have difficulty. They don't really know how to react. . . . I think that it's really a *cultural* problem. We in France, we are just not used to [this]. There was a law at the beginning of the century that truly separated religion and the state, and . . . as a result, it's just that people are uncomfortable.

A CNRS researcher in biology[78] described for us the time a Muslim researcher applied to join his lab:

I did an interview with her through Skype. I could see that she was Muslim because she had the veil. I kind of went through her skills and stuff. . . . We had a lab meeting and then I said, "OK, I interviewed this woman. She seems OK" . . . and then I brought up the issue that she was a Muslim with a veil, and then the reaction of the colleagues were like pretty diverse actually. Some [researchers] didn't want to have it at all because they thought that they didn't want that in the lab. They think it will interfere with the work . . . and actually it end[ed] up as a debate.

It is clear the applicant's religious identity and expression shaped how colleagues evaluated her. In the end, the researcher told us, this applicant was not the best for the position, but "it would have been much more of an issue" if she were, he said. When asked if there have been any conflicts related to religion in his department, Michel, whom we met earlier,[79] talked about what happened in an adjacent lab when a Muslim student was made to remove her hijab. Because the scholarship for her doctorate was provided by the state, she was told that wearing the head covering would violate laws related to secularity.[80] Not everyone agreed with how the student was treated, Michel said. He explained,

> She eventually accepted not to wear it anymore. . . . Giving up wearing the veil was a strict application of the law . . . but some of us were thinking that since this person had no contact with the public in the framework of her PhD, she didn't really have a representative role of the French State, so she ought not to renounce her religious signs. . . . In some cases, there is a strict interpretation of the law of neutrality of the State representatives, and in other cases, this rule is applied in a less strict manner, and Muslim females are allowed to wear the veil in laboratories that have no real contact with the public. It is a tolerance.

Context, whether it is a scientist's role or the feelings of the scientist's boss or lab group, seems to matter a great deal when it comes to tolerance of religious expression in the workplace. One CNRS researcher in physics[81] told us about a Tunisian student who was pressured into wearing a hat instead of a hijab, but after a period of time went back to a hijab with no sanctions. Other scientists reported that Muslim colleagues wearing hijabs experienced no problems at all.[82]

While this perspective was less prevalent in our interviews, we did hear from some scientists that nonreligious scientists exercise more deference to Muslims and other non-Western religious groups than Catholics or Jews, showing greater religious accommodation. A Catholic physicist[83] we interviewed, for instance, told us that in her lab it was common for organized lunches to avoid serving pork in consideration of Muslim researchers, but a nonmeat alternative was not provided for Catholics during Lent. She also told us of the reaction she faced after offering her colleagues *dragées*—candy-coated almonds commonly offered at weddings, christenings, and first communions in France:

> I just put them there [in the common room where people have coffee] and I said it's for the communion of my son, that's all. And they accused me of proselytism. Wow! . . . I didn't put anything on it [related to religion], I just said it's for people. . . . If an Asian or a Hinduist brought something, they would say, "Oh, it's nice. It is their tradition." With Christianity and for Jews, it's difficult.

It is important to note here that more than 60 percent of French scientists who are Muslim say they have experienced religious discrimination to some extent. Even though less than 3 percent of French scientists are Muslim, Islam was mentioned many times in our interviews when French scientists talked about fear of religious influence or suppressing religion. This may be because required visual symbols of faith and adornment of specific clothing is uncommon across most other religious traditions, and thus it is female Muslim scientists whom nonreligious scientists tend to focus on, and who generally face more difficult decisions related to religious identity and expression in the French scientific workplace.

Religious Accommodation for Students?

The separation of religious and public life is a core principle in France, and many French scientists react strongly to religious symbols or expression in the workplace. Yet, like scientists in other regions we studied, they seem to accommodate the religious practices of graduate and undergraduate students (though, as we have demonstrated, female Muslim students are often an exception). This is somewhat surprising, given how uneasy and uncomfortable some nonreligious French scientists appear to be with religiosity among their colleagues. Overall, we see that French scientists are generally more permissive of the religious needs of their undergraduate and graduate students than those of their colleagues. At the undergraduate level, this mainly involves faculty affiliated with CNRS laboratories, as it is primarily here that scientists not only conduct research but also teach undergraduates.[84] A director of research at a physics laboratory[85] told us:

> We have Jewish students, so we have to bear in mind that they don't work on Saturdays. We have students from Northern Africa who are Muslims. We have a lot of them—a lot. We have to take into account that some of them wish to pray [daily]. We have a place in the library where they can come and pray. Praying is not forbidden, nor is doing Shabbat. Catholics pose no specific problem in terms of work organization. Muslims practice Ramadan, so we have to enable them to do it during the Ramadan period. If they come at work, one mustn't push them to drink or eat, and work hours have to fit in the Ramadan day. . . . These are arrangements so that students can practice their religion.

Other French scientists described helping students secure religious clothing for safety when using Bunsen burners or allowing certain religious students to abstain from experiments involving the death of animals in research.

With university students, as we saw with graduate students, Muslims sometimes draw the ire of French scientists—a clear parallel to scientists' reactions to conservative Christian undergraduates in the United States. One director of research in biology,[86] for example, said of Muslim students, "These people openly tell me that the Earth was created 6,000 years ago. . . .

It's a waste of my time to try and teach them." Another director of research in biology[87] also talked about the beliefs of Muslim students but suggested that he planned to directly address the issue:

> My intention in the near future for one of my lectures on the role of the viruses in evolution is to open a debate . . . not at all provocatively, just to discuss. . . . I'll ask them how they perceive the subject matter of my class with respect to their religious ideas. For now, I think that a literal reading of the sacred scriptures is totally incompatible with a scientific approach.

The notion of opening a discussion of religion with religious students is not unique within our study—some scientists in other regions made similar references—but it was relatively rare in France, where religion is avoided as a topic of conversation in the scientific workplace.

Religion Pushing Through the Wall of Science

As we have seen, France's culture and laws, which seek to protect public institutions from the influence of religion and prohibit religious expression in the public sphere, have the effect of suppressing religion in the scientific workplace. Consequently, religion has greater opacity among scientists in France—its impact is primarily private, personal, and less transparent than in most of the other nations we studied. And yet, for many French religious scientists, ethics influenced by religion are an important component of how they approach their work and their colleagues. For example, when asked how religion comes up in his work, a Catholic CNRS researcher in physics[88] answered:

> Actually mainly in ethics. . . . As a religious person, I must respect the truth, because truth exists and I have to find it. I must also be vigilant . . . that applications of my research do not lead to increasing the wrong and problems on our Earth with regard to my human fellows. However, where all this does not come up at all is on the fact that my scientific work has to be conducted with an independent scientific reason. I mean that the scientific truth is not a revealed truth—even if, on the other hand, for me as a Christian, there is a revealed truth that we call the Word of God.

This physicist also told us that religion leads him to "taking care of students with attention and empathy."

Nonreligious scientists also talked about how unobservable expressions of faith and spirituality—such as wonder, reverence, and inspiration—could have a positive impact on the feelings and qualities religious scientists bring to their work. When we asked a nonreligious professor of physics[89] who studies cosmology whether he thought being religious might discourage someone from pursuing a scientific career, he responded, "No, not really. I guess it depends what science. For my science, I would think it might even help. We are talking about the birth of everything and if you're a very religious person that might intrigue you." In response to the same question, a nonreligious scientist in physics[90] replied, "If a child has a religious education and is serious about it, it means that he or she has a taste for reading, for reflection, and this can help in his or her scientific academic studies." When we asked a director of research in physics who is spiritual but not religious[91] how religion or spirituality comes up in his work, he told us,

> Physics has shown that each time we think, we discover absolutely extraordinary things. . . . Discovering the laws of nature and how they are organized gives a kind of religious feeling. That's how I feel it. It is a vague feeling, and it won't make me say or write an equation differently. It is pure awe in nature.

While, as we've seen, laïcité suppresses outward religious expression in the scientific workplace, we also see how scientists may still express their religious identity, values, and feelings in less visible and apparent ways.

Conclusions

France's assertive secularism defines the relationship between science and religion in the country. As we expected, scientists in France are less religious than scientists in all the other countries we studied. It is the only nation in which more than half of scientists identify as convinced atheists. Perhaps because the culture and law protects public institutions from the influence of religion, our interviews found that French atheist scientists do not tend to critique their religious colleagues or disparage religion more generally. Rather, they seem to exercise a degree of humility in understanding how their colleagues can be religious in some respect, and even benefit from religion in some way. To be sure, there are still French scientists who criticize religious colleagues, but it would seem the assertive secularism and official state policy of laïcité minimizes the potential for conflict between science and religion by separating church and state and suppressing religious expression in the public sphere.

Laïcité disproportionately affects Muslim women in science. The French policy of laïcité applies to all religions, *but* we often heard from French scientists of different faith traditions that it can be exercised on prejudicial grounds, discriminating against Muslims in particular—especially Muslim women who wear head coverings of any kind. In part, this is driven by the fact that headscarves are a very visible symbol of religious identity. We also found that laïcité is not applied consistently in all contexts, suppressing or prohibiting religious expression in some environments but not others, and there is ambiguity as to where the law applies. Of all the issues between science and religion we explored in France, we believe that how Muslim women are treated in science has the most potential to escalate conflict. (It is worth mentioning that the felt presence of Islam in French science is much larger than the actual presence of Islam in the French science community). One survey finds, for example, that more than 70 percent of the French public would support banning Muslim veils from university campuses.[92] Even though Muslim women are a small minority of the French scientific community, if female Muslim scientists feel they have to choose between their work and what they see as a requirement of their faith, it could lead to greater conflict between science and religion in France.

There seems to be little opportunity for dialogue between science and religion in France. In France, laïcité keeps religion from public debates, relegating it to the private sphere to avoid conflict. Most French scientists don't feel free to express their religious beliefs or to discuss religion in any meaningful way in the workplace. Only a small minority of scientists—7 percent—can imagine science and religion helping each other, and given the spirit of secularism in France, we are unlikely to see public dialogue between religious and scientific communities. Yet as France becomes more religiously diverse, greater discussion of religious identity and expression might be more necessary, especially within the scientific community, to better understand the tensions religious minorities face and promote religious tolerance.

CHAPTER 6 | Italy
A Distinctively Catholic Religion and Science

AS WE WALKED THE streets of Milan, one of the cities we visited to speak with Italian scientists, it was easy to imagine how the country where Galileo developed observational astronomy might have looked in his time. Many of the original picturesque buildings still stand.

It was Galileo who insisted that the Earth revolved around the sun, not the other way around. Although he claimed that his scientific findings did not conflict with his Catholic faith, the people in charge did not agree.[1] Today, he is as famous for his run-in with the Catholic Church as he is for his extraordinary contributions to astronomy, and his story is often invoked as a symbol of the science–religion conflict. Yet in present-day Italy, we find a more supportive relationship between the Catholic Church and science. For example, the Vatican Observatory, staffed by Jesuit priests trained in astronomy, aims to serve as a "bridge between science and the Catholic Church."[2]

In Italy we found that *Catholicism is everywhere* and scientists have a love-hate relationship with the Catholic Church. For many Italian scientists, being Catholic is a beautiful way of life, but they also feel the Church sometimes encroaches on science when scientific developments impinge on Catholic notions of what it means to be human. Italian scientists generally think Catholicism and science should be kept separate, but we found that the two realms often overlap. Italian scientists sometimes draw on their Catholicism for notions of morality and beauty in science. We also found that because science funding is stagnant in Italy, few scientists are migrating there from other national contexts to work at Italian universities. In addition, Italy has less international coauthorship and copatenting than other developed countries.[3] Consequently, Italian scientists are less exposed to religiously different scientists, and thus tend to have a distinctively Catholic way of understanding the relationship between science and religion.

Cultural Context of Science and Religion in Italy

When we look at the scientific culture in Italy, two issues stand out. First, Italian scientists point to a lack of job prospects and limited opportunities for promotion. The economic downturn starting in 2008, as well as a recession in 2011, led the Italian government to pass a series of austerity measures.[4] As a result, Italy froze academic salaries and career progression to contain public spending for several years.[5] This policy caused many highly qualified scientists to pursue better opportunities abroad.[6] It also flattened research and development budgets at approximately $30 billion per year. When we interviewed scientists in the United States, the United Kingdom, and France, we consistently encountered scientists who had emigrated from Italy. (Several scientists noted that the Berlusconi government, which was responsible for cutting science funding, claimed that Italy's strength, and key to economic revival, lay not in science and technology, but in arts and culture.) Italian scientists who migrate to these contexts seldom plan to return, because they find better working conditions and systems that support scientific research.[7]

Second, many Italian scientists complained about the hiring process in academic science, claiming it is often not based on merit but rather "who you know."[8] Scientists said that Italians who are part of certain Catholic groups are believed to gain access more easily to funding, jobs, and other opportunities because of their religious networks. For example, some scientists in Milan mentioned the political clout of Comunione e Liberazione, a conservative Catholic movement whose members occupy prominent positions across institutional sectors.[9] Universities were also regularly criticized for academic inbreeding, predicated on financial or family connections, or the connections of the person a scholar worked with for doctoral studies. And the scientists we spoke with often mentioned "academic nepotism." As one biologist[10] explained,

If you are a son of someone, you [advance] in your career, and if you are a commoner, it's very hard [to have a career]. . . . [I have] an example of a person that is not really a brilliant scientist, but since his surname is an important name or [he] is the son of a professor, son of a politician and so on, this person for 90 percent will become a professor, will become faculty of the institute, and so on. This has happened, and during these decades it's very common here in Italy.

While many of the scientists we interviewed were critical of Italy's scientific culture, they largely shared a positive view of the role of religion in society. Atheist scientists in Italy tend to be more anticlerical than antireligious, and Italian atheists do not typically harbor negative attitudes toward religion in general.[11]

Though institutional religious participation has gradually declined in Italy, religious affiliation and belief are still strong and widespread in the country and a seemingly indelible piece of what it means to be Italian. Catholicism remains eminent in Italy.[12] The majority of the population retains selective aspects of Catholicism—particular religious beliefs, ideals, education, and spiritual resources for coping with life's challenges. Even though religion in Italy today is marked—especially among the intellectual elite—by growing individualism in people's spiritual search, that individuality is deeply embedded in the communal teachings and traditions of Catholicism. Italians become "spiritual but not religious" in a specifically Catholic way. According to sociologist Franco Garelli, Italy exhibits a distinctive "version of religious modernity," which is for the most part a "flexible, easygoing, selective, 'made to measure'" Catholicism.[13] The dominance of Catholicism, both historically and today, has implications for scientists.

Religion and Science in the Public Sphere

Italian scientists did criticize the Catholic Church when it came to what some see as the Church's political role in science-related issues. Scientists provided examples of issues at the national level that religion seeks to influence, especially the use of fertilized human eggs for in vitro fertilization (IVF) and human embryonic stem cell (hESC) research.

The Catholic Church opposes IVF and hESC research, a position consistent with its overall teaching about reproductive technologies and birth control.[14] The Church believes that the "life and identity" of an embryo should be in the hand of God instead of doctors. After hESCs were isolated in 1998, the Catholic Church engaged in debates opposing hESC research on ethical and moral grounds due to the fact that human embryos are destroyed in the process. In 2008, Pope Benedict XVI issued an encyclical that addressed the ethical issues related to research on human embryos and the use of hESCs.[15]

In 2004, Italy passed a law that recognized embryos as imbued with rights from the moment of conception, which had an impact on how IVF was implemented.[16] For example, the law forbade fertilizing more than three eggs during treatments and required all viable embryos to be implanted simultaneously—they could not be frozen for later use as is the practice in other countries. Italian scientists played a prominent role in challenging the law in the Constitutional Court in 2005. (Some of the scientists we interviewed mentioned their involvement.) As a result of the 2005 case, the Court overturned restrictions on the number of implantations, the freezing of embryos, and the use of donor sperm and eggs.[17]

Yet we did not leave our interviews with the sense that scientists believe the Catholic Church controls or heavily influences government funding of science or that the impact of the Church on science is always negative. The Italian scientists we spoke with were almost in universal agreement that the Catholic Church is not antagonistic to the teaching of evolution, an issue that evokes the most conflict between science and religion in places like Turkey, the United States, and the United Kingdom. Italian scientists reminded us that several Church pronouncements and documents express the compatibility of evolution, and scientific inquiry more generally, with the Catholic faith.[18] In 1996, for example, Pope John Paul II stated, "new knowledge leads us to recognize in the theory of evolution more than a hypothesis."[19] More recently, Pope Francis stated before the Pontifical Academy of Sciences,[20]

[The] Big Bang, which today we hold to be the origin of the world, does not contradict the intervention of the divine creator but, rather, requires it. Evolution in nature is not inconsistent with the notion of creation, because evolution requires the creation of beings that evolve.

Italian scientists we spoke with also mentioned that in 2004, when Letizia Moratti, then Italian minister of education, removed the teaching of evolutionary theory from junior high school curricula, prominent scientists quickly launched a petition, collecting more than 45,000 signatures from citizens concerned that this measure would promote creationism and impede scientific education. As a result, Moratti reconsidered her proposal, reinstated instruction about evolution, and appointed a commission of scientists to oversee its teaching.[21]

Religion Among Italian Scientists

"As probably the 100 percent of Italians, my background is Catholic and that is almost needless to say," one Italian scientist[22] told us. Italian scientists operate in a national context in which to be religious means to be Catholic, and being Catholic is a way of life. As one biologist who grew up in southern Italy[23] explained, "you cannot avoid being Catholic in a context like that. You don't even question the idea of being Catholic." Most Italian scientists were raised in religious households, given religious education, and confirmed in the Catholic Church as teenagers. When defining religion, they have the country's dominant religion in mind; unlike scientists in other national contexts, the majority of Italian scientists did not talk about a diversity of religions.

Italian scientists, like scientists in other countries, view religion as a set of beliefs about the transcendent or sacred. More than one-quarter of Italian scientists we interviewed defined religion as a belief in the transcendent—usually a personal God, sometimes with specific personalities, such as prophets and founders, who communicate teachings and rules. Italian scientists who adhere to classical conceptions of the Christian God often talked about transcendent experiences. One such respondent, a professor of astronomy and a devout Catholic who experienced a religious conversion through a charismatic Catholic prayer group later in life,[24] defined religion in the following way:

> [I]t's the way of believing in something that is beyond the normal knowledge of your mind. It's part of your knowledge in any case, but it's beyond the normal knowledge of science as we define as scientists. As you know, it's not just experiencing something that someone told you or taught you, but it is really experiencing something for yourself.

We also found, because of the deep influence of Catholicism, two types of definitions that stood out as distinctively Italian: religion as a system of rituals and practices (rather than a source of personal identity and meaning), and religion as a communal activity that must have organized aspects. Religion "is just a bunch of laws that have been put together to control the more aggressive instinct of human beings and make possible social living," said one associate professor of biology.[25] "[I]n a religion, there are a lot of laws." Many scientists similarly defined religion by focusing on its function in a person's life or society. Most often, these scientists talked about religion as a source of "moral issues and regulations" to which people had to conform.[26] They also often spoke as if the structure and organization of religion is almost too rigid, sometimes leading to conflict.

None of the negative aspects attributed to religion were mentioned when Italian scientists discussed spirituality, however. While they associated concepts like "conflict" and "irrationality" with religion, they never associated these concepts with spirituality. This would suggest that Italian scientists perceive religion and spirituality differently, with spirituality viewed more positively. According to our survey, 29 percent of Italian scientists (three times more than the general Italian population) consider themselves spiritual but not religious.

When we asked Italian scientists what they meant by spirituality, they emphasized individualism. The majority focused on personal beliefs or the inner self rather than organized structure and beliefs. As social scientists Stefano Sbalchiero and colleagues have argued, Italian scientists tend to see spirituality as dynamic and largely compatible with science.[27] They also consider spirituality to be disconnected from specific religious teachings and institutions. As an associate professor of biology[28] explained: "[Spirituality] lacks . . . the structure of religion. . . . I think religion is spirituality plus this like . . . construction around it, so priests, the Church, and codification of behaviors, what's right, what's wrong." A physicist[29] expressed it this way:

> Spirituality can be in every person, even inside or outside the institution, so maybe there are a lot of people who don't like the institutional Church and they live their faith on their own because they hate, or they don't like, what priests do.

The form of spirituality that Italian scientists articulated, believe in, and practice nearly always seemed to us to be a direct response to the Catholic Church—more specifically, an antidote to what some Italian scientists perceived as the Church's organized nature, rigid rules, certitude, and judgments.

It comes as little surprise, given the pervasive presence of Catholicism in Italy, that we found a greater degree of religiosity among Italian scientists than among scientists in the other Western nations we studied. Fifty-two percent of scientists in Italy—compared with 31 percent of scientists in the United States and only 15 percent of scientists in France, for example—see themselves as religious (Table 6.1). Still, Italian scientists are less religious than the Italian public: 86 percent of the general population say they are religious. We also found that while 44 percent of the Italian population consider themselves both religious *and* spiritual, only 16 percent of scientists see themselves in this way (see Appendix A, Table A.7, on Italy).

We also observed patterns of religiosity by academic discipline, gender, and institutional status in Italy. For instance, 58 percent of Italian biologists describe themselves as religious, compared with 47 percent of Italian

TABLE 6.1. Self-professed religiosity in Italy independent of religious attendance.

RELIGIOUS IDENTITY	POPULATION (%)	SCIENTISTS (%)
A religious person[a]	85.8	51.8
Not a religious person	9.1	16.9
An atheist[b]	2.6	24.5
Don't know	2.5	6.8
Total Respondents	1,012	1,348

NOTES: Based on weighted data. Values exclude nonresponse.
[a] RASIC data includes options for "slightly religious," "moderately religious," and "very religious."
[b] The World Values Survey category asks if the respondent is "A convinced atheist," whereas RASIC asks only if the respondent is "An atheist."
SOURCE: World Values Survey Italy 2005; RASIC Italy Survey 2014.

TABLE 6.2. Religious affiliation in Italy.

RELIGIOUS TRADITION	POPULATION (%)	SCIENTISTS (%)
Roman Catholicism	87.5	58.0
Protestantism	–	0.5
Orthodoxy	–	1.3
Judaism	–	0.0
Islam	–	1.8
Hinduism	0.1	0.5
Buddhism	0.2	0.5
Other	0.2	3.0
None	12.0	34.4
Total Respondents	1,011	1,351

NOTES: Based on weighted data. Values exclude nonresponse.
SOURCE: World Values Survey Italy 2005; RASIC Italy Survey 2014.

physicists[30] (see Appendix A, Table A.8). Based on our data, we also found that 46 percent of men in science identify as religious, compared with 61 percent of women in science,[31] and 47 percent of scientists at elite institutions are religious, compared with 58 percent of scientists at nonelite institutions.[32]

In terms of religious tradition, about 34 percent of Italian scientists say they are not affiliated with a religion, compared with only 13 percent of the general Italian population. Perhaps unsurprisingly, Italian scientists have the highest proportion of Roman Catholics when compared with scientists in all the other national contexts we studied (see Table 6.2). While only

TABLE 6.3. Belief in God in Italy.

BELIEF ABOUT GOD	POPULATION (%)	SCIENTISTS (%)
I don't believe in God.	5.9	20.2
I don't know whether there is a God, and I don't believe there is any way to find out.	7.5	22.6
I don't believe in a personal God, but I do believe in a Higher Power of some kind.	6.8	14.7
I find myself believing in God some of the time, but not at others.	13.6	5.0
While I have doubts, I feel that I do believe in God.	25.3	20.6
I know God really exists and I have no doubts about it.	41.0	16.7
Total Respondents	1,078	1,325

NOTES: Based on weighted data. Values exclude nonresponse.
SOURCE: International Social Survey Programme 2008: Religion III (Italy); RASIC Italy Survey 2014.

12 percent of scientists in the United Kingdom and 22 percent of scientists in France are Catholic, for example, 58 percent of scientists in Italy affiliate with Catholicism. Even still, this figure is somewhat smaller than that of the Italian public, among whom nearly nine in ten (87.5 percent) identify as Roman Catholic.

Scientists in Italy also differ from the general public with regard to their belief in God (Table 6.3). National surveys find that more than 80 percent of Italians declare some belief in God, and more than two in five claim to be "totally convinced" beyond doubts.[33] Only 40 percent of scientists, however, say they have some belief in God. Roughly 23 percent of Italian scientists are agnostic—meaning they don't know if God exists and don't believe there is any way to find out—and one in four are atheist. Only 12 percent of the general Italian population expresses either of these two views. Nevertheless, in a global science context, Italian scientists are notable for their *high level of religious belief*. In fact, Italy is among the subset of countries where a majority of scientists—here, about 57 percent—have at least some belief in a higher power.

Communal religious practice is integral to the expression of religiosity among Italian scientists and the general public alike. When we look at religious service attendance (Table 6.4), we see that 27 percent of scientists say they attend services once a month or more. This means Italian scientists have a relatively high level of religious service attendance compared with scientists

TABLE 6.4. Religious service attendance in Italy.

FREQUENCY	POPULATION (%)	SCIENTISTS (%)
More than once a week	7.4	1.8
Once a week	24.0	15.1
Two–three times a month[a]	–	5.7
Once a month	22.6	4.4
Only on special holy days	24.9	19.3
Once a year	4.1	5.3
Less often	5.0	4.2
Never, practically never	11.7	44.3
Total Respondents	1,004	1,348

NOTES: Based on weighted data. Values exclude nonresponse.
[a] Not a response category on the World Values Survey.
SOURCE: World Values Survey Italy 2005; RASIC Italy Survey 2014.

in countries like the United Kingdom, the United States, and France: Only 17 percent of scientists in the United States, 11 percent of scientists in the United Kingdom, and just 5 percent of scientists in France say they attend religious services as frequently as once a month or more. Seventeen percent of Italian scientists say they attend religious services every week.

By comparison, however, about double the proportion of the general Italian public —31 percent—attends religious services every week. Members of the general Italian public are also nearly four times less likely than Italian scientists to say they do not attend services at all: More than 40 percent of Italian scientists say they never attend religious services, compared with less than 12 percent of the general population in Italy.

Relationship Between Science and Religion for Italian Scientists

At about 22 percent, the proportion of scientists in Italy who view the relationship between science and religion as one of conflict (Table 6.5) is the lowest of any Western country we studied. Fifteen percent of Italian scientists perceive science and religion as collaborative, believing it possible for each to be used to help support the other. Notably, 21 percent of scientists at nonelite institutions hold the collaboration view compared with 11 percent of scientists at elite institutions,[34] where scientists may think it's more in keeping with the identity of a scientist to view religion and science as being in conflict. And even more interesting is that 21 percent of biologists hold the

TABLE 6.5. Perceived relationship of science and religion among scientists in Italy.

RELATIONSHIP	%
Conflict; I consider myself to be on the side of religion	0.0
Conflict; I consider myself to be on the side of science	21.1
Conflict; I am unsure which side I am on	0.4
Independence; They refer to different aspects of reality	57.8
Collaboration; each can be used to help support the other	15.1
Don't know	5.6
Total Respondents	1,285

NOTES: Based on weighted data. Values exclude nonresponse.
SOURCE: RASIC Italy Survey 2014.

collaboration view compared with 11 percent of physicists[35] (see Appendix A, Table A.9, on Italy).

Among the Italian scientists we surveyed, 58 percent said they see science and religion as independent, referring to "different aspects of reality." This is nearly the same proportion of scientists who hold this view in France, where 57 percent of scientists surveyed said they see science and religion as independent realms. The only national or regional context we studied in which a greater proportion of scientists hold this view is Taiwan, where 63 percent of scientists embrace the independence perspective. "Understanding better what the domain of science is has led me to the conclusion that science and religion are mostly complementary and not one against the other," a nonreligious physicist[36] we interviewed said.

While a greater proportion of biologists than physicists see science and religion as having the ability to collaborate, which is not what we expect given that most of the recent global conflicts between religion and science have involved biology not physics, we find the opposite with the independence view of science and religion: 61 percent of physicists and 53 percent of biologists see science and religion as independent of each other, though the difference is not statistically significant.[37] We also find that, at 60 percent, a greater proportion of scientists at elite institutions than those at nonelite institutions—55 percent—view science and religion as independent, though again, the difference was not statistically significant.[38] More complicated statistical analyses that allow us to compare the odds that a survey respondent selects a particular response relative to multiple other response options reveals that patterns by discipline and organizational status were significant net of one another and while keeping other things constant (see Appendix A, Table A.10, on Italy).[39] A number of scientists we spoke to in Italy referred to some version of Stephen Jay Gould's idea of nonoverlapping magisteria[40] to explain how science and religion can coexist without interacting. As one professor of biology,[41] who admitted to being a "great fan" of Gould's theory, told us, "They do not overlap . . . in principle, they do not overlap. Religion is based on faith; science is based on facts . . . methodology and facts."

"I'm not getting from religion any piece of information that can be immediately useful for my science," said Maurizio, a tenured professor of biology who heads a research institute on the outskirts of a major metropolitan center in Italy.[42] "Science works with different kinds of instruments and different, also, purposes."

Maurizio is a tall man with youthful features masked by graying hair and a thick goatee. His office was sectioned off from the rest of his molecular biology lab, a small room with conference posters, pictures of his children plastered on the walls, and a conspicuous wooden cross, which hung above the door. "I'm Catholic; I know you can see," he said, gesturing to the cross. "I'm not going to in any way deny it." His faith, he explained, is and always has been a vital part of his personal life. "I grew up in a Catholic country," he said, "and I've been always, I would say, fed by religion. At a certain point of my life, I have also chosen by myself to adhere to this belief."

Maurizio was born into a conventionally religious Catholic family typical of Italy. He grew up in a small village in northern Italy, where "religion was a common part of life," he said, and Sunday mass and religious education played a central role in the socialization of children. He admitted that his faith has had its "ups and downs," particularly as he went through high school and university and began spending time with "people that do not think like you." He told us,

> I was struggling with the principle behind these impossible phenomena in the physical world, for example the conception of Jesus Christ, the virginity of Holy Mary, the miracles, the resurrection, you know? . . . How can you explain it? . . . So the real point is whether I was believing . . . in the holiness of Jesus. And if the answer to the question was yes, then I don't have to explain it rationally—the miracles, the resurrection or anything else.

Maurizio clearly values his commitment to Catholicism, and religion is a central part of his family life, he said. Yet when it comes to the question of "whether religion is important as part of my job, and if it gives me any clue or any piece of information that I can use particularly," his answer is an emphatic no. For him, religion and science play distinct roles. Throughout much of our discussion, he stressed all the ways that religion does *not* affect his scientific research. He also mentioned the notion of nonoverlapping magisteria,[43] which he finds "a particularly agreeable view." As a result, "every time the Church [makes] a statement on purely scientific matters, I feel a little bit uncomfortable because I think it is going beyond the boundaries," he admitted. He continued:

> And most of the cases, the statements are maybe made by some people within the Church, but they are not official positions. The same way I feel when scientists are making hard statements about something that is not science, for example about religion.

For Maurizio—like the vast majority of Italian scientists, as our survey indicates—science and religion are seen as inherently separate spheres. Given how religious Italy is as a nation, we were surprised to find the independence view of science and religion so predominant, even among scientists who professed strong religious commitment to Catholicism.

In spite of his view of faith and science as completely independent, Maurizio, like many of the Catholic scientists we interviewed in Italy, does believe his faith influences the way he relates to those around him and his ethical approach toward research. He is especially concerned for his students, and he wants to help secure funding and jobs for them in the midst of the difficult Italian economy. "I feel responsible for them. And I feel responsible for them because, generally speaking, I have some positive attitude toward other people, which I think is also influenced by my religion," he suggested. "I'm not saying that only those that are sharing my beliefs are like that," he quickly added. "I derive my moral principles mainly from my religion as much as some atheist can derive his own or her own moral principle from something else."

When Italian scientists talk about the independence of science and religion, there are features of their narratives that are specific to the national context. Two in particular stand out. First, consistent with the pervasiveness of Catholicism in Italy and the "everyone's Catholic" perception, scientists situate their views on science and religion in the context of Catholic thought. Among Italian scientists, Catholic doctrine is perceived as progressive, lacking the literalist tradition found in some corners of Protestant thought, which Italian scientists perceive as fostering conflict between religion and science in other countries. For one thing, as Maurizio referenced, Catholicism is widely seen as perfectly compatible with evolution: "We are all 100 percent

Darwinists," he told us. When we asked an associate professor of biology[44] whether she agreed with scientists who perceive a conflict between being religious and being a scientist, she responded,

> Luckily, my religion doesn't ask that I have to believe that [the science–religion relationship] is happening in that way. . . . I think the Catholic religion is rather progressive in some ways, also. It's not so rigid. . . . No, I keep them [science and religion] distant. . . . In my work as a scientist, I don't feel any conflict.

Interestingly, some scientists in Italy attribute rivalry between science and religion primarily to specific elements of Catholicism and the Catholic Church, which they see as religion's most structured and sometimes most unscientific form, said one professor of biology.[45] According to him, the Catholic Church is "very keen on supporting ideas about miracles and things like that"—ideas which he believes "make little sense" and that, as a scientist, make him "much more skeptical" of religious beliefs.

Of course, not all Italian scientists identify as Catholic. A second country-specific feature of the independence perspective on science and religion in Italy is that the view also originates from scientists who identify as more spiritual than religious. Consider, for example, our conversation with a post-doctoral scientist studying theoretical physics.[46] When asked if he perceives a conflict between being a scientist and being religious, he commented,

> It depends on what you mean by religious. If by religious you mean that you believe in a guy with a long beard that punishes people when they don't do what is ordered, then OK, I must admit that it's hard to be a scientist and at the same time be religious. But *I repeat*, if by being religious you mean a daily fight to increase your consciousness level and become more aware of what is going on inside of you and outside of you and in relation to you, to make order inside yourself, to create a certain kind of harmony inside yourself, and that's between yourself and the universe, I think there is no problem with being a scientist.

One physics graduate student[47] explained how he believes religion, loosely defined, can be compatible with science, as long as religion does not produce rigid theories that go against the reasoning of scientific thought. For this scientist and others like him, religious belief that is not strict but, rather, compromising and fluid can be compatible with science. Religious beliefs that are more spiritual than structured or dogmatic allow the scientific method to monopolize the process of producing rigid taxonomies and definitions of the material world. Thus, this type of spiritual belief does not rival science in any way.[48] As this Italian graduate student[49] sees it,

> maybe science can live with some light, very light definition of religion, but I think they [scientists] cannot believe in religion in the strict sense. I always tend to leave some space because I find it very difficult to end up with just some definite theory.

He went on to explain,

> I think you cannot do science if you believe in religion in a strict sense. Meaning that you believe literally in every word, which is written in the Bible, let's say for instance. So, the idea is that if you are in science, you make your religious beliefs smoother [sic] and you just drop many things making the space for religion as little as possible.

Religion in the Italian Scientific Workplace

Claudia, an associate professor of biology,[50] is what we might call a "cultural Catholic," someone who was raised Catholic and might identify as Catholic but no longer practices. She does not consider herself personally religious, seldom attends church, and doesn't pray, and yet she has retained many traditional Catholic beliefs. In recent years, after getting married to a "very Catholic man" and having a daughter, religion has begun to play much more of a role in her life. She has felt a growing desire to become more involved in church, and as her daughter approaches the age of First Communion, she thinks it might be an occasion to become more active in her parish. What attracts her to religion, in large part, is the sense of community it can offer.

Claudia doesn't see any conflict between being a scientist and being religious, and she rejects the idea that religion is somehow antithetical to scientific inquiry. Like Maurizio, she sees science and religion as separate realms. "I don't feel that religion affects my science," she said. "I don't think of religion as an alternative way to answer the questions that science cannot. It's just an additional overview of life for me. So it's not alternative. It's an added value," she explained. At the same time, she feels put off by the Church's role in public life in Italy, and mentioned in particular the attempts of religious groups to influence money and politics related to science and to restrict reproductive rights. "I would like them far from science," she said.

She doesn't think her work environment is in any way hostile to religion though. "We don't have any kind of pressure at work" either to disclose or conceal religious views, she explained. She also doesn't see religion influencing any of her students, but she recalls a woman she worked with in her previous position who was a devout Catholic. "I was impressed by her way of being, mostly," Claudia remembered. She continued,

> I love the way she was very tolerant, open to people. So if we think about religion as a human being, I may say that I feel the Catholic religion [is a] way of being open, tolerant, [and in] friendship with people around.

Claudia admitted that she doesn't know enough about other religions because in Italy "we don't have a lot of possibility to interact with the diversity of religions."

In many countries, religion is considered an impolite topic of conversation in the workplace, and religious identity is regarded as an intensely private matter. Not so in Italy. "I know exactly who is Catholic and who is not," said an associate professor of physics.[51] Most scientists know colleagues who are religious, and religion does not seem to be a taboo topic among them. Religion is a common topic of conversation, perhaps more so than in any other country we studied. The pervasiveness of Catholicism fosters an environment in which religion is a relatively mundane cultural referent, and religion is strongly coupled with public life.[52] In the words of one physicist[53] we interviewed, "inside our minds as Italians, [religion] is deeply predicated in our culture."

According to our survey data, only 16 percent of Italian scientists indicated that they would be somewhat or very uncomfortable letting others in their university department know their views on religion, whatever those views may be (Table 6.6). Compare this to Turkey, where nearly 22 percent of scientists say they would be somewhat or very uncomfortable letting people in their department know their views on religion, or to the United States, where 24 percent of scientists say the same.

When asked about his level of comfort with sharing his views on religion among colleagues and students, a professor of biology who identifies as Catholic[54] explained,

> I'm perfectly comfortable with it. . . . I may be more afraid or more reluctant to open up myself especially if I was seeing if other people were not sharing my thoughts. . . . [G]enerally speaking, I even sometimes prefer to make things very clear from the beginning. I'm not going around, you know, with a cross in my hand, but let's say if it comes to a certain point where it is appropriate to say, "Well, I think so because *I am Catholic*," I have no problem saying that.

TABLE 6.6. Scientists' degree of comfort with letting colleagues know about their views on religion in Italy.

RESPONSE	%
Very comfortable	28.4
Somewhat comfortable	40.5
Somewhat uncomfortable	11.8
Very uncomfortable	4.3
I have no views on religion	15.0
Total Respondents	1,287

NOTES: Based on weighted data. Values exclude nonresponse.
SOURCE: RASIC Italy Survey 2014.

When Italian scientists have conversations about religion, we found they are almost exclusively related to Catholicism. Most commonly, Italian scientists mentioned that current and former popes were the objects of these "chats" among colleagues, and these conversations were typically in response to news events rather than about the relationship between religion and science. As one associate professor of biology[55] explained, she and her colleagues discuss "events in the news, like the Pope, but it's mostly whenever religion comes in the way of some social aspects, or political aspects, but never in the work . . . it never impacts the work."

In very rare cases, however, the volume of conversation and news coverage related to religion can influence decisions scientists make about their work. For example, a molecular biologist[56] was discussing how religious debates in the political sphere come up in conversation with her colleagues when she added:

I've been being led to study stem cells much more than I would probably have done otherwise hadn't there been specific debates on the use of stem cells, so the fact that there was a specific political debate on that . . . led me to study that issue more than I would have done otherwise. So it has awakened my curiosity.

In Italy, religion in the scientific workplace is rarely tied to tension or controversy, though some scientists did mention a 2008 incident involving Pope Benedict XVI. The pope canceled a visit to the prestigious La Sapienza University in Rome after professors and students planned a protest and wrote a petition to withdraw his invitation to speak, because his views on abortion, homosexuality, and medical research "offend and humiliate us," they said.[57]

When asked if there have ever been conflicts about religion in their academic department, only 8 percent of Italian scientists we surveyed answered in the affirmative. A large majority of scientists indicated that there has *never* been a conflict related to religion in their department. Because there were so few incidents of religious conflict in the workplace, our interviews in Italy did not result in data on the types of religious conflicts we heard about from scientists in other national contexts, such as conflicts related to immigrant or minority religions. As we mentioned earlier, religious pluralism within the scientific community in Italy is low, just as it is in broader Italian society.

The Workplace Morality of a "Catholic" Science

Sociologist John E. Tropman, who wrote about how Catholic theological beliefs work themselves out in daily life, argued "the Catholic ethic is a community-centered pattern of values" and that Catholic theology prioritizes the community of individuals over any one individual.[58] While Italian scientists seldom see religion overlapping with their work lives, we observed this type of helping ethic among many of the Catholic scientists we studied in Italy. For these scientists, Catholicism is a source of morality that leads them to place the good of the group over their own needs and to care for colleagues and students in a way that goes beyond seeing them as only functionally useful to the scientific enterprise.

When asked if religion comes up in his work, one Catholic professor of biology,[59] for example, told us,

> I define myself as a Catholic. . . . You try to keep behavior that is loyal . . . because that is the heritage of my religion. . . . So, if somebody comes here and tries to talk to me because he or she has problems and so on, I'm not closing the door. . . . I am available for discussion, probably too much, because that burns a lot of my time.

It was not only Catholic scientists who emphasized this type of community-oriented ethic when discussing how faith influences the work of religious scientists. Nonreligious scientists also cited this ethic in characterizing their Catholic peers. For example, when asked if she sees any differences between religious and nonreligious scientists in the workplace, an associate professor of biology[60] responded,

What I've noticed is that . . . Catholic progressive professor[s] who we had, they also took a lot of care for the community, to meet the needs of the people and the needs of the community. . . . They took care of everything in the department, from the very silliest stupid things to the important things . . . because they were also religious and they grew up with certain principles.

Beauty in Scientific Work Among Italian Scientists

A number of Italian scientists spoke too about seeing great beauty in science, and some described this beauty in a somewhat spiritual way.[61] They talked about scientific research, experiments, and formulas allowing them to see the natural world, experience spiritual moments, and understand the meaning of life. For example, when discussing the picture we have of elementary particles developed in the twentieth century, a postdoctoral fellow in physics[62] said,

I would stretch to say that it is a kind of a dramatic wonder because you know that it's not going to last forever. . . . So in a sense, in a romantic way, I would say that the present state of where we are in particle physics is like a picture of life itself. It's a great beauty, then it's going to crumble, to change its form. Of course, the results will stay. There will be a great legacy of our present understanding of elementary particles, but it's going to fade away sooner or later.

Another scientist[63] reflected,

As you feel beauty in nature, you feel beauty in physics because there is not so much difference. When you see the sunset, you say it is beautiful, but also, when you see particles in light, it is just the same. It's nature in my opinion. And if you represent nature with formulas, so even formulas can be beautiful.

A researcher in biology[64] told us that doing science is

something that looks a bit like what happens in meditation—if one relaxes and clears his mind, that doesn't mean that they don't think of anything and become an amorphous being [laughs]. But it's basically there that one has the possibility of developing and coming up with new intuitions and new advancements. . . . Again, these intuitions are moments of extreme joy, just as if one has been inspired in some way, as if you truly connected to the universe.

Several scientists claimed that their scientific work opened them up to larger questions of meaning. An Italian physicist,[65] for example, told us that his work gives him a sense of ultimate meaning and purpose. When doing science, he said, he feels "that it is a very intimate way of discovering the world. It is something which is an emotion which is comparable to the emotion of being in front of an outstanding piece of art." He told us he "would die with this work" and that he "cannot live without this work."

Networks of "Robed Barons"

The Italian higher education system has long adhered to a patronage model in which gaining access to jobs and promotions requires the support of "barons" or well-connected tenured faculty.[66] The influence and clout fundamentally rest in the hands of the individuals who control hiring and who tend to hire family members and friends.

The only time we heard Italian scientists reference a specific pernicious influence of religion in the workplace was as part of a broader critique about networks and politics in science. A majority of Italian scientists we interviewed expressed concerns that funding and appointment decisions in science were sometimes influenced by political networks rather than based on merit. Some scientists at universities and institutes in the northern region of Italy speculated that certain Catholic organizations, such as Comunione e Liberazione, influence dynamics in science, and that members of these groups can more easily gain access to funding, jobs, and other opportunities.

One biologist[67] explained it this way:

[These kinds of organizations] have a very strong political influence and can influence funding as well, so we have some way of getting funding to research that doesn't go through peer reviews and is allocated on the basis of not very transparent criteria, and these kind of organizations, you know, also can influence how this funding is distributed.

A physics professor[68] told us, "These kinds of groups have some facilities with which they have command . . . and there is kind of a network in which they can discuss and be a little bit more [influential]." When asked specifically about Comunione e Liberazione, as a way of us following up on what other Italian scientists had told us, another physicist[69] in the same region responded:

I had some colleagues who said that this was some kind of physics organization, it deals with Catholics and they have a lot of power here and basically if you are in it you are guaranteed to have a job. How should I say what guarantee means? When [a job] becomes available, if you are in this organization, you are going to get an extra point—not officially, but just by prejudice—extra points from someone of comparable weight.

"The funny thing is that the mafia in science is something subliminal," Maurizio told us. It's common, he said, for two or three employees in a lab to come from the same specific network, and that such networks are often specifically religious.

The veracity of such claims is difficult to determine. None of the scientists we interviewed indicated involvement with organizations that combine religious and political interests in this respect. One scientist,[70] however, introduced us to a colleague in her lab who belonged to the Comunione e Liberazione movement. We did not conduct a formal interview with her, as she was not in our study sample. But in our conversation with this scientist, she denied that the movement had any particular clout in science, and stated that scientists who are members need to find and rely on supportive "barons" just like other Italian academic scientists do.

If scientists belong to a religious movement, it may be an added bonus in certain cases, but the power and favoritism in science does not stem from these religious movements per se. Nevertheless, concerns about the influence of religious networks in academic science are very real in Italy, and it's easy to imagine how conflict (although rare) would emerge as a result, especially in an environment in which there are broader concerns about job opportunities and funding.

Conclusions

Monolithic Catholicism shapes the science and religion interface in Italy. Religion—specifically Catholicism—is pervasive and familiar within the Italian scientific community. In biology and physics departments at universities and research institutes across the country, we find little tension between science and Catholicism, largely because the majority of scientists share the same religious background and affiliation, and religion is seen as totally independent from the realm of science. (It also helps that evolution, which the Catholic Church supports, is not a highly contentious issue in Italy.[71]) Even those scientists who consider themselves spiritual but not religious are rather indifferent to religion in the workplace.

Religious and nonreligious groups do not threaten the independence view of science and religion. Most Italian scientists see science and religion as referring to different aspects of reality. This perspective is primarily driven by two groups of scientists—those who are Catholic and those who are spiritual but not conventionally religious. Because both groups perceive their approach to religion as progressive, and because they live in a place where there is little presence of other faiths that might be viewed as literalist, the independence perspective is allowed to persist and flourish, more so than among scientists in other national contexts.

Italy provides a model for interaction between science and religion. Although the majority of Italian scientists view science and religion as separate and independent spheres, we also found examples of Catholic scientists integrating science and faith in productive ways. An Italian scientist[72] we interviewed talked about an agreement between a theological school and the university where he works to promote students' understanding of both science and religion and facilitate dialogue about the science and religion interface:

> Here, we have several occasions to discuss science and faith. . . . Students from here can get credits attending the theological school. I don't know how widespread it is in Italy, but these are good characteristics of our city. We have both ties, university [science] and the theological school. And as a consequence, there are conferences [and discussions] attended by theologians and by scientists.

Indeed, more than one-fifth of the Italian biologists we surveyed perceive collaboration between science and faith. While not the majority of Italian scientists, to the extent that collaboration between science and faith is indeed desirable, Italian scientists may be leading the way in promoting it.

| Turkey
The Politics of Secular Muslims

ISLAM PERVADES TURKEY, the only predominantly Muslim nation we studied. Anywhere in Istanbul, the call to prayer can be heard five times a day. Yet, while almost everyone in Turkey identifies as Muslim and religion remains an important component of the personal lives of many Turkish citizens, Turkey is officially secular. Mustafa Kemal Ataturk, the founder of modern Turkey, established a secularist state modeled after France during a sweep of nationalism across the Middle East in the aftermath of World War I, the fall of the Ottoman Empire, and the weakening of European colonialism. Turkey has no state religion, and its constitution calls for freedom of religion. Based on its politics and demographics, it is what scholars call a "secular Muslim" nation. Indeed, there are many Muslims, both in the general public and in science, for whom Islam is a component of national identity but does not entail religious practice.

Yet, with the ascendency of a more conservative, specifically religious government now in power, the role of religion in society and the national influence of Islam are growing. For example, Turkish secularists have criticized current President Recep Tayyip Erdogan's lifting of restrictions on wearing a headscarf in public institutions; for them, greater freedom to don this Islamic dress is not a sign of religious freedom so much as a sign of actively "pushing an Islamist agenda" and betraying Turkey's strict separation of private religion and public life.[1] Scientists we interviewed noted a change in the visibility of religious symbols at academic institutions in recent years. "Effectively you cannot kick a girl out of class for wearing a headscarf," one biologist[2] said of his university, "but there are definitely faculty who would."

Today, scientists we interviewed in Turkey are deeply concerned about the impact of Islam on the education system and the country's scientific research and development, an issue that was particularly salient at the time we were writing this book.[3] After a military faction unsuccessfully attempted to overthrow the Erdogan's more Islamic government in 2016, tensions came to a head in a state of emergency. The Turkish government began targeting academics: arresting, suspending, and forcing them from the academy. The presidents of four Turkish universities and more than 1,500 university deans were asked to resign, and 167 staff members were reportedly dismissed from Turkey's Scientific and Technological Research Council (TÜBİTAK). According to a 2016 article in *Inside Higher Education*, "The space for academic freedom in Turkey has by many accounts been shrinking in recent years against what observers describe as increasing authoritarianism and a drift away from secularism."[4]

Aysel, a professor of biology,[5] echoed many of the same apprehensions about the current mix of religion and politics in Turkey expressed by other scientists. On the wall behind her desk hung a framed iconic picture of Ataturk, a strong supporter of science—wearing a pinstriped suit with a vest, a handkerchief tucked into his jacket pocket, his hair slicked straight back, and his face slim and handsome, clearly from the 1920s or 1930s. In Aysel's opinion, the government is now more religious than it has been in the entire history of modern Turkey. While she believes Islam preaches good things, including that knowledge is inherently important, she also believes the government is not practicing Islamic teaching in its true spirit. Because her research on human genetic diseases touches on evolution, deemed controversial by the government, she is even apprehensive that her phone might be tapped.

The government has increased emphasis on mandatory courses on Islam for young children, she said, even though the European Court of Human Rights, of which Turkey is a member, ruled against it. She also described how she sees the government corrupting the education system by appointing to certain key positions people who are close to the government or agree with its religious views, including the rector of the public universities.[6] She is a member of the Turkish Academy of Sciences, which used to function the way the National Academies does in the United States, meaning new members were elected by their peers. Now, the Turkish prime minister appoints people to the Academy based on their allegiance to the government or alignment with its views. Some of the new members do not have the publication record or qualifications that were expected previously, diminishing the overall quality of the Academy. As a result, many Academy members have resigned in protest. Aysel also said it is difficult for scientists to get government funding, as it is highly politicized. We heard similar concerns from other scientists we spoke with, who talked about corruption in science funding and the need to be connected to certain political parties or organizations in order to receive support from the government.

Aysel takes an interest in the young women who come to the university wearing head coverings. She discusses the Qur'an with them and encourages these young women to read it themselves. Her goal is to open their eyes to what the Qur'an really says. She believes the Qur'an can empower women—including women in science—but that sometimes Islam has been used in ignorance to oppress women. She thinks the secularism of previous Turkish governments was better for women's equality than the current, more religiously influenced government. Overall, Aysel does not see Islam itself as the problem, but rather the way people use religion. In this way, she represents a group of modern Turkish scientists who believe that science in Turkey is threatened less by religion as an idea and more by how intertwined religion and politics have become.

Cultural Context of Science and Religion in Turkey

Turkey has a complex history of both science and religion. After stagnating for a period, Turkey's public science infrastructure has undergone major reforms over the past decade to improve quality and relevance.[7] Sociologist Alper Yalçinkaya's analysis of science and religion during the Ottoman Empire finds that scientific practices and knowledge were much less controversial for Ottoman citizens than the characteristics of scientists. According to Yalçinkaya, the "entire debate was about what kind of people the Ottomans were (and were not) and what kind of people they should (and should not) become."[8] That is, when Muslim Ottomans discussed science, they were more concerned with virtues associated with the possession of scientific knowledge and how possession of such knowledge might change someone than they were with scientific knowledge itself and its relation to religion.

Turkey is home to more than 102 research institutes and universities, and employs more than 95,000 scientists out of a population of 76 million people.[9] Turkish scientists outpublish many of their neighbors in the Middle East (with the exception of Israel and Iran), but Turkey has been outpaced by several East Asian societies, including China, Japan, South Korea, and Taiwan.[10] Turkey spent $16.6 billion USD on research and development in 2015, which is approximately 0.88 percent of its GDP and significantly lower than the OECD average of 2.38 percent.[11] Indeed, a major difficulty of the Turkish higher education system more broadly has been the combination of limited subsidies from the government and a rapid and unplanned increase in the number of universities and students—with many universities suffering from a lack of staff.[12] Accordingly, vast discrepancies can be found between elite and nonelite universities.

Turkey is also one of the most religious nations we studied, when measuring the several commonly used indicators of religiosity, such as affiliation, identification, and belief. According to the 2012 World Values Survey, 99 percent of Turkish respondents identified as Muslim, and 68 percent reported that religion is "very important" in their life. When measuring commonly used indicators of religiosity, the United States and Turkey are the *most* religious of the eight national contexts we studied. A larger share of the Turkish population regularly attends religious services, as well. About one in three said they attend religious services once a week or more, with only 25 percent reporting that they never attend religious services. Eighty-four percent of people in Turkey described themselves as a religious person, with less than 1 percent identifying as an atheist. On a scale of 1 (not at all important) to 10 (very important), nearly 70 percent rated the importance of God in their life as a 10.

Almost half of World Values Survey respondents in Turkey agreed or strongly agreed that all religions should be taught in public schools, and more than 70 percent agreed that people who belong to different religions are "probably just as moral" as those in their own tradition. Yet, nearly 76 percent of respondents agreed or strongly agreed that their religion is the only acceptable religion. When asked if religion is *always* right whenever science and religion conflict, 70 percent agreed to some extent that religion is always right.

Secularism in Turkey differs from the other national contexts we studied. Scholars Angel Rabasa and F. Stephen Larrabee note that Ataturk, the founder of modern Turkey, wanted a nation that "insisted on the control of religion by state institutions," a concept of secularism that drew on the French concept of *laïcité*.[13] Religion, according to this ideal, was intended to be completely separate from and subordinate in matters of public administration.[14] To keep religious matters under the purview of the government, a public institution known as the Directorate for Religious Affairs, called the *Diyanet* in Turkey, was established in 1924 to manage the nation's mosques and propagate Islamic knowledge in accordance with the state's wishes.[15] It might seem odd that there exists a government ministry to manage religious affairs in an officially secular state, but in Turkey, there is not true separation of state and religion as we commonly think of it in the American context: The state controls religion. The precise reason for the Directorate of Religious Affairs is to ensure that Islamic religious activity remains within and is disseminated according to state-prescribed boundaries.

Religion and Science in the Public Sphere

As we traveled across Turkey to speak with a wide range of the country's scientists, we found most of them are afraid of the impact that a religiously motivated political regime will have on Turkey's scientific research and development and their academic freedom. "The National Academy of Sciences in America is autonomous; the US president doesn't interfere with their activities," one Turkish scientist[16] told us. She went on to say that "Turkey is already not strong in science in the world, and the little position it has, has been pushed even farther down the scale and this is really, really upsetting."

When we interviewed Turkish scientists in 2012 and 2015, several of them mentioned the government being involved in determining the science curriculum and suppressing the teaching of evolution. A biologist who considers herself secular[17] told us, for example,

> [The] government brings their own men into administrative positions from high school to universities. These people do not like the issues about evolution. One of our professors wanted to prepare a science workshop in a high school. The name of the workshop was "Evolution," and her request was declined. Then she changed the name of the workshop to "Adaptation," after which it was accepted.

Scientists also talked about how the government has in recent years interfered with the way evolution is taught in public schools. These recent events in Turkey underscore the challenges Turkish scientists face as they strive to increase the country's scientific development and influence. One wonders how Erdogan's wish to create a "pious generation" by promoting religiosity among Turkish citizens might affect science education and, in turn, Turkey's prestige within the global science infrastructure.[18]

Religion and Spirituality Among Turkish Scientists

When Turkish scientists defined religion, three characteristics figured prominently, namely the prevalence of Islam in the nation, the high level of religiosity in the region and among its scientists, and the relative absence of other religious traditions in the country. Similar to scientists in Christian contexts, scientists in Turkey highlighted the concept of a higher power in their descriptions of religion, though they often allowed for flexibility in interpreting exactly what this meant or the form it takes. In some cases, the intricacy and beauty of nature is taken as evidence that such a higher power exists. For example, one physicist[19] said:

> There must be a power, an energy. But you may call this Allah, or energy, or you'll give it a different name. But there *is* something, though. A design, a symmetry within that design, the movement of the sky aligning with the movement of atoms, especially, it's like an embroidery, [detailed] like a honeycomb, like the magnificence of a spiderweb. I mean, there are so many things.

Rituals are central to how Turkish scientists define religion, which is unsurprising given the importance of such practices to Muslims. While all religions can be characterized by the presence of rituals, Islam has certain sacred practices, called the Five Pillars of Islam, which are expected of every Muslim. These include a confession of faith, ritual prayer (five times a day), almsgiving, fasting during the month of Ramadan, and—at least once in a Muslim's lifetime—a pilgrimage to Mecca. One doctoral student in biology[20] explained that for her religion means "rituals . . . are directed at finding yourself, listening to yourself, realizing yourself." Another doctoral student in biology[21] similarly focused on the importance of rituals and practices, saying that religion involves things like "rightful duties [and] the meaning behind fasting. These kind of things, to me, actually seem like understanding the concept of living and living better."

When compared with scientists in more religiously pluralistic contexts, we found that relatively few scientists in Turkey defined religion in negative terms. When one religious physicist[22] noted, "there are people who think that religion is a form of opium that puts the public to sleep," he was referring to a view of religion that he does not personally embrace.

By and large, spirituality was not a meaningful concept for the Turkish scientists we interviewed; it is mainly recognized as a component of religion. "We accept spiritual values, you know, we accept a set of customs. . . . There are certain things with our religious beliefs, we accept those," one scientist[23] told us. "For me, it's not really something that can be separated into two different frameworks. . . . I don't see a difference [between religion and spirituality]." For the few Turkish scientists who did draw a strong distinction between religion and spirituality, it seemed to be based on exposure to how these terms are defined in other national contexts rather than a specific form of spirituality birthed from Turkish forms of Islam. Their descriptions of spirituality as separate from religious traditions and institutions reminded us of understandings of spirituality that have become popular in Western countries, where we see more religious individualism. In the words of one Turkish scientist,[24]

> Religion is more defined, more institutionalized, more organized. . . . And the rules are maybe more written down . . . you can practice spirituality within the institutionalized form of religion . . . maybe this is one way to understand it. Sort of, spirituality should be a part of—or can be a part of—religion, while spirituality can also be separate from any institutions, very personal or in small groups, something like that.

Despite the fact that many Turkish scientists feel that their careers could be marginalized by a new religion-infused political climate, Turkish scientists do not seem to eschew religious belief. Among the Turkish scientists we surveyed, 59 percent reported they are religious, making them more likely to be religious than scientists in most of the other national contexts we studied. Eighty-five percent of Turkish scientists reported they are Muslim (Table 7.1), while, perhaps most notably, less than 10 percent said they are atheists. Among Muslim scientists in Turkey, 42 percent say they do not belong to a particular denomination within Islam. Of those that do belong to a particular denomination and provided a write-in response, a vast majority (more than 90 percent) identified as Sunni or a specific religious school within Sunni Islam, such as Hanafi, Maturidi, Salafi, and Shafi'i. Another 4 percent identified as Shia, Alawi, or Bektashi. We did find differences in religiosity between scientists working at elite universities

TABLE 7.1. Religious affiliation in Turkey.

RELIGIOUS TRADITION	POPULATION (%)	SCIENTISTS (%)
None	0.7	13.3
Orthodox	–	0.22
Islam	99.1	84.8
Judaism	0.1	0.0
Other	0.1	1.7
Total Respondents	1,603	595

NOTES: Based on weighted data. Values exclude nonresponse.
SOURCE: World Values Survey Turkey 2011; RASIC Turkey Survey 2015.

and those working in less elite institutions. Approximately 17 percent of scientists at elite institutions reported no religious affiliation compared with 9 percent of scientists at nonelite institutions.[25]

By several measures, we find Turkish scientists are nearly as religious as the general Turkish population, although it's important to note that in Turkey being Muslim has long been characterized as essential to being Turkish. When we look at belief in God or a higher power, we see that more than 95 percent of the Turkish population reported at least some belief in one or the other, compared with approximately 85 percent of Turkish scientists (Table 7.2). While Turkish scientists are substantially less likely than members of the general Turkish population to be wholly convinced of the existence of God (61 percent vs. 93 percent), we find that another 9 percent of Turkish scientists feel they do believe in God though they have some doubts, and another 13 percent said they believe in some kind of higher power.

Our survey also shows that a greater proportion of biologists than physicists identify as atheist or agnostic.[26] Moreover, physicists are more likely to express an uncompromised belief in God; 68 percent of physicists said they are convinced of God's existence compared with around 56 percent of biologists.[27] When we look at scientists at different types of institutions, we find that 51 percent of scientists at elite institutions reported having no doubts of God's existence compared with 73 percent of scientists at nonelite institutions.[28]

TABLE 7.2. Belief in God in Turkey.

BELIEF ABOUT GOD	POPULATION (%)	SCIENTISTS (%)
I don't believe in God.	1.9	6.3
I don't know whether there is a God, and I don't believe there is any way to find out.	0.8	8.8
I don't believe in a personal God, but I do believe in a Higher Power of some kind.	1.4	12.9
I find myself believing in God some of the time, but not at others.	1.0	1.6
While I have doubts, I feel that I do believe in God.	1.8	9.1
I know God really exists and I have no doubts about it.	93.1	61.3
Total Respondents	1,448	513

NOTES: Based on weighted data. Values exclude nonresponse.
SOURCE: International Social Survey Programme 2008: Religion III (Turkey); RASIC Turkey Survey 2015.

About the same proportion of scientists and the general population in Turkey—one in three—attend religious services once a week or more (Table 7.3). The most significant discrepancy we observed between the two groups was when we looked at the proportion who almost never attend religious services: 25 percent of the general population reported a complete or near-complete lack of participation in religious services, while 40 percent of Turkish scientists reported the same. In both cases, these are significant numbers, despite the difference, perhaps revealing that being part of a religious tradition and belief in God are more important to Muslim scientists than attending religious services.

Our survey data largely do not reveal substantial gender differences in the belief and practice of religion among Turkish scientists. Roughly equal proportions of male and female scientists reported either rejecting or strongly adhering to belief in God, with approximately 62 percent of both groups reporting that they believe in God without any doubt.[29] Male and female scientists were also about the same in the extent to which they do not believe in God (7 percent vs. 6 percent).[30] More female scientists than male scientists reported they don't believe in a personal God but instead believe in a higher power (16 percent vs. 10 percent).[31] On one measure, however, we did find substantial and statistically significant differences between men and women. Namely, we found that female scientists were far more likely than male scientists to say they never or practically never attend religious services (54 percent vs. 30 percent),[32] perhaps reflecting cultural norms in Islam.

TABLE 7.3. Religious service attendance in Turkey.

FREQUENCY	POPULATION (%)	SCIENTISTS (%)
More than once a week	14.0	14.7
Once a week	19.7	16.1
Once a month	4.0	2.2
Only on special holy days[a]	29.0	16.1
Once a year	2.6	5.8
Less often	5.3	4.8
Never, practically never[b]	25.4	40.3
Total Respondents	1,581	599

NOTES: Based on weighted data. Values exclude nonresponse.
SOURCE: World Values Survey Turkey 2011; RASIC Turkey Survey 2015.
[a] Wording on the World Values Survey: "Only on holy days."
[b] Wording on the World Values Survey: "Never."

TABLE 7.4. Frequency of prayer in Turkey.

FREQUENCY	POPULATION (%)	SCIENTISTS (%)
Several times a day	49.5	41.0
Once a day	14.6	12.2
Several times a week	17.4	8.7
Every week	–	0.9
Nearly every week	–	4.1
2–3 times a month	–	3.2
About once a month	–	2.0
Several times a year	–	5.6
Only when attending religious services	3.3	–
Only on special holy days	9.1	–
About once or twice a year[a]	1.2	3.2
Less than once a year	1.3	1.7
Never	3.6	17.3
Total Respondents	1,577	540

NOTES: Based on weighted data. Values exclude nonresponse.
SOURCE: World Values Survey Turkey 2011; RASIC Turkey Survey 2015.
[a] Response reads "Once a year" on the World Values Survey.

While levels of religious attendance among scientists in Turkey mirror closely that of the general public, perhaps even more significant given the Five Pillars of Islam are differences between the public and scientists in the frequency of prayer (Table 7.4). That is, a smaller share of scientists when compared with members of the general public pray regularly, and a larger share of scientists (when compared with members of the public) never pray. While about half of the Turkish population pray several times a day and 82 percent pray at least once a week, only 41 percent of scientists pray several times a day, with about 63 percent praying at least once a week. Conversely, less than 4 percent of the Turkish public never pray, compared to more than 17 percent of scientists.

Relationship Between Science and Religion for Turkish Scientists

When asked about the impact of their scientific knowledge and training on their faith, 28 percent of Turkish scientists—the most in any region (the next highest was Hong Kong at 17 percent)—reported that their scientific background had actually made them *more* religious.[33] Half of Turkish scientists said their scientific training had no effect on their religiosity, while only 22 percent said their training made them less religious. We again found a striking discrepancy between physicists and biologists. As we saw, a greater proportion of biologists than physicists in Turkey said they are atheist or agnostic. We also found that a greater—though not significantly greater— proportion of physicists than biologists (32 percent vs. 24 percent)[34] reported that science made them more religious (see Appendix A, Table A.11, on Turkey). These findings could suggest that there is a better climate for being religious in physics than in biology, or at least Turkish scientists perceive there is such a difference. Perhaps this perception stems in part from the sense that physics is not as encumbered by ideas that conflict with religious beliefs, such as the theory of evolution. In Turkey, where the vast majority of the population is Muslim, acceptance of evolution is low (in a 2006 *Science* study, it was found to be even lower than in the United States[35]), and there have been reports of Turkish scientists who are pro-evolution getting death threats.

We also found that a much larger share of female scientists (59 percent) than male scientists (44 percent) said their scientific knowledge and training had no effect on how religious they are.[36] Male scientists were more than twice as likely as female scientists to say their training made them *much* less religious (20 percent vs. 9 percent).[37]

As with the other regions we studied, the largest share of scientists in Turkey—34 percent—view science and religion as having an independent relationship (Table 7.5). But among all the national contexts we studied, Turkey has the largest share of scientists who perceive the relationship between science and religion as one of collaboration. Nearly a third of Turkish scientists

TABLE 7.5. Perceived relationship of science and religion among scientists in Turkey.

RELATIONSHIP	%
Conflict; I consider myself to be on the side of religion	1.9
Conflict; I consider myself to be on the side of science	24.3
Conflict; I am unsure which side I am on	0.1
Independence; they refer to different aspects of reality	34.4
Collaboration; each can be used to help support the other	31.8
Don't know	7.6
Total Respondents	460

NOTES: Based on weighted data. Values exclude nonresponse.
SOURCE: RASIC Turkey Survey 2015.

reported believing that science and religion can collaborate or be used to support each other. The conflict view was the least popular, with 26 percent of Turkish scientists saying they see science and religion as having a conflictual relationship.

About 29 percent of male scientists compared with 18 percent of female scientists in Turkey see science and religion as in conflict, and they are on the side of science,[38] while more female scientists than male scientists think the relationship between science and religion is one of independence, such that they refer to different aspects of reality[39] (see Appendix A, Table A.12, on Turkey). Female scientists had lower odds than male scientists of affirming the conflict view rather than the independence view. Scientists at elite institutions were more likely than those at nonelite institutions (31 percent vs. 17 percent) to view science and religion as having a conflict relationship.[40] Scientists at nonelite institutions were more likely than those at elite institutions (42 percent vs. 23 percent) to perceive science and religion as having a collaborative relationship in which each can be used to support the other.[41] And Turkish scientists at elite institutions had lower odds than those at nonelite institutions of affirming the collaboration view rather than the independence view (see Appendix A, Table A.13, for Turkey).

In line with our other findings and likely for similar reasons—namely, the controversial nature and treatment of evolution in Turkey—our data show that physicists are more likely than biologists in Turkey to believe science and religion can be collaborative (37 percent of physicists vs. 28 percent of biologists)[42] and biologists are more likely than physicists to espouse a conflict view of science and religion. Thirty percent of biologists and only 19 percent of physicists in Turkey described their understanding of the science and religion relationship as one of conflict.[43] And biologists had significantly higher odds than physicists of affirming the conflict view rather than the independence view. Many scientists who hold the conflict view pointed to current tensions surrounding teaching human origins as evidence of such a conflict; in fact, it was the example scientists brought up most often when discussing why there is a conflict. Turkish scientists raise some concerns about religion sometimes being too "dogmatic" in its approach to the natural world. "I think this is more of religious people's problem rather than scientists' problem," said an associate professor of physics[44] when talking about conflict between science and religion. Different from scientists in other national contexts who view religion and science as in conflict, a large minority of the Turkish scientists we interviewed who hold the conflict perspective *do not* see science as having to be *inherently* in tension or conflict with religion.

Turkish scientists who said they see science and religion as potentially collaborative stressed aspects of Islamic theology that encourage scientific work. For example, one associate professor of biology[45] noted that she formerly believed science was in conflict with religion, before she came to the realization that "religion is for me asking good questions of who I am and if God created me" and that these questions paralleled those she asked as a biologist. As such, "they are in agreement right now, my scientist side and religious side," she said. Other scientists who hold the collaboration view also don't perceive their Muslim faith as discouraging scientific investigation and draw inspiration for their scientific work from the Qur'an, seeing religion and science as compatible because they are both divinely ordered. "God created everything in some order in the sciences," one graduate student[46] told us, "and [the] Qur'an actually encourages people to explore." A doctoral student in biology[47] explained how she sees Islam as motivating learning:

In Islam, from what I've read—I mean, the first word [of the Qur'an] is, "Read"— . . . there's really no other way to explain it. That means that it's telling you to not think narrowly. Don't look at anything with blindfolds on. You will read. You will learn. And you will adapt accordingly. That being the case, that means that other people interpret religion differently, hence their alienation from science. Therefore, I don't think that sort of thing is necessary.

For other Turkish scientists, their belief in science and religion collaboration seems to stem from seeing science as inherently limited. One assistant professor of physics[48] explained that his view is that "science cannot explain everything," rooted in an expansive notion of Islam. This rationale was also commonly cited by scientists holding the view that science and religion are independent, with several of these scientists arguing that science cannot ultimately explain religious belief. An assistant professor of biology[49] noted, "you don't have to put [religious belief] through any scientific methodology," in wondering aloud why some scientists remain unsatisfied with their inability to explain everything in naturalistic terms. An associate professor of physics[50] explained that for him, science and religion are "equally self-consistent" ways of conceptualizing human existence, resembling the model of "nonoverlapping magisteria."

Religion in the Turkish Scientific Workplace

Mehmet,[51] an assistant professor of biology, identifies as a religious man, yet maintains that religious belief can interfere with scientific work in a detrimental way. He views religion as largely a personal matter to be kept separate from intellectual and professional pursuits. In fact, he views religion as so private that he does not even discuss it with his wife. His grandmother, who is his inspiration, was a *hatime*, a religious woman who had read the entire Qur'an, he said, yet she also held loyal to the secularist ideology of Ataturk, the Turkish republic's founder.

Mehmet began by inquiring about the confidentiality of the study, and once assured, he graciously supplied us with numerous details on his personal life and thoughts on religion and science. He made it clear that he sees religion as serving a functional purpose on two levels. One, it compels individuals to treat one another with empathy and reinforces ideals of charity and kindness. In his view, the "Golden Rule" and its manifestations in Islam have socially positive benefits:

> I maybe see religion as . . . the criteria for being a good person. So not going to bed if your neighbor is hungry. What does that mean? So my financial situation is good, but my neighbor is going to sleep hungry. If then, I am sharing a piece of bread with this person, . . . that's what religion is to me.

Second, he sees religion as shedding light on concepts that seem to escape human knowledge, serving a spiritual function. He paints religion as "an argument people use in their own lives to fill a spiritual void." For him, "the scientific data we have, the occurrences in nature are generally not enough to explain" certain phenomena. As a result, "the concept of God, the concept of Allah, the concept of religion, are important."

Given Mehmet's belief that religion is necessary to explain and comprehend the world around us, you might expect him to consider religion to be integral to his scientific undertakings. On the one hand, he does not view science and religion as inherently in conflict. "Why should [my research] oppose my religious views or feelings?" he stated. "I mean, to this day, I've never had that contradiction. The scientific work that I've done hasn't put me in any difficulty with my beliefs." At the same time, he believes there can indeed be a conflict between religion and science if religion weakens a scientist's sense of objectivity. In other words, Mehmet values religion for its overall ethos, for its ability to give people comfort and to coax them toward socially benevolent actions, but he also believes religion can overtake a scientist's intellectual honesty if it becomes too intertwined with scientific work. For all the positive aspects that he believes religion holds, the particularities of a person's religious belief and practice should not enter into the scientific workplace, he argues, for this could jeopardize the pursuit of truth with objective rigor. He is concerned that "for people where religion outweighs everything or they're left under the influence of religion, I think it can affect their scientific work." In his view, "the biggest obstacle for the institutions and establishments doing science in a scientific way is religious groups."

Not all of the scientists at Mehmet's public university think religion should remain outside the laboratory at all times. Rather, he is acquainted with colleagues who undertake *namaz*, or daily Islamic prayers, in their offices and attend Friday prayers together as a group. Some students will discuss going to *iftar* celebrations during Ramadan and will perform *abdest*, or ritual ablutions, in university restrooms. Some professors even integrate religious ideas into their discussions of evolution, something that Mehmet views as antithetical to a scientific environment. When asked whether religion enters his classroom, he replied:

> Absolutely not. I keep these two completely separate anyway. Like I said in the very beginning, when I first begin my lesson, I draw it on the board: religion, science, politics. I say, "As a scientist, I am obligated to tell you the scientific truth, and . . . if it's clashing with your beliefs, your spirituality, I won't even make an argument of it when you're going to criticize me, or ask me something." I warn them, "keep religion and spirituality out of it completely, direct the question itself at scientific truths."

In science, Mehmet said, "the truth is singular," unlike the variegated value systems found across religion and politics. Religion, he claims, is a "subset" of spirituality that helps individuals feel a sense of rejuvenation and cope with difficulties when they arise in life. Science, on the other hand, is "the reality of life . . . it is life itself."

A number of Turkish scientists talked to us about the need for distinct separation between science and religion in the workplace. A Muslim[52] physics professor[53] expressed his view that religion should not encroach on scientific research by stating, "A scientist should maybe work like an atheist. She or he can be inspired from his or her religious beliefs but act like an atheist when conducting scientific research." Another physicist who identifies as religious[54] told us he had read the Qur'an a number of times but religion "has nothing to do" with his research pursuits, and he would equally disapprove of a "nonreligious or atheist" colleague raising religious topics in a classroom as he would a religious colleague. "This isn't a theology class, it's a physics class," he said. A biology professor[55] said that while she would welcome conversations about religious topics outside of her lab and coursework, religion "would not interfere with my academic work or with my teaching. Nor would it affect my relation to my students in the lab or in the classroom." When discussing religion and science, "I keep the two of them really separated in my head," another biologist[56] said, while yet another scientist[57] explained, "I see them as basically living side by side, at least in the type of science I do." Many scientists in Turkey referenced this type of compartmentalization when asked if and how their religious commitments informed their scientific work.

Other Turkish scientists described for us instances in which religious beliefs could detrimentally affect the scientific work of others. It is important to note that many of the scientists who said that they see the potential for religion to negatively influence the scientific work of their colleagues are themselves Muslim. One biology doctoral student[58] spoke of how some scientists might display intellectual curiosity but then reject certain conclusions that conflict with their preexisting religious beliefs, thus hindering their scientific practice. How Turkish scientists view the influence of religion (generally they are talking about Islam) in the scientific workplace seems to parallel how they view conflict between science and religion. Just as they tend to see such conflict as due to the personal religious beliefs of certain scientists rather than intrinsic to the realms of science and religion, so do they tend to believe it is the strength and dogmatism of a given scientist's religious beliefs, rather than religious beliefs in the general or abstract, that hamper scientific practice. In other words, Turkish scientists tend to individualize the influence of religion on science rather than take the position that religion is inherently opposed to science. There were some scientists, however, who did argue that religious belief inherently inhibits science and thus religion is not compatible with the scientific workplace. "When you are religious, you don't question much," one biologist[59] said. "When you don't question much, you can't be a successful scientist."

Our survey data support the idea that Turkish scientists largely do not see innate conflict between religion and scientific practice. Less than 10 percent of Turkish scientists said they believe religion has an impact on the research of their colleagues (Table 7.6). Of the group who hold this belief, 28 percent think religion has a positive influence on scientific research or are unsure whether the impact is positive or negative. Almost 70 percent of Turkish scientists believe their religious colleagues have not been influenced, either

TABLE 7.6. Perceived influence of religion on scientific research among scientists in Turkey.

NOW THINKING ABOUT YOUR RELIGIOUS COLLEAGUES, DO YOU THINK THAT THEIR RELIGIOUS VIEWS INFLUENCE THEIR RESEARCH?	%
Yes	9.2
Positive influence (% of "Yes")	17.6
Negative influence (% of "Yes")	71.8
Don't know whether influence is positive or negative (% of "Yes")	10.7
No, because none of my religious colleagues are engaged in research.	1.6
No, their religious views do not influence their research	67.4
No religious colleagues	6.1
Don't know if religion influences colleagues' research	15.7
Total Respondents	393

NOTES: Based on weighted data. Values exclude nonresponse.
SOURCE: RASIC Turkey Survey 2015.

constructively or detrimentally, by their religious beliefs. Notably, only 6 percent of scientists we surveyed reported not having religious colleagues.

More than 20 percent of Turkish scientists reported that there has been conflict about religion in their academic department—a proportion greater than in any of the other national contexts we studied. Some scientists explained that they fear scientific work will be influenced by political and religious ideologies of the government. "Kind of jokingly, but we say, 'Oh, pretty soon we'll be teaching creationism instead of evolution' and things like that," one biologist[60] told us. "We do joke around this quite a bit, and buried behind these jokes we're actually fearful that it's going to come to that." Another biologist[61] admitted wariness and influence:

> maybe when I don't feel free, when I should give a lecture and when I have to think twice saying something about evolution. I mean, I think it's not yet the case, but it's going in this direction, so it doesn't make me feel very easy.

A postdoctoral fellow in biology[62] was even more pointed in expressing his concern about religiously influenced politics affecting science, stating that the conservative government led by Erdogan had caused "a suppression of the science- and the fact-based institutions." The significance of these words should not be lost.

We also found that 22 percent of Turkish scientists reported they were uncomfortable letting people in their department know their views on religion, a figure that is higher only in the United States (24 percent) among the nations we studied. For comparison, 15 percent of scientists in the United Kingdom and 16 percent of scientists in India, Italy, and Taiwan expressed the same sentiment. Our interviews show that *both* religious and nonreligious scientists in Turkey feel this discomfort. One assistant professor of biology[63] suggested that, different from other contexts where many scientists are afraid of being perceived by peers as too religious, some scientists in Turkey worry that access to research resources might be limited if it is perceived they are not religious *enough*.[64] This biologist said,

> [B]ecause there is this battle between the two camps, I feel that many people are also scared of telling their standing points. There is a lot of hush going on. And Turkey is unfortunately going to more authoritarian-style regime. So if you were to go around saying you are an atheist, you don't believe in this and that, the word can spread around and your grants might not be funded.

Conversations About Religion

Nearly all of the Turkish scientists we interviewed reported having conversations about religion at work. In certain instances, religion arises as a topic of conversation when colleagues or students casually discuss their involvement in routine religious practices. One professor of biology[65] noted that she has colleagues who openly tell other faculty members that they attend Friday prayers, and that certain colleagues make a point of asking whether other professors are fasting so as not to eat or drink in front of them. A nonreligious professor of physics[66] told us "everyone knows" scientists in her department fast during Ramadan, and she would not let certain religious professors know she is stepping out to lunch if they have told her they are fasting. Another biologist[67] recounted how a student hoping to attend Friday prayers during her class time had approached her openly with the request. Given that religion is a salient topic in many aspects of Turkish life, scientists accordingly seem to expect that basic discussions of religious practices will arise among faculty and students.

One biologist who identifies as a nonreligious Muslim[68] told us he commonly witnesses colleagues praying, and estimates from his discussions with his fellow scientists that about "30 percent of [his] colleagues may believe that religion is as important as science." In his opinion, conversations on religion might be avoided not out of a desire to elevate scientific discourse above religion, but rather to give deference to religious colleagues who might be unsettled by discussing controversial topics related to their faith. "If [your colleague] is a religious person, you cannot go and tell him about evolutionary stuff, it's not really kind and so you keep it for yourself," he said. An astrophysicist at an elite university who identifies as religious[69] claimed that issues such as what her colleagues do or wear during Ramadan are "otherworldly matters" that she "would not interfere with" in her "work life." While many Turkish scientists perceive conflict between science and religion in the workplace, it appears there might be some attempt made to accommodate the religious beliefs or practices of colleagues, even if such practices and beliefs are shared by only a minority of students or faculty.[70] The importance assigned to accommodation of religious belief can be observed more broadly in an April 2018 memorandum from Turkey's Higher Education Council (YÖK), which instructed universities to reschedule activities to allow students and staff to attend Friday prayers.[71] Only 7 percent of Turkish scientists said they felt religiously discriminated against often or very often, though 29 percent—the most of any region we examined—claimed to have experienced at least some degree of religious discrimination. And only 10 percent of scientists in Turkey said they felt instances of discrimination rarely took place. While a number of Turkish scientists spoke of witnessing religious discussions among colleagues and students, few of them displayed any outright hostility toward religious beliefs.

Conclusions

The role of religion is changing in Turkey. There has long been tension in the "secular Muslim" nation between the secularism the state was founded on and particular forms of Islam, the religion practiced by the majority of the nation's citizens. And yet a strict secular/religion distinction is in no way represented by the Turkish case. When we spoke with Turkish scientists, transitions within Turkey's political infrastructure were simmering, and they have since erupted. Our conversations with these scientists, marked by great concern about government intervention in academic work, foreshadowed the unrest and turmoil that followed. It is indeed a very particular and highly politicized form of Islam that scientists are concerned about rather than Islam more broadly. Since the failed coup by members of the Turkish military against Erdogan, the president has cracked down on dissent in various segments of Turkish government and society. Many see Erdogan's government as trying to inject a specific version of Islam into politics and the national identity, reshaping Turkey away from its secular tradition and into a more religious country with more open religious expression and a more religious ideology, education system, and public life. Ultimately, the prevalence of religious scientists in Turkey shows that scientists do not always view Islam in itself as the biggest threat to their science. The *politicization* of Islam, on the other hand, is what they think poses challenges to the expansion of science in Turkey perhaps greater than ever before seen in the country's history.

Erdogan's government and the political unrest within Turkey are having an enormous impact on the country's scientific community. In an article for the scientific journal *Nature*, Alison Abbott writes that Erdogan's purges have halted what was an upward trajectory of Turkey's scientific development, based on research funding that became more plentiful in 2005 when Turkey began its negotiations to join the European Union.[72] TÜBİTAK, Turkey's key research funding agency, was disbanded following the coup. There is widespread apprehension among scientists. While the government-controlled Turkish Council of Higher Education (YÖK) has been pursuing initiatives to make universities more competitive—including organizing research competitions for colleges to be granted the title of "research university," which would afford them more freedom in creating courses and approving new professors, and "has also opened 2,000 new Ph.D. positions to ensure a future generation of scientists" —many Turkish scientists have expressed concern about a "brain drain" from Turkey. Scholars Ibrahim Sirkeci and Jeffrey Cohen claim that many scientists are choosing to leave Turkey, using academic connections (as opposed to applying for asylum, as many businesspeople and artists have done), and they note that 15 Turkish universities have been closed since the coup and Turkish science conferences have tapered off.[73] It is increasingly difficult to attract doctoral and postdoctoral students; many of Turkey's best and brightest are leaving for positions in Europe or the United States. These trends point to a nervousness among Turkish scientists and a feeling that life in the scientific diaspora will provide them with a more certain future.

| India

Science and Religion as Intimately Intertwined

IN NOVEMBER 2013, on the island of Sriharikota—nestled between Pulicat Lake and the Bay of Bengal—India successfully launched its first Mars orbiter into space. A colleague who was at the launch reported that, before the liftoff, the chairman of the Indian Space Research Organization (ISRO), Koppillil Radhakrishnan, had taken miniature replicas of the rocket and orbiting spacecraft to the Venkateswara temple in Tirupati, about a three-hour drive from the launchpad, placed them at the feet of a deity, and offered pujas (devotional rituals). "We know we have done a great job," an ISRO scientist told *The Times of India*, "but let's not complain if there is a little divine intervention."[1]

The morning that the spacecraft, called Mangalyaan (Hindi for "Mars-craft"), was set to enter the orbit of Mars, religious groups prayed for its successful entry.[2] One group in Thiruvananthapuram, for example, offered coconut, lotus, and delicacies to the deity at the famous Pazhavangadi Ganapathy Temple. The orbiter was a highly visible symbol of a rapidly advancing infrastructure for scientific research in India, and South Asia more generally—and still, religious rituals were all around.

Public religious blessing of a scientific endeavor was not without precedent in India. Madhavan Nair, Radhakrishnan's predecessor at ISRO, had prayed at the Venkateswara Temple before the launch of Chandrayaan 1, India's historic 2008 moon mission.[3] Upon the 1917 founding of the scientific institute in Calcutta that now bears his name, distinguished experimental physicist J. C. Bose declared, "This is not a laboratory, but a temple."[4] Following the launch of the Mars orbiter, most people in India seemed less concerned with the prayers and religious offerings than with the $70-million price tag for the mission, which many regarded as difficult to justify in a country where hunger and poverty are widespread.[5] Yet the religious acts did cause some acrimony among certain public constituencies. The director of the Federation of Indian Rationalist Associations stated that Radhakrishnan was "unfit to occupy the position of the head of the space mission and should be immediately sacked."[6]

During our fieldwork in India, we saw an intertwined relationship between science and religion reflected in the lives of many scientists. More than in any other region we studied, the boundaries between science and religion in India are fluid and overlapping—though much of what we would consider religious goes largely unnoticed by the average Indian scientist. A number of scientists participate in religious festivals or prayer practices. At one university we visited, a termite hill being used by geologists for an ecological study was also used as a prayer site for campus staff (see Figure 8.1).[7] Yet on our survey, many Indian scientists said they generally see science and religion as independent.

India is considered a developing country but has a strong emerging research and development (R&D) infrastructure. It spends only 0.63 percent of its GDP on R&D, estimated to be $50 billion in 2015. Furthermore, unlike several other countries and regions we studied (the United States, the United Kingdom, France, and Hong Kong), where 65 to 70 percent of the work is conducted in industry, India's R&D is performed predominately in higher education (60 percent). As a result, India is more focused on basic and applied research than experimental development.

To talk in depth with Indian scientists about how they view the relationship between science and faith, we traveled as far north as the capital of New Delhi, west to Mumbai at the edge of the Arabian Sea, south to the center of India's high-tech industry in Bangalore, and as far east as Kolkata. Our fieldwork took us beyond the city limits of metropolitan areas to universities in smaller towns, and when we were not able to travel to a destination, we conducted remote interviews via Skype and telephone.

We met Sanjay, a reader in physics who identifies as a devout Hindu,[8] at the gates of the science institute where he works. To gain entry, we had to register our laptops and have our photos taken, and we were told we could not take photos during our visit—security more elaborate than we usually encountered, signifying the elite and prestigious status of the institute. Sanjay was welcoming and cheerful, smiling often. He wore rings with stones around a couple of his fingers and an orange thread around his right wrist. Such astrological gemstones and sacred threads (this orange

FIGURE 8.1. A termite hill being used for an ecological study and as a prayer site.
Photo credit Brandon Vaidyanathan.

one, the *kalava*, typically worn to ward off evil) are not uncommon in India.
On a narrow ledge along the wall by his desk sat a couple of religious idols,
and pinned on a cabinet were two photocopies of what looked like poems
in Hindi script; on one was the face of Nobel laureate Rabindranath Tagore,
and on the other Hindu monk Swami Vivekananda. Sanjay's religious background is on display to all who enter his office.

Although he is now religious, Sanjay feels religion was not important to his family when he was growing up. As is "standard procedure" among middle-class families, he says, they only did a daily puja, washing their hands and feet and then lighting a lamp while reciting a Sanskrit verse that according to Sanjay means, "This lamp lights our lives. May our knowledge remove ignorance and push back darkness." To Sanjay, there is "nothing religious" about this practice, illustrating how complex it can be for researchers to determine which activities and behaviors should and should not be characterized as religious.

Sanjay became a serious Hindu quite recently, after he and his wife both faced serious health issues. In the ICU, he started asking himself questions: "What have I achieved? What difference does it make?" Sanjay felt compelled to reinvestigate his faith. His doctors suggested he meditate regularly. He laughs when he says, "They ask you to close your eyes and concentrate. . . . If you are having trouble, this is like an aspirin."

Sanjay now sees religion as a way of life with certain practices that give people "moral principles so you don't create a nuisance to others," encouraging respect for teachers and the elderly. He rejects distinctions between religions, believing that all prophets and "God-men" across cultures have common basic experiences and that all religious practices are essentially the same. But he draws a clear line between religion and science, he says. Religion is for home life only, he explains, not the life of science. He says he never discusses religion in the course of his scientific work, and he thinks other scientists are similarly private about their beliefs. Yet he does feel religion strengthens his scientific work by guiding his moral compass and making him more ethical, he tells us, and he believes nonreligious scientists are "mechanical" in their interactions with students, lacking a "human touch." He further describes them as, on average, "highly untrustworthy." As he talks, we glance around at all the religious artifacts in his office and on his person and think: It looks and sounds like science and religion are not as separate as Sanjay believes.

Given our perception of India as a spiritual place, we expected most Indian scientists would see unity or compatibility between science and religion. But we found something different: Scientists in India often try to separate or compartmentalize science from religion—even though religion often overlaps with science in ways that scientists don't recognize. In India, we found science and religion are intertwined and hard to disentangle.

Cultural Context of Science and Religion in India

Although India is officially a secular state, religion permeates nearly every aspect of life.[9] India embraces a form of secularism that is distinct from secularism in the West, referring not to the absence of religion in public spaces but to the accommodation and tolerance of all religions.[10] The origins of contemporary secularism in India began with the partition of the British Indian Empire in 1947, which divided the colony into two distinct sovereign states: Hindu-majority India and Muslim-majority Pakistan. What ensued was one of the largest mass migrations in history. Scholars estimate that roughly 15 million people migrated from their native land—Muslims to Pakistan and Hindus and Sikhs to India—and close to 80 percent of these immigrants became homeless.[11] In the aftermath of the partition, India experienced profound religious and cultural conflict, and religion became a sensitive topic.

The nation's first prime minister upon independence, Jawaharlal Nehru, was an ambitious rationalist who emphasized the importance of scientific development and viewed science as a "great liberator from superstition."[12] Nehru was certain that with scientific education and economic development, the problems of religious communalism would dissolve. But Gandhi, who led the country's independence movement, saw all religions as equal, and it was his view that the nation would constitute a community of religious communities.[13] From its very foundations, the country has attempted to chart a course between a commitment to rationalistic, scientific progress and faithfulness to ancient traditions.

In 1976, the Indian National Congress passed the controversial 42nd Amendment to the Indian Constitution.[14] Among other changes, the Amendment altered the preamble to define the country as a "sovereign socialist *secular* democratic republic." The Amendment also made it the fundamental duty of every Indian citizen to "develop the scientific temper, humanism and the spirit of inquiry and reform."[15] Since then, India has maintained an official dedication to secularism, prohibiting state-sponsored religion and requiring that all religions are equally welcome and accommodated within the public sphere. This particular understanding of secularism has created a unique situation for scientists here: India self-ascribes as a secular state, and science is largely perceived as a secular institution, and yet the cultural context makes science and religion completely inseparable.

There also has long been an emphasis on locating the origins of scientific knowledge in Hindu texts and traditions. As historian Gyan Prakash writes of the "Hindu intelligentsia" in the late nineteenth century: "Denying that science was alien to India, they argued with remarkable ingenuity and deep cultural learning that the ancient Hindus had originated scientific knowledge, and that this justified the modern existence of Indians as a people."[16] Books such as *The Positive Sciences of the Hindus* by philosopher Brajendranath Seal and *History of Hindu Chemistry* by chemist Prafulla Chandra Ray argue that Hindus constructed a scientific heritage alongside, and even before, Arabs and Europeans. Scholars argue that the reaction to Darwin's *On the Origin of Species* in India, where the book generated little attention and no controversy, reveals the compatibility between science and Hinduism.[17] The widely acclaimed intellectual Swami Vivekenanda[18]—who asserted a fundamental indivisibility between science and religion—wrote,

> The theory of evolution, which is now the foundation of almost all the Indian schools of thought, has now made its way into the physical sciences of Europe. It has been held by the religions of all other countries except India that the universe in its entirety is composed of parts distinctly separate from each other. God, nature, [humanity]—each stands by itself, isolated from one another. . . . [But] knowledge is to find unity in the midst of diversity—to establish unity amongst things, which appear to us to be different from one another.

We expected contemporary Indian scientists would view science and religion as compatible given the history of the relationship between science and religion in India, the Hindu belief in the unity of all existence, the country's acceptance of evolution and Darwinism, and the number of public intellectuals asserting and promoting an overlap perspective.

Science and Religion in the Public Sphere

India also lacks the recurring controversies between science and religion that are characteristic of other religious national contexts, such as the United States and Italy. India's brand of secularity may quell conflicts of this nature by creating a climate that embraces a diversity of religious views. India also lacks public figures who use the media to fan the flames of conflict between science and religion.

One science–faith controversy that did emerge in the country surrounded an attempt to introduce astrology in higher education. Indian astrology has been around since the early nineteenth century and remains extremely popular. One professor of physics[19] explained to us that in India "many people consult astrologists about the future." Astrology in India has roots in the Vedic period of Hinduism, when priests relied on observations of the sun, moon, and planets for timing religious performances, marriages, and festivals.[20] Today, it is still held in high religious esteem, and individuals in India rely on astrology to determine auspicious times for important life events. This type of astrology attempts to associate different heavenly characteristics with earthly affairs to make predictions and provide advice. In 2001, the Indian University Grants Commission decided to offer funding for university departments of Vedic astrology. Scientists, however, reacted strongly to this decision. "Leading researchers have condemned the move as an attempt to legitimize pseudo-science and superstition," reported the science journal *Nature*, "and some have said that it undermines India's scientific credibility."[21] Other critics argued that astrology would take India "backwards towards medieval times."[22] Twice, organizations have attempted to challenge the 2001 ruling; in 2004, a group of skeptics filed a petition in the Supreme Court to suspend funding for astrological studies, and skeptics made an appeal to the Mumbai High Court in 2011, attempting to code astrology as false advertising. Both efforts failed.[23] One professor of biology[24] we interviewed told us,

> I was one of the protestors, saying that, look, government resources cannot be spent on such pursuits. . . . What astrology tries to do is to say that [the sun, moon, and planets] influence your day-to-day life. That is irrational, and most of our objections are from that point.

"Astrology, I think, is a fun pastime," said another biologist.[25] "I don't think that one should invest research money in it."

Some Indian scientists acknowledge that they follow astrology in some traditional sense but do not see it as scientific. Most scientists in India reject astrology for the same reasons scientists in other countries reject creationism. Both have origins in religion and attempt to use scientific logic to make claims about possible realities outside the natural world. "My mom believes in it," said a graduate student in physics[26] who sees no scientific basis for astrology, adding, "I think the basis to astrology is kind of mathematical, [but] I don't know that that's there to make it look more believable or whether it's really out there."

Religion Among Indian Scientists

When we surveyed Indian biologists and physicists about their views on religion, we found that many Indian scientists see the cosmos and its laws as a religion. For some, religion is a private practice exercised primarily in their homes with their families. Others view religion merely as social participation in festivals, without embracing specific religious beliefs.[27]

In terms of religious affiliation, Indian scientists stand out in two key respects when compared with scientists in all the other nations and regions we examined: magnitude and match with the general public. In India, 94 percent of scientists identify with a religious tradition (Table 8.1), making India the region with the highest level of religious affiliation among scientists in our study. The share of religiously affiliated scientists, in fact, is 19 percent higher than in Turkey, the nation with the next highest share of religious affiliation among scientists. Moreover, scientists in India are particularly likely to identify as religious. More than half (53 percent) describe themselves either as "religious and spiritual" or "religious but not spiritual" (Table A.14), a share of scientists second only to that in Turkey (71 percent).

We also find that while levels of religious affiliation differ vastly between scientists and the public in most regions we studied, scientists in India

TABLE 8.1. Religious affiliation in India.

RELIGIOUS TRADITION	POPULATION (%)	SCIENTISTS (%)
Hinduism	72.3	79.0
Islam	14.0	6.3
Buddhism	1.5	0.8
Sikhism	–	1.79
Jainism	–	0.33
Roman Catholic	0.8	2.6
Protestant	2.4	1.6
Orthodox	1.7	0.3
Judaism	1.6	0.0
Other[a]	2.7	1.2
None	–	6.2
Total Respondents	1,581	1,606

NOTES: Based on weighted data. Values exclude an oversample of members from the Indian Academy of Sciences.
[a] "Other" responses from the World Values Survey include "Christian" and "Other; Not Specific."
SOURCE: World Values Survey India 2014; RASIC India Survey 2014.

largely mirror the country's general population in terms of their religious affiliations.[28] Like members of the Indian public, Indian scientists overwhelmingly identify as Hindu, and at similar margins. Specifically, nearly three-quarters (72 percent) of the Indian public affiliate with Hinduism, compared to 79 percent of Indian scientists. Islam represents the second largest religious tradition among groups, though the share of the public (14 percent) identifying as Muslim is nearly twice as large as the share of Muslim scientists (6 percent).

The overall proportion of scientists who express at least some belief in God (or a god) is also higher in India than in most of the other places we studied. Seventy-eight percent of Indian scientists say they have some form of belief in a higher power (Table 8.2).[29] Relative to other nations, India is characterized by some of the lowest shares of both atheist scientists (11 percent)—or those who do not believe in God—and agnostic scientists (11 percent)—or those who say they don't know whether there is a God and don't believe there is any way to find out. According to the 2005 World Values Survey, only 4 percent of the Indian general public does not believe in God or a god. This suggests that while Indian scientists are more religious than scientists in a number of other countries, they are a bit less religious than the general population in their country.

More sophisticated analyses we conducted reveal that scientists at elite universities and institutes in India are significantly less likely to believe in God than their counterparts at lower-ranked organizations.[30] It is possible that individuals who become elite scientists in India are more likely

TABLE 8.2. Belief in God in India.

BELIEF ABOUT GOD	%
I don't believe in God.	11.1
I don't know whether there is a God, and I don't believe there is any way to find out.	10.8
I don't believe in a personal God, but I do believe in a Higher Power of some kind.	38.4
I find myself believing in God some of the time, but not at others.	4.9
While I have doubts, I feel that I do believe in God.	8.5
I know God really exists and I have no doubts about it.	26.4
Total Respondents	1,606

NOTES: Based on weighted data. Values exclude an oversample of members from the Indian Academy of Sciences.
SOURCE: RASIC India Survey 2014.

than those who work in less prestigious institutions to travel for doctoral or postdoctoral training abroad, to less religious regions where they might be exposed to the ideas of antireligious science popularizers. Some of the elite scientists we interviewed did mention their fondness for British atheists such as Richard Dawkins and Christopher Hitchens, and admitted to becoming less religious after living abroad. Religious disbelief may also be part of how elite scientists in India construct their professional identity, distinct from a national context of powerful religious belief.[31]

What truly sets Indian scientists apart from scientists in the other nations we studied is the large number of them—close to 40 percent—who express belief in a higher power but not a personal God. Our interviews with these scientists suggest that one of the key religious doctrines underlying this belief is pantheism, derived from the Greek roots *pan* (all) and *theos* (God). Although it lacks a single codified position, pantheism at its most general may be understood as the view that God and the cosmos are identical. In other words, nothing exists that is outside of God.[32] India is "a country where . . . we see God in every living being, in every form," a research scientist in biology[33] told us.[34]

Many of the Indian scientists we spoke with referenced the idea that the cosmos is an impersonal and immanent divinity. They also expressed seeing God as abstract, embodied in all reality, including the self. Some scientists expressed this idea in general terms, using phrases like "God is just a state of being."[35] A graduate student in physics[36] explained that, "God means, to me, it is my good work." One biologist[37] captured the concept this way:

> For me God is nothing. God is just a spiritual understanding of yourself. So if you understand yourself, you'll find a god. . . . The message, which I got from the books which I have read, from the Upanishads and Vedas, is God is everywhere. . . . God lives within you. So . . . your inner self, your spirit, is actually a god.

Another Indian scientist[38] explained that he did not believe in "an anthropomorphic god," but saw God as

> an intelligence, which is operating in nature, which is not born of the human mind. Yes, I don't believe in it but I see it around me and it seems to me that that's a fact. That there is a tremendous intelligence operating in nature. It is operating in my body right now.

An associate professor of physics[39] told us: "God is everything. That includes science also. . . . God is not a human being. God is not a thing. God is a philosophy. God is a path of life. . . . You don't have to differentiate a god from anything."[40]

We also found that religious practices, independent of belief in God or a higher power, are central to religion for Indian scientists. Most of the religious scientists we spoke with in India emphasized that they tend to eschew religious rituals per se, but participate in religious festivals and household pujas. Participation in these activities is driven largely by Hindu tradition and Indian culture more broadly, rather than religious belief. For example, a graduate student in biology[41] said his "normal religious family" is:

> not obsessive about all the rituals . . . but we do observe fasts on days like Hanuman Jayanti, Rama Navami, or the Sravana month . . . the entire holy month we celebrate the Hindu festivals and all. During the Navratri, [we] do this aarti and the puja every night for goddess Durga and these things. But everything is normal. . . . That has helped me grow into a balanced Hindu when it comes to religion, not being too away from it and not being too much into it.

Over the course of our interviews, it was hard to determine how Indian scientists distinguished between religious practices and cultural norms or beliefs that are not specifically religious. Consider, for example, our conversation with a physics graduate student who says he is nonreligious[42] but still participates in pujas as "a social thing with his family":

> INTERVIEWER: *And while you're doing that . . . everyone is praying, so do you at that point try to sincerely pray?*
> GRADUATE STUDENT: Yeah, yeah. I'm not strictly, staunchly atheist.
> INTERVIEWER: *So you're not just pretending to pray.*
> GRADUATE STUDENT: No, no. I'm praying.

Family and gender play a major role in influencing religious practice among Indian scientists, especially those who are nonreligious. Our survey data show that a significant proportion of Indian scientists who say they are not religious (mainly men) have a religious spouse at home. Many male scientists we interviewed mentioned that their wives are "more religious" or that they lead household pujas to expose their children to the culture they grew up in. For example, an assistant professor of physics who says he is personally nonreligious[43] told us his wife leads pujas at home "out of a sense of continuity because she's been exposed to these things from when she was a child." A principal scientist in biology[44] described his practices as "prayer for sure, just to keep everybody happy in the family."

TABLE 8.3. Religious service attendance in India.

FREQUENCY	POPULATION (%)	SCIENTISTS (%)
More than once a week	12.5	16.7
Once a week	12.0	8.9
Once a month	23.9	5.4
Only on special holy days	26.5	27.1
Once a year	7.1	4.9
Less often	11.1	17.9
Never, practically never	5.2	19.2
Total Respondents	1,581	1,606

NOTES: Based on weighted data. Values exclude an oversample of members from the Indian Academy of Sciences.
SOURCE: World Values Survey India 2014; RASIC India Survey 2014.

Indian scientists participate in religious practices, including household pujas, more than scientists in most of the other regions we studied. While in most national contexts scientists exhibit lower levels of religious practice than the general public, Indian scientists report levels of religious practice that are similar to the general Indian population in many respects (Table 8.3). When we look at active participation, Indian scientists and the general Indian public are nearly indistinguishable: One in four attend religious services or rituals once a week or more. The proportion of those who practice only on special holy days or once a year is also similar among Indian scientists and the public. We find the biggest difference when we look at those who engage in religious practices the least: Nearly 40 percent of Indian scientists attend religious services or rituals "less often" than once a year or "practically never," while only 16 percent of the Indian public match those levels of religious participation.

Relationship Between Science and Religion Among Indian Scientists

While Indian scientists stand out from scientists in other countries with regard to their religious beliefs and practices, their views on the relationship between science and religion are not as different. Forty-four percent of Indian scientists see science and religion as independent, referring to different aspects of reality, making this the most frequent response (Table 8.4)—perhaps a reflection of the number of scientists we met who try to compartmentalize religion from their work by restricting it to their

TABLE 8.4. Perceived relationship of science and religion among scientists in India.

RELATIONSHIP	%
Conflict; I consider myself to be on the side of religion	0.7
Conflict; I consider myself to be on the side of science	18.1
Conflict; I am unsure which side I am on	1.3
Independence; they refer to different aspects of reality	44.1
Collaboration; each can be used to help support the other	28.7
Don't know	7.0
Total Respondents	1,606

NOTES: Based on weighted data. Values exclude an oversample of members from the Indian Academy of Sciences.
SOURCE: RASIC India Survey 2014.

private life at home. Nearly 20 percent of Indian scientists embrace a conflict view of science and religion; among the nations we studied, the proportion of scientists who hold this view is lower only in Hong Kong and Taiwan. An even smaller share—12 percent—of female scientists hold the conflict view, a share that is significantly smaller than that of male scientists (21 percent; see Appendix A, Table A.15, on India).[45] Twenty-nine percent of Indian scientists believe science and religion can be used to support one another. Only in Turkey did we find a greater proportion of scientists holding this collaboration perspective. Of course, how scientists view the relationship between science and religion depends greatly on how they conceptualize religion. In particular, the ideas an individual holds about the nature and role of God in the world greatly impact whether that person adopts a conflict perspective. As we've seen, many Indian scientists have a view of God as a "state of being" or "path in life," and this helps them see religion as compatible with science. As a Hindu professor of physics[46] explained,

[The conflict view] is itself born out of this wrong definition of religion. You have called religion as belief and belief is anathema to science. Therefore, there is this contradiction between the two. But when you look upon it as a quest for truth, then they become two complementary quests for truth.

When we asked a professor of physics who identifies as both Hindu and nonreligious[47] about those who see a conflict between being religious and being a scientist, he responded, "[This view] comes because people confuse rituals with believing in God. OK? The conflict is between science and the ritual. OK? So, if you don't follow any rituals, there is no conflict." In his view, God is not irrational in the same way some religious rituals are, and thus not incompatible with science in the same way. Ethnographic research by the sociologist Renny Thomas similarly shows that many Indian scientists tend to eschew narratives of conflict as well as complementarity.[48]

Another interesting finding emerged through more complex statistical analyses of the survey data: Hindu, Sikh, and Muslim scientists in India are significantly more likely than religiously unaffiliated scientists to see the science and religion relationship as one of collaboration rather than independence or conflict.[49] Our interviews help us understand the role these faith traditions play in framing the relationship between religion and science. Among Hindus, pantheism encourages a collaboration perspective, and Sikh and Muslim scientists believe that religious texts can motivate or even foreshadow scientific discovery. A Sikh professor of biology[50] told us,

> We should take science and religion together rather than going our different paths. . . . For example, 500 years back, it was written in the religious scripture that there are a large number of universes in this world and it was followed only later. So, I see it that religion is not inseparable from science. [Religion] should be connected with science, in order that both can flourish in their own way.

Citing an example we heard numerous times from Muslim scientists, an associate professor of biology[51] explained, "When Europe was in the Dark Age, it was the Muslim who carried out research in the field of science. . . . There's no controversy. Rather, [the Qur'an] encourages that Muslims should go to learn." Another scientist[52] said, "It is also true that if we study science . . . then we can understand more about the Qur'an."

And our statistical analysis also revealed that female scientists have significantly lower odds than male scientists of seeing science and religion as in conflict rather than independent (see Appendix A, Table A.16, on India). We speculate that, given that married women in India play a pivotal role in their family's household religious practices, female Indian scientists may see a strong association between home and religion and, in turn, separate science and religion as part of a broader distinction between work life and family life.

Religion in the Indian Scientific Workplace

When we compare Indian scientists with scientists in the other countries we studied, we find that they rank high in religious affiliation, religious practice, and belief in God. We also found that many Indian scientists try to separate religion from their work, often by restricting religious practice to the home. So how and when, if at all, does religion overlap with the scientific work of Indian scientists?

Institutional Sanctioning

In India, some overlap between science and religion is sanctioned by official actions of the state or public religious expressions by representatives who wield high levels of formal authority in the scientific community. In this respect, India is very different from France, for example, where state policy prohibits religious expression in government and other state organizations. When the chairman of ISRO blesses the Mars orbiter or the Indian government funds astrology departments at universities around the country, they are sanctioning the overlap of science and religion. Institutional sanctioning is much more common in highly religious contexts, such as India, than in more secular contexts like the United Kingdom, where it is largely absent. As one Indian scientist[53] shared,

> Certainly when I was in the US, I can't think of a single conference that I attended where anything religious came up. But in the last five years that I've been in India, there was one conference that I went to where the first thing that happened in the conference was an invocation of a particular god. . . . So the goddess Saraswati is supposed to be the Goddess of Learning, and this particular conference, which was actually one of the meetings of the Indian Academy of Sciences, which is the largest scientific academy in the country . . . I remember that the first thing that happened was an invocation of this goddess and then there was this song and hymn that was sung in praise of this goddess, Goddess Saraswati. And then the rest of the scientific program commenced. So once the science started, there wasn't any other mention of religion. And this was not really a very uncommon thing in a sense that if you go to many schools in India, for instance, you will see that the morning assembly often starts with such a prayer. But I did find it a little odd that a scientific conference—especially one that was being conducted by the largest scientific academy in the country—would start in a similar manner.

Our interviews with Indian scientists revealed a number of examples of institutional sanctioning. Most nonreligious scientists in India have no issue with religious events on campus they perceive as primarily social, but they do have a problem when scientists appear to make an official acknowledgment or endorsement of religion. An associate professor of physics,[54] for example, noted that to commemorate the newest campus of the prestigious

Tata Institute of Fundamental Research, the institute's director arranged for then Prime Minister Manmohan Singh to deliver a bhumi puja—a Hindu prayer ceremony—to inaugurate a new site for the construction of a building. The ceremony provoked protests by many Indian scientists. When we asked about his own level of comfort with the ceremony, the physicist responded,

> Symbolism has a very strong role. When you are doing a bhumi puja, how are you going to teach rational thinking to your students? What is the role of bhumi puja in science? . . . One has to draw the line between one's professional duties, where one has to maintain a nonreligious stand, even if your belief, personal belief, is religious. If this same person had done it when making his own house somewhere, that would have been fine with me.

Not all examples of institutional sanctioning are as highly visible. Institutional sanctioning can also take the form of a statement bearing organizational authority in a less public setting. A nonreligious graduate student in biology at an elite research institute[55] told us of one experience he had when a new director joined the institute, who had

> published in very good journals, *Nature, Nature Chemical* . . . all of those. . . . The first week of his joining . . . his first meeting as a director and a scientist, and he did not invite any scientists . . . just students . . . and the first slide he showed was of modern intelligent design. He said, "I don't believe evolution works," and for the next 30 minutes, he kept on talking about why evolution does not work.

When we asked this graduate student how other scientists reacted when they learned about the meeting, given that nearly all scientists in India think evolution is the best way to explain the development of life on earth, the student responded, "if you're publishing good papers and . . . you are positioned, nobody can [talk] about any of [these] things." In other words, certain ideas, including those bearing on the relationship between science and religion, can be sanctioned by the status of the scientist delivering them.

Personal Practices in the Workplace

As we traveled around the world interviewing scientists, we seldom encountered referents to religion in their offices. Here are a few rare exceptions: One US scientist had a newspaper article on her door with the headline, "Why God Did Not Create the World." A British scientist had a picture of a Buddha that read, "Relax: Nothing is in Control." An Italian scientist had put up a picture of Samuel L. Jackson's character in the movie *Pulp Fiction* pointing a gun toward the camera, with the words: "Say God Particle One More Goddamned Time!"

In India, however, we more frequently observed religious symbols in the offices of scientists, particularly images and statues of Hindu deities. These artifacts came up in our interviews, too. "One of my earlier bosses [had] Ganesh's idol in front of him and whenever he enters his lab he used to touch [the idol's] feet and then start working," a Hindu research scientist in biology[56] told us. A Sikh assistant professor of biology[57] explained that a Hindu student in her lab "put up a photo of his Guru and . . . another Hindu in the group, he also put a small photo up. We don't comment. It's OK with us."

Most Indian scientists we interviewed had never seen their colleagues pray in the workplace, but we did meet some who admitted to praying. "Before starting my work, I make a small prayer. So I have a picture of an Indian god sitting right in my office," a research scientist in biology[58] shared. "I do pray for work going well," a graduate student in biology[59] acknowledged, "but I don't depend on that."

Festivals

Major religious festivals occur throughout the year in India with a frequency unparalleled among the other national contexts we studied. When discussing religion in India, scientists referred to a number of Hindu festivals, such as Pongal, Saraswati Puja, Holi, Ganapati Puja, Vishwakarma Puja, Durga Puja, and Diwali, as well as Ramadan and Christmas. As we've seen, for many Indian scientists, these public festivals are their main form of religious participation—though, as they see it, participation in these festivals does not necessarily entail or require religious belief or identification. In their view, they are engaging in a social event in a social way. Consequently, many Indian scientists take for granted that they will participate in religious festivals, without any discussion of religion. A graduate student in physics who identifies as both Hindu and nonreligious[60] explained it this way:

> A lot of religious festivals are not just because of the religion . . . they are essentially social festivals. Things like Diwali, for example, you'll find if you walk into [my institute] the canteen is probably decked up. . . . But it's got no sense of the religion. It's more of a social thing and a celebration.

A graduate student in biology[61] shared a similar view, explaining, "Though there are instances where students celebrate certain festivals on campus and most of them are Hindu festivals because Hindus are the majority . . . it's more of a celebration than anything."

The social component of religious participation was especially salient when Indian scientists talked about the festival of Vishwakarma Puja, a day of celebration for a Hindu god varyingly revered as a divine engineer, architect, or carpenter. The festival is primarily celebrated in working-class communities, where people have jobs in factories and industrial areas, but it is also commonly observed in the scientific community by technicians and engineers in labs. It entails, among other ceremonies, the cleaning and worship of tools and prayers for the smooth functioning of machines. Many Indian scientists mentioned this festival, including a prominent female scientist[62] who said she donates funds for the Vishwakarma Puja because she wants her lab staff to look on her favorably and get things done. At one of the premier universities in India, an associate professor of physics who said he is not at all religious[63] explained:

> Vishwakarma is the mechanic god. So [the technicians and engineers] celebrate Vishwakarma in a reasonably big way. . . . Once in a while, they invite me to come there to take . . . what is called prasad. Prasad is the offering after you perform the puja. . . . And so, I once in a while attend that. Because there are many of the machinists whose services I use, and I'm very fond of them, because they are very good machinists.

"Vishwakarma day, of course I worship," said another professor of physics[64] who noted he never goes to temple. "But not otherwise." A similar festival called Ayudha Puja is conducted in South India, even in campuses of elite scientific institutes, as documented by ethnographers Renny Thomas and Robert Geraci.[65]

Among the Indian scientists we interviewed, only a minority said they do not support religious festivals at scientific institutes. Opposition can emerge if it is believed the traditions of certain religions are favored over others. Opposition also emerges among those who feel that religious festivals, even if they are cultural traditions, are still very much religious in nature and practice. For example, a graduate student in biology[66] said that religious celebrations "should be allowed for all religions or it should not be allowed for any." To explain his objection to religious festivals at his institution, he referenced the annual Hindu festival Durga Puja, which celebrates the goddess Durga:

> They bring this idol of goddess Durga and then they pray . . . exactly the way it is done in a temple. . . . I don't mind if you just say yes, I have to go do Durga

Puja . . . but they do it with that detail the way people who are religious [would] do it in the temples.

Accommodation

In our interviews with Indian scientists, we heard fewer stories about accommodating religious beliefs in the workplace than we heard in countries where scientists are far less religious. One possible explanation is the country's distinctive brand of secularism based on equal treatment of all religions. This kind of secularism motivates religious diversity and prescribes religious accommodation, so allowing for the religious beliefs and practices of students and colleagues in the workplace is assumed and expected, and thus not noteworthy. When we asked Indian scientists whether they were aware of any discrimination toward religious individuals in science, not one concrete account emerged.

As a Hindu research scientist in biology[67] described,

> We have students who will wear headscarves, students who wear caps and want to keep a long beard and do not want to wear shoes or want to pray five times a day. And that is perfectly fine, we have no qualms about it, and we don't question it. And all that we expect from students is that they do not impinge upon their own research productivity because of these—this is a very personal affair, and it's a very personal choice that they make.

A nonreligious professor of biology[68] said that, in her lab,

> If an experiment is planned and it happens to be a big religious festival for any religion . . . on that day we don't do that experiment, depending on the student who's doing it. . . . I have people of all faiths in my lab, so I have Muslims, I have Christians, Hindus of course. . . . So some of them come and tell me, "Today is Eid. I won't be coming." And I say, "Yeah, OK, don't come."

Another factor normalizing religious accommodation in the scientific workplace is the regularity of Hindu festivals throughout the year and Muslim practices throughout the day. In Western contexts, formal religious practices tend to be isolated to the weekends and weeknights, but Indian scientists are constantly running up against the religious practices of campus staff, colleagues, and students during the workday.

Religious accommodation in the scientific workplace is also driven, in some small part, by Indian scientists with a profound and personal commitment to the socialization and success of their students. In particular, a number of male scientists we interviewed described a special relationship between teacher and student—the established scientist as a mentor and kind of spiritual guide to the younger scientist. This kind of relationship was not found in any other nation we studied.

A reader in physics[69] explained it this way:

> You have this guru shishya—that is, a "guru and a disciple," a teacher and a disciple. . . . Because that kind of responsibility from religion is there . . . you will find there are some sets of people who will view that very strongly, so they will work like a very dedicated person.

"There is a guru and student relation," said an associate professor of physics[70] speaking about his graduate students. "It's more like a family. More than a son and father." He told us the following story about working with one of his Muslim graduate students:

> It is very difficult to understand their emotions and their [prayer] times. . . . I am familiar with Christians and I am very much familiar with Hinduism. . . . But I don't have too many Muslims with me. But I don't want to do any mistake . . . because he is adopted as my son. . . . I had the books [the Qur'an and other books about Islamic teaching] and whenever I got time, I am reading those things. . . . I had to respect his thing. . . . I think I know Islam more or less now.

Separation

Even though religion is everywhere, Indian scientists do not see it as a problem for the scientific enterprise. Although they often find themselves surrounded by religious colleagues, festivals, and symbols, scientists in India do not tend to view religion as permeating the practice of science. This is different from how scientists view the relationship between religion and science in the United States and United Kingdom, where they believe the two realms often clash. A nonreligious assistant professor of biology who trained in the United States[71] explained that in India

> Religion is a separate thing. I think almost every student on the campus or wherever I've seen in India understands that. Now, I understand because I've been in the US for about 11 years, I understand that creationism, evolution, these are things that people bring into classrooms.

Many of the scientists we interviewed in India talked about how they draw boundaries between their scientific work and their religious beliefs and practices. "Now it depends on how you practice, how you define that religion and define your science," said a principal scientist in biology,[72] adding that "most of the people, they manage a kind of coexistence with that and, as I told you, they have a kind of a separation between [religion and science]." A professor of biology[73] told us that, in his view, science and religion (or spirituality)

are separate issues. Science is professional and religion and spirituality, they are personal attitudes. A person can justify being a good scientist, he can also be spiritual, he can also believe in religion or in God. For me, they don't interfere, these two fields.

It is interesting to note that Indian scientists used language and narratives similar to those we heard from scientists in other countries when discussing the separation of science and religion. This similarity suggests that the separation approach to science and religion may largely be transnational. In contrast, collaboration, inseparability, and overlap between science and religion often take national, cultural, and locally specific forms.

That said, one topic showed up in the data on the separation of science and religion that is unique to India: astrology. A few Indian scientists we met, such as Sanjay, wear rings with astrological gemstones. Some of them do so even though they do not believe in the practice. "I wear astrological rings for my parents' happiness but not because I believe in it," asserted one graduate student in biology.[74] While many nonreligious scientists participate in religious practices, such as pujas to appease their families, or religious festivals organized on campus, they draw a line when it comes to astrology. As a doctoral student in biology[75] relayed,

My boss is an atheist. He doesn't like all these things. He doesn't even like [that] some people wear stone rings. . . . He will be saying: "Why are you wearing this and that, this doesn't mean something, this doesn't do something."

We believe this reaction to astrology among scientists is due to its history in India—specifically, the government's 2001 decision to fund university astrology departments: The scientific community unsuccessfully fought against the decision, and thus many scientists are now especially motivated to demarcate science from what they see as pseudoscience. The subject has become a lightning rod.

Conclusions

Indian secularism reflects a unique model of openness to religion. As we have discussed, India's brand of secularism stresses religious accommodation, without stirring the kind of complaints we hear among scientists in places like the United Kingdom. Even religiously affiliated universities in India strive to be welcoming to people of all religions in the name of such secularism. We also found examples of professors at all types of universities who make the time and effort to familiarize themselves with the religious traditions of their students in order to better support them. Even in the scientific environment, Indian secularism affirms diversity of religious expression.

India is a growing science superpower. At the time we were writing this book, the Indian Institute of Science became the first Indian university to be ranked among the top ten globally.[76] If the historical development of universities in OECD countries is a measure, Indian universities will continue to increase in number, become home to more and more international scholars, and send greater numbers of their own scholars to international conferences and positions at universities around the world. As Indian scientists increasingly study and work in other national contexts—where the conflict between scientific and religious communities is generally greater—we have to wonder if they will begin to call for more separation between science and religion, or whether they might lead scientists in other parts of the world to see more overlap between the two realms.

At the same time, however, funding for research and development in India is still low. India spends only about 0.6 percent of its GDP on R&D, a number that has remained fairly static over recent years, making the nation's investment in scientific research significantly lower than many developed countries. In August 2017, scientists in cities across India participated in their own March for Science, concerned that "science in India is facing the danger of being eclipsed by a rising wave of unscientific beliefs and religious bigotry, and scientific research is suffering serious setback due to dwindling governmental support," according to a statement by organizers.[77] The demonstration called for at least 3 percent of the country's GDP to go to scientific research and 10 percent to education. The demands also included a call for evidence-based science policies and to "stop propagation of unscientific, obscurantist ideas and religious intolerance, and develop scientific temper, human values and spirit of inquiry in conformance with . . . the Constitution."[78]

Indian scientists connect religion to morality in science. The anticipation of India as a software and science superpower clashes with the country's immense poverty and sometimes shoddy infrastructure. Outside the pristine campuses of elite universities, we saw trash piled on the side of streets, and in many areas, burning is a common method of disposal. The country still faces challenges when it comes to basics like energy, food, and health care. "If you walk out of campus . . . you will see a bunch of kids with no clothes on their backs," said a biologist[79] we interviewed. "So you think immediately, I just spent a million dollars . . . I better get something out of it which hopefully is useful for somebody in the future." Indian scientists at times draw on religious frameworks to understand the moral importance of their work. Among the physicists and biologists we interviewed in India, being a "good scientist" often means doing work that alleviates poverty and human suffering. "Spirituality makes a man soft and kind toward humanity," said one biologist[80] we talked with, adding, "Spirituality helps me to understand the problem of the poor people." Of his research group, a professor of physics[81] said,

> Our institute is the temple. So all the time we pray here in our own lab so that God can bless us. Physically, we do not pray, but working here is like praying to God. So we are always trying to find something new . . . that will be useful for our society.

Religion plays a significant role in family life for Indian scientists, even those who consider themselves nonreligious. In many cases, female scientists who identified as nonreligious felt obliged to practice traditional religious ceremonies at home as part of their duties as a Hindu wife and mother. Male scientists often admitted their spouses were quite religious and that they participated in religious ceremonies in order to maintain traditions and appease their families.

Religion and science inevitably overlap in India. The majority of Indian scientists see science and religion as separate realms. Yet given the importance and presence of religion in India, separation is hard to implement. Because India is such a religious nation—77 percent of individuals consider themselves "a religious person" and 76 percent believe in a god—we expected commentary on religion to occur more naturally than in contexts where people are less religious.[82] Instead, scientists we interviewed in India were hesitant to make claims about religion or even to define religion. It reminded us of David Foster Wallace's essay "This Is Water," in which two fish on a swim are asked how the water is and one later turns to the other and says, "What the hell is water?"[83] In a sense, this is what it is like to ask about religion in India. Religion is all around, so abundant that it almost goes unnoticed. In India, we found nonreligious scientists organizing religious festivals on campus (as ethnic celebrations) and sponsoring pujas (to remain in the good graces of their more religious staff). We found examples of public religion in the inaugurations of university buildings and scientific events. And at one school, we found the same area being used for both an ecological study and a prayer site. To us, it appears that science and religion in India are much more intimately intertwined than many Indian scientists realize.

| # Hong Kong and Taiwan
A Science-Friendly Christianity and Folk Religion

HONG KONG AND TAIWAN are both broadly defined as "Chinese societies" and share an underlying Confucian cultural and philosophical ethos, and because of this and other similarities, we explore the views of scientists in these regions together. The island of Taiwan, with a population of 23 million people, has been governed as a region independent from mainland China since the 1940s, and democratized as well since the 1980s.[1] Hong Kong, on the other hand, has a population of just 7 million people. It became free from British colonial rule in 1997, but is a special autonomous region within mainland China, with only a partially representative electorate.[2]

Thus both regions share a complex interplay of Western and Japanese colonial history, and both have a cultural and linguistic identity distinct from that of the Chinese mainland. Both Hong Kong and Taiwan also have plans to become global leaders in science and technology. Taiwan spent $33.5 billion on research and development (R&D) in 2015.[3] This accounts for 3.05 percent of its gross domestic product, which is higher than the other countries and regions in the study, including the United States. In addition, Hong Kong spent approximately $2 billion in 2015, or 0.76 percent of its gross domestic product.[4] Both societies are establishing modern scientific communities through governmental investment in research and development and communication between their scientists and scientists in the West.

For Taiwanese and Hong Kong scientists, mainland China's scientific establishment is omnipresent. Many laboratories in Hong Kong house graduate students from the mainland, and many graduate students in Taiwan spoke openly about seeking job opportunities in the mainland after graduation. Taiwan and Hong Kong are both so small that young scientists face constant pressure to leave their homelands for advanced training, postdocs, and other early career research positions in the West. They are thus required to be transnational in their communication style, work ethic, and worldview in ways that may not be necessary for mainland Chinese scientists.

Moving to other countries can also have an impact on the religious beliefs of these scientists, their views on secularism, and their personal lives. Many scientists in Hong Kong and Taiwan spoke about the challenges of being separated from their families to advance their careers, sometimes compounded by the emphasis their religious traditions put on having a strong family life.

Both regions have at least a residual history of Christianity in the best primary and secondary schools (in Hong Kong it is more mainstream), where budding scientists first receive their training. And in their large public research universities both Christian and Buddhist groups proselytize among students and faculty. In Hong Kong, many scientists mentioned attending educational institutions founded by Christians, where they had to read the Bible and sing hymns in the morning. Although these institutions have become more secular, several scientists said Christians still control the school boards. We also found the perception exists among scientists that a Christian elite controls science education and research funding. One scientist, for example, told us she believes there was a Christian conspiracy to deny research funding and advancement to atheists as well as Chinese from the mainland.[5] A significant minority of Hong Kong scientists also mentioned they were likely to meet science faculty and administrators at their Christian churches, and that churches are good places for networking that helps their scientific careers.[6]

In Taiwan, the three most prevalent faith traditions are Buddhism, Daoism, and folk religion (which often overlaps with the others), all linked to Chinese culture.[7] Buddhism has become increasingly institutionalized in Taiwan thanks to the Orthodox Buddhist Movement and the emergence of humanistic Buddhism. Daoism and folk religion are still diffuse religions in Taiwan.[8] While nearly everyone in Taiwan integrates Daoism and folk religion into their daily lives to some extent, they do so without affiliating with a specific religious community centered on these traditions.

Cultural Context of Science and Religion in Hong Kong and Taiwan

As societies with religious freedom, Hong Kong and Taiwan are usually perceived as "important manifestations of contemporary Chinese faith and practice."[9] Yet defining religion is not always easy in Hong Kong and Taiwan. Western ideas of religion have shaped how previous scholars have measured religion in the East, but perhaps the greatest issue is that religiosity in Chinese societies is sometimes manifested more through lived experience than through religious participation. Ethnic Chinese people usually practice "non-theistic religions," which are based on "inactive supernatural essences or forces that govern human life but are not regarded as accessible or engaged in partnership with humankind and therefore can inspire only meditation, ritual, and magic."[10] Hence, religious individuals in Chinese cultures, such as Buddhists or believers in folk religion, may not participate in collective rituals, but burn incense or pray to a shrine at home.[11] Furthermore, in Chinese societies, religiosity is nonexclusive; Eastern and Western religions sometimes intermingle.[12] Folk religion, for example, can be practiced with other religions, such as Buddhism or Christianity.[13] (One example is *feng shui*, a type of Chinese geomancy that regards people's luck as dependent on the arrangement of a physical space.[14]) It is possible that the mixing of Christianity with Eastern faiths creates a context that makes it easier for science, also a Western invention, to mingle with Eastern religions in these regions.

There are, however, some important differences between the religious contexts in Hong Kong and Taiwan. Although both regions are religiously diverse, Protestant, Catholic, and atheist communities are growing in Hong Kong.[15] The increasing number of Protestants and Catholics could be partially attributed to the influx of immigrants from predominantly Christian countries, as well as Protestant and Catholic evangelization efforts. Many Christian schools and philanthropic organizations were established and sponsored by Protestant and Catholic congregations.[16] The increase in atheists can be partly attributed to an influx of immigrants from mainland China, a country with state-sponsored atheism. It is also the case that many mainland Chinese who either immigrated and settled in Hong Kong or are studying at universities have converted to Christianity. And Hong Kong is very much an immigrant society, with the majority of the population living in Hong Kong only since the 1950s.

Largely because of restrictive immigration policies, Western religions are considerably less present in Taiwan relative to Hong Kong.[17] Therefore, immigration has less of an impact on the religious landscape in this region. A large share of Taiwanese practice folk religion[18] with practices such as ancestral worship exhibiting aspects of Chinese culture, including the concept of five elements (*wu xing*) and the theories of *yin/yang*.[19] Formal Buddhism in Taiwan dates back to a movement in the 1960s and 1970s.[20] Unlike those who practice popular Buddhism, which integrates folk religion and Daoist practices, the leaders of formal or Orthodox Buddhists want their lay believers to differentiate themselves from practitioners of folk religions, Daoists, and other Buddhists, who they see as practicing less serious forms of the tradition.[21]

Religion and Science in the Public Sphere

Public debates about science and religion only occasionally arise in Taiwan and Hong Kong.[22] In 2009, there was a debate in Hong Kong over science education and the teaching of evolution[23] when the Education Bureau enacted a new curriculum guideline for senior biology students that stated, "in addition to Darwin's theory, students are encouraged to explore other explanations for evolution and the origins of life." Scientists criticized this guideline, accusing the bureau—which had Christian members—of encouraging schools to teach creationism. In response, the Education Bureau backpedaled and "clarified" that the instructional emphasis was intended to be on Darwin's theory and other explanations of evolution that do not include creationism and intelligent design. In one newspaper report, this resolution was portrayed as a "Victory of Darwin."[24] Interestingly, while English-language newspapers reported on this public debate, it received less press in the area's influential Chinese-language newspapers, perhaps because evolution has been much less publicly controversial and heated in Chinese-speaking contexts than in some English-speaking nations like the United States and the United Kingdom. Public debate about evolution emerged again in the region in 2014, when the Sheng Kung Hui Welfare Council—one of the largest social service organizations of the Anglican Communion in Hong Kong—facilitated the organization of the Hong Kong science festival[25] at the Solar Tower at Mawan Park, which advocates creationism. Scientists and science enthusiasts interpreted this decision as an affront to science and the goals of the festival.

In Taiwan, Buddhism figures more prominently in public debates between science and religion, which largely center on concerns about using animals and cadavers in scientific experiments and research. Buddhists feel these practices do not uphold respect for all living things.[26] According to Buddhist teaching, all lives are equal and killing any living thing is forbidden.[27] The Life Conservation Association recently promoted the passage of a draft amendment of the Animal Protection Law to prevent using animals in biological experiments. Tzu Chi University, a Buddhist University in Taiwan, created a special program for cadaver experiments, in which the bodies are called "silent teachers" and students meet and pray with members of the donor's family before dissection and perform religious ceremonies afterward. Tzu Chi University established this program as part of an intentional effort to show that religion does not have to be a barrier to conducting biological experiments but rather can be used to infuse experiments with compassion and benevolence, the essence of Buddhism.

Religion Among Scientists in Hong Kong and Taiwan

In most regions of the study, scientists are less religious than the public. Yet, in both Hong Kong and Taiwan, measures of religiosity mirror or *exceed* those of the general public. Looking at religious affiliation (Table 9.1), we see that 69 percent of both scientists and the general public in Hong Kong are religiously unaffiliated. In no other region does the proportion of scientists and members of the public who are unaffiliated match up like this.

Because 58 percent of the scientists we surveyed in Hong Kong are from other regions, immigration is important to understanding religious affiliation there. In particular, the proportion of religiously unaffiliated individuals in Hong Kong may be driven to some degree by immigration from mainland China. As one biologist from mainland China currently working in Hong Kong[28] explained,

> I credit [my nonreligion] to my upbringing in communist China and because they at least told us the truth: that there was no God, depend on yourself to achieve whatever you wish to achieve, don't depend on God who plans everything for you. And that definitely is the truth. The Chinese communist government told us [to believe that] rather than being deceived by the Western religions.

TABLE 9.1. Religious affiliation in Taiwan and Hong Kong.

RELIGIOUS TRADITION	TAIWAN		HONG KONG	
	POPULATION (%)	SCIENTISTS (%)	POPULATION (%)	SCIENTISTS (%)
Roman Catholic	1.2	0.7	3.1	5.8
Protestant/ Christian (non-Catholic)	5.3	10.7	15.7	12.7
Orthodox	–	–	–	0.5
Judaism	–	–	–	0.3
Islam	–	–	0.1	0.7
Hinduism	–	–	0.1	1.9
Buddhism	26.5	18.0	11.3	5.7
Folk beliefs / folk religion	17.9	18.1	–	–
Taoism/Daoism	21.8	5.8	–	–
Yiguan Dao	3.6	1.3	–	–
Other	1.3	2.9	1.1	2.8
None	22.0	42.7	68.6	69.5
Total Respondents	1,237	830	999	299

NOTES: Based on weighted data. Values exclude nonresponse.
SOURCE: World Values Survey Taiwan 2012; RASIC Taiwan Survey 2015; World Values Survey Hong Kong 2013; RASIC Hong Kong Survey 2014.

While our statistical data preclude our ability to identify with confidence what share of nonnative scientists immigrated from China, we can state that nonnative scientists in Hong Kong—generally—are significantly less likely to be religiously affiliated relative to scientists from Hong Kong.[29] Immigration is less important to understanding religion in Taiwan, however, because only 5 percent of our survey sample is nonnative.

In Hong Kong, we also see a similarity in religious affiliation when we look at the proportion of scientists and the general population who identify as Protestant, in both cases roughly 15 percent. In Taiwan, we note that a substantially *higher proportion* of scientists identify as Protestant (11 percent) than do members of the general public (5 percent). We also find a sizable minority of scientists in Taiwan identify with Eastern religious traditions, such as Daoism and Yiguan Dao. Furthermore, in most regions of our study, Buddhists rarely exceed 2 percent of the scientific community. In Taiwan, 18 percent of scientists identify as Buddhist. We also find that 18 percent of Taiwanese scientists are affiliated with folk religion, matching the proportion of folk religion followers in the general population. These folk beliefs seem localized to Chinese societies, particularly Taiwan.[30] Scientists who identify with a folk religion are seldom found elsewhere in our sample.

Among Taiwanese scientists, folk religion is so integrated into their everyday lives and backgrounds that they can hardly point to specific practices, affiliations, or beliefs that are distinctively "religious." Thus, it can be hard to identify who exactly is affiliated with a folk religion. One Taiwanese professor of biology,[31] for example, identified himself as being affiliated with folk religion and said that for him "basically religious belief is merely taking a piece of incense and *bai bai* [worship] to the shrine" and that he will "go in to [temples] and pray for good luck" when he experiences "some stress and throwback" at work. He also prays "to the god of wealth" to "win a lottery." Another biologist[32] talked about participating in similar practices in her daily life, such as what she thought of as "ancestor worship" but unlike her colleague, she identified as nonreligious, and sees the practices as not necessarily being "related to religion." Her family is "more like the so-called typical folk religious family," she said, explaining, "we do pay respect to our ancestors, but then actually my parents aren't devout believers of any religion." She told us that for the anniversary of her father's death:

> we'd buy food that he liked and pay respects to him. Would you think that he would really come and eat? We don't know. But psychologically, we think that as we do this we are establishing a connection with him anew. It's a warm feeling.

The way scientists in Hong Kong and Taiwan define and understand religion is influenced by the different religions in their region. When Hong Kong scientists describe religion, it tends to have a more Christian-centric flavor than when Taiwanese scientists discuss religion. For example, an associate professor of biology in Hong Kong[33] told us he conceptualizes religion as "the idea of having a God" and the belief that "there's a Creator; we are created" and "we have limitations." Similarly, his colleague in physics[34] thinks that religion provides answers to the following questions: "Why are we here? Where are we going to? How are we created?" Such definitions are very much informed by Christianity.

In Taiwan, the percentage of scientists who believe in folk religion is much higher than of those who are affiliated with Christianity, and thus the ways Taiwanese scientists define religion tend to be less Christian-centered. Taiwanese scientists usually regard religion as related to worshipping at temples and belief in some type of god form, and claim that this belief has an impact on people's everyday practices. "When I was a kid, before I had mystical experiences, I have always thought that religion is going to *bai bai* [worshipping gods in temples], to plead gods and ask for oracles," a physicist in Taiwan[35] said, explaining that it was her "identity as a Taiwanese" that gave her such a definition of religion. One of her colleagues[36] struggled when trying to define religion. He paused and said, "I have tried Buddhism and Daoism. How do I define religion? I just cannot define it. I think it just gives me anything which can make me compromise my ego and then maybe support me to carry on." He then emphasized, "I think it cannot be defined." In Taiwan, religion among scientists is sometimes more integrated, lived, and hard to isolate than the religion scientists in Hong Kong describe. That said, scientists in both regions commonly describe religion as something that guides people's behaviors and teaches them "the importance of being kind, and not being evil," as one scientist[37] put it, while also motivating them to participate in charitable activities.[38] In this way, scientists interpret religion as having secular, ethical, and moral standards that leave an impact on people's everyday lives.

We found that most scientists in Hong Kong and Taiwan did not find the word "spirituality" intuitive. The particular way that "spirituality" manifests itself in the West is not really found in the vernacular of scientists in these regions. Most scientists in Hong Kong and Taiwan, especially those who have not been exposed to Christianity, found the term confusing. For example, an associate professor of physics in Hong Kong[39] said that he is not sure what "spirituality" means, but—like some other scientists in the region— later offered that it might be associated with ethics and morality. Similarly, an associate professor of biology in Hong Kong[40] said she sees spirituality as "morality and a sense of consciousness toward others." We did speak with several scientists in Hong Kong and Taiwan who have a more concrete understanding of spirituality, framing the concept as connected with the individual and the inner self. A biology professor in Hong Kong,[41] for example, said she understands spirituality as "a personal definition" and "some essence of being that is a part of me." An associate professor of physics in Hong Kong[42] said, "Religion is the institution and spirituality is the heart and mind." We also encountered some scientists who self-identify as Christian and offer distinctively Christian conceptions of spirituality. One Taiwanese scientist who was a Buddhist but later became a Christian[43] said, "[Spirituality] is about that person's relationship with God. It is good or bad. It is about the relationship that person has with God and that he has with other people." Likewise, an associate professor of biology in Hong Kong[44] said spirituality means wanting "to do what you consider to be good [in] the eyes of God."

TABLE 9.2. Belief in God or gods in Taiwan and Hong Kong.

BELIEF ABOUT GOD OR GODS	TAIWAN (%)	HONG KONG (%)
I don't believe in any God or gods.	10.6	26.1
I don't know whether there is a God or gods, and I don't believe there is any way to find out.	15.3	20.3
I don't believe in a personal God, but I do believe in a Higher Power of some kind.	31.7	26.2
I believe there is only one God.	11.7	19.5
I believe there may be many gods.	30.7	8.0
Total Respondents	820	294

NOTES: Based on weighted data. Values exclude nonresponse.
SOURCE: RASIC Taiwan Survey 2015; RASIC Hong Kong Survey 2014.

We also examined how scientists in Hong Kong and Taiwan describe their beliefs about God (Table 9.2), finding variations that reflect differences in religion within and between the regions. In Hong Kong, 26 percent of scientists reported that they don't believe in any God or gods and another 20 percent said they don't know whether God or gods exist and don't believe there is any way to find out. Smaller shares of scientists in Taiwan affirmed these positions, with about 11 percent saying they don't believe in any God or gods and another 15 percent saying they don't know whether there is a God or gods and don't think there's any way to find out.

Monotheism is more popular in Hong Kong, where Christianity is more popular. Here, about 20 percent of scientists report they believe in only one God. Only about 12 percent of scientists in Taiwan report the same. Polytheism is more prevalent in Taiwan, where nearly a third of scientists said they believe in many gods. In Hong Kong, in comparison, 8 percent of scientists hold this belief. In both regions, however, the largest share of scientists—26 percent in Hong Kong and 32 percent in Taiwan—said they don't believe in a personal God, but they do believe in a higher power of some kind.

Note that we are limited in our ability to compare belief in God among scientists in Hong Kong and Taiwan to their respective publics because of either the availability or the wording of nationally representative survey data in these regions.[45] Our new question allowed for respondents to affirm belief either in many gods (polytheism) or only one God (monotheism).

When we look at religious affiliation and belief in God, we see that Hong Kong scientists closely mirror the general population in the region, while in Taiwan, scientists are less likely than the general population to affiliate with

TABLE 9.3. Religious service attendance in Taiwan and Hong Kong.

FREQUENCY	TAIWAN		HONG KONG	
	POPULATION (%)	SCIENTISTS (%)	POPULATION (%)	SCIENTISTS (%)
More than once a week	4.0	3.8	4.3	3.9
Once a week	3.8	7.8	6.9	8.5
Once a month	6.5	5.6	4.8	2.1
Only on special holy days	27.5	37.1	8.3	12.0
Once a year	3.7	7.8	3.4	1.5
Less often	25.0	16.0	24.6	26.0
Never, practically never	29.1	21.9	47.6	46.1
Total Respondents	1,238	830	999	299

NOTES: Based on weighted data. Values exclude nonresponse.
SOURCE: World Values Survey Taiwan 2012; RASIC Taiwan Survey 2015; World Values Survey Hong Kong 2013; RASIC Hong Kong Survey 2014.

a religion or believe in God. Yet, our findings with regard to religious service attendance suggest that scientists are not necessarily less religious than the general public in Taiwan (Table 9.3). For example, 12 percent of scientists in Taiwan attend religious services once a week or more,[46] while only 8 percent of the general population report the same. Of all the contexts we studied, Taiwan has the largest gap in attending religious services once a week or more often where scientists attend *more frequently* than the general public (perhaps due to the overrepresentation of Protestants in the Taiwanese scientific community). Taiwanese scientists are also more likely than the general public in the region to attend services on special holy days and once a year, and less likely to attend services "never" or "less often." When we compare across national contexts, scientists in Taiwan are more likely to attend services only on special holy days (37 percent) than are scientists in the other regions we studied (in India, the next highest, 27 percent of scientists attend at this level, followed by 19 percent of scientists in Italy). The high proportion of Taiwanese scientists who attend religious services only on special holy days could be attributed to the majority status of folk religion in Taiwan and how much folk religion is integrated into people's everyday lives (as opposed to reflected in specifically religious practices like service attendance).[47]

While public discourses and scholarly discussions may assume that scientists are generally less religious than their counterparts in the general public, in Taiwan and Hong Kong we have observed a reverse pattern. In Taiwan, specifically, attendance once a week or more is higher in the scientific community (11.6 percent) than among the general public (7.8 percent). Hong Kong is the only other context we studied in which the proportion of scientists who attend religious services weekly (12.4 percent) exceeds the proportion of the general public who attend services weekly (11.2 percent). Holy day attendance is also higher among Hong Kong scientists than the general public. Hong Kong is the *only* context we studied in which the percentage of scientists and members of the general public who attend services "never" or "less often" is very similar.

Additional statistical analysis shows that in both Hong Kong and Taiwan, immigrant status is significantly associated with both belief in God and religious service attendance. When compared with native-born scientists, scientists who are immigrants to Hong Kong and Taiwan are more likely to not believe in God[48] and to never or practically never attend religious services.[49] We also discovered that scientists who are immigrants to both regions are likely to be more secular and much more likely when compared to native-born scientists to believe there is little truth in any religion.[50]

Relationship Between Science and Religion Among Taiwanese and Hong Kong Scientists

The conflict view of science and religion is lower among scientists in Hong Kong and Taiwan than in any other national context where we studied scientists. Only 16 percent of scientists in Hong Kong and 9 percent of scientists in Taiwan view science and religion as in conflict and take the side of science (Table 9.4). It's worth pointing out that in no country we studied did more than one-third of scientists hold this conflict view. India, where 18 percent of scientists hold the conflict perspective, is the only country that comes close to matching the relative lack of perceived conflict between science and religion found among scientists in Hong Kong and Taiwan.

We met some scientists who see science and religion as conflicting because they think the nature of science discourages them from being religious. A professor in Hong Kong[51] told us he could hardly find a pastor who is able to deliver "convincing sermons," and a biology professor in Hong Kong[52] explained,

> I always needed, from the time I was very young, to see the evidence, the proof, the tangible side of things. I needed that. And so for me, although I did have a Christian upbringing in England, I always had a problem because, at some level, it required giving in, I suppose in a sense, to just believing what you were told. And I guess . . . so that always made it difficult.

TABLE 9.4. The perceived relationship of science and religion among scientists in Taiwan and Hong Kong.

RELATIONSHIP	TAIWAN (%)	HONG KONG (%)
Conflict; I consider myself to be on the side of religion	0.4	0.3
Conflict; I consider myself to be on the side of science	8.7	16.3
Conflict; I am unsure which side I am on	0.5	1.2
Independence; they refer to different aspects of reality	62.8	43.6
Collaboration; each can be used to help support the other	20.7	23.4
Don't know	7.1	15.3
Total Respondents	799	290

NOTES: Based on weighted data. Values exclude nonresponse.
SOURCE: RASIC Taiwan Survey 2015; RASIC Hong Kong Survey 2014.

For some of these scientists, their scientific training provides them with a critical lens to examine religion. As a Taiwanese research fellow in biology[53] said, "I should say that everything should develop according to scientific rules. . . . However, some things cannot be explained, such as deities and ghosts. . . . Supposing that we are able to explain these things eventually, this should be science." Based on the scientific method, he said, he does not have absolute answers to the question of whether supernatural power exists. In his view as an agnostic and biologist, it is "meaningless" to talk about supernatural phenomena, such as ghosts and deities, unless such experiences can be proved by science.

In both Hong Kong and Taiwan, most scientists see science and religion as independent. When talking about the science and religion interface, several scientists said science and religion "are not closely related."[54] Slightly less than half of Hong Kong scientists and approximately two-thirds of Taiwan scientists perceive science and religion as referring to different aspects of reality. The proportion of scientists who hold the independence perspective of science and religion is higher in Taiwan (63 percent) than in any other region in our study.

The second most popular view of science and religion in Hong Kong and Taiwan is collaboration. In both regions, a large minority of scientists—23 percent in Hong Kong and 21 percent in Taiwan—think science and religion have the potential to collaborate. The proportion of scientists who hold the collaboration view is only higher in India (29 percent) and Turkey (32 percent). Notably, a significantly larger share of biologists (31 percent) than physicists (14 percent) hold this view in Hong

Kong.[55] And biologists had higher odds than physicists of affirming the collaboration view rather than the independence view (see Appendix A, Table A.19, on Hong Kong). In Taiwan, however, we observed the opposite pattern; biologists had lower odds than physicists of affirming the collaboration view rather than the independence view (see Appendix A, Table A.20, on Taiwan).

The proportion of scientists who hold the collaboration perspective rarely exceeds 10 percent in other countries, suggesting there might be a special relationship between science and non-Western religious traditions, which leads adherents to see ways the two realms can be used to support one another. From our conversations with scientists in Hong Kong and Taiwan, we also speculate that the diverse religious landscape of these two regions—especially Taiwan—blurs the boundaries between religion, spirituality, and nonreligion, and thus also between science and religion.

"Sure, I'm a Buddhist," a physicist in Taiwan[56] told us, when reflecting on the extent to which religion or spirituality comes into his scientific work. "Actually, it's very difficult to claim that I am a Buddhist," he continued. "In Taiwan, our belief is very complex." While he reads Heart Sutra, a sacred book in Buddhism, he also follows "a [Daoist] tradition" when back home. He went on to say that he "needs religion to support [his] living and research." For many scientists in Taiwan and Hong Kong, religion is more a philosophy than theology. As another Taiwanese physicist[57] explained, Taiwan has

> Lots of kinds of religion, although people will say we have Confucianism or Buddhism, but they are more like a philosophical type of religion. So we don't have much theology to follow. So in general, my impression is that scientists in Taiwan like myself treat religion as a theory, and this kind of theory is difficult to prove, but we don't necessarily reject the idea or see it as a conflict either.

"I consider myself as a Buddhist," a biologist in Hong Kong[58] informed us, but "somebody once told me that Buddhism does not really count as a religion in the sense that they think it's more like a philosophy," which is different from "those Judeo-Christian religions," he said. He thinks his scientific training helped him to detach the supernatural connotations from Buddhism, making his religiosity even more "philosophical." Whether there is any conflict between science and religion really "depends on the [specific type of] religion," he said, and he sees the religions he has been exposed to—Buddhism, with an integration of Daoism—as being entirely compatible with science.

Religion in the Hong Kong and Taiwan Workplace

Professor Sun⁵⁹ was born and raised in Hong Kong. He got his doctorate from one US university, and followed that with a postdoctoral fellowship at another. Sun then returned to Hong Kong and accepted a position as a biology professor at an elite university. He explained that, with God's leading, he is fortunate enough to do research and teaching as a university professor and get paid "to do something [I am] interested in."

Today, Sun is a committed Christian. Growing up, he remembers his family believing in Chinese folk religion, a mixture of Daoism, Buddhism, and related local religions that are a part of the cultural fabric of Hong Kong. He now describes the practice of folk religion as "just a way to make you feel better by asking for good"; as an example, he tells us his parents sought a fortuneteller to bring good to his life and future. His religious transition to Christianity began during his college years, when he met Christian classmates who invited him to church and talked with him about what it would mean to become a Christian. At first, he was just trying to be friendly so he accepted their invitation, hoping not to offend. But then he started to realize that Christianity might be something good for him and eventually adopted the faith as his own. When he was growing up, his father had two wives, he told us, and there were often fights and arguments between the two; he wondered whether there could ever be such a thing as unconditional love and whether God existed. He admitted, "at the beginning, [it was] very much [self-oriented] and maybe using [Christianity] as a way out [of the struggles in life]," not really a spiritual connection with God. But, suddenly, "my life changed more and I transformed my view of the world and everything," and, at this point, "I feel more connected with God," he explained. His faith as a Christian motivates his scientific research and enhances his moral and ethical standards; he said,

> I would say having religion may at least [make you] a little more aware that there is a God, and [. . .] you will have to account for what you are doing, and you have to be more aware of acting justly in the world.

Sun generally does not hide his faith in the workplace. He prays at meals with colleagues and peers with whom he maintains close relationships; they are all aware that he is a Christian. Even at academic conferences, where "there are opportunities that we know that there will be other Christians," he talks about religion-related issues with other biologists. Yet, he is also aware there are boundaries regarding religion in the workplace. In his words, religion often occurs in conversations that have "become very personal during dinner" or leisure time—and usually such conversations do not "deal with science." He generally does not discuss his personal faith beliefs with other biologists who are not his close friends and who do not know his religious identity, except, he added, "when they discuss the purpose of life and when they discuss evolution."

Religion does not come up in his teaching very often, he said. "Of course the evolutionary perspective is always used in textbooks," and "of course you'll be using all the textbooks," he told us. Yet as a Christian who embraces elements of creationism, he personally believes, "Definitely there is no mega-evolution. There may be micro-evolution." According to him, even though "the seven days may not be exact," "the creator is beyond and outside and [encompasses] everything that can be explained by science." Hence, in his teaching, particularly in his lectures to high school students as part of scientific outreach, he would "mention the mystery of life" and "talk about different issues, not directly, but hinting the complexity and some [order in] the mystery of life." Seeing his work as a search for order (by which he means the ordered world created by God) is implicitly linked to his views of religion and science as a Christian.

Sun believes some Hong Kong academics may be hostile to "creation scientists . . . on some subtle issues." He said,

> I don't want to name names, but [there is a] very prominent agnostic astrobiologist, and . . . he's wholeheartedly for the idea of introducing more evolutionary perspectives [and] astrology into secondary textbooks or in the syllabus. [This scientist] tries to put away the creation scientists or something related to the possibility of a god in the textbook. . . . They regard religion as something bad for science. They are very against it. . . . I can feel something like that, that there's some subtle discrimination.

In his view, mentioning different perspectives on creation could be an approach to "retain diversity," by which he means draw more Taiwanese Christians into biology.

Freedom and Accommodation

When asked about their comfort sharing their views of religion with colleagues, 45 percent of scientists in Hong Kong and 23 percent of scientists in Taiwan said they have "no views on religion." This is significantly more than we see in other national contexts: for example, 6 percent of scientists in Turkey and 9 percent of scientists in both the United Kingdom and the United States reported they have no views on religion.

Very few scientists in Hong Kong and Taiwan reported they are uncomfortable sharing their views on religion in the workplace. In Hong Kong, 36 percent of scientists said they were very comfortable discussing religion, while about 48 percent of scientists in Taiwan said the same. The *lack* of concern about religious self-expression in the workplace is noteworthy. Scientists in Hong Kong and Taiwan are much more comfortable sharing their views on religion with colleagues than are scientists in other regions. Only 1 percent of scientists in Hong Kong and 2 percent of scientists in Taiwan said they would be very uncomfortable sharing their views on religion with scientists in their academic department. Scientists in Turkey (6 percent), the United States (8 percent), and France (11 percent) were much more likely to report feeling very uncomfortable about sharing their views about religion with colleagues.

In Hong Kong and Taiwan, there is no expectation of informal sanctions for expressing religious identity. "Yes, I would invite people [to dinners at my church]. Some would come, some would oppose," one Taiwanese physicist[60] told us. "Usually if I see classmates in trouble, for example if they can't finish a report or something, I might also say, 'I'll pray for you.'" She usually would not avoid talking about her religious beliefs with her colleagues in the scientific field and tells us, "normal Christians usually would not avoid [talking about their faith]. They might even very obviously want to talk about it." She also talked about how she identifies the religious beliefs of her colleagues through her conversations with them:

> Daoists will talk about karma and reincarnation. . . . Buddhists will observe this gratefulness, benevolence. . . . Christians are a bit more complicated. . . . Christianity has a lot of, you know, a lot of branches, and they have different opinions on every topic.

Another Taiwanese physicist[61] told us she would invite her nonreligious colleagues to a Bible study:

> We have just started a Bible study group for professors. We Christian professors lead this group and we invite some non-Christian professors in our department to participate. Some of them are interested in it. They want to know more about the Bible. They have some needs. So, we invite them to read the Bible with us.

In other national contexts, religious scientists are reluctant to express their beliefs so freely.

Given that scientists we interviewed told us that they were fairly comfortable discussing religion in the scientific workplace in Hong Kong and Taiwan, we were surprised that religious symbolism was not as visible in the labs and offices we visited in these regions as in other contexts. The same physicist who invited others to Bible study[62] also had a framed piece of calligraphy on her wall: "Love is patient, love is kind," an excerpt from the first book of Corinthians in the Bible. But for the most part, personal religious decorations or effects weren't found.

Accommodation of religious beliefs is not as salient as it is in the other national and regional contexts that we have visited. The relative lack of public discourse on the religion and science interface in Hong Kong and Taiwan, on the one hand, creates an institutional norm in science that does not necessarily situate science and religion in tension and subsequently provides scientists with more room to express their religiosity in the workplace. On the other hand, however, scientists in the two contexts do not necessarily perceive the need to accommodate religious beliefs and practices. In Taiwan, we sometimes heard scientists talk about accommodating religious beliefs and practices in the workplace. "There was a certain period of time when I chose one small research room to take naps in, and then there was this group of people [Muslims] walking in and praying there," a Taiwanese biologist[63] recounted. "I was just like, if you aren't going to ask me to go away then I'll just continue sleeping." She believes it is necessary to accommodate Muslim scientists' needs to pray and that the time "they want to talk to you about research, they want to meet, and they need you to do an experiment" should not "disrupt their worship time." Such accommodation, she explained, is easy to do. "Their worship time is also really short," she told us, requiring breaks that are "just like the time you use to go to the restroom."

Another Taiwanese biologist[64] spoke with us about accommodating religious beliefs regarding respect for life:

> I have two students who are Christians. . . . We have to kill a lot of mice. But [they] refused to do so. . . . So one of them could only design an experiment . . . that had nothing to do with neuro cells. The other one had to ask my assistant to [kill the mice]. My assistant didn't have such an issue. He did it for the student. . . . As a result, I was criticized by another colleague who said: "How could you let the assistant help students do what they were supposed to do?" But we had no choice. It's [the student's] religious belief.

Surprisingly, accommodation of religious practices and beliefs was not a topic that emerged in our conversations with scientists in Hong Kong. It may be that in Hong Kong, where significantly more scientists are religiously unaffiliated than in Taiwan, there is more conversation about the place of religion in the workplace than accommodating religion.

Religion as a Resource to Overcome Challenges in Research and Mentoring

Professor Tsai[65] is a practitioner of folk religion. Similar to many academic scientists in Taiwan, he received his doctorate outside the region, in his case in Australia. His work as a scientist includes two essential components, he told us. The first is about research, "looking at the origins of the species and the reasons why these species have lasted until now from the perspective of evolution and ecology." The second is "education and promotion on the protection of our environment." Science outreach is one of his passions.

He explained his lifelong involvement in Taiwanese folk religion. "Both my parents do *bai bai* [worship]," he said. "I have been familiar with religion since I was very young." In addition to the worship, he has also visited temples and participated in religious rituals with his parents, and still goes to ritualistic gatherings in temples where he "always sheds tears involuntarily." Religion "has actually been with me all along in my personal upbringing and it still is," he explained. He not only believes in a supernatural god, but also has "personal experiences encountering such [supernatural] matters," he said. "I have been a follower of the Third Prince [a deity in Chinese folk religions]." Tsai told us that he has interacted with deities and spirits from the time he was a child.

Tsai thinks he is not the only academic in Taiwan who has had supernatural experiences with folk religion deities. "I believe that a lot of those who work in . . . higher education, they probably all have the same beliefs I do," he said. "It's just that they wouldn't talk about it." He is not worried about whether science is able to detect interactions with these deities because he knows that the current scientific methodology "is incapable of really detecting matters of the [supernatural] aspect of reality." He continues:

Even if you use the most accurate and sophisticated methodology with global collaboration to try to detect the smallest particle, even that, at the end of the day, is incapable of getting to even the fringes of [the realms of deities and spirits].

Tsai described for us certain events from his fieldwork. He detailed:

I am a person who works underwater. . . . I have had the experience of some—unexpected incidents underwater. And, then, I could feel the more evil energies affecting me. But the thing is that there were some unobservable forces by my side that were helping me.

When the waves became too high in the sea, Tsai said he would "ask the Third Prince to assist me and see if the problem gets resolved in the end." He believes he overcame the dangerous situation by relying on the assistance of the Third Prince deity, but he has "never told anybody about this." He also believes the deity intervenes in his academic research articles. He explained:

As the deity comes down he would help me. He would take the ink brush and the cinnabar, and he would make edits. He would be like: "Look, you wrote this poorly, and there's something wrong there." And I would have been a little careless, and once I carefully looked into it I would discover that I really did make a mistake.

Other scientists in Taiwan and Hong Kong talked about how they see religion potentially helping scientists resolve difficulties in their scientific research. The Taiwanese physics professor who has a framed scripture from the biblical book of Corinthians in her office[66] told us how she relies on the religious text when faced with a challenge in her role as an instructor:

[Some] students don't necessarily like physics that much. Maybe they just want to get a degree. . . . There are huge gaps here between my expectations, or criteria, and that of the students. . . . When I [find] the gap overwhelming, I rely on my faith to learn how to be patient. God is patient with us. So, you can see the quote here. This is a quote from First Corinthians in the Bible about love. Love suffers long and is kind. As a teacher, I have to have this character.

When she was a graduate student, she recounted, she came up with results that conflicted with a famous theoretical physicist. "It was a really surprising result. . . . I thought God allowed me to know it," she said. A theoretical physicist flew to her lab to assess her findings, and she drew on her religious beliefs:

My advisor and other professors were really nervous. They were scared, because that guy was obnoxious. . . . I had prayed beforehand. I was so calm and peaceful at that time. I was not scared by him. I presented facts honestly.

I answered his questions faithfully. He found that there were no flaws in my experiments.

Most of the scientists in Taiwan and Hong Kong who rely on religion to overcome challenges attribute the help from religion to the transformation of their attitudes after practicing religion. In Hong Kong, for instance, we encountered a physicist who had converted to Christianity about one year ago.[67] He reflected on how religion changes the way in which he deals with difficulties in his work and said, after he was baptized, he has "been more positive and active." These positive and active attitudes also reflect on how he does scientific work: "I don't feel depressed even though I have faced difficulties. Instead, I would think about it."

Scientists in Hong Kong and Taiwan may perceive that religion helps them in different ways. Religion—Christianity, folk religions, and Buddhism—can help scientists to cope with challenges in the workplace by providing supernatural support, by calming them down, and by helping them to maintain positive and active attitudes in scientific work. Regardless of *how* religion helps them to cope with challenges, they believe that "the power of religion enables a person to receive some sort of intangible support in one's unstable life."[68] And to many academic scientists in Hong Kong and Taiwan, this unstable life refers to the difficulties and challenges in scientific explorations and the stress of being in academia.

Research Ethics

Both religious and nonreligious scientists in Hong Kong and Taiwan have the sense that religious scientists may have a different ethical standard in their research than nonreligious scientists do. As a biologist in Taiwan reflected,[69] "these religious colleagues usually have a more serious attitude. . . . No matter what religion he believes—Buddhism, Catholicism, or whatever."

Some religious scientists in Taiwan spoke about how religion influences their research ethics in a way that goes beyond the basic academic ethics that focus on plagiarism, fabrication, and falsification—often taking into consideration the needs of disadvantaged groups (an idea central to the Christian faith tradition, for example). When asked about potential differences between religious and nonreligious scientists, a Taiwanese biologist who self-identifies as Catholic[70] said,

> The [scientists who are religious] generally care more about minorities, in my opinion, through the process of our interactions. And then also in terms of

research topic choices, they are willing to do some trade-offs. And then when publicizing their research findings, regarding the application of findings, [they will emphasize] how to achieve equality in society. Or in nutrition, because many of our research findings will transform into materials for promotion in the society. Then in the process of promotion, [they will emphasize] how to take care of all people, and not just some particular interest groups.

This biologist continued to explain that, guided by her religion, she believes science should benefit the disadvantaged in society. As a biologist, she does research on nutrition. Most of the previous studies on nutrition, however, only focus on healthy people. As she explained:

> When I am doing [research], I discover that although we get funds from the government to do these jobs, our targets are still healthy people. . . . There are a lot of disadvantaged groups, such as these who live in remote areas, which are not completely taken care of. Most of the studies do not care about people who have disabilities and do not care about people who are suffering in some special diseases and people who have special needs. This way I will think that if we keep on doing this, we are actually ignoring people who need more help in the society. . . . So when I explore research topics, what I want or do not want to do, I think [religion] has some influence.

For some scientists in Taiwan and Hong Kong, research ethics becomes an important locus where science and religion intersect with each other. On the one hand, religious scientists perceive themselves to have an expanded ethical standard that motivates them to use science to benefit and help others, especially the underprivileged in society. On the other hand, religious ethical standards can lead to moral struggles in the workplace, constraining the scientific topics or types of experiments that scientists want to or will pursue. In Hong Kong, we interviewed a biologist who was exposed to Buddhism and Daoism, converted to Christianity in high school, went back to Buddhism, and now identifies as a religious person who believes in deities but does not practice a religion.[71] "Their interpretation of findings can be deeply colored by their religious views," he said of his religious colleagues. "Well, I think they may self-impose some constraints on the kind of work they might want to take, maybe in their religious views it's considered unethical," he added. "It's just some areas which they don't want to tread." According to him, the differences between religious ethical standards and secular ethical standards may create some tensions for religious scientists in the workplace.

In Hong Kong and Taiwan, we found the tensions between religious and secular ethical standards are most salient in biology and often center on the issue of killing animals. In Taiwan, we talked with a female physicist who identified as "not a religious person" on our survey but occasionally goes to a temple for folk religions to pray.[72] When the interviewer asked her if religion or spirituality influences her own research, she hesitated for a moment and said, "Well, I'm not sure if this is related to religion, but I don't like doing biology things." She then continued and said that she tries to avoid using animal models in biological experiments, explaining,

> When I think of using [animals] in biological experiments, although it is for [the benefit of] a bigger number of people, or whatever it is, but I just do not want to do it. It is a very agonizing feeling to me.

"Buddhism is about not killing," a Buddhist biologist in Taiwan[73] told us. "When I am designing my research, if I can avoid using animals, I would do so. And in that way religion is related to my research."

Separation of Religion from the Scientific Workplace

Most scientists in Hong Kong and Taiwan believe science and religion refer to different aspects of reality. These scientists say they exclude religion from the workplace. They explicitly informed us that they "just deal with work or purely science"[74] and religious views should be expressed "out of class time, outside of work."[75] To some extent, scientists in Hong Kong and Taiwan are still constrained by the institutional norm of secularity in science. Nevertheless, as we see in other national contexts, science and religion are not always kept apart in the day-to-day work of scientists.[76]

A professor of physics who migrated to Hong Kong from China[77] reflected on a colleague who wanted to have a science class from a Christian perspective:

> I do not support this class. If you want to propagandize these [religious] thoughts in private domains or after the class, I will not have a reason to oppose it. But if you want to have it on campus, how should I put it, I think this is inappropriate.

He mentioned times when he was invited by his religious colleagues to attend parties at their houses, and said that one colleague "propagandizes something about God and miracles. I think these things are a bit ridiculous." Yet, he does appreciate the scientific abilities of his religious colleagues and does not discredit their work because of their religious views, believing "they are real scientists, and they have made great achievements in their scientific research." In his view, expression of religion by his scientist colleagues is acceptable if in a private domain.

We talked directly with some religious scientists in Hong Kong who try to keep religious influence to the more private and nonscientific domains of their workplaces, such as individual meetings with students or informal conversations with colleagues. Most of these scientists would not bring up religion or religious issues in the classroom or in discussions directly related to science. For example, an associate professor of physics from Hong Kong[78] explained,

> I am a Catholic. I don't think there is a conflict because of religion. . . . We ask questions. For example, say: What's the purpose of existence? What's the meaning of life? Where do we come from? These kinds of questions. So science, what we do, in my opinion, is we observe the physical universe, try to conclude, make models, and try to use the models to predict. . . . So I think it's completely two aspects for me. It's two separate things.

This physicist does not mention religion while teaching. At most, he may, in certain cases and small groups, recognize religion among his colleagues. "There may be some occasions, maybe of just one or two guys," he said. "If he's also a Christian. So sometimes, just we come across, 'Oh, you are Christian! Oh!' That's just very brief, not at all in a deep interpretation or discussion."

In Taiwan, nonreligious scientists also seem to accept some limited and confined integration of religion in the workplace by their religious colleagues. A nonreligious professor of physics,[79] for example, told us that he accepts the occasional interjection of religion in conversations among his colleagues, as long as the conversations are limited to "an exchange of experiences." Specifically, he said,

> I know that my colleagues, some of them, are Buddhists, some are, say [practitioners of] Occultism. Some are Christians. They have different religious beliefs and they would share their experiences. I would be open to this information. But these are their belief[s]. I would probably not be able to go one step further and share my opinions with them.

While he allows a small space where the expression of religion is acceptable, he also defends a generally secular workplace.

Religious scientists in Taiwan also rarely talk about religion publicly in the workplace. A Buddhist professor in biology[80] we interviewed described how she is really careful about limiting conversations about religion to private spaces with students:

> Often times, it is when they have problems that I make use of my religious concepts or thoughts to talk with them. . . . I would tell them that this is from the Buddhist book. . . . The professors that I know, including myself, most of us would not be the one to tell our students what our religious beliefs are. However, in discussion, since we take up positions as mentors who counsel students, as we talk privately with students, or when we publicly talk about certain problems, we would deliver to them what we think and may be related to our religious beliefs.

Conclusions

Scientists in Hong Kong and Taiwan have a different understanding of the science and religion interface than scientists in the West. The belief that there is inherent conflict between science and religion is a largely Christian-centric concept found heavily in Western public discourse[81] but is not as salient in Hong Kong and Taiwan, where there is low level of endorsement of the "conflict" perspective of science and religion among scientists. Among scientists in these regions, we also observed a freer expression of religion in the scientific workplace.

Perhaps due in part to the lower levels of tension between science and religion in these two societies, we find scientists there who are in some ways religiously similar to the general public. In both Hong Kong and Taiwan, we believe the religiosity found among scientists can be explained partially by a lack of public discourse on the tension between science and religion. In Hong Kong, we find that the religious practices of scientists largely mirror those of the general public, and we don't see the secularization of science that we find in the West. We also find that public discourse on conflict between science and religion is much less salient here than in Western societies, particularly the United States. (As we mentioned earlier, the 2009 public debate about teaching creationism was a somewhat surprising and isolated incident that was rarely reported by local media in Chinese.) In Taiwan, we find scientists are more likely to attend religious services weekly and to attend religious services on holy days than are members of the general public. The high proportion of scientists who attend services on a weekly basis possibly can be explained by the overrepresentation of Protestants working in science in Taiwan when compared with the general population. We also speculate, given how folk religious practices embody the symbolic meanings of ethnicity, culture, and family union in Taiwan,[82] that attending religious services on holy days is a way in which Taiwanese scientists maintain a connection with the local and traditional culture of their society.

The science–faith interface materializes more saliently in the scientific workplace in Hong Kong than in Taiwan. Hong Kong combines a Christian legacy from earlier colonialism and a mainstream modern-day commitment to Christianity with an influx of atheists from mainland China. And as a result, the interface of science and religion is more salient than in Taiwan. We see this reflected, for example, in atheist scientists' perception that their Christian colleagues control the academic resources and some Christian scientists, such as Professor Sun, who integrate a creationist perspective in teaching and scientific outreach. In Taiwan, where folk religion is prevalent if not dominant, the interface between science and religion in the scientific workplace is subtler. Religious scientists sometimes integrate religion into their research, teaching, and mentoring, but nonreligious scientists defend a certain degree of secularity in the workplace by setting up boundaries regarding when, where, and to what extent conversations about religion are acceptable.

CHAPTER 10

An Integrated Global Science
and Religion

AS WE HAVE SEEN through our survey and interviews with scientists in the eight
national and regional contexts examined in this book, a variety of conditions
and conceptions govern the relationship between science and religion as
scientists see it. These characteristics include the nature of the country's scientific community, the norms regarding public displays and discussion of
religion, and the personal religious views and beliefs of the nation or region's
scientists. Together, the contexts we studied provide us with a more holistic
perspective on the science and religion relationship and the factors that have
an impact on and shape how scientists view this relationship.

Nations and Regions at a Glance

We can begin to crystallize this more comprehensive perspective by breaking
down and then pulling together the key factors and findings from each national context. Here we consider each context, in the order in which they
appeared in the book. We then turn to broader conclusions by looking at the
similarities and differences among these regions.

United States

Nature of the Scientific Community. US scientists tend to see the US religious public as evangelical biblical literalists who are antiscience, and
this has a significant impact on how they view the nature of the relationship between science and religion. The hostility that nonreligious
scientists have toward religious scientists seems to be driven—at least

in part—by an erroneous view of how religious individuals think about science that is promulgated in the public sphere.

Religious Views and Beliefs of Scientists. US scientists are much more likely to be atheist or agnostic than are members of the general population in the United States. Almost half of scientists who are Protestant, the largest religious group in the US scientific community, feel they have experienced discrimination.

Perspective on the Science and Religion Relationship. The conflict perspective is very popular here (more so than in all the other countries we studied except the United Kingdom). Most scientists see the conflict as originating from certain religious groups or beliefs (namely, biblical literalism) rather than from the science community or an innate conflict between science and religion. Most religious scientists in the United States compartmentalize their work and faith.

Looking Forward. Religious discrimination in the scientific workplace could be an issue when it comes to recruiting and retaining women and minorities, as these groups are more likely than white males to be religious.

United Kingdom

Nature of the Scientific Community. The United Kingdom is experiencing a decline in religiosity and increasing religious diversity resulting from immigration; nearly half of scientists in the United Kingdom originate from other nations.

Religious Views and Beliefs of Scientists. Greater diversity among students pursuing science careers in the United Kingdom is leading to some disconnect between older Christian scientists and their younger, more religiously diverse and devout students.[1] Even as scientists here make accommodations for religious graduate students and postdoctoral researchers, Islam nevertheless seems to be a particular challenge for many UK scientists. Biologists, for example, worry about Muslim students bringing antievolution sentiments into the scientific community.

Perspective on the Science and Religion Relationship. Debates regarding the proper relationship between science and religion feature prominently in UK public life. The dominant view among UK scientists is that the two realms are separate and independent. Yet, the most vocal scientists promote the conflict perspective. New Atheists, who actually represent a small portion of the population, receive a disproportionate share of media attention (as do religious fundamentalists). The conflict perspective is more pronounced in the United Kingdom than in any other nation, with 35 percent of scientists embracing this view.

Looking Forward. UK scientists will have to grapple with a public and scientific community that is becoming increasingly more diverse with regard to religious traditions and beliefs.

France

Nature of the Scientific Community. France is defined by assertive secularism, and it is the only nation we studied in which more than half of scientists are convinced atheists.

Religious Views and Beliefs of Scientists. Scientists in France are less religious than scientists in the other countries we studied. *Laïcité* keeps religion from public debates, relegating it to the private sphere. Most French scientists don't feel free to express their religious beliefs or discuss religion in any meaningful way in the workplace.

Perspective on the Science and Religion Relationship. While the assertive secularism of France minimizes conflict between science and religion by suppressing religious expression in the public sphere, the proportion of scientists who see science and religion as having a conflict relationship is similar to the proportion in the United States. Among all the nations and regions of our study, scientists in France are the least likely to hold the collaboration perspective.

Looking Forward. Given the spirit of secularism in France, we are unlikely to see public dialogue between religious and scientific communities. Yet, as France becomes more religiously diverse, greater discussion of religion within the scientific community might be necessary to understand the tensions religious minorities face—particularly Muslim scientists—in the service of promoting even a thin version of religious tolerance.

Italy

Nature of the Scientific Community. The majority of Italian scientists share the same religious background and affiliation, Catholicism.

Religious Views and Beliefs of Scientists. Religion, specifically Catholicism, is pervasive in the scientific community. Constant news coverage of the Church contributes to the strong coupling of religion and culture, thereby normalizing the presence of religion among scientists.

Perspective on the Science and Religion Relationship. Most Italian scientists see religion as totally independent from the realm of science. The independence perspective is more popular here than in other national contexts we studied. We believe this is because most scientists in Italy are Catholic or spiritual but not religious, and thus there is little to no presence of biblical literalism that creates conflict or tension between science and religion.

Looking Forward. We found little conflict related to religion in the scientific workplace in Italy, and the majority of scientists are comfortable sharing their religious views with colleagues. As with the broader society, religious pluralism in the scientific community is low, and we believe tension or controversy related to religion in the scientific workplace will continue to be low.

Turkey

Nature of the Scientific Community. Many scientists we spoke with were concerned that new government policies were injecting Islam into the national identity and education system, moving Turkey away from its "secular Muslim" roots and into a more religious country with more public religious expression.

Religious Views and Beliefs of Scientists. The vast majority of Turkish scientists identify as Muslim, and scientists here are more likely to be religious than are scientists in most of the other national contexts we studied. When compared with scientists in more religiously pluralistic nations, we found that relatively few scientists in Turkey defined religion in negative terms. More scientists here than in any other region reported their scientific background made them *more* religious.

Perspective on the Science and Religion Relationship. The independence perspective is the most popular, as in other regions, but Turkey has the largest share of scientists who see the science and religion relationship as one of collaboration, stressing aspects of Islamic theology they see as encouraging scientific work or pointing to what they see as the limitations of science.

Looking Forward. The public role of religion is changing in Turkey. The politicization of Islam poses challenges to the expansion of science in the nation, and many of Turkey's top academics are leaving for positions in Europe or the United States.

India

Nature of the Scientific Community. India is defined by a religion-friendly secularism that stresses religious accommodation. In the scientific community, Indian secularism affirms diversity of religious expression. We found a number of scientists had tried to familiarize themselves with the religious traditions of their students in order to better support them.

Religious Views and Beliefs of Scientists. Religion plays a big role in family life for Indian scientists, even for those who don't consider themselves religious. Scientists expressed feeling as if they had to participate in religious ceremonies to maintain traditions, as part of their familial duty, or to appease their families.

Perspective on the Science and Religion Relationship. The majority of Indian scientists see the two realms as independent. Yet, given the importance and presence of religion in India, separation between the two realms is hard for them to implement and science and religion are more intertwined than many scientists seem to realize. Indian scientists often connect religion to morality in science, seeing being a "good scientist" as doing work that alleviates poverty and human suffering.

Looking Forward. As universities increase in number and attract greater numbers of international scholars, it is possible the relationship between science and religion in the nation will begin to change and there will be greater calls for actual separation between the two realms.

Hong Kong and Taiwan

Nature of the Scientific Community. Though these two regions are small, they are both developing modern scientific communities.

Religious Views and Beliefs of Scientists. In these regions, scientists are, according to some measures, religiously similar to the general public. We also observed a freer expression of religion in the workplace among scientists in these regions. We believe the religiosity found among scientists can be partially explained by a lack of public discourse on science–religion conflict, which is much less salient here than in Western societies.

Perspective on the Science and Religion Relationship. Support for the conflict view is lower among scientists here than in any other national context we studied. In both regions, most scientists see science and religion as independent.

there is the simple fact that there are greater proportions of atheists in these regions. Even though, as we've seen, not all atheist scientists are antireligion or view science and religion as in conflict, they are nevertheless more likely to embrace the conflict perspective of science and religion.

Though the majority of scientists we surveyed epistemologically see science and religion as independent and separate, and want to keep religion out of the scientific workplace, our interviews revealed the numerous ways in which religion comes up in the workplace, both for religious scientists who try to compartmentalize their faith and for nonreligious scientists. In practice, we found powerful examples of religion entering the scientific workplace in all of the national contexts of our study, in region-specific ways. In the United States scientists sometimes face university students who are more religious than they are and might raise religiously based opposition to certain foundational ideas in science, such as evolution. In the United Kingdom and France we found scientists trying to make accommodations for the religious beliefs and practices of Muslim students. In India and Taiwan we found Hindu scientists (even those who see a Hindu identity as more cultural than religious) performing the Vishwakarma Puja, blessing the tools of their work to appease the more religious technicians in their laboratories. In Taiwan, Hong Kong, and Italy we heard from scientists who said they wanted to keep their religious lives completely distinct and separate from their scientific lives, but then sometimes offered to pray with students about personal concerns in the scientific workplace, had large crosses or Bibles in their offices, or had malas—Buddhist prayer beads—wrapped around their wrists. Then there are the regions where scientists see religion entering the scientific workplace in more institutionalized ways: in Italy, where belonging to religious networks and organizations may matter for funding; in Turkey, where some scientists are not seen as religious in the right way to appeal for government funding; and in Hong Kong, where Christian faith is sometimes linked to the institutions where scientists are likely to get their degrees.

In all the national contexts we studied, we found scientists who used religiously infused words, like "calling" in a Christian context or "mission" in a Jewish sense, to explain why they chose a career in science. We also found scientists who used their faith to make ethical decisions about scientific work; even scientists who were not currently religious drew on the faith of their childhood. We met Buddhist and Hindu scientists who avoided types of science that rely heavily on animal models in experiments. We spoke with evangelical Christian, Jewish, and Catholic scientists who used aspects of their faith traditions to justify declining funding from a source that might use their research to contribute to nuclear proliferation or harm the environment. We also heard religious scientists describe indirectly using their faith beliefs to select research that will benefit society, maintain positive relationships with colleagues, or bring religiously promoted virtues into the workplace. We found scientists using their faith traditions to think of creative ways that scientific work could help alleviate poverty, contribute to innovative medical treatments to help those who are suffering, or connect to a larger sense of beauty in the world. Faith was also found to provide some scientists with various resources, such as an identity apart from a scientific environment that values competition and success as evidenced by publications and funding above all else, a predisposition for treating their lab technicians and students more humanely, motivation to keep going in the midst of family changes, or infusing meaning in mundane work.

Concluding Thoughts

As we noted at the beginning of this work, our research provides insight into the major theoretical issues related to religious change and the relationship between science and religion. Our goal was to begin to develop a more global understanding of how science is related to secularization among scientists and how scientists in different kinds of institutions in different regions think about religion and its relationship to science. Our analyses uncovered key factors that have an impact on and change how scientists perceive the relationship between science and religion, globally and locally, and how this relationship manifests itself in the scientific workplace.

Religious Pluralism Versus Homogeneity

State policies related to religion have consequences for how scientists—both religious and nonreligious—navigate religion in the workplace. At one end of the spectrum are states that have more established religious structures (e.g., the United Kingdom, Italy), and at the other end are states characterized by assertive secularism (e.g., France). In between are countries like India and the United States that are characterized by passive secularism or a commitment to religious pluralism (sometimes both). States that have established religions create a condition in which policy normalizes religious culture. The extreme case we find is Italy, where religion is so pervasive, homogeneous, and coupled with culture that it can almost coexist independently and harmoniously with science. In the United Kingdom, however, where there is growing religious pluralism but one religion is normalized, perceived differences between native religious traditions and immigrant religious traditions can be amplified, leading to tensions and conflict with religion in the public sphere, including the scientific workplace.

In the United States, where there is high religious pluralism, 29 percent of religious scientists indicated they have experienced some level of religious discrimination in the workplace. (Among the regions we studied, it was only in Turkey that a greater proportion of scientists reported experiencing religious discrimination.) Among US scientists, reports of discrimination were highest among Muslims (57 percent) and Protestants, including evangelical Christians (40 percent), the largest religious group in science and in the US public.

Religious pluralism is very closely associated with a region's position in the global science infrastructure. Religious differences, and the challenges that can be related to them, are most pronounced in the scientific communities of core countries, such as the United Kingdom (even though it has a dominant religion), France (even with its assertive secularism), and the United States, because the professional opportunities in these countries attract scientists from around the globe. These immigrant scientists often bring religious traditions from their home country to their new country and scientific community. In Italy, where there is a jobs crisis in science and high religious homogeneity, we did not hear stories of tension due to the religious practices of immigrant scientists.

We also find in religiously pluralistic national contexts that rather than develop a deep understanding of the complex religious landscape, scientists tend to select one tradition and overgeneralize about that religion to make it an exemplar of what is "problematic" about religion. In France, for example, the focus is on traditional Muslims. Recent terror attacks by extremist religious groups have led to overt discrimination against Muslim students and scientists. Some Muslims in France feel laws regarding public expression of religion are applied more to them than Catholics, and female Muslim scientists face ambiguity surrounding the acceptability of headscarves in laboratories where the boundaries between public scientific institutions and universities are permeable. In the United States, as we pointed out, scientists tend to focus on evangelical Protestantism (even if they don't specify it) when they speak about the conflict they see between religion and science.

The Lived Religions of Individual Scientists

Still today, in the minds of many people, a professional scientist is *not* religious. Thus, it is the boundary between scientist and nonscientist that a religious scientist may threaten.[5] By threatening this boundary, religious scientists may experience instances of hostility and discrimination from their colleagues—or *fear* they will experience such hostility and discrimination.

Religious scientists who are highly respected in their profession have the potential to act as *boundary pioneers*.[6] We find that working closely with a religious scientist who has developed a successful career seems to illustrate to a nonreligious scientist that science and religion do not necessarily conflict with one another. Among scientists, one of the most prevalent justifications we heard for why there is not innate conflict between being religious and being a scientist was that they had worked with a successful religious scientist. Although this mechanism does not evince region-specific patterns, we find it is an especially powerful influence in elite scientific institutions, where the most successful scientists are located.

If scientists are afraid that sharing their religious beliefs will lead to hostility and discrimination, it can have a chilling effect, however. Scientists who are boundary pioneers between science and religion not only reconcile their faith and work but also openly discuss and display how they do so. They provide a public example of how science and religion can be compatible. If they fear doing so will have negative repercussions, they are more likely to hide their religiosity or faith. If, on the other hand, a greater number of well-respected scientists were to discuss how they maintain integrity in both science and religion and how they reconcile their faith and work, we predict prejudice against religious scientists would decrease.

Key Findings for Moving Forward

Whether science and religion *should* be viewed as conflicting, independent, or collaborative is not a question we can answer with the kind of empirical data we have here. Having spent years conducting research on this topic, we recognize that not all scientists or members of publics see reason for or want collaboration between religion and science. And under certain conditions there are good reasons for keeping science and religion separate. *But* for those who do want to connect faith and science in ways that serve common goals and goods, we do see potential for certain groups of scientists, in particular, to lead such aims.

Religious scientists who are most likely to see science and religion as having a collaborative relationship are: physicists in Taiwan, biologists in Turkey, and scientists at nonelite institutions in Turkey. Traditionally religious scientists, particularly those who see the relationship between science and religion as one of collaboration or independence, are most open to science–faith discussions and thus a key constituent in the science-and-religion dialogue.

Spiritual scientists who see science and religion as having a collaborative relationship are a nontrivial minority in the United Kingdom, the United States, Taiwan, and France. Although spiritual but not religious scientists exhibit relatively low levels of traditional belief, they may be fertile ground for the practice of new forms of what they see as science-consistent spirituality.[7] Many scientists identify as spiritual but not religious in order to construct meaning in ways they perceive as consistent with scientific practice. Accordingly, spiritual scientists, especially those who view the relationship between science and religion as one of independence or collaboration, are perhaps the most open to discussions of science as related to purpose and meaning.

Scientists who are atheist or agnostic, do not identify with a religion, or do not identify as religious or spiritual are located primarily in Western countries: France, the United Kingdom, and the United States. These groups of scientists appear to be the least receptive to engaging in dialogue on the relationship between science and religion, yet they represent an important opportunity for dialogue because they are most likely to be purveyors of scientism (the idea that science is the best or only way of knowing).[8] Across national contexts, these scientists tend to be disproportionately male, at elite institutions, and in advanced stages of their careers. Although powerful now by virtue of their institutional status and career stage, we believe these scientists will not be leaders in the future science and religion dialogue.

It is vitally important that scholars take a distinctively social scientific approach to examining the nature of the relationship between science and religion— on a global scale, taking into account epistemologies, cultural traditions, histories, political agendas, and lived experience. Looking at science and religion in a number of national contexts around the world offers a new perspective on the science–religion interface that could not be attained by studying any one context alone. The United States, the United Kingdom, France, Italy, Turkey, India, Hong Kong, and Taiwan exhibit distinctive religious characteristics and contribute a unique outlook on the relationship between science and religion. Here we have illustrated how characteristics of regions, the nature and norms of their scientific communities, and their religious identity and traditions shape the science–religion relationship for the scientists who live there. We also showed how important it is to hear the stories of scientists from various religious traditions, scientific disciplines, and career stages, to listen to them describe in their own words how they experience and navigate science and religion in their lives and work. We hope and believe this work is an important first step in broadening our perspective of the science and religion relationship beyond our local communities, media reports, and common stereotypes. For, as we have seen, the relationship between science and religion is a nuanced, diverse, and ever-changing paradigm that requires systematic examination and an integrated international approach.

APPENDIX A | Detailed Tables

Chapter 3

UNITED STATES

TABLE A.1. Comparing the perceived relationship of science and religion among scientists in the United States.

RELATIONSHIP	MEN (%)	WOMEN (%)	PHYSICISTS (%)	BIOLOGISTS (%)	NONELITE (%)	ELITE (%)
Conflict, side of religion	0.5	0.0	0.7	0.2	0.3	0.4
Conflict, side of science	33.0	19.1	28.3	28.8	27.4	30.3
Conflict, unsure which side	0.3	0.1	0.4	0.1	0.2	0.3
Independence	45.5	63.3	44.5	54.2	51.6	49.8
Collaboration	12.1	11.4	16.9	9.6	12.8	11.0
Don't know	8.6	6.2	9.4	7.2	7.7	8.2
Total Respondents	1,016	802	939	891	919	911

NOTES: Based on weighted data. Values exclude nonresponse.
SOURCE: RASIC United States Survey 2015.

TABLE A.2. Multinomial logit modeling perceived relationship of science and religion among scientists in the United States.

INDEPENDENT VARIABLE	CONFLICT VS. INDEPENDENCE		COLLABORATION VS. INDEPENDENCE	
	ODDS RATIO	STANDARD ERROR	ODDS RATIO	STANDARD ERROR
Gender (female = 1)	.32***	.20	.84	.24
Discipline (biology = 1)	1.17	.19	.42***	.22
Status (elite = 1)	1.00	.18	.88	.24
Rank 1 (reference)	—	—	—	—
Rank 2	.94	.24	1.46	.24
Rank 3	1.08	.25	.63	.31
Married	.63*	.21	.89	.25
Immigrant	.99	.19	.88	.24
Religiously affiliated	.33***	.23	3.54***	.27
Atheist	3.76***	.19	.18***	.38

NOTES: $N = 1,645$. Data were weighted. *$p < .05$, **$p < .01$, ***$p < .001$ (two-tailed tests).

Chapter 4

UNITED KINGDOM

TABLE A.3. Comparing the perceived relationship of science and religion among scientists in the United Kingdom.

RELATIONSHIP	MEN (%)	WOMEN (%)	PHYSICISTS (%)	BIOLOGISTS (%)	NONELITE (%)	ELITE (%)
Conflict, side of religion	0.2	0.3	0.0	0.3	0.6	0.1
Conflict, side of science	37.4	30.0	35.4	34.2	34.3	34.7
Conflict, unsure which side	0.1	0.3	0.2	0.2	0.5	0.1
Independence	42.5	53.8	46.4	47.0	40.8	48.2
Collaboration	13.2	9.2	13.0	11.1	13.8	11.2
Don't know	6.6	6.3	4.9	7.2	10.1	5.7
Total Respondents	847	684	768	763	539	992

NOTES: Based on weighted data. Values exclude nonresponse.
SOURCE: RASIC United Kingdom Survey 2014.

TABLE A.4. Multinomial logit modeling perceived relationship of science and religion among scientists in the United Kingdom.

INDEPENDENT VARIABLE	CONFLICT VS. INDEPENDENCE		COLLABORATION VS. INDEPENDENCE	
	ODDS RATIO	STANDARD ERROR	ODDS RATIO	STANDARD ERROR
Gender (female = 1)	.71	.21	.49*	.32
Discipline (biology = 1)	1.09	.21	1.12	.27
Status (elite = 1)	.95	.21	.68	.24
Rank 1 (reference)	—	—	—	—
Rank 2	.77	.25	.40**	.35
Rank 3	.88	.31	.27**	.40
Married	.70	.22	1.97	.34
Immigrant	.93	.21	.71	.29
Religiously affiliated	.31***	.27	3.50***	.32
Atheist	2.63***	.22	.56	.43

NOTES: $N = 1,410$. Data were weighted. $*p < .05$, $**p < .01$, $***p < .001$ (two-tailed tests).

Chapter 5

FRANCE

TABLE A.5. Comparing the perceived relationship of science and religion among scientists in France.

RELATIONSHIP	MEN (%)	WOMEN (%)	PHYSICISTS (%)	BIOLOGISTS (%)
Conflict, side of religion	0.0	0.0	0.0	0.0
Conflict, side of science	28.5	22.4	22.3	33.5
Conflict, unsure which side	0.2	0.2	0.1	0.0
Independence	55.4	62.3	58.4	55.0
Collaboration	6.6	7.4	8.2	4.3
Don't know	9.4	7.7	11.1	6.8
Total Respondents	337	327	330	344

NOTES: Based on weighted data. Values exclude nonresponse.
SOURCE: RASIC France Survey 2015.

TABLE A.6. Binary logistic regression modeling the conflict perspective.

INDEPENDENT VARIABLE	ODDS RATIO	STANDARD ERROR
Gender (female = 1)	.68	.24
Discipline (biology = 1)	2.43***	.25
Rank 1 (reference)	–	–
Rank 2	.60	.36
Rank 3	.68	.37
Married	1.05	.27
Immigrant	.93	.36
Religiously affiliated	.50*	.32
Atheist	3.04***	.29
Pseudo R-squared[a]	.10	

NOTES: $N = 648$. Data were weighted. Estimates based on listwise deletion of nonresponse. $*p < .05$, $**p < .01$, $***p < .001$ (two-tailed tests).
[a] Pseudo R-squared values were obtained by replicating the logistic procedure with the nonsurvey logistic command in Stata, considering the trimmed weights as "importance weights" rather than "sampling weights."

Chapter 6

ITALY

TABLE A.7. Religious and spiritual identity of scientists in Italy.

IDENTITY	%
Religious and spiritual (RAS)	15.9
Religious but not spiritual (RBNS)	29.0
Spiritual but not religious (SBNR)	9.6
Neither religious nor spiritual (NRNS)	32.6
Don't know	12.8
Total Respondents	1,322

NOTES: Based on weighted data. Values exclude nonresponse.
SOURCE: RASIC Italy Survey 2014.

TABLE A.8. Comparing the self-reported religiosity (independent of service attendance) of scientists in Italy.

RELIGIOUS IDENTITY	MEN (%)	WOMEN (%)	PHYSICISTS (%)	BIOLOGISTS (%)	NONELITE (%)	ELITE (%)
A very religious person	4.1	7.9	4.0	7.7	8.0	3.7
A moderately religious person	29.1	32.2	27.7	33.5	33.5	27.5
A slightly religious person	12.9	20.5	15.3	16.8	16.2	15.8
Not a religious person	16.2	17.2	18.6	14.7	15.7	17.9
An atheist	30.6	16.7	27.9	20.0	19.9	29.1
Don't know	7.0	5.6	6.5	7.2	7.8	6.0
Total Respondents	683	598	618	720	697	641

NOTES: Based on weighted data. Values exclude nonresponse.
SOURCE: RASIC Italy Survey 2014.

TABLE A.9. Comparing the perceived relationship of science and religion among scientists in Italy.

RELATIONSHIP	MEN (%)	WOMEN (%)	PHYSICISTS (%)	BIOLOGISTS (%)	NONELITE (%)	ELITE (%)
Conflict, side of religion	0.0	0.0	0.1	0.0	0.1	0
Conflict, side of science	21.0	21.2	23.8	17.2	15.8	25.2
Conflict, unsure which side	0.1	0.8	0.2	0.6	0.7	0.1
Independence	60.2	55.2	61.1	53.3	55.2	60.0
Collaboration	12.9	18.5	10.7	21.2	20.5	10.8
Don't know	5.9	4.3	4.1	7.7	7.7	4.0
Total Respondents	682	595	598	687	665	620

NOTES: Based on weighted data. Values exclude nonresponse.
SOURCE: RASIC Italy Survey 2014.

TABLE A.10. Multinomial logit modeling perceived relationship of science and religion among scientists in Italy.

INDEPENDENT VARIABLE	CONFLICT VS. INDEPENDENCE		COLLABORATION VS. INDEPENDENCE	
	ODDS RATIO	STANDARD ERROR	ODDS RATIO	STANDARD ERROR
Gender (female = 1)	1.17	.28	.68	.35
Discipline (biology = 1)	1.38	.25	2.27**	.30
Status (elite = 1)	.99	.24	.54*	.27
Rank 1 (reference)	–	–	–	–
Rank 2	.46*	.39	.44	.42
Rank 3	.43*	.34	.46	.48
Married	1.01	.32	1.72	.40
Immigrant	.58	.47	.56	.53
Religiously affiliated	.29***	.28	7.51***	.48
Atheist	3.06***	.29	.31	.64

NOTES: $N = 1{,}021$. Data were weighted. $*p < .05$, $**p < .01$, $***p < .001$ (two-tailed tests).

Chapter 7

TURKEY

TABLE A.11. Comparing the perceived impact of science on religion among scientists in Turkey.

IMPACT OF SCIENCE	MEN (%)	WOMEN (%)	PHYSICISTS (%)	BIOLOGISTS (%)	NONELITE (%)	ELITE (%)
Made you become much more religious	13.8	7.9	15.0	7.8	12.4	9.8
Made you become slightly more religious	16.8	14.6	17.4	16.1	21.5	12.3
Had no effect on how religious you are	43.8	58.8	48.0	51.6	51.6	48.5
Made you become slightly less religious	6.0	9.3	5.6	8.5	5.7	8.6
Made you become much less religious	19.5	9.4	13.9	16.0	8.7	20.8
Total Respondents	256	189	229	238	205	262

NOTES: Based on weighted data. Values exclude nonresponse.
SOURCE: RASIC Turkey Survey 2015.

TABLE A.12. Comparing the perceived relationship of science and religion among scientists in Turkey.

RELATIONSHIP	MEN (%)	WOMEN (%)	PHYSICISTS (%)	BIOLOGISTS (%)	NONELITE (%)	ELITE (%)
Conflict, side of religion	2.5	1.0	0.9	2.7	2.4	1.4
Conflict, side of science	28.6	17.8	18.0	29.5	17.1	30.9
Conflict, unsure which side	0.0	0.3	0.0	0.2	0.0	0.2
Independence	26.7	45.1	34.9	34.0	31.4	37.1
Collaboration	33.2	30.5	36.9	27.6	41.5	22.9
Don't know	8.9	5.3	9.3	6.1	7.6	7.5
Total Respondents	259	192	225	235	203	257

NOTES: Based on weighted data. Values exclude nonresponse.
SOURCE: RASIC Turkey Survey 2015.

TABLE A.13. Multinomial logit modeling perceived relationship of science and religion among scientists in Turkey.

INDEPENDENT VARIABLE	CONFLICT VS. INDEPENDENCE		COLLABORATION VS. INDEPENDENCE	
	ODDS RATIO	STANDARD ERROR	ODDS RATIO	STANDARD ERROR
Gender (female = 1)	.32**	.38	.61	.32
Discipline (biology = 1)	2.16*	.38	.81	.32
Status (elite = 1)	1.77	.35	.52*	.31
Rank 1 (reference)	—	—	—	—
Rank 2	1.97	.51	.64	.38
Rank 3	3.16*	.48	.45*	.39
Married	1.18	.43	1.34	.36
Immigrant	1.41	.87	1.41	.64
Religiously affiliated	.14***	.51	10.07**	.84
Atheist	8.90*	.95	5.23	1.45

NOTES: $N = 399$. Data were weighted. $*p < .05$, $**p < .01$, $***p < .001$ (two-tailed tests).

TABLE A.14. Religious and spiritual identity
of scientists in India.

IDENTITY	%
Religious and spiritual (RAS)	18.9
Religious but not spiritual (RBNS)	43.9
Spiritual but not religious (SBNR)	7.9
Neither religious nor spiritual (NRNS)	21.0
Don't know	8.3
Total Respondents	1,606

NOTES: Based on weighted data. Values exclude
nonresponse.
SOURCE: RASIC India Survey 2014.

TABLE A.15. Comparing the perceived relationship of science and religion among
scientists in India.

RELATIONSHIP	MEN (%)	WOMEN (%)	PHYSICISTS (%)	BIOLOGISTS (%)	NONELITE (%)	ELITE (%)
Conflict, side of religion	0.6	1.1	0.6	0.8	1.1	0.3
Conflict, side of science	21.1	12.3	19.5	17.0	17.9	18.3
Conflict, unsure which side	1.6	0.9	1.1	1.5	1.3	1.4
Independence	42.0	48.1	41.3	46.4	41.6	47.3
Collaboration	27.7	30.6	29.3	28.3	30.5	26.5
Don't know	7.0	7.1	8.2	6.1	7.5	6.4
Total Respondents	1,147	459	815	791	950	656

NOTES: Based on weighted data. Values exclude nonresponse.
SOURCE: RASIC India Survey 2014.

Multinomial logit modeling perceived relationship of science and religion among scientists in India.

INDEPENDENT VARIABLE	CONFLICT VS. INDEPENDENCE		COLLABORATION VS. INDEPENDENCE	
	ODDS RATIO	STANDARD ERROR	ODDS RATIO	STANDARD ERROR
Gender (female = 1)	.57*	.23	1.00	.18
Discipline (biology = 1)	.93	.20	.87	.16
Status (elite = 1)	.75	.19	.80	.16
Rank 1 (reference)	–	–	–	–
Rank 2	.68	.27	1.16	.21
Rank 3	.69	.27	1.20	.21
Married	1.24	.24	.77	.18
Immigrant	2.06	.94	2.36	.72
Religiously affiliated	.64	.41	4.51**	.47
Atheist	6.56***	.27	.81	.38

NOTES: $N = 1,448$. Data were weighted. $*p < .05$, $**p < .01$, $***p < .001$ (two-tailed tests).

Chapter 9

HONG KONG AND TAIWAN

TABLE A.17. Comparing the perceived relationship of science and religion among scientists in Hong Kong.

RELATIONSHIP	MEN (%)	WOMEN (%)	PHYSICISTS (%)	BIOLOGISTS (%)
Conflict, side of religion	0.4	0.0	0.0	0.5
Conflict, side of science	20.0	5.6	21.3	12.0
Conflict, unsure which side	0.9	2.1	1.0	1.3
Independence	40.4	52.2	46.4	41.3
Collaboration	24.4	22.9	14.1	31.5
Don't know	13.9	17.2	17.3	13.5
Total Respondents	239	44	152	138

NOTES: Based on weighted data. Values exclude nonresponse.
SOURCE: RASIC Hong Kong Survey 2014.

TABLE A.18. Comparing the perceived relationship of science and religion among scientists in Taiwan.

RELATIONSHIP	MEN (%)	WOMEN (%)	PHYSICISTS (%)	BIOLOGISTS (%)	NONELITE (%)	ELITE (%)
Conflict, side of religion	0.3	0.6	1.1	0.1	0.2	0.4
Conflict, side of science	9.2	7.0	10.4	7.9	4.7	10.1
Conflict, unsure which side	0.3	0.8	1.0	0.2	0.2	0.5
Independence	59.3	69.3	52.6	67.2	62.4	62.9
Collaboration	22.8	17.2	27.4	17.8	23.2	19.8
Don't know	8.1	5.2	7.6	6.8	9.2	6.3
Total Respondents	571	221	311	488	250	549

NOTES: Based on weighted data. Values exclude nonresponse.
SOURCE: RASIC Taiwan Survey 2015.

TABLE A.19. Multinomial logit modeling perceived relationship of science and religion among scientists in Hong Kong.

INDEPENDENT VARIABLE	CONFLICT VS. INDEPENDENCE		COLLABORATION VS. INDEPENDENCE	
	ODDS RATIO	STANDARD ERROR	ODDS RATIO	STANDARD ERROR
Gender (female = 1)	.28	.85	.42	.69
Discipline (biology = 1)	.76	.50	2.77*	.48
Rank 1 (reference)	–	–	–	–
Rank 2	.78	.65	.48	.73
Rank 3	1.31	.66	.77	.70
Married	.69	.61	.59	.61
Immigrant	.90	.51	2.10	.52
Religiously affiliated	.77	.51	5.30**	.47
Atheist	3.62*	.57	.29	.85

NOTES: $N = 228$. Data were weighted. $*p < .05$, $**p < .01$, $***p < .001$ (two-tailed tests).

TABLE A.20. Multinomial logit modeling perceived relationship of science and religion among scientists in Taiwan.

INDEPENDENT VARIABLE	CONFLICT VS. INDEPENDENCE		COLLABORATION VS. INDEPENDENCE	
	ODDS RATIO	STANDARD ERROR	ODDS RATIO	STANDARD ERROR
Gender (female = 1)	.75	.52	.73	.38
Discipline (biology = 1)	.81	.44	.44*	.33
Status (elite = 1)	1.54	.54	.68	.32
Rank 1 (reference)	–	–	–	–
Rank 2	.77	.62	.35	.56
Rank 3	.84	.57	.55	.57
Married	.68	.44	1.93	.51
Immigrant	.86	.52	1.24	.56
Religiously affiliated	.44	.43	2.76**	.30
Atheist	4.62**	.45	.07*	1.09

NOTES: $N = 706$. Data were weighted. $*p < .05$, $**p < .01$, $***p < .001$ (two-tailed tests).

APPENDIX B | Survey and Interview Sampling Procedures and Response Rates

T HIS BOOK IS BASED on data from the Religion Among Scientists in International Context (RASIC) study. The purpose of the study was to examine how scientists—specifically biologists and physicists—in different national and regional contexts encounter and engage with religion, as well as how their religious identities, practices, and beliefs influence their professional ethics and the role of gender, race, and family in the scientific enterprise. The study included a survey of 22,525 scientists in eight national and regional contexts: the United Kingdom, India, Italy, Hong Kong, Taiwan, the United States, France, and Turkey. Pilot interviews and sampling occurred over a two-year period between 2011 and 2012, and data collection related to the survey occurred between 2013 and 2015. Two independent global research firms, GfK NOP and Abt SRBI, were contracted to implement the surveys, while the research team conducted the in-depth interviews. We received a total of 9,422 survey responses and conducted 609 in-depth interviews with scientists. The survey achieved an overall response rate of 42 percent with region-specific response rates ranging from 39 percent (Turkey) to 57 percent (Italy and the United States).[1]

Members of our advisory boards also assisted with our research through their contributions. We consulted an advisory board of ten social scientists familiar with social science research in each national context in our study. We also consulted a separate advisory board of twenty-nine in-country natural scientists, which provided valuable information about the scientific landscape in each regional context, such as the relative prestige of research institutions in our sampling frame and the importance of endorsements from highly respected scientists for legitimating our research to potential respondents.

Sample Frame Construction

The research team constructed the sample frame—which we define as "the universe of scientists eligible to participate in the study"—through a two-stage process. At the first stage, we selected organizations, and at the second stage, we selected individual scientists. Generally, we stratified institutions by discipline (biology/physics) and status (elite/nonelite), and we stratified individuals in terms of career stage and gender. We then weighted the results of the survey so the profile of respondents matched the population in terms of institutional status, gender, and career stage, and took into account the process of oversampling.

We provide greater detail for both stages of sample frame population, stratification, and sampling in the sections that follow. We then discuss particularities in the sampling procedure, survey design, and interview data collection for each of the national or regional contexts in our study.

SAMPLING SCIENCE ORGANIZATIONS

The RASIC sampling process was designed to generate data that is representative of biologists and physicists at various career stages at "elite" and "nonelite" organizations in a variety of national contexts. The experience and expression of religion among scientists is nested within a social context, like universities within nations—which is to say that context could influence how scientists responded to our study. This meant that the first phase of sampling entailed identifying relevant research organizations in biology and physics, rather than simply identifying scientists themselves. We also sampled on organizations rather than individuals largely because organizational context heavily influences scientific careers. Organizations vary in many ways, particularly in terms of mission, prestige, norms and values, standards of achievement, and demographics. In addition, there are different conditions of practice that enable and constrain opportunities for research productivity. These conditions of practice include financial resources, such as startup funds and external funding, technological instrumentation, laboratory space, teaching loads, technical support staff, the number and quality of postdoctoral scientists and graduate students, and the doctoral and postdoctoral origins of colleagues. Scientists thus experience different opportunities for achievement, interaction, and rewards by virtue of the organizational context in which they work. We began collecting data nearly eighteen months before fielding the survey, starting with the development of a list of all organizations where biologists and physicists work in each of the eight national contexts in our study.

When selecting organizations from which to draw biologists, we typically excluded hospitals both because they generally emphasize clinical research and because of difficulties we encountered attempting to identify eligible scientists in these institutions. We did draw from medical schools when selecting biologists, provided scientists at the medical school worked in a field corresponding to our definition of biology. This definition includes a number of subfields, selected on the basis of definitions used by *Open Biology*, a peer-reviewed journal published by the Royal Society in the United Kingdom, and the National Research Council in the United States, with input from author Kirstin R. W. Matthews and other members of our research team and advisory board of natural scientists. For the purpose of this study, we included the following subfields in our definition of biology: cell biology, developmental biology, structural biology, molecular biology, biochemistry, neuroscience, immunology, microbiology, genetics, plant science/botany, animal-related research/ zoology, physiology, nutrition, ecology, evolution, infectious disease, and other very specific medical research (i.e., cancer, diabetes, etc.). We excluded any subfield outside of these listed categories, including areas of research that are sometimes included within biology but overlap with other disciplines, as well as the following subdisciplines:[2] biomaterials, bionanotechnology, pharmacology/pharmaceutical research, clinical trials, health sciences, translational biomedicine, mathematical biology, computation biology, agriculture and environment, and cognitive science. Given the interdisciplinary nature of these subfields, we thought it best to exclude them to avoid potentially having a sample that included scientists from disciplines quite different from biology.

Determining eligible organizations from which to draw physicists was more straightforward. In general, physics departments are clearly named and easily identified. We excluded ambiguous cases (i.e., materials science) and overtly interdisciplinary departments from the sampling frame. Across our regions of interest, we encountered departments that combined physics with other disciplines, such as astronomy, engineering, and earth sciences. When possible, we excluded scientists from these other related disciplines from the sampling frame and sample of scientists—especially if they were housed in distinct subunits within a mixed department—using information we gleaned from their doctoral degrees, courses taught, and publications. We did include astronomers from mixed physics and astronomy departments if they were not in a distinct "astronomy" division or academic cluster. If a department did not contain a majority of evident physicists, the department was excluded.

In each of the eight regions in our study, we first generated lists of research institutions for biology and physics using Thomson Reuter's Web of Science database. Importantly, we sought to include less-research-productive departments as well as research-intensive departments, which meant we could not rely solely on published ranking systems. Such rankings are generally biased toward larger research organizations and often include only universities, thus excluding other potentially relevant institutes. The Web of Science contains articles from more than 12,000 scientific journals worldwide—albeit mostly English-language journals, though they do make concerted efforts to include regional journals, which casts a wider net in terms of the range of research productivity. For each region, after an initial search for articles published between 2001 and 2011, we generated a list of up to 500 organizations (the most that Web of Science searches allow) with which authors of articles were affiliated, and ranked these organizations by the number of articles per institution. After aggregating different versions of names for the same institution to eliminate duplicates and removing schools and institutes from outside the regions of interest, sample frames for the larger nations generally contained about 200 to 300 organizations per discipline. This method yielded smaller lists for smaller regions, but the finished sample frames typically extended to organizations that publish frequently as well as those that publish very infrequently.

Representing the views of a range of scientists means sampling across a wide swath of universities and research institutions, including those not necessarily highly ranked or active in publishing research. Due to the cross-national nature of our study, however, creating a system for identifying relative institutional ranking proved difficult. A universally accepted system of ranking organizations across national contexts does not exist, nor does a governing bureaucracy to create such a list.

Had we simply relied on existing rankings, two problems would undermine our approach. First, our study would have lacked a universal sampling strategy due to variation in measures by different in-country ranking systems. For example, the US National Research Council and the Research Excellence Framework in the United Kingdom employ different measures to rank organizations. Second, relying on these rankings would not allow us to identify less-research-oriented institutions.

Therefore, to ensure inclusion of less-research-oriented institutions in the sample, we stratified institutions into "elite" and "nonelite" categories using a process of triangulation. That is, to classify organizations, we relied on three sources of information. First, we considered research productivity, as measured by Web of Science. While we assumed organizations with more publications are more elite, this measure alone was problematic for two reasons. Namely, we were unable to scale for the size of organizations, and the measure marginalizes high-quality organizations that might focus more on training activities than publication. To address the first issue, we added a second source of information: publication rankings. Here, we gave much more weight to local and discipline-specific rankings than to general cross-national rankings—using the latter only if no other information was available. To address the second issue, we also considered insider perspectives, our third source of information. Due to the difficulty of evaluating institutional quality from afar, and because neither research productivity nor publication rankings can capture every characteristic of an institution, we also consulted with members of our advisory board as well as scientists within each region of our study who were familiar with the scientific landscape in that region.

From the stratified lists of research institutions, we sampled enough elite and nonelite organizations to draw large enough samples of scientists to make statistically significant and theoretically interesting inferences about the sample frames. We aimed for the minimum number of organizations that would generate 2,000 scientists per discipline. The number of institutions needed to generate samples of this size varied widely by regional context, due to differences in the kind and size of organizations in each context. Since elite organizations are typically larger than non-elite organizations, we generally needed to select more non-elite organizations than elite organizations. When necessary, we included all organizations in a particular stratum; if it was obvious from the start that including every eligible organization in the sample frame would yield not much more than 2,000 scientists at most, we included every organization in the sampling frame. For instance, in Taiwan, we simply took a census of all biology organizations in our sampling frame because it was difficult to find pure "biology" departments in the region. Typically, however, we randomly sampled organizations until we had enough to populate a sample of 2,000 scientists per discipline. We randomly sorted the organizations and selected a few elite and a few nonelite organizations for the sampling frame. After constructing sampling frames of scientists from these preliminary organizations, we had a better sense of the size of elite and nonelite organizations, and continued to add organizations to the sampling frame as necessary to achieve our target number of scientists in the sampling frame of scientists.

In addition to ensuring representation by regional context, discipline, and institutional status, we also wanted our sampling frame to represent both male and female scientists at all stages of a scientific career. Within each sampled organization, we compiled a list of scientists as provided on relevant department websites, from which we identified both sex—that is, male, female, or unknown (gender identity was later self-classified on our survey)—and career stage. Generally, we conceptualized the career pipeline in terms of three distinct and consecutive phases, or "academic ranks." The first rank (Rank 1) comprises scientists in the training phase, such as graduate students (either at the doctoral or master's level). Rank 2 scientists are practicing scientists who have completed their training—earned a doctorate—such as postdoctoral fellows, early-career instructors, and tenure-track faculty members. Rank 3 scientists are practicing scientists in the advanced stages of their career, such as tenured professors. Due to regional differences in academic and research positions, operationalizing these concepts entailed some degree of variation. We include classification of nation-specific job titles in the sections that follow.

For each discipline in each region, we apportioned scientists into one of 12 strata defined in terms of institutional status, gender, and career stage:

2 institutional statuses (elite/non-elite) × *2 genders (male/female)*
× *3 academic ranks* = *12*

As mentioned earlier, we determined gender and rank based on scientist profiles on university and department websites. Scientists in the unknown gender strata were assigned to other, fully defined strata once they disclosed their gender upon taking the survey (we allowed for multiple gender classifications on the survey). In several nations, we had to create additional rank categories to capture scientists whose positions and titles were unclear or impossible to determine from their website listing.

Ideally, the sampling frame of scientists would include at least 100 scientists in each stratum, so that—assuming a response rate of 50 percent—we would have 50 responses for analysis. One hundred scientists in each of the 12 strata translated to a sampling frame of 1,200 scientists per discipline. However, we aimed for a larger sampling frame of scientists when possible for several reasons. The desired response rate of 50 percent was likely to be unattainable in many cases. Further, we anticipated that a number of scientists would prove unreachable because they had moved to a new institution or had incorrect or insufficient contact information listed online. Therefore, as a general rule, we attempted to compile a sampling frame of at least 2,000 scientists for each discipline in each nation if possible, for a total sampling frame size of 4,000 scientists per nation, aiming for approximately an equal number of scientists in each status-gender-rank stratum. In some of the national contexts, however, we were unable to achieve this number of scientists.

Because of extreme differences in gender representation among scientists, for example, especially at higher academic ranks and in physics, we often needed to draw scientists from many more organizations than otherwise would be necessary to construct a sampling frame of 2,000 scientists. The true constraint, therefore, is not the total sampling frame size, but the size of the smallest strata—typically those including Rank 3 female scientists. Thus, we continued to include organizations until there were approximately 167 (= 2,000/12) scientists in the stratum that was most difficult to populate (or less if there were unknown gender cases that might bolster the count in that stratum upon disclosure of the gender and reassignment of the scientist according to later self-classification). Target sample sizes were not always reached due to insufficient numbers of scientists in certain strata, in which case all scientists in that organization-level stratum were selected for inclusion.

While we did provide an option for respondents to take the survey by telephone, we intended for Internet-based surveys to be the primary mode of data collection for budgetary reasons. For practical reasons, then, we removed scientists from our sample frame who did not have e-mail addresses available on their department or university website. It tended to be graduate students who lacked contact information. Once we populated the sample frame of individual scientists, we provided contact details, including e-mail address, postal address, and phone number (if available), as listed on institutional websites, to a survey firm for data collection. GfK NOP (for the United Kingdom and India) and Abt SRBI (for the remaining regions) then administered online and telephone surveys, which we offered in both English and the official language of the country or region studied.

Qualitative Interview Sampling

We asked all survey respondents whether the research team at Rice University could contact them for a follow-up interview. We considered those who answered affirmatively as our interview sample frame, and we then mapped the overall geographic dispersion of possible interview candidates to identify cities/regions with a high concentration of interview candidates. Because religion was the central focus of the study, we prioritized stratifying the interview sample frame in terms of self-reported religiosity. Specifically, the survey asked, "Independent of whether you attend religious services or not, would you say you are . . . " with possible responses including 1 = "A very religious person," 2 = "A moderately religious person," 3 = "A slightly religious person," 4 = "Not a religious person," 5 = "A convinced atheist," and 6 = "Don't know." We identified respondents who selected either the first or second response as "religious," those who selected response 3 as "slightly religious," and those who selected response 4 or 5 as "nonreligious." We employed this approach for three reasons. In highly religious countries, such as Turkey, it would have been difficult to sample nonreligious scientists. In highly secular countries, such as France, it would have been difficult to sample religious scientists. Third, sampling those who are "slightly religious" ensured that the broadest range of religious views would be included. We also found that those who identify as "slightly religious" are more likely to be spiritual, and spirituality was another concept and quality we wanted to explore among scientists. Within these three categories of religiosity, we then attempted to maintain a balance among the other core analytic dimensions of discipline, organizational status, gender, and rank.

As with the survey, participants were offered the opportunity to conduct the interview in English or the official language of their country or region. In Appendix D, we provide a copy of the interview guide used in the United Kingdom. The wording and structure of this particular interview guide are characteristic of the protocols followed in all other regions. We departed from these protocols in only one instance. In France, we rearranged the sequence of the interview questions to begin with questions about ethics in the workplace before asking questions on religion. We believed that beginning an interview with questions about religion in this intensely secular context could have made scientists less open to speaking in detailed terms about their views of religion. By beginning with questions on ethics, we were able to facilitate conversation with ease before turning to what French scientists may have viewed as more difficult or threatening questions. Ultimately, like scientists in all the other countries in our study, scientists in France were quite open to speaking in depth about their views of religion. In the sections that follow, we identify specific challenges we faced in each of the national contexts we studied in the order we examined them.

Quantitative Data Collection in the United Kingdom

The United Kingdom was the first national context in which we surveyed scientists, and the process there differed from the other regions we studied in important ways. For one, instead of generating a sampling frame of *organizations*, in the United Kingdom we generated a sampling frame of *suborganizational units* (frequently departments at universities). Using the online Web of Science database, we downloaded citation information for all articles published in the United Kingdom from 2001 to 2011 in the disciplines of physics and biology. We then drew a random sample of 500 to 2,000 articles (depending on the region in the United Kingdom and the number of citations) and extracted department data from the articles, combining duplicate departments, to create a list of unique departments.

While often strongly correlated, university prestige and departmental prestige (a proxy for research intensity) do not always perfectly align. Consider an example from our own discipline of sociology in the United States. According to the 2017 *U.S. News & World Report* rankings of top universities, Yale University is the third-best university in the country. The same ranking system, however, places its sociology department at 22nd among the top nearly 100 graduate sociology programs offering doctorates. In an attempt to be thorough, we sought at the outset of the study to capture such a fine distinction by using the subjective rankings of our advisory board of in-country natural scientists. The Research Excellence Framework in the United Kingdom allowed us to examine discipline-specific rankings as a means of triangulating these insider rankings of departments. Yet, we could not identify discipline-specific rankings in all of the subsequent countries. Because of the strong correlation between departmental prestige and university prestige, and a stronger capacity to triangulate insider rankings at the university level, we abandoned sampling on departments after the United Kingdom. Also particular to the UK context, we further stratified the department sample frame by region (England, Northern Ireland, Scotland, Wales), resulting in sixteen first-stage strata: 2 disciplines (biology/physics) × 2 statuses (elite/nonelite) × 4 regions. We attempted to sample equal numbers of departments for each discipline and status, and to sample each region roughly in proportion to the total population of the region. Departments were then randomly sampled from within strata. Additionally, for both biology and physics, certain prestigious and large departments in the elite strata were sampled with probability of 1 (i.e., "with certainty").

Not all of the departments listed in the sampling frame were eligible. Many physicists in the United Kingdom are housed in a "Physics and Astronomy Department." If the department contained a subunit delineated for astronomy, we removed this subunit. In cases where the department was not parsed into smaller subunits or research groups, a sampling frame of scientists for the whole department was collected. While subunits and research groups are an integral part of the physics infrastructure, we discovered that research groups are not as important to the structure of biology. Biology departments in the United Kingdom typically provide a centralized online list of all department members, rather than dividing them by research group or theme. Typically, we included standard university departments as well as departments in hospitals associated with a university, while excluding scientists working in industry, museums, hospitals not associated with a university, or research institutes that do not grant doctorate degrees. A summary of organizational sampling in the United Kingdom is provided in Table B.1.

TABLE B.1. Sampling of institutions in the United Kingdom.

INSTITUTIONAL STRATA	SAMPLE FRAME	INELIGIBLE ORGANIZATIONS	SAMPLE FRAME OF ELIGIBLE ORGANIZATIONS	ORGANIZATION SAMPLE SIZE
England				
Elite biology	68	11	57	15
Nonelite biology	41	5	36	15
Elite physics	34	13	21	21
Nonelite physics	24	11	13	13
Northern Ireland				
Elite biology	4	0	4	1
Nonelite biology	2	2	0	0
Elite physics	1	0	1	1
Nonelite physics	1	1	0	0
Scotland				
Elite biology	16	2	14	1
Nonelite biology	10	0	10	1
Elite physics	8	5	3	1
Nonelite physics	13	9	4	1
Wales				
Elite biology	4	0	4	1
Nonelite biology	4	0	4	1
Elite physics	2	1	1	1
Nonelite physics	4	3	1	1

We determined individual-level career stage and gender based on scientist profiles on institutional websites and later self-classification. The three career stages included the following titles:

Rank 1: graduate students (i.e., postgraduates)

Rank 2: assistant professors, postdoctoral fellows, lecturers, readers, and research fellows/associates/assistants/academic staff with a PhD. The Rank 2 category acts as a catchall for scientists who have a PhD but do not have easily definable titles.

Rank 3: associate professors, full professors, Royal Society Fellows, "Named" Fellows, research fellows with prestigious grants (i.e., early-career grants), and "statutory professors"

Ineligible: emeritus professors, emeritus readers, emeritus lecturers, or others who have retired. We invalidated research fellows, assistants, and support staff who did not have doctorate degrees (unless these individuals were graduate students, in which case we classified them as Rank 1). Biology researchers with an MD but not a PhD were ineligible. Joint appointments or adjuncts were also considered ineligible unless their home department and university were drawn in the sample. Although rare, we also decided to invalidate individuals with titles akin to "research sister" and "research nurse," as found in biology, specifically medical schools. These individuals tend to conduct more clinical, patient-related work than research work. It was unclear to what extent these individuals are involved in the research process.

For departments where we could not contact graduate students due to lack of available contact information or student listings, we still sampled the Rank 2 and Rank 3 members of the department. We randomly assigned a gender to scientists for whom gender was unclear in proportion to the gender representation of each career-stage stratum in their particular department.

Pilot Cognitive Testing in the United Kingdom

Before implementing the full study, the UK data collection firm GfK NOP and Rice University administered a two-phase pilot study involving cognitive interviews followed by a quantitative pilot survey. The purpose of the pilot study was to test respondent understanding of questions and answer categories. Between July 29 and August 7, 2013, a total of 33 scientists participated in cognitive interviewing, generally split in terms of discipline, gender, and career stage. A total of 300 respondents from the sample frame were randomly selected to participate in the quantitative pilot study: 151 to complete the survey online, and 149 to complete the survey by telephone. From September 5 to September 9, 2013, a total of 48 scientists completed the survey, 30 online and 18 by telephone. The primary adjustment to the survey instrument due to results from the pilot study related to how long it was, as the initial version exceeded the length recommended by GfK NOP.

Data collection for the full survey occurred from September 19 to October 16, 2013. From the sample frame of 3,393 scientists, 1,604 scientists completed the survey. Of these, 1,581 were eligible scientists and 23 were ineligible. To boost response rate, we elected to provide a preincentive in the form of a £5 note sent along with a letter

TABLE B.2. Final dispositions for the UK survey sample.

CODE[a]	DISPOSITION	n
1.0	Interview	1,689
1.1	Completed Interview	1,581
2.0	Eligible noninterview	1,263
2.10	Refusal and break-off	1,202
2.11	Explicit Refusal	506
2.12	Implicit Refusal	118
2.3	Other	1
3.0	Unknown eligibility/noninterview	754
3.10	Nothing known about respondent/contact information	0
4.0	Ineligible	193

[a] Codes refer to the American Association for Public Opinion Research (AAPOR) disposition codes.

of appreciation. Table B.2 reports final dispositions for the UK sample. Taking into account postsurvey adjustments, we achieved a response rate of about 50 percent. The majority completed the survey online; less than 1 percent elected to complete the survey by phone.

Fellows of the Royal Society in the United Kingdom

We conducted a separate survey-based study nested within our broader survey to examine the views of Royal Society Fellows (RSFs), a prestigious collective of scientists who have made substantial contributions to the field. We compiled a census of RSFs residing in the United Kingdom from 2010 to 2013, excluding those who are part of the Commonwealth, honorary fellows, or international fellows. We also excluded RSFs who were not actively scientists, such as CEOs of corporations, and retired scientists. Unlike the main sample frame, we did not limit scientific disciplines to biology and physics. We classified all RSFs in the field of medicine, as well as neuroscientists and zoologists, under biology. As part of the main RASIC study, we sampled thirteen RSFs whom we coded as Rank 3 and excluded from the separate study. An additional forty RSFs completed the separate study, and we designated them as Rank 4. These scientists should not be considered when weighting the main sample of scientists.

Qualitative Data Collection in the United Kingdom

Of the 1,604 eligible and ineligible scientists who completed the survey, 643 agreed to be contacted by Rice University for a follow-up in-depth interview. The interview sample was made up of 295 women (46 percent) and 348 men (about 54 percent), and 415 of these scientists were at elite universities (65 percent) while 228 were at nonelite universities (35 percent). A total of 131 professors and 196 graduate students agreed to participate in interviews; the remainder of participants included postdoctoral scientists, lecturers, and readers.

The research team conducted 137 interviews (including 39 during the pilot stage), with about equal numbers in each of the three religious categories—nonreligious, slightly religious, and religious. Participants were also roughly equally split between the two disciplines, institutional statuses, and genders, as well as across career ranks. The scientists were evenly distributed across Central and Northern England, with small clusters in Scotland and Northern Ireland. Because of this geographic dispersion, in-person interviews were conducted only in three areas, characterized by a high density of respondents: London, OxBridge (Oxford and Cambridge), and the cluster of Coventry, Birmingham, and Leicester in the West and East Midlands region of England. Logistically, we struck a balance between maximizing in-person interviews and cost-effectiveness. We ultimately interviewed eighty-nine scientists in person (65 percent), thirty-three by telephone (24 percent), and fifteen by Skype (11 percent). All interviews were completed in English.

Quantitative Data Collection in India

In India, we sampled 119 organizations for physics and 53 organizations for biology (Table B.3). We did not take a census of organizations for either discipline but rather drew organizations until we reached a sampling frame population with a satisfactory number of female scientists, balancing this effort with time and labor constraints. The disproportionate number of organizations sampled in physics compared with those sampled in biology can be attributed to the dearth of senior (Rank 3) female scientists in physics.

At the individual level, we were unable to assign a gender for more than 1,000 scientists in our India sampling frame, largely due to a lack of cultural knowledge regarding naming conventions. We assigned career stages in accordance with the following:

Rank 1: graduate students (i.e., students seeking a PhD, MSc, MD/PhD, integrated PhD, or integrated MSc degree), junior research fellows without a PhD, senior research fellows without a PhD, and assistant professors without a PhD

Rank 2: assistant professors with a PhD, postdoctoral fellows, principle scientific officers, senior scientific officers, senior program officers, research assistants, research associates, research scholars, Scientists B-D, lecturers, readers, junior research fellows with a PhD, and senior research fellows with a PhD

Rank 3: associate professors, professors, senior professors, Scientists E-H, and heads of division

TABLE B.3. Sampling of institutions in India.

INSTITUTIONAL STRATA	SAMPLE FRAME	INELIGIBLE ORGANIZATIONS	SAMPLE FRAME OF ELIGIBLE ORGANIZATIONS	ORGANIZATION SAMPLE SIZE
Elite biology	34	4	30	19
Nonelite biology	252	33	219	34
Elite physics	27	5	22	20
Nonelite physics	193	70	123	99

TABLE B.4. Final dispositions for the Indian survey sample.

CODE[a]	DISPOSITION	n
1.0	Interview	1,763
1.1	Completed Interview	1,763
2.0	Eligible noninterview	1,115
2.10	Refusal and break-off	1,074
2.11	Explicit Refusal	311
2.12	Implicit Refusal	763
2.2	Noncontact	39
2.3	Other	2
3.0	Unknown eligibility/noninterview	1,265
3.10	Nothing known about respondent/ contact information	779
4.0	Ineligible	335

[a] Codes refer to the American Association for Public Opinion Research (AAPOR) disposition codes.

Ineligible: technicians, engineers, administration or support staff, emeritus or retired Rank 2 and Rank 3 positions, and adjuncts not housed in biology or physics

The survey field dates spanned from February 20 to April 21, 2014. Midway through the survey fieldwork period (largely because of low return of response to the survey), we began to offer a gift card to the Indian online store Flipkart worth Rs. 350 (approximately $5 US) as a reward for participating in the study. From a sample frame of 4,478 scientists, 1,763 scientists completed the survey. Table B.4 reports final dispositions of the sample collected in India. After adjusting for known and unknown eligibility, we yielded a response rate of 40 percent.

Indian Academy of Sciences Survey

There are three national academies in India that elect fellows who are roughly equivalent to Royal Society Fellows in the United Kingdom: the Indian National Science Academy in Delhi, the National Academy of Sciences in Allahabad, and the Indian Academy of Sciences (IAS) in Bangalore. In order to investigate perspectives associated with the most elite scientists in India, we identified among our survey respondents members of the IAS and designated them as such for analysis. Approximately eighty-four of our responding scientists in India were affiliated with the IAS and our sampling frame included an additional twenty-nine IAS scientists. We also conducted a census of the IAS scientists, excluding any scientist who has an affiliation with the IAS but is housed outside of India.

Qualitative Data Collection in India

Our research team conducted eighty in-depth interviews with scientists in India. For the most part, interviews were conducted in English, though two interviews included some degree of Sanskrit, Arabic, and Hindi. We conducted sixty-eight interviews in person (85 percent), six by telephone (7.5 percent), and six by Skype (7.5 percent). In-person interviews were conducted during two separate trips to India. During the first trip, made in March 2014, we interviewed eleven professors and graduate students, divided roughly equally in terms of gender and career rank—though eight of the interviews were with scientists in biology and only three were with scientists in physics. We offered all Indian respondents who participated in an interview, whether in person or by phone or Skype, a Rs. 500 gift card to Flipkart. A few participants declined to be sent the incentive. During the second trip, lasting ten days in May 2014, we completed forty-nine interviews in four cities across India, including large, urban areas and one rural town. Most of the institutions visited during the second trip were classified as "elite."

Quantitative Data Collection in Italy

In Italy, we found physicists are often housed in mixed departments that also contain mathematics, earth science, astronomy, and/or technology, and biologists are often situated within interdisciplinary departments, many of which overlap with medical departments. Further, some organizations had labs in multiple branch locations, which we attempted to identify as thoroughly as possible. All said, we sampled 38 institutions for biology and 38 for physics (Table B.5).

Some organizational websites in Italy list positions ambiguously or lack position information entirely. Thus, we added intermediate categories to the three standard career ranks. We therefore assigned career ranks in accordance with the following:

Rank 1: graduate students/*dottorando* (i.e., students seeking a PhD, MSc, or MD/PhD degree), technicians enrolled in graduate studies, *formazione*, (junior researchers), *specialiazzando* (clinical fellowship or training)

Rank 2: assistant professors, postdoctoral fellows, *assegno di ricerca* (nontenured researchers), *ricercatore* (researchers), *assegnista* (research associates), research scientists, and *borista* (fellows)

Rank 3: *professore associate* (associate professors), *professore orindario* (full professors), *primo ricercatore* (first researchers), senior researchers, and *dirigente di ricerca* (directors of research)

Rank 5: Not enough information to determine ranking. Position considered between ranks 1 and 2

TABLE B.5. Sampling of institutions in Italy.

INSTITUTIONAL STRATA	SAMPLE FRAME	INELIGIBLE ORGANIZATIONS	SAMPLE FRAME OF ELIGIBLE ORGANIZATIONS	ORGANIZATION SAMPLE SIZE
Elite biology	20	3	17	17
Nonelite biology	78	18	60	21
Elite physics	67	1	66	15
Nonelite physics	44	21	23	23

TABLE B.6. Final dispositions for the Italian survey sample.

CODE[a]	DISPOSITION	n
1.0	Interview	1,411
1.1	Completed Interview	1,411
2.0	Eligible noninterview	212
2.10	Refusal and break-off	200
2.11	Explicit Refusal	91
2.12	Implicit Refusal	109
2.3	Other	12
3.0	Unknown eligibility/noninterview	1,000
3.10	Nothing known about respondent/ contact information	1,000
4.0	Ineligible	249

[a] Codes refer to the American Association for Public Opinion Research (AAPOR) disposition codes.

Rank 6: Not enough information to determine ranking. Position considered between ranks 2 and 3 and usually has a PhD
Rank 7: Not enough information to determine ranking
Ineligible: *professore a contratto* (temporary appointments)

Surveys were fielded in Italy by Abt SRBI from June 9 to August 12, 2014. A total of 2,872 scientists populated the sample frame, and 1,411 scientists completed the survey. The response rate—adjusted for known and unknown eligibility—was 56.7 percent. Table B.6 provides a description of the final dispositions for the Italian sample.

Qualitative Data Collection in Italy

We conducted eighty-one in-depth interviews with scientists in Italy, fifty-nine of them in person (73 percent), eight by phone (10 percent), and fourteen by Skype (17 percent). In September 2014, we took two trips to Italy to conduct these interviews. During the first trip, we interviewed twenty-five Italian scientists in the cities of Rome, Florence, and Modena. During the second trip, additional interviews were performed in Milan, Pavia, Trieste, and Torino. Of the eighty-one interviews, fifty-eight were conducted entirely in English, twenty were conducted entirely in Italian, and three involved both English and Italian (including one that also contained some French).

Quantitative Data Collection in Hong Kong

Due to Hong Kong's size, the sampling frame for this region was relatively small. We therefore chose to take a census for our sample. Many of the organizations generated by the Web of Science process were centers or institutes that were part of larger organizations also listed by Web of Science. These suborganizations were removed from the sampling frame of organizations, but we still included scientists from these suborganizations in the sampling frame of scientists. In total, we sampled

TABLE B.7. Sampling of institutions in Hong Kong.

INSTITUTIONAL STRATA	SAMPLE FRAME	INELIGIBLE ORGANIZATIONS	SAMPLE FRAME OF ELIGIBLE ORGANIZATIONS	ORGANIZATION SAMPLE SIZE
Elite biology	6	0	6	6
Nonelite biology	10	9	1	1
Elite physics	6	0	6	6
Nonelite physics	19	19	0	0

seven biology organizations and six physics organizations, nearly all of which were considered "elite" (Table B.7). Most organizations classified as "nonelite" were invalidated during the sampling stage because they did not fit a definition of a valid organization. That is, we removed hospitals and companies that appeared in our sampling frame.

Names of scientists were drawn from English versions of Hong Kong organizational websites. Given that most Chinese names are only loosely gendered, we were typically unable to stratify by the gender of scientists. This did not prove problematic for sampling purposes, since we ended up taking a census of the contactable population. We defined three career stages in accordance with the following:

Rank 1: graduate students (i.e., students seeking a PhD, MSc, or MD/PhD degree) and research assistants without a PhD

Rank 2: assistant professors, postdoctoral fellows, research associates with a PhD, research assistants with a PhD, honorary professors, and research professors

Rank 3: associate professors, professors, and named chairs

Ineligible: technicians, engineers, administration or support staff, emeritus or retired Rank 2 and Rank 3 positions, adjuncts not housed in biology or physics, lecturers, teaching faculty, adjunct faculty

The survey was open from August 20 to November 21, 2014. All said, we compiled a sample frame of 919 scientists, and 326 scientists completed the survey (Table B.8). The adjusted response rate was 40.1 percent. While the survey completion numbers for Hong Kong (and Taiwan, see later) were lower than originally expected, we received feedback from regional experts that this is fairly typical of quantitative studies in these regions, and our response rates were actually higher than those of most surveys. We did, however, attempt to develop strategies to improve response rates as much as possible under the circumstances. In the final weeks of survey fieldwork in Hong Kong, we offered a postincentive to survey respondents, which took the form of a charitable donation of 38 HKD ($5 US) to the International Red Cross on behalf of the person who participated. The exact amount was chosen because the numbers 3 and 8 are auspicious in Chinese culture. Upon implementing the incentive, we observed that response rates did increase slightly.

TABLE B.8. Final dispositions for the Hong Kong survey sample.

CODE[a]	DISPOSITION	n
1.0	Interview	326
1.1	Completed Interview	326
2.0	Eligible noninterview	361
2.10	Refusal and break-off	359
2.11	Explicit Refusal	101
2.12	Implicit Refusal	258
2.3	Other	2
3.0	Unknown eligibility/noninterview	143
3.10	Nothing known about respondent/ contact information	143
4.0	Ineligible	89

[a] Codes refer to the American Association for Public Opinion Research (AAPOR) disposition codes.

Qualitative Data Collection in Hong Kong

A total of twenty-nine in-depth interviews were conducted in Hong Kong, twenty-four of them in person (83 percent) and five of them by telephone (17 percent). Nine of the in-person interviews were part of the pilot study, though we also conducted in-person interviews across Hong Kong during a trip in December 2014. We faced challenges securing participation due to the Umbrella Revolution protest movement[3] affecting universities around the region at the time and we were only able to interview fifteen scientists in person. Eight of the interviews were conducted entirely in Chinese, fifteen were conducted entirely in English, and six were conducted in both Chinese and English.

Quantitative Data Collection in Taiwan

Due to the limited number of organizations in Taiwan, we again took a census of the available physics and biology organizations in our sampling frame. Although we identified 58 nonelite physics organizations and 169 nonelite biology organizations in our sampling frame, we determined that most were ineligible (Table B.9).

TABLE B.9. Sampling of institutions in Taiwan.

INSTITUTIONAL STRATA	SAMPLE FRAME	INELIGIBLE ORGANIZATIONS	SAMPLE FRAME OF ELIGIBLE ORGANIZATIONS	ORGANIZATION SAMPLE SIZE
Elite biology	13	2	11	11
Nonelite biology	169	142	27	27
Elite physics	14	1	13	13
Nonelite physics	58	46	12	12

In this context, institutes of applied physics and biology were common, but research institutions focusing on fundamental physics or biology were rarer. Specifically, we invalidated many organizations because they did not have physics departments (instead, physics education was nested within engineering and technology departments). Similarly, we also invalidated a large number of hospitals and health professional prep organizations initially identified as biology departments, especially if they provided only healthcare or training services.

As in Hong Kong, we encountered substantial difficulty determining the gender of scientists from their institutional websites. That said, for both physics and biology, we needed to take a census of eligible scientists due to the limited number of eligible organizations. Three career stages were defined as follows:

Rank 1: graduate students (i.e., students seeking a PhD, MSc, or MD/PhD degree) and research assistants enrolled in graduate programs

Rank 2: postdoctoral fellows, research fellows, assistant professors, assistant investigators, and assistant research fellows

Rank 3: associate professors, professors, chaired professors, senior professors, investigators, associate investigators, distinguished investigators, and research fellows

Ineligible: technicians, engineers, administration or support staff, emeritus or retired Rank 2 and Rank 3 positions, lecturers, instructors, adjunct faculty, and adjunct associate professors and professors

The survey was fielded by Abt SRBI from July 31, 2014, to April 23, 2015. Because we initially experienced low rates of response, we decided to offer a postincentive of 388 TWD. The numeral eight, in Taiwan, represents prosperity, and 88 resembles the character for happiness; this amount had a positive meaning in this Chinese context and was in parity with the amount of incentive that we gave in the other societies in this study. Ultimately, we distributed 7-11 gift cards with a value of 400 TWD to 431 randomly selected scientists as an experiment to increase response rate. The incentive had a modest effect. That is, 27 percent of the sample not offered the incentive completed the survey compared with 33 percent of those who were offered the incentive. From a sample frame of 2,824 scientists, 892 scientists completed the survey, and the response rate adjusted for known and unknown eligibility was 39.2 percent. Final dispositions of the Taiwanese sample are represented in Table B.10.

Qualitative Data Collection in Taiwan

We conducted 52 in-depth interviews with scientists in Taiwan, forty-four in person (85 percent), seven by telephone (13 percent), and one by Skype (2 percent). We hired an in-country subcontractor who performed thirty in-person interviews during the fall of 2014 and the spring of 2015. To round out the interviews in this region and bring us closer to our target number, we also traveled to Taiwan for two weeks in early November 2014 and conducted almost twenty interviews in Taipei, Taichung City, and Tainan City. We conducted thirty-two interviews in Chinese only, eight in English only, and twelve in a combination of English and Chinese.

TABLE B.10. Final dispositions for the Taiwanese
survey sample.

CODE[a]	DISPOSITION	n
1.0	Interview	892
1.1	Completed Interview	892
2.0	Eligible noninterview	603
2.10	Refusal and break-off	434
2.11	Explicit Refusal	302
2.12	Implicit Refusal	132
2.3	Other	169
3.0	Unknown eligibility/noninterview	970
3.10	Nothing known about respondent/ contact information	970
4.0	Ineligible	359

[a] Codes refer to the American Association for Public Opinion
Research (AAPOR) disposition codes.

TABLE B.11. Sampling of institutions in the United States.

INSTITUTIONAL STRATA	SAMPLE FRAME	INELIGIBLE ORGANIZATIONS	SAMPLE FRAME OF ELIGIBLE ORGANIZATIONS	ORGANIZATION SAMPLE SIZE
Elite biology	44	2	42	11
Nonelite biology	245	2	243	15
Elite physics	40	0	40	17
Nonelite physics	174	8	166	35

Quantitative Data Collection in the United States

As with other regions, we used the Web of Science procedure to populate a sampling
frame of organizations in the United States. A few government agencies and health
centers were excluded, but on the whole, most organizations identified were eligible
(Table B.11).

We defined three career stages based on the following titles:

Rank 1: graduate students (i.e., students seeking a PhD, MSc, or MD/PhD degree),
junior research fellows without a PhD, senior research fellows without a PhD,
and assistant professors without a PhD

Rank 2: postdoctoral fellows, assistant professors, research professors, research
scientists, and researchers of all ranks unless housed at a nonuniversity institute (in which case they may be Rank 3)

Rank 3: associate professors and professors

TABLE B.12. Final dispositions for the US survey sample.

CODE[a]	DISPOSITION	n
1.0	Interview	1,989
1.1	Completed Interview	1,989
2.0	Eligible noninterview	361
2.10	Refusal and break-off	431
2.11	Explicit Refusal	187
2.12	Implicit Refusal	244
2.3	Other	13
3.0	Unknown eligibility/noninterview	1,202
3.10	Nothing known about respondent/ contact information	1,202
4.0	Ineligible	354

[a] Codes refer to the American Association for Public Opinion Research (AAPOR) disposition codes.

Ineligible: part-time scientists, technicians, engineers, administration or support staff, emeritus or retired Rank 2 and Rank 3 positions, lecturers, and doctors of medicine without a PhD

We delivered a sampling file containing names and information for 3,989 scientists to Abt SRBI. They fielded the survey in the United States between January 14 and March 23, 2015. We provided a $5 US preincentive to sampled individuals to encourage participation (this means that everyone we asked to participate in the survey received $5 in the mail). A total of 1,989 scientists completed the survey, yielding an adjusted response rate of 57.1 percent. Final dispositions for the US sample are represented in Table B.12.

Qualitative Data Collection in the United States

We conducted 100 in-depth interviews in the United States. Of these, we conducted fifty-five interviews in person, thirty-eight by telephone, and seven by Skype. Our research team conducted these interviews with US scientists during multiple trips. In-person interviews were conducted in North Carolina, Maryland, Texas, California, and New York. Phone interviews were conducted with scientists throughout the United States. We conducted these phone interviews in April and May 2015. The sample had an even number of male and female scientists; scientists in biology and physics; scientists at elite and nonelite institutions; and scientists at ranks 1, 2, and 3 career stages. In total, ninety-nine interviews were conducted in English and one was conducted in Chinese.

Quantitative Data Collection in France

In French universities, there is an academic profession consisting of tenured scholars who are "teaching only" academic staff or *enseignants-chercheurs*, those whose work includes both teaching and research. Scientific research in France is primarily organized through the Centre Nationale de la Recherche Scientifique (CNRS), a research organization that has approximately 26,000 staff members (of which 40 percent are full-time researchers) and about 1,300 laboratories. Importantly, most research occurs in CNRS "mixed research units" (UMRs) that bring together CNRS scientists and academic scientists.[4] The overlap between universities and research laboratories presented a significant sampling challenge because it is nearly impossible to know where a CNRS laboratory ends and a university begins. After much consultation with in-country experts and representatives of the CNRS, we elected to use physics and biology laboratories of the CNRS as our sampling frame for two key reasons. First, they account for most of the basic research in France in these two disciplines. Second, the CNRS has a directory that enables identification of all scientists working therein. Given that the CNRS is one nonhierarchical organization, this necessary sampling decision meant we were unable to sample on elite versus nonelite institutional status in France.

We populated a sampling frame of CNRS UMRs (which mix university and CNRS staff) and UPRs (*unités propres de recherche*, which exclusively employ CNRS staff) located primarily in the Institute of Physics, Institute of Nuclear Physics, and Institute of Biology. We randomly selected UMRs and UPRs to compile a sampling frame of scientists (Table B.13).

The CNRS directory classifies different types of researchers: CNRS researchers, non-CNRS researchers, CNRS engineers, non-CNRS engineers, and nonpermanent members. Based on consultations with representatives of the CNRS, we sampled on three categories of scientists to capture CNRS scientists, university faculty (professors and those with the title *maître de conférence*), and scientists in training (such as post-doctoral scientists):

Rank 1: nonpermanent researchers
Rank 2: non-CNRS researchers
Rank 3: CNRS researchers

Ineligible: retired scientists, engineers, doctors, managers, technicians, and visiting scientists

The survey was fielded by Abt SRBI from May 21 to July 19, 2015. We created a sample frame of 1,977 scientists, and 779 scientists completed the survey (Table B.14) for an adjusted response rate of 45.9 percent.

TABLE B.13. Sampling of institutions in France.

INSTITUTIONAL STRATA	SAMPLE FRAME	INELIGIBLE ORGANIZATIONS	SAMPLE FRAME OF ELIGIBLE ORGANIZATIONS	ORGANIZATION SAMPLE SIZE
Biology	36	0	36	36
Physics	42	0	42	42

TABLE B.14. Final dispositions for the French survey sample.

CODE[a]	DISPOSITION	n
1.0	Interview	779
1.1	Completed Interview	779
2.0	Eligible noninterview	401
2.10	Refusal and break-off	393
2.11	Explicit Refusal	125
2.12	Implicit Refusal	268
2.3	Other	8
3.0	Unknown eligibility/noninterview	601
3.10	Nothing known about respondent/ contact information	601
4.0	Ineligible	196

[a] Codes refer to the American Association for Public Opinion Research (AAPOR) disposition codes.

Qualitative Data Collection in France

We conducted a total of eighty in-depth interviews with French scientists from March 2012 through September 2015. Altogether, we carried out twenty-nine interviews in person (36 percent), thirty-nine interviews over the phone (49 percent), and twelve interviews via Skype (15 percent) during fall 2015. Although many scientists were reluctant to discuss the topic of religion with us, we were surprised at the overall willingness of French scientists to participate in an interview. Interviewers conducted thirty-eight interviews in French, allowing us to hear from scientists from more varied backgrounds than we might otherwise. Of the remaining interviews, thirty-nine were in English and three were mostly in English with some French.

Quantitative Data Collection in Turkey

After consolidating a list of organizations via the Web of Science database, we removed organizations not located in Turkey or that did not conduct some type of research, including social organizations, governmental health institutions, and the ministry of education. Ultimately, we sampled forty-seven biology organizations and thirty-eight physics organizations (Table B.15).

Early on, we determined that we would need to take a census of members from each of the selected biology departments, as these departments tended to be small and had few graduate students and postdoctoral fellows with an online presence. We classified scientists into the following career stages:

Rank 1: graduate students (i.e., students seeking a PhD, MSc, or MD/PhD degree) and *araştırma görevlileri* (research assistants) without a PhD
Rank 2: postdoctoral fellows, *yardımcı doçent öğretim* (assistant professors), *araştırma görevlileri* (research assistants) with a PhD, and *uzman*
Rank 3: *doçent öğretim* (associate professors) and *professor öğretim* (professors)

TABLE B.15. Sampling of institutions in Turkey.

INSTITUTIONAL STRATA	SAMPLE FRAME	INELIGIBLE ORGANIZATIONS	SAMPLE FRAME OF ELIGIBLE ORGANIZATIONS	ORGANIZATION SAMPLE SIZE
Elite biology	22	0	22	22
Non-elite biology	79	8	71	25
Elite physics	23	4	19	15
Non-elite physics	52	14	38	23

Ineligible: lecturers, instructors, part-time scientists, technicians, engineers, administration or support staff, emeritus or retired Rank 2 and Rank 3 positions, doctors of medicine without a PhD

During the period of data collection, Turkey faced considerable political unrest caused by controversial and increasingly stringent government policies, which possibly limited the success of our survey and interview fieldwork there.[5] Members of our advisory boards who are Turkish natives or had scholarly area studies experience in Turkey advised us that Turkish scientists would be hesitant to participate in an international study on religion, particularly one led by researchers outside Turkey if the impartiality or confidentiality of the study were in doubt. While we emphasized confidentiality and explicitly stated in our invitation letter that we were not affiliated with any government body, many Turkish scientists wrote to us saying they viewed the study with suspicion. Many objected to participation based on what they consider the private nature of religion, with one scientist[6] writing, "Thank you for your invitation. However I consider my moral and religious convictions to be in my private domain and consider answering questions on these issues inappropriate. Under these circumstances, I will not be able to participate in your survey."

Due to delays in presurvey setup, we were forced to launch the survey during the summer months of 2015—a time when many scientists would be on vacation or out of the country. The survey also happened to fall during Ramadan, the fasting season that many Muslims in Turkey observe. For this religious holiday, many adherents work alternate or reduced hours because of the physical and mental toll fasting takes. An initially low rate of participation reflected the realities of the social context. To account for these difficulties, we kept the survey open slightly longer than anticipated in order to ensure the highest participation rate possible. The survey was fielded by Abt SRBI from June 17 to October 5, 2015. Of the sample frame of 1,990 scientists, 684 scientists completed the survey (Table B.16). Our adjusted response rate in Turkey was 39.3 percent, an accomplishment given the number of unforeseen challenges in our final country.

Qualitative Data Collection in Turkey

Securing interviews in Turkey was particularly challenging due to the political climate at the time. As with the survey, Turkish scientists were especially reluctant to

TABLE B.16. Final dispositions for the Turkish survey sample.

CODE[a]	DISPOSITION	n
1.0	Interview	684
1.1	Completed Interview	684
2.0	Eligible noninterview	311
2.10	Refusal and break-off	300
2.11	Explicit Refusal	92
2.12	Implicit Refusal	208
2.3	Other	11
3.0	Unknown eligibility/noninterview	852
3.10	Nothing known about respondent/ contact information	852
4.0	Ineligible	143

[a] Codes refer to the American Association for Public Opinion Research (AAPOR) disposition codes.

participate and discuss the topic of religion with a non-Turkish researcher. We also had trouble reaching scientists during the summer vacation months, which meant we had to contact a much higher volume of respondents in Turkey than in the other regions of our study. Ultimately, we had to break from our standard procedure of contacting only scientists who had taken our survey and given permission for further contact because that pool of scientists was quite small. In addition to those who took our survey and gave us permission to reach out to them again, we also contacted other scientists in our sampling frame who had not been asked to take our survey, had not responded to our survey invitation, or had begun but not finished the survey (partial completes).

In all, we conducted fifty in-depth interviews with scientists in Turkey, thirty-two in person (64 percent), thirteen by phone (26 percent), and five by Skype (10 percent). In person interviews were conducted primarily during May 2015—in Ankara and in Istanbul. In total twenty-seven interviews were conducted in Turkish, one was mostly in English with some Turkish, and the remaining interviews were conducted in English.

Final Programmed Main Survey

ENGLISH QUESTIONNAIRE

Religion Among Scientists in International Context

In this survey we are interested in your experiences and opinions as a scientist. This is an academic research study designed by researchers at Rice University. The survey is conducted by the independent research organization Abt SRBI and will cover a variety of topics, reflecting our broad interest in the relationship between society and science.

Your responses will be kept strictly confidential by both Abt SBRI and Rice University. Your identity will not be disclosed in any findings disseminated from this study nor will your responses be associated with your institution in particular.

Please click "Continue" to begin the survey.

First, some general questions about your educational background and present-day work life.

CURRENTAFF: Current affiliation

CURRENTAFF. Are you currently affiliated with <Organization>?[1]

    <1> Yes
    <0> No (Please enter name of your current institution) {CURRENTAFF_TXT}[2]

PROFPOS: Professional position

PROFPOS. Which one of the following best describes your professional position?[3]

    <1> Graduate Student
    <2> Postdoctoral Fellow
    <3> Assistant Professor

<4> Associate Professor
<5> Full Professor
<6> Professor with named chair
<7> Other [specify]

TENURE: Permanence of position

[ASK IF PROFPOS > 2]

TENURE: Which of the following best describes the nature of your professional position?[4]

<1> My position is permanent (e.g., tenure or equivalent)
<2> I am moving toward a permanent position at this institution (e.g., tenure-track or equivalent)
<3> My position is on a finite or renewable contract basis (non-tenure-track)

PHDDISC1–PHDDISC4: Discipline of PhD granted

PHDDISC1–PHDDISC4. In what discipline did you receive a PhD (or an equivalent doctorate)? [RESPONDENT MAY NOT SELECT <0> AND <1>, <2>, OR <3>]

<0> I do not have a PhD (phddisc1 = 1)

You may select more than one of the following

<1> Biology   (phddisc2 = 1)
<2> Physics   (phddisc3 = 1)
<3> Other [specify]   (phddisc4 = 1){PHDDISC_TXT}[5]

CURRDISC1–CURRDISC4: Current discipline

CURRDISC1–CURRDISC4. Which one of the following best describes your main academic discipline currently?[6]

<1> Biology   (phddisc1 = 1)
<2> Physics   (phddisc2 = 1)
<3> Other previously mentioned (phddisc3 = 1)
<4> Other [specify]   (phddisc4 = 1)

PHDYEAR2–PHDYEAR4: Year PhD received

[ASK IF PHDDISC1 IS NOT EQUAL TO 1 OTHERWISE GO TO MD]

PHDYEAR2–PHDYEAR4: What year did you receive your PhD in [INSERT SUBJECT FROM PHDDISC2–PHDDISC4]?

<1> [specify] (Answer must be an integer from 1930 up until year of survey)
<3> PHDCNTRY2–PHDCNTRY4: Country of PhD

[ASK IF PHDDISC1 IS NOT EQUAL TO 1 OTHERWISE GO TO MD]

PHDCNTRY2–PHDCNTRY4: In what country did you receive your PhD in [INSERT SUBJECT FROM PHDDISC2–PHDDISC4]?[7]

<102> Austria
<103> Belgium
<106> Denmark
<108> Finland
<109> France
<110> Germany
<116> Greece
<117> Hungary
<119> Ireland
<120> Italy
<126> Netherlands
<127> Norway
<128> Poland
<129> Portugal
<134> Spain
<136> Sweden
<137> Switzerland
<139> England
<140> Scotland
<141> Wales
<142> Northern Ireland
<148> Czech Republic
<151> Croatia
<163> Russia
<207> China
<209> Hong Kong
<210> India
<212> Iran
<214> Israel
<215> Japan
<217> Korea
<226> Malaysia
<235> Saudi Arabia
<240> Taiwan
<243> Turkey
<301> Canada
<303> Mexico
<360> Argentina
<362> Brazil
<363> Chile

<414> Egypt
<449> South Africa
<501> Australia
  <515> New Zealand
<998> Other (specify)
<999> United States

MD: Medical doctor

MD. Do you have a medical degree such as a Doctor of Medicine (MD)?[8]

<1> Yes
<0> No

PUBS: Publications

PUBS. Please indicate the number of your writings (solo authored or coauthored) that have been published or have been accepted for publication within the past 3 years in refereed journals (not counting abstracts).

<0> 0
<1> 1 to 3
<2> 4 to 6
<3> 7 to 10
<4> 11 to 20
<5> 21 to 50
<6> 51 to 100
<7> 101 to 200
<8> More than 200

<3>*FUNDING: Research funding*

FUNDING. Which of the following best characterizes how much research funding you have had, in the past 3 years, relative to other researchers in your discipline at universities in the United States?

<1> No research funding
<2> Below average research funding
<3> Average research funding
<4> Above average research funding
<.d> Don't know

Turning now to some questions about your personal experiences as a scientist.

DSCR*: Experiences of Discrimination

DSCR. How often have you felt discriminated against in your work life as a scientist because of the following: [ITEMS AND THEN ASK]: Is that very often, often, sometimes, rarely, or never? [STATEMENTS RANDOMIZED]

(DSCRREG) Your regional background[9]
(DSCRRACE) Your ethnic background[10]

(DSCRLANG) Your language or accent[11]
(DSCRRLG) Your religion
(DSCRCASTE) Your caste[12]
(DSCRGNDR) Your sex or gender
(DSCRORGN) Your national origin
(DSCRMAR) Your marital status[13]
(DSCRSEX) Your sexual orientation (e.g., heterosexual, homosexual, bisexual)
  <1> Very often
  <2> Often
  <3> Sometimes
  <4> Rarely
  <5> Never

HRS: Hours worked per week

HRS. How many hours a week do you usually work as a scientist?

  <1> [Specify]

HRSPRF: Preferred hours of employment

HRSPRF. If you could work just the number of hours in paid employment that you would like, how many hours per week would that be?

  <1> [Specify]

TMALCACTL_0*: Actual time allocation

TMALCACTL. We would like to know the percentage of your work time devoted to undergraduate instructional activities, graduate instructional activities, research activities, and all other activities. If you are not sure, give your best estimate. The percentages should sum to 100. Zero is a valid answer. What percentage of your work time is usually devoted to . . .

  (TMALCACTL_01) Undergraduate instructional activities: [specify] percent
  (TMALCACTL_02) Postgraduate instructional activities: [specify] percent[14]
  (TMALCACTL_03) Research activities: [specify] percent
  (TMALCACTL_04) All other activities: [specify] percent

TMALCDSRD_0*: Desired time allocation

TMALCDSRD. We are interested in what would be your ideal work arrangement as a scientist. Thinking about the four categories just discussed, please report the percentage of your work time you would prefer to devote to the following activities. The percentages should sum to 100. Zero is a valid answer.

  (TMALCDSRD_01) Undergraduate instructional activities: [specify] percent
  (TMALCDSRD_02) Postgraduate instructional activities: [specify] percent[15]

(TMALCDSRD_03) Research activities: [specify] percent
(TMALCDSRD_04) All other activities: [specify] percent

ETHDIFF: I often face ethical difficulties

ETHDIFF. I have faced ethical difficulties in my work as a scientist. Do you . . .

    <1> Strongly agree
    <2> Somewhat agree
    <3> Have no opinion
    <4> Somewhat disagree
    <5> Strongly disagree
    <.d> Don't know

ETHTEXT: Ethical difficulties faced

[ASK IF ETHDIFF < 5]

    ETHTEXT. Please describe briefly in one or two sentences the kinds of ethical difficulties you have faced as a scientist:[16]

    <1> [specify]

SCIMORAL1–SCIMORAL2: Stem cell research[17]

Please indicate the extent to which you agree or disagree with the following statements.
    SCIMORAL1. Scientists should be able to create human embryos for medical research purposes.

    <1> Strongly agree
    <2> Somewhat agree
    <3> Have no opinion
    <4> Somewhat disagree
    <5> Strongly disagree
    <.d> Don't know

SCIMORAL2. The government should support research using cells derived from lab-created human embryos.

    <1> Strongly agree
    <2> Somewhat agree
    <3> Have no opinion
    <4> Somewhat disagree
    <5> Strongly disagree
    <.d> Don't know

Please answer the following questions about commercialization of science, by which we mean the conversion of scientific knowledge into technologies that can be sold.

COM: Commercial activities compromise

Please indicate the extent to which you agree or disagree with the following statement.

COM. The engagement of academic scientists in commercial activities harms a university's commitment to knowledge production. Do you . . .

<1> Strongly agree
<2> Somewhat agree
<3> Have no opinion
<4> Somewhat disagree
<5> Strongly disagree
<.d> Don't know

PTNTOPIC: Patenting and topic of research

PTNTOPIC. Please evaluate what you believe has been the overall impact of patenting activities by scientists with regard to the freedom to choose research topics according to scientific criteria. Would you say it has been . . .

<1> Very negative
<2> Somewhat negative
<3> No effect
<4> Somewhat positive
<5> Very positive
<.d> Don't know

PTNOPENSCI: Patenting and norms of open science

PTNOPENSCI Please evaluate what you believe has been the overall impact of patenting activities by scientists with regard to the norms of open science (i.e., freely sharing research with other scientists). Would you say it has been . . .

<1> Very negative
<2> Somewhat negative
<3> No effect
<4> Somewhat positive
<5> Very positive
<.d> Don't know

PTNT_N: How many patents

PTNT_N. How many patents, if any, do you have?

<1> [specify]

The following questions are about family and gender.

WORKTOFAM: Work-to-family conflict

WORKTOFAM. In the past three months, how often have you not had enough time for your family (however you define it) because of your job? Is that . . .

<1> Very often
<2> Often
<3> Sometimes
<4> Rarely
<5> Never
<.d> Don't know

FAMTOWORK: Family to work conflict

FAMTOWORK. In the past three months, how often have you not had enough time for your job because of your family? Is that . . .

<1> Very often
<2> Often
<3> Sometimes
<4> Rarely
<5> Never
<.d> Don't know

WOMANHOME: Better if man earns money and woman stays home

WOMANHOME. Please indicate the extent to which you agree or disagree with the following statement. It is much better for everyone involved if the man earns the money and the woman takes care of the home and children. Do you . . .

<1> Strongly agree
<2> Somewhat agree
<3> Have no opinion
<4> Somewhat disagree
<5> Strongly disagree
<.d> Don't know

Now a few questions about your opinions of the social composition of science . . .

WIS*: Women in science

WIS. Researchers have found that there are differences in the proportion of women and men in different science fields. For example, in most countries there are far fewer women in physics than in biology.

(Telephone: I am going to list) (Online: We have listed below) some possible explanations as to why there are differences in the proportion of women and men in different science fields. Please say whether you think each of the following explanations for this difference is true or false.

(WISABLTY) Women seem to have more natural ability in biology than in physics
(WISPRF) Women seem to prefer biology more than physics
(WISFND) There is a lot more funding support specifically for women in biology than in physics

(WISDSCRM) Women are discriminated against more in physics than in biology
(WISMNTRS) There are fewer mentors for women in physics than in biology

<1> True
<2> False
<.d> Don't Know

WISOTHR: Women in Science: Other

WISOTHR. Apart from the things already mentioned, is there anything else which you believe explains the fact that there are far fewer women in physics than in biology?

<1> Nothing else
<2> Other explanation(s) [specify] {WISOTHR_TXT}[18]
<.d> Don't know

Please answer the following questions about your research collaborations, i.e., working with other scientists in the course of conducting scientific research.

CLBPRC: Percentage of international collaborators

CLBPRC. Among collaborators you have worked with in the past 12 months, about what percentage of them were from institutions located in a different country?[19] Your best estimate is fine.

<1> I have not collaborated in the past 12 months
<2> None of my collaborators were from institutions located in a different country
<3> 1 to 25 percent
<4> 26 to 50 percent
<5> 51 to 75 percent
<6> 76 to 100 percent
<.d> Don't know

CLBPUBS: Publications with international collaborators

CLBPUBS. Please estimate what percentage of your publications is coauthored with scientists from institutions located in a different country?[20]

<0> I don't have any publications
<1> Zero percent
<2> 1 to 10 percent
<3> 11 to 25 percent
<4> 26 to 50 percent
<5> 51 to 75 percent
<6> 76 to 100 percent
<.d> Don't know

CLBIMP: Importance of international collaborators

CLBIMP. How important is it to your success as a scientist to try to collaborate with scientists from institutions located in a different country?[21]

<o> I'm not a researcher
<i> Very important
<2> Somewhat important
<3> Not very important
<4> Not at all important
<.d> Don't know

CLBBARYN: Experienced barriers to collaboration

CLBBARYN. Have you ever encountered any barriers to collaborating with scientists from institutions located in a different country?[22]

<i> Yes
<o> No [GO TO RLGAFF1]

BRCL*: Barriers to collaboration

[ASK IF CLBBARYN = 1. ALL OTHERS GO TO WORDING BEFORE RGLAFF1]
 BRCL. Have you encountered any of the following barriers to international collaboration? [STATEMENTS RANDOMIZED]

(brclvisa) Getting visas for myself or collaborators
(brclang) Language
(brclfnd) Funding for collaborative research
(brclclndr) My academic calendar is inconsistent with my collaborators
(brclfm) Separation from family and friends prevents international travel
(brclplt) Differences in political beliefs among collaborators makes collaboration difficult
(brclgndr) Gender discrimination
(brclsex) Discrimination because of my sexual orientation
(brclrlg) Religious differences among collaborators
(brcleth) Differences in ethical standards for scientific work
(brclintl) Differences in enforcement of intellectual property rights
(brclzone) Difficulty finding a time to communicate because of time zone differences
<i> Yes
<o> No
<.d> Don't Know

BRCLOTHR: Barrier to Collaboration: Other

[ASK IF CLBBARYN = 1. ALL OTHERS GO TO WORDING BEFORE RLGAFF1]
 BRCLOTHR. Have you experienced any other barriers to international collaboration?

<i> Yes [Specify—what were the barriers?] {BRCLOTHR_TXT}[23]
<o> No

Broadly speaking, this survey is interested in your views on science and society. Religion is a major part of society, so we'd like to ask you a few questions about your personal perspective on religion.

RLGAFF1: Religious affiliation

RLGAFF1. Do you belong to a religion or religious denomination? If yes, which one?

<0>	I do not belong to a religion	[GO TO ATTEND]
<1>	Roman Catholic	[GO TO RLGAFFCL]
<2>	Protestant	
<3>	Orthodox (Russian/Greek/etc.)	
<4>	Jew	
<5>	Muslim	
<6>	Hindu	
<7>	Buddhist	
<10>	Folk beliefs / folk religion	
<11>	Taoism	
<12>	Yiguan Dao	[GO TO RLGAFFCL]
<99>	Other [specify]	{RLGAFF1_TXT}[24]

RLGAFF2: Religious denomination

[ASK IF rlgaff1 > 1]
RLGAFF2. Do you belong to a particular denomination[25] within . . .

[INSERT "Protestantism"	IF RLGAFF1 = 2
INSERT "Orthodoxy"	IF RLGAFF1 = 3
INSERT "Judaism"	IF RLGAFF1 = 4
INSERT "Islam"	IF RLGAFF1 = 5
INSERT "Hinduism"	IF RLGAFF1 = 6
INSERT "Buddhism"	IF RLGAFF1 = 7
INSERT "folk religion"	IF RLGAFF1 = 10
INSERT "Taoism"	IF RLGAFF1 = 11
INSERT "Yiguan Dao"	IF RLGAFF1 = 12
INSERT "verbatim answer"	IF RLGAFF1 = 99]

<1> Yes [specify] {RLGAFF2_TXT}[26]
<0> No

RLGAFFCL: Religious affiliation: Conservative or Liberal

RLGAFFCL. Would you describe yourself as a conservative/traditional

[INSERT "Catholic"	IF RLGAFF1 = 1
INSERT "Protestant"	IF RLGAFF1 = 2
INSERT "Orthodox"	IF RLGAFF1 = 3
INSERT "Jew"	IF RLGAFF1 = 4
INSERT "Muslim"	IF RLGAFF1 = 5
INSERT "Hindu"	IF RLGAFF1 = 6
INSERT "Buddhist"	IF RLGAFF1 = 7

INSERT "folk religion"	IF RLGAFF1 = 10
INSERT "Taoism"	IF RLGAFF1 = 11
INSERT "Yiguan Dao"	IF RLGAFF1 = 12
INSERT "verbatim answer"	IF RLGAFF1 = 99

or a liberal/progressive . . .? PROBE IF NECESSARY: Is that very or somewhat . . .?

[INSERT "Catholic"	IF RLGAFF1 = 1
INSERT "Protestant"	IF RLGAFF1 = 2
INSERT "Orthodox"	IF RLGAFF1 = 3
INSERT "Jew"	IF RLGAFF1 = 4
INSERT "Muslim"	IF RLGAFF1 = 5
INSERT "Hindu"	IF RLGAFF1 = 6
INSERT "Buddhist"	IF RLGAFF1 = 7
INSERT "folk religion"	IF RLGAFF1 = 10
INSERT "Taoism"	IF RLGAFF1 = 11
INSERT "Yiguan Dao"	IF RLGAFF1 = 12
INSERT "verbatim answer"	IF RLGAFF1 = 99

- \<1\> Very conservative/traditional
- \<2\> Somewhat conservative/traditional
- \<3\> Somewhat liberal/progressive
- \<4\> Very liberal/progressive
- \<5\> The words conservative/traditional and liberal/progressive don't mean anything to me in this religious context
- \<.d\> Don't know

ATTEND: Attendance of religious services

ATTEND. Apart from weddings and funerals, about how often do you attend religious services these days?[27]

- \<1\> More than once a week
- \<2\> Once a week
- \<3\> Once a month
- \<4\> Only on special holy days
- \<5\> Once a year
- \<6\> Less often
- \<7\> Never, practically never

PRAY: Frequency of prayer

PRAY. Now thinking about the present, about how often do you pray?[28]

- \<1\> Never
- \<2\> Less than once a year
- \<3\> About once or twice a year
- \<4\> Several times a year

<5> About once a month
<6> 2–3 times a month
<7> Nearly every week
<8> Every week
<9> Several times a week
<10> Once a day
<11> Several times a day

MEDITATE: Meditation

MEDITATE. Do you currently practice any form of meditation?

<1> Yes
<0> No

RLGPERSN: Religious person

RLGPERSN. Independently of whether you attend religious services or not, would you say you are?

<1> A very religious person
<2> A moderately religious person
<3> A slightly religious person
<4> Not a religious person
<5> A convinced atheist[29]
<.d> Don't know

RLG_EXCL: Religious exclusivity

RLG_EXCL. Which of the following statements comes closest to your own views?

<1> There is very little truth in any religion
<2> There are basic truths in many religions
<3> There is truth only in one religion
<.d> Don't know

GOD: Belief in God[30]

GOD. Please indicate which statement below comes closest to expressing what you believe about God. Would you say . . .?

<1> I don't believe in God.
<2> I don't know whether there is a God and I don't believe there is any way to find out.
<3> I don't believe in a personal God, but I do believe in a Higher Power of some kind.
<4> I find myself believing in God some of the time, but not at others.
<5> While I have doubts, I feel that I do believe in God.
<6> I know God really exists and I have no doubts about it.

GOD1–GOD2: Belief in God or gods[31]

GOD1. Please indicate which statement below comes closest to expressing what you believe about God.

<1> I don't believe in any God or gods.
<2> I don't know whether there is a God or gods, and I don't believe there is any way to find out.
<3> I don't believe in a personal God, but I do believe in a Higher Power of some kind.
<4> I believe there is only one God.
<5> I believe there may be many gods.

[ASK IF GOD1 > 3]
  GOD2. Please indicate which statement comes closest to expressing what you believe about God or gods.

<1> I find myself believing in God/gods some of the time, but not at others.
<2> While I have doubts, I feel that I do believe in God/gods.
<3> I know God really exists (or that gods really exist) and I have no doubts about it.
<4> None of the above.

MIRACLES: God performs miracles

[ASK IF GOD > 1. IF GOD = 1 GO TO INSTRUCTION BEFORE BIBLE]
  MIRACLES. Please indicate the extent to which you agree or disagree with the following statement. God performs miracles. Do you . . .

<1> Strongly agree
<2> Somewhat agree
<3> Have no opinion
<4> Somewhat disagree
<5> Strongly disagree
<.d> Don't know

QURAN: Views on the Qur'an[32]

QURAN. Which of these statements comes closest to describing your feelings about the Qu'ran?

<1> The Qur'an is the actual word of God and is to be taken literally, word for word.
<2> The Qur'an is the inspired word of God but not everything should be taken literally, word for word.
<3> The Qur'an is an ancient book of fables, legends, history, and moral precepts recorded by Man.
<4> This does not apply to me.
<.d> Don't know

READQUR: Read Qur'an[33]

READQUR. How often have you read any of the following religious texts in the past 12 months? The Qur'an

- <1> Several times a day
- <2> Once a day
- <3> Several times a week
- <4> Once a week
- <5> Less than once a week
- <6> Never

BIBLE: Views on Bible[34]

[ASK IF RLGAFF1 = 1, 2, OR 3][35]

BIBLE. Which of these statements comes closest to describing your feelings about the Bible?

- <1> The Bible is the actual word of God and is to be taken literally, word for word.
- <2> The Bible is the inspired word of God but not everything should be taken literally, word for word.
- <3> The Bible is an ancient book of fables, legends, history, and moral precepts recorded by Man.
- <4> This does not apply to me.
- <.d> Don't know

READBIBLE: Read Bible[36]

[ASK IF RLGAFF = 1, 2, OR 3]

READBIBLE. How often have you read the Bible in the past 12 months?

- <1> Several times a day
- <2> Once a day
- <3> Several times a week
- <4> Once a week
- <5> Less than once a week
- <6> Never

READGITA: Read Bhagavad Gita[37]

READGITA. How often have you read any of the following religious texts in the past 12 months? The Bhagavad Gita

- <1> Several times a day
- <2> Once a day
- <3> Several times a week
- <4> Once a week
- <5> Less than once a week
- <6> Never

READVED: Read Vedas[38]

READVED. How often have you read any of the following religious texts in the past 12 months? The Vedas

- <1> Several times a day
- <2> Once a day
- <3> Several times a week
- <4> Once a week
- <5> Less than once a week
- <6> Never

READGUR: Read Guru Granth Sahib[39]

READGUR. How often have you read any of the following religious texts in the past 12 months? Guru Granth Sahib

- <1> Several times a day
- <2> Once a day
- <3> Several times a week
- <4> Once a week
- <5> Less than once a week
- <6> Never

READTAO: Read Tao Te Ching[40]

READTAO. How often have you read any of the following religious texts in the past 12 months? Tao Te Ching

- <1> Several times a day
- <2> Once a day
- <3> Several times a week
- <4> Once a week
- <5> Less than once a week
- <6> Never

READSUTRA: Read Buddhist Sutras[41]

READSUTRA. How often have you read any of the following religious texts in the past 12 months? Buddhist Sutras

- <1> Several times a day
- <2> Once a day
- <3> Several times a week
- <4> Once a week
- <5> Less than once a week
- <6> Never

READOTH: Read Other Religious Text[42]

READOTH. How often have you read any of the following religious texts in the past 12 months? Other religious text [specify] {READOTH_TXT}[43]

<1> Several times a day
<2> Once a day
<3> Several times a week
<4> Once a week
<5> Less than once a week
<6> Never

SPRTLTY: Spirituality versus religious

SPRTLTY. What best describes you?

<1> I follow a religion and consider myself to be a spiritual person interested in the sacred and the supernatural
<2> I follow a religion, but don't consider myself to be a spiritual person interested in the sacred and the supernatural
<3> I don't follow a religion, but consider myself to be a spiritual person interested in the sacred and the supernatural
<4> I don't follow a religion and don't consider myself to be a spiritual person interested in the sacred and the supernatural

The following questions ask about your religious beliefs and affiliation when you were 16 years old.

GOD16: Belief in God at age 16[44]

GOD16. Please indicate which statement below comes closest to expressing what you believed about God at age 16.

<1> I didn't believe in God
<2> I didn't know whether there is a God and I didn't believe there is any way to find out
<3> I didn't believe in a personal God, but I did believe in a Higher Power of some kind
<4> I found myself believing in God some of the time, but not at others
<5> While I had doubts, I felt that I did believe in God
<6> I knew God really exists and I had no doubts about it

GOD116–GOD216: Belief in God or gods at age 16[45]

GOD116. Please indicate which statement below comes closest to expressing what you believe about God at age 16.

<1> I didn't believe in God or gods.

<2> I didn't know whether there is a God or gods, and I didn't believe there is any way to find out.

<3> I didn't believe in a personal God, but I did believe in a Higher Power of some kind.

<4> I believed there is only one God.

<5> I believed there may be many gods.

[ASK IF GOD116 > 3]

GOD216. Please indicate which statement comes closest to expressing what you believed about God or gods at age 16.

<1> I found myself believing in God/gods some of the time, but not at others.

<2> While I had doubts, I felt that I did believe in God/gods.

<3> I knew God really exists (or that gods really exist) and I had no doubts about it.

<4> None of the above.

RLG16AFF1: Religious affiliation at age 16

RLG16AFF1. Did you belong to a religion or religious denomination at age 16? If yes, which one?

<0> I did not belong to a religion [GO TO RLGPERSN16]

<1> Roman Catholic [GO TO RLGPERSN16]

<2> Protestant

<3> Orthodox (Russian/Greek/etc.)

<4> Jew

<5> Muslim

<6> Hindu

<7> Buddhist

<10> Folk beliefs / folk religion

<11> Taoism

<12> Yiguan Dao

<99> Other [specify] {RLG16AFF1_TXT}[46]

RLG16AFF2: Religious denomination at age16

[ASK IF RLF16AFF1 > 1]

RLG16AFF2. At age 16, did you belong to a particular denomination within . . .

[INSERT "Protestantism"	IF RLG16AFF1 = 2
INSERT "Orthodoxy"	IF RLG16AFF1 = 3
INSERT "Judaism"	IF RLG16AFF1 = 4
INSERT "Islam"	IF RLG16AFF1 = 5
INSERT "Hinduism"	IF RLG16AFF1 = 6
INSERT "Buddhism"	IF RLG16AFF1 = 7
INSERT "folk religion"	IF RLG16AFF1 = 10
INSERT "Taoism"	IF RLG16AFF1 = 11

INSERT "Yiguan Dao"   IF RLG16AFF1 = 12
INSERT "verbatim answer" IF RLG16AFF1 = 99
INSERT "verbatim answer" IF RLG16AFF1= 99]

    <1> Yes [specify] {RLG16AFF2_TXT}[47]
    <0> No

RLGPERSN16: Religious person at age 16

RLGPERSN16. At age 16, independently of whether you attended religious services or not, would you have said you were . . .

    <1> A very religious person
    <2> A moderately religious person
    <3> A slightly religious person
    <4> Not a religious person
    <5> A convinced atheist[48]
    <.d> Don't know

SCIREL: Perceived impact of science on religion

SCIREL. Would you say that your scientific knowledge and training has . . .?

    <1> Made you become much more religious
    <2> Made you become slightly more religious
    <3> Had no effect on how religious you are
    <4> Made you become slightly less religious
    <5> Made you become much less religious

Please answer the following questions about your perspectives on religion and your professional life as a scientist.

RLGINFLINT: Religion influences interactions

[ASK IF RLGAFF1 > 0]

    RLGINFLINT. How strongly do you agree or disagree with the following statement: My spiritual or religious beliefs have a positive influence on how I interact with colleagues and students in my department. Do you . . .

    <1> Strongly agree
    <2> Somewhat agree
    <3> Have no opinion
    <4> Somewhat disagree
    <5> Strongly disagree
    <.d> Don't know

RLGOUT: Letting colleagues know about views on religion

RLGOUT. How comfortable would you be letting people in your department know about your views on religion (whatever those views may be)? Would you be . . .

<1> Very comfortable
<2> Somewhat comfortable
<3> Somewhat uncomfortable
<4> Very uncomfortable
<5> I have no views on religion

RLGPEERS: Religious peers

RLGPEERS. Please estimate the percentage of colleagues in your department who are very religious.

<0> Zero percent
<1> 1 to 20 percent
<2> 21 to 40 percent
<3> 41 to 60 percent
<4> 61 to 80 percent
<5> 81 to 100 percent
<.d> Don't know

RLGINFLCLGS: Research influenced by religious views

[ASK IF RLGPEERS > 0. OTHERWISE GO TO DPTCNFL]

RLGINFLCLGS. Now thinking about your religious colleagues, do you think that their religious views influence their research?

<1> No, because none of my religious colleagues are engaged in research
<2> No, their religious views do not influence their research
<3> Yes
<.d> Don't know

RLGINFLCLGS2: Research influenced positively or negatively

[ASK IF RLGINFLCLGS = 3]

RLGINFLCLGS2. In your opinion, do you think that their religious views positively or negatively influence their research?

<1> Positively influence
<2> Negatively influence
<.d> Don't know

DPTCNFL: Department conflict about religion

DPTCNFL. Have there ever been conflicts about religion in your department (that you are aware of)? [IF YES] Is that just once or twice, a few times, or many times?

<0> No
<1> Just once or twice
<2> A few times
<3> Many times

NEGRLG: Scholars have negative attitude toward religion

NEGRLG. Please indicate the extent to which you agree or disagree with the following statement. In general, I feel that scholars in my discipline have a negative attitude toward religion. Do you . . .

  <1> Strongly agree
  <2> Somewhat agree
  <3> Have no opinion
  <4> Somewhat disagree
  <5> Strongly disagree
<.d> Don't know

SCIRLG: Relationship of science and religion

SCIRLG. Please indicate which statement best represents you. For me personally, my understanding of science and religion can be described as a relationship of . . .

  <1> Conflict; I consider myself to be on the side of religion
  <2> Conflict; I consider myself to be on the side of science
  <3> Conflict; I am unsure which side I am on
  <4> Independence; they refer to different aspects of reality
  <5> Collaboration; each can be used to help support the other
<.d> Don't know

For each of the following statements, please indicate if it is true or false. If you don't know, you may indicate so.

EVLTN: Evolution

EVLTN. Human beings, as we know them today, developed from earlier species of animals.

  <1> True
  <o> False
<.d> Don't know

BIGBANG: Big bang

BIGBANG. The universe began with a huge explosion.

  <1> True
  <o> False
<.d> Don't know

Next, some questions about your personal values.

PVQ*: Personal values

PVQ. How much does each of the following statements sound like you? [ITEMS AND THEN ASK] Is it very much like you, like you, somewhat like you, a little like you, not like you, or not like you at all?

(pvqporich) I want to have a lot of money and expensive things.

(pvqunequ) I think it is important that every person in the world be treated equally. I believe everyone should have equal opportunities in life.

(pvqporspct) It is important to me to get respect from others. I want people to do what I say.

(pvqunlstn) It is important to me to listen to people who are different from me. Even when I disagree with them, I still want to understand them.

<1> Very much like me
<2> Like me
<3> Somewhat like me
<4> A little like me
<5> Not like me
<6> Not like me at all

And finally, please answer some basic questions about yourself.

GENDER: gender

GENDER. What is your gender?

<1> Female
<2> Male
<3> Transgender

YOB: Year of birth

YOB. What year were you born?

<1> 19[specify]

CNTRYORIGN: Country of origin

CNTRYORIGN. In what country did you spend the majority of your childhood, that is ages 16 or under? [49]

<100> Albania
<101> Andorra
<102> Austria
<103> Belgium
<104> Bulgaria
<105> Czechoslovakia
<106> Denmark
<107> Faroe Islands
<108> Finland
<109> France
<110> Germany
<115> Gibraltar
<116> Greece

<117> Hungary
<118> Iceland
<119> Ireland
<120> Italy
<121> Jan Meyan
<122> Liechtenstein
<123> Luxembourg
<124> Malta
<125> Monaco
<126> Netherlands
<127> Norway
<128> Poland
<129> Portugal
<130> Azores Islands
<131> Madeira Islands
<132> Romania
<133> San Marino
<134> Spain
<135> Svalbard
<136> Sweden
<137> Switzerland
<139> England
<140> Scotland
<141> Wales
<142> Northern Ireland
<143> Guernsey
<144> Jersey
<145> Isle of Man
<146> Vatican City
<147> Yugoslavia
<148> Czech Republic
<149> Slovakia
<150> Bosnia and Herzegovina
<151> Croatia
<152> Macedonia
<153> Slovenia
<154> Serbia
<155> Estonia
<156> Latvia
<157> Lithuania
<158> Armenia
<159> Azerbaijan
<160> Belarus
<161> Georgia
<162> Moldova
<163> Russia

<164> Ukraine
<165> USSR
<167> Kosovo
<168> Montenegro
<200> Afghanistan
<201> Bahrain
<202> Bangladesh
<203> Bhutan
<204> Brunei
<205> Myanmar (Burma)
<206> Cambodia
<207> China
<208> Cyprus
<209> Hong Kong
<210> India
<211> Indonesia
<212> Iran
<213> Iraq
<214> Israel
<215> Japan
<216> Jordan
<217> Korea
<218> Kazakhstan
<219> Kyrgyzstan
<220> South Korea
<221> North Korea
<222> Kuwait
<223> Laos
<224> Lebanon
<225> Macau
<226> Malaysia
<227> Maldives
<228> Mongolia
<229> Nepal
<230> Oman
<231> Pakistan
<232> Paracel Islands
<233> Philippines
<234> Qatar
<235> Saudi Arabia
<236> Singapore
<237> Spartley Islands
<238> Sri Lanka
<239> Syria
<240> Taiwan
<241> Tajikistan

<242> Thailand
<243> Turkey
<244> Turkmenistan
<245> United Arab Emirates
<246> Uzbekistan
<247> Vietnam
<248> Yemen
<250> East Timor
<300> Bermuda
<301> Canada
<302> Greenland
<303> Mexico
<304> St. Pierre & Miquelon
<310> Belize
<311> Costa Rica
<312> El Salvador
<313> Guatemala
<314> Honduras
<315> Nicaragua
<316> Panama
<320> Anguilla
<321> Antigua & Barbuda
<322> Aruba
<323> Bahamas
<324> Barbados
<325> British Virgin Islands
<326> Cayman Islands
<327> Cuba
<328> Dominica
<329> Dominican Republic
<330> Grenada
<331> Guadeloupe
<332> Haiti
<333> Jamaica
<334> Martinique
<335> Montserrat
<336> Netherlands Antilles
<337> St. Barthelemy
<338> St. Kitts-Nevis
<339> St. Lucia
<340> St. Vincent & the Grenadines
<341> Trinidad and Tobago
<342> Turks & Caicos Islands
<343> West Indies
<360> Argentina
<361> Bolivia

<362> Brazil
<363> Chile
<364> Colombia
<365> Ecuador
<366> Falkland Islands
<367> French Guiana
<368> Guyana
<369> Paraguay
<370> Peru
<371> Suriname
<372> Uruguay
<373> Venezuela
<400> Algeria
<401> Angola
<402> Benin
<403> Botswana
<404> British Indian Ocean Territory
<405> Burkina Faso
<406> Burundi
<407> Cameroon
<408> Cape Verde
<409> Central African Republic
<410> Chad
<411> Comoros
<412> Congo
<413> Djibouti
<414> Egypt
<415> Equatorial Guinea
<416> Ethiopia
<417> Eritrea
<418> Europa Island
<419> Gabon
<420> Gambia
<421> Ghana
<422> Glorioso Islands
<423> Guinea
<424> Guinea-Bissau
<425> Ivory Coast
<426> Juan de Nova Island
<427> Kenya
<428> Lesotho
<429> Liberia
<430> Libya
<431> Madagascar
<432> Malawi
<433> Mali

<434> Mauritania
<435> Mayotte
<436> Morocco
<437> Mozambique
<438> Namibia
<439> Niger
<440> Nigeria
<441> Reunion
<442> Rwanda
<443> Sao Tome & Principe
<444> Senegal
<445> Mauritius
<446> Seychelles
<447> Sierra Leone
<448> Somalia
<449> South Africa
<450> St. Helena
<451> Sudan
<452> Swaziland
<453> Tanzania
<454> Togo
<455> Tromelin Island
<456> Tunisia
<457> Uganda
<458> Western Sahara
<459> Democratic Republic of Congo (Zaire)
<460> Zambia
<461> Zimbabwe
<501> Australia
<502> Christmas Island, Indian Ocean
<505> Cook Islands
<506> Coral Sea Islands
<507> Heard & McDonald Islands
<508> Fiji
<509> French Polynesia
<510> Kiribati
<512> Micronesia
<513> Nauru
<514> New Caledonia
<515> New Zealand
<516> Niue
<517> Norfolk Island
<518> Palau
<519> Papua New Guinea
<520> Pitcairn Islands
<521> Solomon Islands

<522> Tokelau
<523> Tonga
<524> Tuvalu
<525> Vanuatu
<526> Wallis & Futuna Islands
<527> Samoa
<528> Oceania
<999> United States

PRNTEDU: Highest education level of mother or father
    PRNTEDU. What is the highest level of education your mother or father (or your primary caregiver during childhood) has attained? Please think of your parent with the highest level of education as you answer this question. [50]

<1> No formal education
<2> Incomplete primary school
<3> Complete primary school
<4> Incomplete secondary school: university-preparatory type
<5> Complete secondary school: university-preparatory type
<6> Some university-level education, without degree
<7> University-level education, with degree
<8> PhD or equivalent
<.d> Don't know

PRNTSCI: Was parent a scientist
PRNTSCI. Was at least one of your parents a scientist?

<1> Yes
<0> No
<.d> Don't know

HISP: Hispanic[51]
HISP. Are you of Hispanic, Latino, or Spanish origin?

<1> Yes
<0> No

ETHN: Ethnic group
ETHN. Please say which of these best describes your ethnicity.

<1> Black, African, Caribbean
<2> Caucasian, White, European
<3> Central Asian / Arab
<4> East Asian (Chinese, Japanese, Korean, Taiwanese,[52] etc.)
<5> South Asian (Indian, Pakistani, Bangladeshi, etc.)
<6> Other [Specify] {ethn_txt}[53]

POL: Political status

POL. In political matters, people talk of "the left" and "the right." Using a scale where "1" means "left" and "10" means "right," how would you place your views on this scale, generally speaking?

<1> Left
<2>
<3>
<4>
<5>
<6>
<7>
<8>
<9>
<10> Right

MAR: Marital status

MAR. Are you currently . . .

<1> Married
<2> Living together as married
<3> Divorced [GO TO KIDS]
<4> Separated [GO TO KIDS]
<5> Widowed [GO TO KIDS]
<6> Single [GO TO KIDS]

PRTOCC: Partner's occupation

[ASK IF MAR = 1/2. OTHERWISE GO TO KIDS]
PRTOCC. Which of the following best describes your spouse or partner's occupation?

<1> An academic scientist
<2> A nonacademic scientist
<3> Other
<4> Does not work for pay

RLGSPAFF1: Spouse religious affiliation

[ASK IF MAR = 1/2]
RLGSPAFF1. Does your spouse or partner belong to a religion or religious denomination? If yes, which one?

<0> Does not belong to a religion
<1> Roman Catholic
<2> Protestant
<3> Orthodox (Russian/Greek/etc.)
<4> Jew

<5> Muslim
<6> Hindu
<7> Buddhist
<10> Folk beliefs / folk religion
<11> Taoism
<12> Yiguan Dao
<99> Other [specify] {RLGSPAFF1_TXT}[54]

KIDS: Number of children

KIDS. How many children have you had?

<0> No children
<1> One child
<2> Two children
<3> Three children
<4> Four children
<5> Five children
<6> Six children
<7> Seven children
<8> Eight or more children

KIDSSCI: Fewer children because of science career

KIDSSCI. Please indicate the extent to which you agree or disagree with the following statement. I have had fewer children than I would have liked because I have pursued a career as a scientist. Do you . . .

<1> Strongly agree
<2> Somewhat agree
<3> Have no opinion
<4> Somewhat disagree
<5> Strongly disagree
<6> This question does not apply to me

KIDSHOME: Kids at home

[ASK IF KIDS > 0]

KIDSHOME. How many children (i.e., 18 years of age and under) are currently living in your household?

<0> No children
<1> One child
<2> Two children
<3> Three children
<4> Four children
<5> Five children
<6> Six children
<7> Seven children
<8> Eight or more children

KIDAGE: Age of youngest kid at home

[ASK IF KIDSHOME > 0. OTHERWISE GO TO SEXORNT]

KIDAGE. What is the age of the youngest child that is currently living in your household? Please round up to 1 if child is less than one year old.

    <1> [specify] year(s) old

KIDATND: Kids religious attendance

[ASK IF KIDSHOME > 0]

KIDATND. Apart from weddings and funerals, about how often does your youngest child attend religious services these days?[55]

    <1> More than once a week
    <2> Once a week
    <3> Once a month
    <4> Only on special holy days
    <5> Once a year
    <6> Less often
    <7> Never, practically never

SEXORNT: Sexual orientation

SEXORNT. Would you consider yourself to be . . .

    <1> Heterosexual
    <2> Bisexual
    <3> Homosexual
    <4> Other
    <.d> Don't know

INCOME: Individual income

INCOME. To better understand your overall experience as a scientist, we need to ask about your income. Please remember, all of your responses will be kept confidential.

In which of these groups did your total family income, from all sources, fall last year, before taxes, that is. Total income includes interest or dividends, rent, Social Security, other pensions, alimony or child support, unemployment compensation, public aid (welfare), armed forces or veteran's allotment.[56]

    <1> Less than $30,000
    <2> $30,000 to $34,999
    <3> $35,000 to $39,999
    <4> $40,000 to $49,999
    <5> $50,000 to $59,999
    <6> $60,000 to $74,999
    <7> $75,000 to $89,999
    <8> $90,000 to $109,999
    <9> $110,000 to $129,999

<10> $130,000 to $149,999
<11> $150,000 to $199,999
<12> $200,000 to $249,999
<13> $250,000 to $499,999
<14> $500,000 to $1,000,000
<15> More than $1,000,000

PERM: Permission for follow-up contact

PERM. Thank you very much for answering all of these questions.

We invite a portion of our respondents to take part in a conversation about these topics. Are you willing to be contacted?

<1> Yes
<0> No

CONTINFO: Contact information for follow-up

[ASK IF PERM = 1. OTHERWISE SKIP TO END]

CONTINFO. Please provide your e-mail address and telephone number for researchers from Rice University to contact you. The information you provide will be kept strictly confidential.

E-mail address: [TEXT ENTRY; CHECK FOR E-MAIL FORMATTING]

Telephone number: [TEXT ENTRY]

Alternate phone number: [TEXT ENTRY]

That is the end of the survey. Thank you very much for taking part. We are very grateful to you for contributing your time to this academic research.

For more information on the study, please visit the Scientists in International Context research initiative website at http://siic.rice.edu/.

APPENDIX D | Main Sample Interview Guide

Interview Guide for Religion Among Scientists in International Context Study

While the interview guide was adapted and translated for each national context, the template below is based on the interview guide used in the United Kingdom. We chose this interview guide as a template because it has the most overlap with the guides in other national contexts.

ACADEMIC AND RESEARCH BACKGROUND

1. To start, could you explain—as you might to a nonspecialist in just one or two sentences—the kind of research you are working on right now and the subfield of science you are in?

RELIGION AND SPIRITUALITY IN SCIENTISTS' WORK

As you know, part of what I am interested in studying is what scientists think about religion and spirituality.

2. Thinking for a moment about your own work as a scientist how does religion or spirituality come up, if at all?
3. How about in teaching? Does religion or spirituality come up at all in interactions with students or teaching? If so, in what kinds of ways? [*If interviewing postdocs ask about interactions with students or mentoring*].
    a. *Probe*: For example, how comfortable are you letting students in your department or institute know about your views on religion?
4. What kinds of informal ways do other scientists in your department talk about religion?
    a. *Probe*: We are trying to figure out the extent to which religion ever is a topic of conversation among colleagues in any kind of way. Do you ever have any casual conversations with colleagues about religion or religious issues?

b. *Probe*: How about more broadly within your discipline?
5. Can you think of a colleague in your area of science for whom religion or spirituality is important? How do you know religion is important to this person?
   a. *Probe*: [*If yes*] In what ways, if any, is the research of your religious colleagues influenced by their religious views?
6. Thinking more generally, to what extent do you see religious scientists as different from nonreligious scientists?

PERSONAL DEFINITION OF RELIGION AND SPIRITUALITY

Now I'd like to ask you about your own understanding of religion and spirituality.

7. Could you give me your working definition of what those terms mean? What is your working definition of "religion," for example?
   [*If the respondent appears to be having difficulties, stress that there are no wrong or right answers. We just want to know their thoughts.*]
8. How about spirituality? Do you have a working definition of the term "spirituality"?
   a. *Probe*: Do you see spirituality as something distinct from religion?
9. And while it may seem obvious, could you in just a few sentences give me your definition of science?
   a. [*If R doesn't understand:* I am interested in your own understanding of science. Can you tell me what that term means to you?]
10. Do you think there are any limits to what science can explain?
    a. *Probe*: How did you come to this position?

SCIENCE POLICY AND RELIGION

Thinking about your national context for a moment (*if the respondent is not a native of the country in which he or she is working then ask both about the country in which he/she is working as well as his/her country of origin*).

11. How does religion come up in conversations about government policies that relate to science?
    a. [*If no awareness*] So religion does not come up in any discussions about funding for science, what should be taught in schools, regulation of science, or national security?

PERSONAL RELATIONSHIP BETWEEN RELIGION AND SCIENCE

I'm also interested in the relationship between religion and your work as a scientist.

12. How does religion (or spirituality) influence the work you do as a scientist, if it does at all? [*If the respondent seems not to think that spirituality is at all relevant then do not mention anymore in the interview guide.*]
    a. *Probe*: Does religion influence your research goals? If so, how?

b. *Probe*: Does religion have any impact on your work with students? If so, how?

13. How about the opposite perspective, how has being a scientist influenced the way you think about religion, if it does at all?

14. Some say, "There is a conflict between being a scientist and being religious." How would you respond to such a statement?
    a. *Probe*: What do you think these people mean?

15. How about books or people? I am wondering if you have read any books or follow any thinkers who have influenced how you think about the religion–science interface?

RELIGIOUS HISTORY

I also have just a few questions about your own religious history.

16. In what ways was religion a part of your life as a child?
    a. *Probe*: In what ways was religion talked about in your family setting?

17. [*Can skip, if redundant.*] Thinking about the arc of your life so far, has there been a time when you experienced a religious shift? Please tell me about that.
    a. *Probe*: It could be a small or large shift from religious to nonreligious, or nonreligious to religious, do you recall ever experiencing such a change?
    b. *Probe*: How about the relationship between religion and science, has there been a shift in how you view the relationship between religion and science?

CURRENT RELIGIOUS IDENTITY, BELIEFS, AND PRACTICES

18. How about now for you personally, how would you describe the place of religion or spirituality in your life? [*Or: if they have already talked about the place of religion or spirituality in their lives, ask*: Do you have anything more to add about the place of religion or spirituality in your life now?]

19. What religious or spiritual beliefs do you hold? How about religious practices?

20. In what ways, if any, is religion a part of your family life now? [*Ask this question even if the respondent is not personally religious.*]

21. How do you answer the big questions of the meaning of life, such as why we are here, what is the meaning of my life? How do you find purpose?

22. Do you believe in God?
    a. *Probe*: Can you tell me a little bit about how you think about God or the concept of a God?

23. [*If no religious beliefs*] Do you believe in anything that is not readily observable?
    a. [*If R doesn't understand, restate*]: Do you have any beliefs about nonmaterial aspects of the world?

24. How about awe and beauty. Can you give me an example of any moments in your life when you have experienced a sense of awe, beauty, or wonder?
    a. *Probe*: How about in your scientific work. Are there occasions in your work that provoke these emotions?

Switching now to the topic of ethics, or what it means to be a responsible scientist.

25. Could you talk to me a bit about your sense of what it means to be a responsible scientist?

26. What does it mean—in your sense of things—for scientists to be responsible to the broader public?

27. Some scientists have mentioned philosophical or religious traditions as important to how they think about developing an ethical perspective toward science. Is anything like that significant for you?

RESEARCH INTEGRITY: OBSERVATIONS AND INTERVENTIONS

28. Without naming names, have you personally known about possible irresponsible or unethical conduct of a scientist? If so, tell me a little bit about that incident. *Note: If R references national/famous cases, ask: How about any cases that you know of personally or have observed?*
   [Be sure to probe about how they learned of the incident, the status of the participants, responses, and outcomes]

29. Thinking more broadly, under what conditions do you think researchers have an obligation to get personally involved in incidents of questionable or irresponsible scientific practices or things that happen in the scientific community that you think of as unethical?
   Note: If R is confused, say By "get personally involved" I mean, intervene in a way that tries to "make right" or rectify the misconduct.

WOMEN, FAMILY LIFE, AND SCIENCE

Another topic we are interested in is the connection between scientific work and family life. So I'd like to turn to some questions on those topics.

30. As you know there are more women in some disciplines of science than others, for instance, biology has more women than physics. Do you have a sense of why that might be the case?

31. Some people have a problem keeping work from infringing on their attention to family and nonwork interests. Is this generally a problem for you? When is it most problematic?

32. How about the way in which you balance time. Would you like to change the number of hours you work? [If yes] In what ways is this problematic and what would you have to change to achieve your preferred hours?

33. Do you think your career in science might have had an impact on your family choices? If so, how?

34. How about children, do you think being a scientist has had an impact on the number of children you've had, if it did at all?

35. Do you think it's more difficult for women than men to be a successful scientist? Could you tell me a little more about why you gave this particular answer?

36. Finally, I wonder if you are satisfied with your career?
    a. *Probe*: If you had to do it all over again, would you still pursue a career as an academic scientist?
    b. *Probe*: What do you find most meaningful about the work you do?

We're coming to the end, just a few more questions.

37. Just to make sure we covered everything, did anything I asked or didn't ask spark anything else you wanted to mention?
38. Just for the record, could I ask some questions about your demographics?
    a. What is your academic title?
    b. Where did you do your PhD work?
    c. Where did you do your postdoc work?
    d. What is your citizenship?

Thank you again for your time. I want to remind you that all your responses are confidential and a report of the research findings will be sent to you after the completion of the study.

NOTES

Chapter 1

1. For an in-depth analysis of why Americans do talk about evolution so much, see Numbers, Ronald L. 2006. *The Creationists: From Scientific Creationism to Intelligent Design*, expanded edition. Cambridge, MA: Harvard University Press. For a perspective on Hindu views, see Subbarayappa, B. V. 2011. "Indic Religions." Pp. 195–209 in *Science and Religion Around the World*, edited by J. H. Brooke and R. L. Numbers. New York: Oxford University Press.

2. For a detailed historical analysis of science and religion around the globe, see Brooke, John Hedley, and Ronald L. Numbers, eds. 2011. *Science and Religion Around the World*. New York: Oxford University Press.

3. Ecklund, Elaine Howard, and Elizabeth Long. 2011. "Scientists and Spirituality." *Sociology of Religion* 72(3):253–274. See also Wagner, Roger, and Andrew Briggs. 2016. *The Penultimate Curiosity: How Science Swims in the Slipstream of Ultimate Questions*. Oxford, UK: Oxford University Press.

4. While more recent studies show that scientists, who were perceived as carriers of secularization, may embody religiosity and spirituality, the picture is far more nuanced and complex than a simple linear version of secularism or not. See Ecklund, Elaine Howard. 2010. *Science vs. Religion: What Scientists Really Think*. New York: Oxford University Press; Di, Di, and Elaine Howard Ecklund. 2017. "Producing Sacredness and Defending Secularity: Faith in the Workplace of Taiwanese Scientists." *Socius: Sociological Research for a Dynamic World* 3:1–15; and Ecklund, Elaine Howard, David R. Johnson, Christopher P. Scheitle, Kirstin R. W. Matthews, and Steven W. Lewis. 2016. "Religion Among Scientists in International Context: A New Study of Scientists in Eight Regions." *Socius* 2:1–9.

5. As sociologist Stephen Kalberg explains, "Ideas are important causal forces of historical change, for Weber . . . only if they are 'carried' by demarcated and influential social groupings, strata, and organizations." See page lxxx of Weber, Max. 2002. *The Protestant Ethic and the Spirit of Capitalism*, 3rd edition. Translated by Stephen Kalberg. New York: Roxbury Publishing Company.

6. See Habermas, Jurgen. 2010. *An Awareness of What Is Missing: Faith and Reason in a Post-Secular Age*. Cambridge, UK: Polity Press; Keysar, Ariela, and Barry A. Kosmin, eds. 2008. *Secularism and Science in the 21st Century*. Hartford, CT: Institute for the Study of Secularism in Society and Culture; and Owen, David, and Tracy B. Strong, eds. 2004. *Max Weber, The Vocation Lectures: "Science as a Vocation," "Politics as a Vocation."* Indianapolis, IN: Hackett Publishing Company.

7. See Ecklund, Elaine Howard. 2010. *Science vs. Religion: What Scientists Really Think*. New York: Oxford University Press.

8. Leuba, James H. 1916. *The Belief in God and Immortality: A Psychological, Anthropological and Statistical Study*. Boston, MA: Sherman, French & Company; and Leuba, James H. 1934. *God or Man? A Study of the Value of God to Man*. London, UK: Kegan Paul, Trench & Trubner.

9. See also Larson, Edward, and Edward Witham. 1997. "Scientists Are Still Keeping the Faith." *Nature* 386(3):435–436; and Stirrat, Michael, and R. Elisabeth Cornwell. 2013. "Eminent Scientists Reject the Supernatural: A Survey of the Fellows of the Royal Society." *Evolution, Education and Outreach* 6(33):1–5.

10. Berger, for instance, argues that because modernity takes varying forms as it intersects with particular cultural histories, the lines between religion and secularity are often drawn in ways that differ from Western democracies. Berger, Peter L. 2014. *The Many Altars of Modernity: Toward a Paradigm for Religion in a Pluralist Age*. Berlin: Walter de Gruyter.

11. We had response rates ranging from 57.1 percent in the United States to 39.2 percent in Taiwan.

12. See Berger, Peter L., ed. 1999. *The Desecularization of the World: Resurgent Religion and World Politics*. Washington, DC: Ethics and Public Policy Center. See also Inglehart, Ronald F., and Pippa Norris. 2004. *Sacred and Secular: Reexamining the Secularization Thesis*. Cambridge, UK: Cambridge University Press; and Stolz, Jorg, and Oliver Favre. 2005. "The Evangelical Milieu: Defining Criteria and Reproduction Across the Generations." *Social Compass* 52(2):169–183.

13. See Dawkins, Richard. 2008. *The God Delusion*. New York: Houghton Mifflin Company. See also McGrath, Alister, and Joanna Collicutt McGrath. 2010. *The Dawkins Delusion? Atheist Fundamentalism and the Denial of the Divine*. Downers Grove, IL: InterVarsity Press; and Polkinghorne, John C. 1998. *Science and Theology: An Introduction*. Minneapolis, MN: Fortress Press.

14. See Pew Research Center. 2015. "Extremism Concerns Growing in West and Predominantly Muslim Countries." Retrieved May 1, 2018 (http://www.pewglobal.org/2015/07/16/extremism-concerns-growing-in-west-and-predominantly-muslim-countries/).

15. Kuru, Ahmet T. 2009. *Secularism and State Policies Toward Religion: The United States, France, and Turkey*. Cambridge, UK: Cambridge University Press.

16. See page 3 of Garelli, Franco. 2014. *Religion Italian Style: Continuities and Changes in a Catholic Country*. Farnham, UK: Ashgate Publishing.

17. See Pace, Enzo. 2006. "Religion as Communication: The Changing Shape of Catholicism in Europe." Pp. 37–50 in *Everyday Religion: Observing Modern Religious Lives*, edited by N. T. Ammerman. New York: Oxford University Press.

18. RASIC_HK08, physics, male, professor, conducted 12/16/14

19. See Ecklund, Elaine Howard. 2010. *Science vs. Religion: What Scientists Really Think*. New York: Oxford University Press.

Chapter 2

1. See page 383 of Tylor, Edward B. 1871. *Primitive Culture: Researches into the Development of Mythology, Philosophy, Religion, Art, and Custom, Vol 1*. London: John Murray.

2. See page 85 of Spencer, Herbert. 1904. *First Principles*. New York: J. A. Hill & Co.

3. See page 197 of Ross, Edward A. 1901. *Social Control: A Survey of the Foundations of Order*. New York: Macmillan.

4. RASIC_UK39, biology, female, professor, conducted 12/6/13

5. RASIC_IND01, biology, female, PhD student, conducted 3/13/14

6. RASIC_UK41, biology, male, lecturer, conducted 12/6/13

7. RASIC_IND05, biology, male, professor, conducted 3/16/14

8. RASIC_TW04, biology, male, research fellow, conducted 10/24/14

9. RASIC_UK02, biology, male, graduate student, conducted 11/26/13

10. RASIC_IND62, physics, male, graduate student, conducted 5/28/14

11. RASIC_TW31, physics, male, PhD student, conducted 11/21/14

12. See page 47 of Durkheim, Emile. 1915. *The Elementary Forms of the Religious Life*. New York: Free Press.

13. See page 372 of Cooley, Charles H. 1909. *Social Organization*. New York: Charles Scribner's Sons.

14. RASIC_IND29, biology, male, associate professor, conducted 5/22/14

15. RASIC_IND71, biology, male, professor, conducted 9/3/14

16. RASIC_TW41, biology, male, assistant research fellow, conducted 1/13/14

17. RASIC_TK31, physics, male, associate professor, conducted 7/10/15

18. RASIC_UK04, physics, male, postdoctoral fellow, conducted 12/2/13

19. RASIC_UK08, biology, male, professor, conducted 12/2/13

20. Riesebrodt, Martin. 2010. *The Promise of Salvation: A Theory of Religion*. Chicago, IL: University of Chicago Press; Smith, Christian. 2017. *Religion: What It Is, How It Works, and Why It Matters*. Princeton, NJ: Princeton University Press.

21. RASIC_TW41, biology, male, assistant research fellow, conducted 1/13/14

22. Dubuisson, Daniel. 2003. *The Western Construction of Religion: Myths, Knowledge, and Ideology*. Baltimore, MD: John Hopkins University Press; McCutcheon, Russell T. 1997. *Manufacturing Religion: The Discourse on Sui Generis Religion and the Politics of Nostalgia*. New York: Oxford University Press; Fitzgerald, Timothy. 2003. *The Ideology of Religious Studies*. New York: Oxford University Press.

23. Schilbrack, Kevin. 2010. "Religions: Are There Any?" *Journal of the American Academy of Religion* 78(4):1112–1138.

24. See page 66 of Hill, Peter C., Kenneth I. Pargament, Ralph W. Hood, Michael E. McCullough Jr, James P. Swyers, David B. Larson, and Brian J. Zinnbauer. 2000. "Conceptualizing Religion and Spirituality: Points of Commonality, Points of Departure." *Journal for the Theory of Social Behaviour* 30(1):51–77.

25. RASIC_UK62, physics, female, unpaid affiliate, conducted 4/14/14

26. RASIC_UK02, biology, male, graduate student, conducted 11/26/13

27. RASIC_TW07, physics, male, assistant research scientist, conducted 11/3/14

28. RASIC_IND12, biology, female, PhD student, conducted 4/23/14

29. RASIC_UK45, biology, female, professor, conducted 12/6/13

30. RASIC_TW27, biology, male, professor, conducted 11/13/14

31. RASIC_IND05, biology, male, professor, conducted 3/16/14

32. RASIC_UK04, physics, male, postdoctoral fellow, conducted 12/2/13

33. RASIC_UK02, biology, male, graduate student, conducted 11/26/13

34. RASIC_TW07, physics, male, assistant research scientist, conducted 11/3/14

35. RASIC_TK32, biology, male, assistant professor, conducted 7/13/15

36. RASIC_IND35, biology, male, assistant professor, conducted 5/23/14

37. Fanelli, Daniele. 2010. "'Positive Results Increase Down the Hierarchy of the Sciences." *PLoS ONE* 5(4):e10068.

38. Wall, Mike. 2018. "Stephen Hawking to Be Interred in Westminster Abbey," *Scientific American*, March 21.

39. See Peterson, Gregory R. 2003. "Demarcation and the Scientistic Fallacy." *Zygon: Journal of Religion and Science* 38:751–761.

40. Some have argued to us that chemistry belonged in our study; most philosophers and sociologists of science, as well as scientists themselves, would view chemistry as a core natural science discipline as well as place it near the top in the hierarchy of disciplines. Given the aims of our study—namely to better understand what scientists think about religion—and the present and historic religious debates about evolutionary theory, we chose to include biology, rather than chemistry. However we should also note that such debates involving biology are a more recent historical phenomenon. For a much more extensive treatment of the development of debates about evolution, see Numbers, Ronald L. 2006. *The Creationists: From Scientific Creationism to Intelligent Design*, expanded edition. Cambridge, MA: Harvard University Press. For an excellent treatment of historical myths surrounding religion and science, see Numbers, Ronald, ed. 2009. *Galileo Goes to Jail: And Other Myths About Science and Religion*. Cambridge, MA: Harvard University Press.

41. Mehta, Sharan Kaur, Elaine Howard Ecklund, and Bob Thomson. 2017. "The Intersection of Gender with Religion and Science." Paper Presented at the Annual Meeting of the Society for the Scientific Study of Religion, October 14, Washington, DC.

42. Scott, Eugenie C. 1997. "Antievolution and Creationism in the United States." *Annual Review of Anthropology* 26:263–289. See also BioLogos. "BioLogos." Retrieved May 3, 2018 (https://biologos.org/), which presents an "evolutionary understanding of God's creation." BioLogos is an organization started by Francis Collins, former head of the Human Genome Project and, at the time of this writing, head of the National Institutes of Health.

43. See Evans, John H. 2018. *Morals Not Knowledge: Recasting the Contemporary U.S. Conflict Between Religion and Science*. Oakland: University of California Press, particularly pages 131–134, where Evans examines the commitment that some groups of conservative Protestants may have to an implicit Baconian science, which stresses fact claims based on the observable.

44. See Evans, John H. 2016. *What Is a Human? What the Answers Mean for Human Rights*. New York: Oxford University Press.

45. See Dooley, James, and Helen Kerch. 2000. "Evolving Research Misconduct Policies and Their Significance for Physical Scientists." *Science and Engineering Ethics* 6(1):109–121. See also Gusterson, Hugh. 2001. "The Virtual Nuclear Weapons Laboratory in the New World Order." *American Ethnologist* 28(2):417–437.

46. Naughton, Barry, ed. 1997. *The China Circle: Economic and Technology in the PRC, Taiwan, and Hong Kong.* Washington, DC: Brookings Institute Press.

47. Ecklund, Elaine Howard, David R. Johnson, Christopher P. Scheitle, Kirstin R. W. Matthews, and Steven W. Lewis. 2016. "Religion Among Scientists in International Context: A New Study of Scientists in Eight Regions." *Socius* 2:1–9.

48. See, for example: Ecklund, Elaine Howard, David R. Johnson, and Kirstin R. W. Matthews. 2016. "Opinion: Turkey's Scientists Under Pressure," *The Scientist*, September 14; Kaiman, Jonathan. 2014. "Hong Kong's Umbrella Revolution—The Guardian Briefing," *The Guardian*, September 30; and Phillips, Tom. 2015. "Hong Kong 'Umbrella Movement' Marks First Anniversary and Vows to Fight On," *The Guardian*, September 28.

49. See also the work of Guy Consolmangno: Ash, Summer. 2016. "Guy Consolmangno, the Vatican's Chief Astronomer, on Balancing Church with the Cosmos," *Smithsonian*, May 31.

50. See Beckford, Martin. 2010. "Atheists Are Wrong to Claim Science and Religion are Incompatible, Church of England Says," *The Telegraph*, February 12.

51. See again Ecklund, Elaine Howard, David R. Johnson, and Kirstin R. W. Matthews. 2016. "Opinion: Turkey's Scientists Under Pressure," *The Scientist*, September 14.

52. Gould, Stephen Jay. 1997. "Nonoverlapping Magisteria." *Natural History* 106:16–22.

53. Casanova, José. 2008. "Public Religions Revisited." Pp. 101–119 in *Religion: Beyond a Concept*, edited by H. DeVries. New York: Fordham University Press.

54. See Scheitle, Christopher P. 2011. "Religious and Spiritual Change in College: Assessing the Effect of a Science Education." *Sociology of Education* 84(2):122–136.

55. Leuba, James H. 1916. *The Belief in God and Immortality: A Psychological, Anthropological and Statistical Study.* Boston, MA: Sherman, French & Company; and Leuba, James H. 1934. *God or Man? A Study of the Value of God to Man.* London, UK: Kegan Paul, Trench & Trubner.

56. See Brown, C. Mackenzie. 2003. "The Conflict Between Religion and Science in Light of the Patterns of Religious Belief Among Scientists." *Zygon: Journal of Religion and Science* 38(3):603–632; Evans, John H., and Michael Evans. 2008. "Religion and Science: Beyond the Epistemological Conflict Narrative." *Annual Review of Sociology* 34:87–105; Merton, Robert K. 1970. *Science, Technology, and Society in Seventeenth Century England.* New York: H. Fertig; Polkinghorne, John C. 1998. *Science and Theology: An Introduction.* Minneapolis, MN: Fortress Press; and Wuthnow, Robert. 1985. "Science and the Sacred." Pp. 187–203 in *The Sacred in a Secular Age*, edited by P. E. Hammond. Berkeley, Los Angeles, and London: University of California Press.

57. See Greeley, Andrew M. 1967. "Religion and Academic Career Plans: A Note on Progress." *American Journal of Sociology* 72(6):668–672; Greeley, Andrew M. 1973. *The New Agenda.* Doubleday; Wuthnow, Robert. 1985. "Science and the Sacred." Pp.

187–203 in *The Sacred in a Secular Age*, edited by P. E. Hammond. Berkeley, Los Angeles, and London: University of California Press; Merton, Robert K. 1970. *Science, Technology and Society in Seventeenth Century England*. New York: H. Fertig; Numbers, Ronald, ed. 2009. *Galileo Goes to Jail: And Other Myths About Science and Religion*. Cambridge, MA: Harvard University Press; and Stark, Rodney. 2003. *On True God: Historical Consequences of Monotheism*. Princeton, NJ: Princeton University Press.

58. Brown, C. Mackenzie. 2003. "The Conflict Between Religion and Science in Light of the Patterns of Religious Belief Among Scientists." *Zygon: Journal of Religion and Science* 38(3):603–632.

59. See, for example, Vaidyanathan, Brandon, David R. Johnson, Pamela Prickett, and Elaine Howard Ecklund. 2016. "Rejecting the Conflict Narrative: American Jewish and Muslim Views on Science and Religion." *Social Compass* 63(4):478–496, for a discussion of Jewish and Muslim perspectives on science and faith.

Chapter 3

1. See Miller, Jon D., Eugenie C. Scott, and Shinji Okamoto. 2006. "Public Acceptance of Evolution." *Science* 313(5788):765–766.

2. See Evans, John H. 2002. *Playing God? Human Genetic Engineering and the Rationalization of Public Bioethical Debate*. Chicago: University of Chicago Press. See also Evans, John H. 2010. *Contested Reproduction: Genetic Technologies, Religion, and Public Debate*. Chicago: University of Chicago Press, which examines how ordinary religious people in the United States talk about reproductive genetic technologies. And see Evans, John H. 2012. *The History and Future of Bioethics: A Sociological View*. New York: Oxford University Press.

3. These two categories are not mutually exclusive and can be overlapping and will be as we progress in our understanding and ability to manipulate the human embryo.

4. Ecklund, Elaine Howard, and Christopher P. Scheitle. 2017. *Religion vs. Science: What Religious People Really Think*. New York: Oxford University Press.

5. Johnson, David R., Christopher P. Scheitle, and Elaine Howard Ecklund. 2016. "Conservative Protestantism and Anti-Evolution Curricular Challenges Across States." *Social Science Quarterly* 97(5):1227–1244.

6. Wuthnow, Robert. 2007. *America and the Challenges of Religious Diversity*. Princeton, NJ: Princeton University Press.

7. Pew Research Center. 2015. "U.S. Becoming Less Religious." Retrieved April 9, 2018 (http://www.pewforum.org/2015/11/03/u-s-public-becoming-less-religious/).

8. Kuru, Ahmet. 2009. *Secularism and State Policies Toward Religion: The United States, France, and Turkey*. Cambridge, UK: Cambridge University Press.

9. Regnerus, Mark, David Sikkink, and Christian Smith. 1999. "Voting with the Christian Right: Contextual and Individual Patterns of Electoral Influence." *Social Forces* 77(4):1375–1401.

10. National Science Board. 2018. "Science and Engineering Indicators 2018." Retrieved April 26, 2018 (https://www.nsf.gov/statistics/2018/nsb20181/).

11. Numbers, Ronald. 1985. "Science and Religion." In *Historical Writing on American Science: Perspectives and Prospects*, edited by S. G. Kohlstedt and M. W. Rossiter. Baltimore, MD: Johns Hopkins University Press.

12. Leuba, James H. 1916. *The Belief in God and Immortality: A Psychological, Anthropological and Statistical Study*. Boston, MA: Sherman, French & Company; and Leuba, James H. 1934. *God or Man? A Study of the Value of God to Man*. London, UK: Kegan Paul, Trench & Trubner.

13. Larson, Edward, and Edward Witham. 1997. "Scientists Are Still Keeping the Faith." *Nature* 386(3):435–436.

14. Ecklund, Elaine Howard, Jerry Z. Park, and Phil Todd Veliz. 2008. "Secularization and Religious Change Among Elite Scientists." *Social Forces* 86(4):1805–1839.

15. See Ecklund, Elaine Howard, and Christopher P. Scheitle. 2017. *Religion vs Science: What Religious People Really Think*. New York: Oxford University Press; Johnson, David R., and Jared L. Peifer. 2017. "How Public Confidence in Higher Education Varies by Social Context." *Journal of Higher Education* 88(4):619–644; Scheitle, Christopher P., and Elaine Howard Ecklund. 2017. "Recommending a Child Enter a STEM Career: The Role of Religion." *Journal of Career Development* 44(3):251–265.

16. Though we do not report it, 6.51 percent of respondents to the International Social Survey Programme (2008) in Hong Kong do not believe in God, compared to 10.6 percent of scientists. We are limited in making comparisons between scientists and general publics in India and Hong Kong, where sampling for the ISSP was not conducted. A related measure was included in the World Values Survey sampled in Hong Kong (2013), however. The measure only offers two response options (Yes/No) to the question "Do you believe in God?," and 41 percent of Hong Kong responded "No." In contrast, only 26 percent of scientists in Hong Kong say that do not believe in any God or gods and another 20 percent say they don't know whether there is a God or gods and they don't believe there is any way to find out. In India, 2.8 percent of respondents to the World Values Survey (2012) reported that they don't believe in God, compared to 11 percent of Indian scientists who don't believe in God and another 11 percent who believe there is no way to find out.

17. RASIC_US29, biology, female, professor, conducted 4/1/15

18. RASIC_US05, physics, female, graduate student, conducted 3/24/15

19. RASIC_US58, biology, female, graduate student, conducted 4/29/15; and RASIC_US56, biology, female, postdoctoral fellow, conducted 4/15/15. Additional analyses of our survey show that 16 percent of female scientists compared with 11 percent of male scientists believe in a higher power of some kind, though the difference is not statistically significant. We also found that 15 percent of graduate students compared with 11 percent of scientists with a doctorate believe in a higher power, but again, the difference is not statistically significant.

20. RASIC_US82, biology, female, professor, conducted 3/25/15

21. RASIC_US49, physics, female, graduate student, conducted 4/8/15

22. RASIC_US73, physics, male, graduate student, conducted 5/1/15

23. Because of the stratified sampling design (see Appendix B), standard errors are sensitive to the manner in which weights are applied. Throughout, we estimated regression models and conducted significance testing with Stata, version 13.1. We applied weights by using the svyset command ("svyset [pweight=trimmed_weight]"), which adjusts estimates for the probability that individual respondents are sampled. $F = 7.05$, $p = .008$

24. $F = 6.80, p = .0092$

25. RASIC_US54, biology, male, professor, conducted 4/13/15

26. RASIC_US52, physics, female, associate professor, conducted 4/10/15

27. RASIC_US06, physics, female, graduate student, conducted 3/24/15

28. $F = 22.15, p = .0000$

29. RASIC_US80, biology, female, postdoctoral researcher, conducted 5/14/15

30. RASIC_US19, physics, male, graduate student, conducted 3/27/15

31. RASIC_US11, physics, female, professor, conducted 3/25/15

32. RASIC_US06, physics, female, graduate student, conducted 3/24/15

33. RASIC_US20, physics, female, postdoctoral researcher, conducted 3/27/15

34. $F = 26.95, p = .0000$

35. RASIC_US74, biology, male, graduate student, conducted 5/4/15

36. $F = 9.52, p = .0021$

37. RASIC_US18, physics, female, graduate student, conducted 3/27/15

38. RASIC_US37, biology, male, graduate student, conducted 4/2/15

39. RASIC_US72, physics, female, associate professor, conducted 4/29/15

40. RASIC_US42, biology, female, professor, conducted 4/3/15

41. RASIC_US74, biology, male, graduate student, conducted 5/4/15

42. RASIC_US80, biology, female, postdoctoral researcher, conducted 5/14/15

43. RASIC_US62, biology, female, postdoctoral researcher, conducted 4/16/15

44. RASIC_US55, biology, male, graduate student, conducted 4/13/15

45. RASIC_US35, physics, female, graduate student, conducted 4/2/15

46. RASIC_US80, biology, female, postdoctoral researcher, conducted 5/14/15

47. RASIC_US85, biology, female, postdoctoral researcher, conducted 5/26/15

48. Scheitle, Christopher P., David R. Johnson, and Elaine Howard Ecklund. 2018. "Scientists and Religious Leaders Compete for Cultural Authority of Science." *Public Understanding of Science* 27(1):59–75.

49. RASIC_US37, biology, male, graduate student, conducted 4/2/15

50. RASIC_US75, biology, male, postdoctoral researcher, conducted 5/11/15

51. RASIC_US41, biology, female, professor, conducted 4/3/15

52. RASIC_US04, physics, male, postdoctoral researcher, conducted 3/12/15

53. RASIC_US03, biology, female, graduate student, conducted 3/2/15

54. RASIC_US37, biology, male, graduate student, conducted 4/2/15

55. Bolger, Daniel, and Elaine Howard Ecklund. 2018. "Whose Authority? Perceptions of Science Education in Black and Latino Churches." *Review of Religious Research* 60:49–70.

56. RASIC_US02, biology, male, graduate student, conducted 3/2/15

57. RASIC_US37, biology, male, graduate student, conducted 4/2/15

58. RASIC_US53, physics, male, professor, conducted 4/13/15

59. RASIC_US57, biology, female, academic professional, conducted 4/15/15

60. RASIC_US22, physics, female, graduate student, conducted 3/31/15

61. RASIC_US41, biology, female, professor, conducted 4/3/15

62. RASIC_US39, biology, female, professor, conducted 4/3/15

63. RASIC_US49, physics, female, graduate student, conducted 5/8/15

64. RASIC_US19, physics, male, graduate student, conducted 3/27/15

65. RASIC_US23, biology, female, graduate student, conducted 4/1/15

66. RASIC_US64, physics, male, graduate student, conducted 4/17/15

67. RASIC_US49, physics, female, graduate student, conducted 4/8/15

68. RASIC_US79, physics, male, associate professor, conducted 5/13/15

69. RASIC_US54, biology, male, professor, conducted 4/13/15

70. RASIC_US29, biology, female, professor, conducted 4/1/15

71. RASIC_US82, biology, female, professor, conducted 3/25/15

72. RASIC_US18, physics, female, graduate student, conducted 3/27/15

73. RASIC_US51, physics, female, research associate, conducted 4/9/15

74. RASIC_US68, biology, female, professor, conducted 4/22/15

75. RASIC_US47, biology, female, associate professor, conducted 4/7/15

76. RASIC_US05, physics, female, graduate student, conducted 3/24/15

77. RASIC_US74, biology, male, graduate student, conducted 5/4/15

78. See Johnson, David R. 2017. *A Fractured Profession: Commercialism and Conflict in Academic Science*. Baltimore, MD: Johns Hopkins University Press. See also Peifer, Jared L., David R. Johnson, and Elaine Howard Ecklund. 2017. "The Moral Limits of the Market: Science Commercialization and Religious Traditions." *Journal of Business Ethics* 1–15.

79. RASIC_US44, biology, male, postdoctoral researcher, conducted 4/3/15

80. RASIC_US46, physics, female, postdoctoral researcher, conducted 4/6/15

81. RASIC_US23, biology, female, graduate student, conducted 4/1/15

82. RASIC_US34, biology, female, graduate student, conducted 4/2/15

83. RASIC_US30, biology, female, associate professor, conducted 4/2/15

84. RASIC_US79, physics, male, associate professor, conducted 5/13/15

85. RASIC_US72, physics, female, associate professor, conducted 4/29/15

86. RASIC_US51, physics, female, research associate, conducted 4/9/15

87. See, for example, Ecklund, Elaine Howard, and Christopher P. Scheitle. 2017. *Religion vs. Science: What Religious People Really Think*. New York: Oxford University Press.

88. For detailed information on the Gallup polls, see Gallup. 2017. "In U.S., Belief in Creationist View of Humans at New Low." Retrieved April 9, 2018 (http://news.gallup.com/poll/210956/belief-creationist-view-humans-new-low.aspx).

89. Hill, Jonathan. 2014. "Rejecting Evolution: The Role of Religion, Education, and Social Networks." *Journal for the Scientific Study of Religion* 53(3):575–594.

90. See, for example, Ecklund, Elaine Howard, and Christopher P. Scheitle. 2017. *Religion vs. Science: What Religious People Really Think*. New York: Oxford University Press.

91. In the full US scientist sample, more women (34 percent) than men (29 percent) and nonwhites (35 percent) than whites (28 percent) describe themselves as religious (although results were not statistically significant). In the full sample, significantly more whites (69 percent) than nonwhites (57 percent) were atheist/agnostic (these comparisons were statistically significant). At elite institutions, more men (70 percent) than women (67 percent) and whites (71 percent) than nonwhites (67 percent) were atheist/agnostic (not significant). At nonelite institutions, significantly more women (39 percent) than men (29 percent) and nonwhites (40 percent) than whites (27 percent) were atheist/agnostic. And at nonelite institutions, significantly more whites (67 percent) than nonwhites (50 percent) were atheist/agnostic.

Chapter 4

1. RASIC_UK81, biology, female, reader, conducted 7/14/14

2. RASIC_UK63, biology, male, professor, conducted 4/15/14

3. For an excellent overview of evolution before and after the impact of Dawkins, see Elsdon-Baker, Fern. 2006. *The Selfish Genius: How Richard Dawkins Rewrote Darwin's Legacy*. London, UK: Icon Books.

4. Alister E. McGrath. "Brief Biography." Retrieved June 29, 2017 (http://alistermcgrath.weebly.com/biography.html).

5. See Kaden, Tom, Stephen H. Jones, Rebecca Catto, and Fern Elsdon-Baker. 2017. "Knowledge as Explanandum: Disentangling Lay and Professional Perspectives on Science and Religion." *Studies in Religion/Sciences Religieuses*. doi: 10.1177/0008429817741448. We should note that the authors draw on data from the multinational study *Science and Religion: Exploring the Spectrum*. For more about this study, see Science and Religion: Exploring the Spectrum. "About." Retrieved April 30, 2018 (http://sciencereligionspectrum.org/about-2/).

6. RASIC_UK22, biology, male, lecturer, conducted 12/4/13

7. See Davie, Grace. 1994. *Religion in Britain Since 1945: Believing Without Belonging*. Oxford, UK: Blackwell Publishers.

8. Bowler, Peter J. 2001. *Reconciling Science and Religion: The Debate in Early-Twentieth-Century Britain*. Chicago, IL: University of Chicago Press.

9. RASIC_UK108, biology, male, postdoctoral fellow, conducted 3/1/11

10. Encylopedia Britannica. 2018. "United Kingdom." Retrieved April 27, 2018 (http://www.britannica.com/EBchecked/topic/615557/United-Kingdom/44685/Religion); Sedghi, Ami. 2013. "UK Census: Religion by Age, Ethnicity and Country of Birth," *The Guardian*, May 16.

11. See Davie, Grace. 1990. "Believing Without Belonging: Is This the Future of Religion in Britain?" *Social Compass* 37(4):455–469.

12. Merton, Robert. 1938. *Science, Technology and Society in Seventeenth-Century England*. Bruges: Saint Catherine Press, Ltd.

13. Anderson, Robert. 2006. *British Universities Past and Present*. London, UK: Bloomsbury Publishing.

14. Village, Andrew, and Leslie J. Francis. 2009. *The Mind of the Anglican Clergy: Assessing Attitudes and Beliefs in the Church of England*. Lewiston, NY: Edwin Mellen Press; White, John. 2004. "Should Religious Education Be a Compulsory School Subject?" *British Journal of Religious Education* 26(2):151–164.

15. Voas, David, and Mark Chaves. 2016. "Is the United States a Counterexample to the Secularization Thesis?" *American Journal of Sociology* 121(5):1517–1556.

16. See Voas, David. 2015. "Religious Involvement over the Life Course: Problems of Measurement and Classification." *Longitudinal and Life Course Studies* 6(2):212–227, for a discussion of the problems inherent in measuring religiosity over the life course.

17. Great Britain refers to all of England, Scotland, and Wales but not Northern Ireland.

18. Crockett, Alasdair, and David Voas. 2006. "Generations of Decline: Religious Change in 20th-Century Britain." *Journal for the Scientific Study of Religion* 45(4):567–584.

19. Survey responses (RASIC UK Survey 2014) indicated that a significantly greater share of immigrants (48 percent) than nonimmigrants (28 percent) reported to be affiliated with a religious tradition. More immigrants (25 percent) than nonimmigrants (16 percent) also pray at least once a month, and a significantly smaller share of immigrants (29 percent) than nonimmigrants (39 percent) believe that the relationship between science and religion is one of conflict.

20. Office for National Statistics. 2013. "Full Story: What Does the Census Tell Us About Religion in 2011." Retrieved June 26, 2017 (http://webarchive.nationalarchives. gov.uk/20160105160709/http://www.ons.gov.uk/ons/dcp171776_310454.pdf).

21. Park, Alison, Caroline Bryson, Elizabeth Clery, John Curtice, and Miranda Philips. 2013. *British Social Attitudes: The 30th Report.* London, UK: NatCen Social Research.

22. Bingham, John. 2013. "Christians Now a Minority in the UK as Half the Population Has No Religion," *Telegraph*, September 10.

23. Martin, Daniel. 2012. "2030: The Year Britain Will Cease to Be a Christian Nation with the March of Secularism," *Daily Mail*, March 2.

24. Park, Alison, Caroline Bryson, Elizabeth Clery, John Curtice, and Miranda Philips. 2013. *British Social Attitudes: The 30th Report.* London, UK: NatCen Social Research.

25. Rienzo, Cinzia, and Carlos Vargas-Silva. 2015. "Targeting Migration with Limited Control: The Case of the UK and the EU." *IZA Journal of European Labor Studies* 4(16):1–19.

26. DailyMail.com. 2011. "Muslim Medical Students Boycotting Lectures on Evolution . . . Because It 'Clashes with the Koran.'" Retrieved April 17, 2015 (http:// www.dailymail.co.uk/news/article-2066795/Muslim-students-walking-lectures-Darwinism-clashes-Koran.html).

27. Jeffries, Stuart. 2007. "Britain's New Cultural Divide Is Not Between Christian and Muslim, Hindu, and Jew. It Is Between Those Who Have Faith and Those Who Don't," *The Guardian*, February 26.

28. Williams, James David. 2008. "Creationist Teaching in School Science: A UK Perspective." *Evolution: Education and Outreach* 1(1):87–95.

29. Branigan, Tania. 2002. "Top School's Creationists Preach Value of Biblical Story over Evolution," *The Guardian*, March 8.

30. Branigan, Tania. 2003. "Dawkins Attacks 'Educational Debauchery' of Creationist Schools," *The Guardian*, April 29.

31. Copson, Andrew. 2012. "Free Schools Are Exploiting Loopholes to Teach Creationism," *The Guardian*, November 30.

32. GOV.UK. "Free Schools." Retrieved July 17, 2017 (https://www.gov.uk/types-of-school/free-schools).

33. See Doward, Jamie. 2012. "Richard Dawkins Celebrates a Victory over Creationists," *The Guardian*, January 14; Walker, Peter. 2012. "Free Schools Must Teach Evolution, Ministers Announce," *The Guardian*, November 30; and Thompson, Evan. 2014. "Picking Holes in the Concept of Natural Selection." *BioScience* 64(4):355–358.

34. See Unsworth, Amy, and David Voas. 2018. "Attitudes to Evolution Among Christians, Muslims, and the Non-Religious in Britain: Differential Effects of Religious and Educational Factors." *Public Understanding of Science* 27(1):76–93.

35. Brinsden, Peter R. 1993. "Reproductive Health Care Policies Around the World: The Effect of the Human Fertilisation and Embryology Act 1990 Upon the Practice of Assisted Reproduction Techniques in the United Kingdom." *Journal of Assisted Reproduction and Genetics* 10(8):493–499.

36. Edemariam, Aida. 2008. "A Matter of Life and Death," *The Guardian*, March 27.

37. China and India have emerged as bigger players in terms of publications. And China outspends the United Kingdom now as well. See National Science Board. 2018. "Science and Engineering Indicators 2018." Retrieved April 26, 2018 (https://www.nsf.gov/statistics/2018/nsb20181/).

38. Zinnbauer, Brian J., Kenneth I. Pargament, Brenda Cole, Mark S. Rye, Eric M. Butter, Timothy G. Belavich, Kathleen M. Hipp, Allie B. Scott, and Jill L. Kadar. 1997. "Religion and Spirituality: Unfuzzying the Fuzzy." *Journal for the Scientific Study of Religion* 36(4):549–564.

39. When discussing belief in God, we omit survey responses of scientists located in Northern Ireland so to better compare with data from the International Social Survey Programme (ISSP), which sampled Great Britain and Northern Ireland separately. Combing ISSP respondents from both regions would bias results, as Northern Ireland has a smaller population than Great Britain but is also characterized by relatively higher degrees of religiosity.

40. See Ecklund, Elaine Howard, Jerry Z. Park, and Phil Todd Veliz. 2008. "Secularization and Religious Change among Elite Scientists." *Social Forces* 86(4):1805–1839. This article examines elite status for US scientists.

41. Among biologists, having at least one child was positively correlated with an ordinal measure of attendance ($r = .15$, $p = .0001$) and being religiously affiliated ($r = .10$, $p = .0069$). Similar relationships were observed among physicists, for whom having at least one child was also positively correlated with attendance ($r = .18$, $p = .0000$) and being religiously affiliated ($r = .14$, $p = .0002$).

42. Considering the combined sample of biologists and physicists, having kids at home was significantly correlated with religious affiliation ($r = .12$, $p = .0000$) and religious attendance ($r = .18$, $p = .0000$) among scientists in the United Kingdom. In the United States, the correlation with religious affiliation was .08 ($p = .0004$) and the correlation with attendance was .15 ($p = .0000$).

43. RASIC_UK71, biology, male, lecturer, conducted 5/8/14

44. Sorrell, Katherine, and Elaine Howard Ecklund. Unpublished Manuscript. "How UK Scientists Legitimize Religion Through Boundary Work"; Ecklund, Elaine Howard, Jerry Park, and Katherine L. Sorrell. 2011. "Scientists Negotiate Boundaries Between Religion and Science." *Journal for the Scientific Study of Religion* 50(3):552–569; Evans, John H., and Michael S. Evans. 2008. "Religion and Science: Beyond the Epistemological Conflict Narrative." *Annual Review of Sociology* 34:87–105.

45. RASIC_UK102, biology, male, professor, conducted 2/28/11

46. RASIC_UK137, physics, female, professor, conducted 7/13/12

47. Gould, Stephen Jay. 1997. "Nonoverlapping Magisteria." *Natural History* 106:16–22.

48. RASIC_UK134, physics, male, professor, conducted 7/13/12

49. RASIC_UK108, biology, male, postdoctoral fellow, conducted 3/1/11

50. RASIC_UK113, biology, male, emeritus senior research fellow, conducted 3/3/11

51. RASIC_UK128, physics, male, reader, conducted 6/11/12

52. RASIC_UK111, biology, female, lecturer, conducted 3/3/11

53. RASIC_UK04, physics, male, postdoctoral fellow, conducted 12/2/13

54. RASIC_UK103, biology, male, research fellow, conducted 2/28/11

55. Alexander, Denis. 2014. *Creation or Evolution: Do We Have to Choose?* Oxford, UK: Monarch Books. For a historical perspective on how ideologies related to science and religion interact with one another, see Alexander, Denis R., and Ronald L. Numbers, eds. 2010. *Biology and Ideology from Descartes to Dawkins.* Chicago, IL: The University of Chicago Press.

56. RASIC_UK134, physics, male, professor, conducted 7/13/12

57. RASIC_UK102, biology, male, professor, conducted 2/28/11

58. RASIC_UK24, physics, male, postdoctoral fellow, conducted 12/4/13

59. RASIC_UK20, physics, male, reader, conducted 12/3/13

60. Bourdieu, Pierre. 1988. *Homo Academicus.* Stanford, CA: Stanford University Press. See also Ecklund, Elaine Howard, Jerry Park, and Katherine L. Sorrell. 2011. "Scientists Negotiate Boundaries Between Religion and Science." *Journal for the Scientific Study of Religion* 50(3):552–569.

61. RASIC_UK114, biology, male, professor, conducted 3/4/11

62. RASIC_UK127, physics, female, lecturer, conducted 6/11/12

63. RASIC_UK09, biology, female, lecturer, conducted 12/2/13

64. RASIC_UK68, biology, male, associate professor, conducted 4/23/14

65. RASIC_UK68, physics, male, senior lecturer, conducted 4/23/14

66. RASIC_UK94, biology, male, professor, conducted 7/25/14

67. RASIC_UK72, biology, female, research scientist, conducted 5/5/14

68. RASIC_UK36, biology, male, professor, conducted 12/5/13

69. RASIC_UK50, biology, female, research associate, conducted 3/3/14

70. RASIC_UK10, physics, female, postdoctoral fellow, conducted 12/2/13

71. RASIC_UK37, biology, female, professor, conducted 12/5/13; given the prominence of the respondent, some nonresearch details have been changed to obscure identity.

72. RASIC_UK21, physics, male, senior research fellow, conducted 12/4/13

73. RASIC_UK06, biology, female, lecturer, conducted 12/12/13

74. RASIC_UK34, biology, male, professor, conducted 12/5/13

75. RASIC_UK09, biology, female, lecturer, conducted 12/2/13

76. RASIC_UK99, biology, male, senior lecturer, conducted 2/28/11

77. RASIC_UK35, biology, female, senior lecturer, conducted 12/5/13

78. RASIC_UK96, biology, female, graduate student, conducted 8/15/14

79. RASIC_UK37, biology, female, professor, conducted 12/5/13

80. RASIC_UK60, biology, male, senior lecturer, conducted 4/1/14

81. Johnson, David, Elaine Howard Ecklund, Di Di, and Kirstin R. W. Matthews. 2016. "Responding to Richard: Celebrity and (Mis)Representation of Science." *Public Understanding of Science* 27(5):535–549. See also, Dawkins, Richard. 2008. *The God Delusion.* New York: Houghton Mifflin Company.

82. RASIC_UK03, biology, female, group leader, conducted 12/2/13

83. RASIC_UK46, biology, female, professor, conducted 12/6/13

84. RASIC_UK24, physics, male, postdoctoral fellow, conducted 12/4/13

85. RASIC_UK02, biology, male, graduate student, conducted 11/26/13

86. RASIC_UK08, biology, male, professor, conducted 12/2/13

87. RASIC_UK04, physics, male, postdoctoral fellow, conducted 12/2/13

88. RASIC_UK22, biology, male, lecturer, conducted 12/4/13

89. RASIC_UK34, biology, male, professor, conducted 12/4/13

90. RASIC_UK53, physics, male, reader, conducted 3/5/14

91. Rivers, Julian. 2010. *The Law of Organized Religions: Between Establishment and Secularism.* Oxford, UK: Oxford University Press.

92. It may have also led to an anti-immigration backlash including the passing of Brexit in 2016, which would remove the United Kingdom from the European Union.

93. RASIC_UK63, biology, male, professor, conducted 4/15/14

Chapter 5

1. Jef Aérosol is the nom de plume of Jean-Francois Perroy.

2. Perroy states, "This gesture is my way of saying, listen to each others and stop for five minutes, listen to things you do not usually hear." As we argue in this chapter, the mural itself makes no apparent comment on religion, but the juxtaposition of the mural alongside a historic Catholic church is open to interpretation, one of which can be on the relationship between Catholicism and secularism. For more on Perroy and this mural, see Forster, Siegfried. 2011. "Jef Aerosol Fait 'Chuuuttt!!!' dans la Grande Symphonie Urbaine de Paris," *Les Voix Du Monde,* June 17.

3. Willaime, Jean-Paul. 1998. "Religious and Secular France Between Northern and Southern Europe." *Social Compass* 45(1):155–174.

4. France. Constitution, 1946. *Préambule de la Constitution du 27 octobre 1946.*

5. RASIC_FR02, physics, female, CNRS researcher, conducted 6/8/15

6. RASIC_FR18, physics, male, maître de conferences, conducted 6/11/15

7. RASIC_FR24, physics, male, maître de conferences, conducted 6/12/15; RASIC_FR08, physics, female, professor, conducted 6/9/15; RASIC_FR07, physics, female, CNRS researcher, conducted 6/9/15

8. RASIC_FR73, physics, female, CNRS researcher, conducted 8/19/15

9. Adam, Charles, and Paul Tannery, eds. 1964–1976. *Oeuvres de Descartes.* Paris: Vrin/CNRS.

10. Clarke, Desmond. 2015. "Blaise Pascal." In *The Stanford Encyclopedia of Philosophy,* Fall 2015 edition, edited by E. N. Zalta. Santa Clara County, CA: Center for the Study of Language and Information, Stanford University.

11. Grimaux, Edouard. 1888. *Lavoisier 1743–1794.* Paris: Arno Press.

12. Kuru, Ahmet. 2009. *Secularism and State Policies Toward Religion: The United States, France, and Turkey.* Cambridge: Cambridge University Press.

13. See, for example, Casanova, José. 2008. "Public Religions Revisited." Pp. 101–119 in *Religion: Beyond a Concept,* edited by H. DeVries. New York: Fordham University Press.

14. Willaime, Jean-Paul. 1998. "Religious and Secular France Between Northern and Southern Europe." *Social Compass* 45(1):155–174. See also Fath, Sebastien. 2007. "Putting God into the City: Protestants in France." Pp. 49–62 in *Politics and Religion in France and the United States,* edited by A. G. Hargreaves, J. Kelsay, and S. B. Twiss. Lanham, MD: Lexington Books.

15. Nolan, Mary Lee, and Sidney Nolan. 1989. *Christian Pilgrimage in Modern Western Europe*. Chapel Hill: University of North Carolina Press.

16. Willaime, Jean-Paul. 1998. "Religious and Secular France Between Northern and Southern Europe." *Social Compass* 45(1):155–174.

17. Lambert, Yves. 1994. "Un Paysage Religieux en Profonde Evolution." Pp. 123–162 in *Les Valeurs des Francais*, edited by H. Riffault. Paris: PUF.

18. Willaime, Jean-Paul. 1998. "Religious and Secular France Between Northern and Southern Europe." *Social Compass* 45(1):155–174.

19. Hargreaves, Alec G., John Kelsay, and Sumner B. Twiss, eds. 2007. *Politics and Religion in France and the US*. Lanham, MD: Lexington Books.

20. Kuru, Ahmet. 2009. *Secularism and State Policies Toward Religion: The United States, France, and Turkey*. Cambridge: Cambridge University Press.

21. Llana, Sara Miller. 2016. "As Demand for Secularism Grows in France, Believers Push Back at Work," *Christian Science Monitor*, November 7.

22. The Economist. 2017. "The State and the Veil." Retrieved April 16, 2018 (https://www.economist.com/news/international/21715679-dispute-over-muslim-womens-attire-helping-nobody-state-and-veil).

23. Reuters. 2016. "Face au Terrorisme, Faire Changer la Peur de Cote, Dit Sarkozy." Retrieved July 26, 2017 (http://fr.reuters.com/article/topNews/idFRKCN10M0CX).

24. Johnson, David R., and Joseph C. Hermanowicz. 2017. "Peer Review: From 'Sacred Ideals' to 'Profane Realities.'" Pp. 485–527 in *Higher Education: Handbook of Theory and Research*, Vol. 32, edited by M. B. Paulsen. Springer.

25. National Science Board. 2018. "Science and Engineering Indicators 2018." Retrieved April 26, 2018 (https://www.nsf.gov/statistics/2018/nsb20181/).

26. Chevaillier, Thierry. 2001. "French Academics: Between the Professions and the Civil Service." *Higher Education* 41:49–75. Compare, for example to INSERM, which focuses on medical research and which has only 2,000 researchers.

27. BioLogos. 2010. "France's Own Evolution Debate." Retrieved July 28, 2017 (http://biologos.org/blogs/archive/france%E2%80%99s-own-evolution-debate).

28. Reuters. 2011. "Muslim Creationists Tour France Denouncing Darwin." Retrieved July 28, 2017 (http://www.reuters.com/article/us-islam-creationism-france-idUSTRE74F3GC20110516).

29. The Economist. 2015. "How Secular France Is Giving Faith a Voice in the Planet's Future." Retrieved April 16, 2018 (https://www.economist.com/blogs/erasmus/2015/11/religion-and-climate-change).

30. Le Parisien. 2015. "Réchauffement Climatique: Qu'en Disentles Religions?" Retrieved July 31, 2017 (http://www.leparisien.fr/environnement/rechauffement-climatique-qu-en-disent-les-religions-28-11-2015-5321335.php#xtref=https%3A%2F%2Fwww.google.com%2F).

31. Religion News Service. 2016. "Catholic Priest's Appointment as University President Stuns French." Retrieved December 22, 2016 (http://religionnews.com/2016/12/22/catholic-priests-appointment-as-university-president-stuns-french/).

32. Grove, Jack. 2016. "Catholic Priest Named as French University Head," *Times Higher Education*, December 20.

33. Nearly 8 percent of Catholics affirm the collaboration view, compared to 6.4 percent of non-Catholics (F = .23, p = .631).

34. RASIC_FR73, physics, female, CNRS researcher, conducted 8/19/15

35. $F = 2.97$, $p = .086$.

36. RASIC_FR18, physics, male, maître de conferences, conducted 6/11/15

37. Fifty-five percent of male scientists and 62 percent of female scientists in France held the independence perspective ($F = 1.83$, $p = .176$), and 58 percent of physicists compared to 55 percent of biologists held this view ($F = .37$, $p = .542$).

38. $F = 3.42$, $p = .065$.

39. RASIC_FR75, biology, female, director of research, conducted 8/25/15

40. RASIC_FR34, physics, male, CNRS researcher, conducted 7/9/15

41. RASIC_FR42, biology, female, scientific officer/research facilitator, conducted 7/15/15

42. A slightly larger share of male scientists (28 percent) than female scientists (22 percent) reported the conflict view, but the difference was not statistically significant ($F = 1.94$, $p = .165$).

43. $F = 5.83$, $p = .016$.

44. RASIC_FR19, physics, male, director of research, conducted 7/11/15

45. RASIC_FR63, biology, male, director of research, conducted 7/31/15

46. $F = 49.16$, $p < .001$.

47. RASIC_FR54, biology, female, director of research, conducted 7/21/15

48. RASIC_FR41, physics, male, postdoctoral researcher, conducted 7/14/15

49. RASIC_FR34, physics, male, CNRS researcher, conducted 6/8/15

50. RASIC_FR73, physics, female, CNRS researcher, conducted 8/19/15

51. RASIC_FR29, biology, male, non-CNRS researcher (graduate student), conducted 7/7/15

52. RASIC_FR02, physics, male, associate professor, conducted 6/2/15

53. RASIC_FR18, physics, male, maître de conférences, conducted 6/8/15

54. RASIC_FR72, physics, male, graduate student, conducted, 8/18/15

55. RASIC_FR58, physics, female, professor, conducted 7/23/15

56. RASIC_FR52, biology, female, CNRS researcher, conducted 7/20/15

57. RASIC_FR07, physics, female, CNRS researcher, conducted 6/9/15

58. Even in a highly secular country, religion can still make its way into science, through ethical debates about technologies for example.

59. Ecklund, Elaine Howard, David R. Johnson, Christopher P. Scheitle, Kirstin R. W. Matthews, and Steven W. Lewis. 2016. "Religion Among Scientists in International Context: A New Study of Scientists in Eight Regions." *Socius* 2:1–9.

60. RASIC_FR42, biology, female, scientific officer/research facilitator, conducted 7/15/15

61. RASIC_FR07, physics, female, CNRS researcher, conducted 6/9/15

62. RASIC_FR20, biology, male, CNRS director of research, conducted 6/11/15

63. RASIC_FR59, physics, female, professor, conducted 7/28/15

64. RASIC_FR15, biology, male, CNRS researcher, conducted 6/10/15

65. RASIC_FR07, physics, female, CNRS researcher, conducted 6/9/15

66. RASIC_FR59, physics, female, professor, conducted 7/28/15

67. RASIC_FR51, biology, female, director of research, conducted 7/17/15

68. RASIC_FR43, physics, female, director of research, conducted 7/15/15

69. RASIC_FR64, biology, female, consultant, conducted 8/5/15

70. RASIC_FR54, biology, female, director of research, conducted 7/21/15

71. RASIC_FR01, physics, female, CNRS researcher, conducted 6/8/15

72. RASIC_FR03, biology, female, CNRS researcher, conducted 6/8/15

73. RASIC_FR17, biology, female, postdoctoral researcher, conducted 6/11/15

74. For context to this claim, see Killian, Caitlin. 2007. "From a Community of Believers to an Islam of the Heart: 'Conspicuous' Symbols, Muslim Practices, and the Privatization of Religion in France." *Sociology of Religion* 68(30):305–320.

75. RASIC_FR17, biology, female, postdoctoral researcher, conducted 6/11/15

76. RASIC_FR34, physics, male, CNRS researcher, conducted 7/9/15

77. RASIC_FR09, physics, male, CNRS researcher, conducted 6/9/15

78. RASIC_FR15, biology, male, CNRS researcher, conducted 6/10/15

79. RASIC_FR34, physics, male, CNRS researcher, conducted 7/9/15

80. There are Muslims who object to equating hijab with the headscarf. See, for example, The Huffington Post. 2016. "Differentiating the Hijab from the Headscarf." Retrieved April 13, 2018 (http://www.huffingtonpost.com/rawan-abushaban/reducing-hijab-to-the-hea_b_9075126.html); or BBC. 2009. "Hijab." Retrieved April 13, 2018 (http://www.bbc.co.uk/religion/religions/islam/beliefs/hijab_1.shtml).

81. RASIC_FR07, physics, female, CNRS researcher, conducted 6/9/15

82. RASIC_FR72, physics, male, graduate student, conducted 8/18/15

83. RASIC_FR73, physics, female, CNRS researcher, conducted 8/19/15

84. Most CNRS scientists work with graduate students but not undergraduates; and because scientific research is centralized primarily in the CNRS, most faculty at French universities do not conduct research unless they are affiliated with a CNRS UMR.

85. RASIC_FR43, physics, female, director of research, conducted 7/15/15

86. RASIC_FR29, biology, male, director of research, conducted 7/7/15

87. RASIC_FR63, biology, male, director of research, conducted 7/31/15

88. RASIC_FR34, physics, male, CNRS researcher, conducted 7/9/15

89. RASIC_FR70, physics, male, professor, conducted 8/12/15

90. RASIC_FR18, physics, male, maître de conferences, conducted 6/8/15

91. RASIC_FR26, physics, male, director of research, conducted 6/12/15

92. *The Economist.* 2017. "The State and the Veil." Retrieved April 16, 2018 (https://www.economist.com/news/international/21715679-dispute-over-muslim-womens-attire-helping-nobody-state-and-veil).

Chapter 6

1. See Machamer, Peter, ed. 1998. *The Cambridge Companion to Galileo.* New York: Cambridge University Press. This volume contains a special focus on Galileo's relationship to the church. In addition, Maurice A. Finocchiaro persuasively dispels the myth that Galileo was incarcerated and tortured for his scientific work. See Finocchiaro, Maurice A. 2009. "That Galileo Was Imprisoned and Tortured for Advocating Copernicanism." Pp. 68–78 in *Galileo Goes to Jail and Other Myths About Science and Religion,* edited by R. L. Numbers. Cambridge, MA: Harvard University Press. It should be noted here that Richard J. Blackwell has argued that this view is an "oversimplified and false view . . . [when] the church had understandable reasons for refusing to reinterpret the Bible in Galileo's favor." See page 105 of Blackwell, Richard

J. 2002. "Galileo Galilei." Pp. 105–116 in *Science and Religion: A Historical Introduction*, edited by G. B. Ferngren. Baltimore, MD: Johns Hopkins University Press. There is a growing literature that challenges the conflict narrative. See, for example, Giberson, Karl, and Mariano Artigas. 2007. *Oracles of Science: Celebrity Scientists Versus God and Religion.* New York: Oxford University Press; Evans, John H., and Michael S. Evans. 2008. "Religion and Science: Beyond the Epistemological Conflict Narrative." *Annual Review of Sociology* 34:87–105; and Collins, Francis S. 2006. *The Language of God: A Scientist Presents Evidence for Belief.* New York: Free Press.

2. Vatican Observatory. 2016. "Science, Religion, Society." Retrieved April 24, 2018 (http://www.vaticanobservatory.va/content/specolavaticana/en/science--religion--society.html).

3. See page 43, figure 29 of Organisation for Economic Co-operation and Development. 2016. "G20 Innovation Report 2016." Retrieved August 23, 2017 (https://www.oecd.org/sti/inno/G20-innovation-report-2016.pdf).

4. International Monetary Fund. 2012. "Italy 2012 Article IV Consultation." Retrieved April 18, 2018 (http://www.imf.org/external/pubs/ft/scr/2012/cr12167.pdf).

5. OECD. 2014. "Italy." In *OECD Science, Technology and Industry Outlook 2014.* OECD Publishing, http://dx.doi.org/10.1787/sti_outlook-2014-en.

6. Guth, Jessica, and Bryony Gill. 2008. "Motivations in East–West Doctoral Mobility: Revisiting the Question of Brain Drain." *Journal of Ethnic and Migration Studies* 34(5):825–841; Sbalchiero, Stefano, and Arjuna Tuzzi. 2017. "Italian Scientists Abroad in Europe's Scientific Research Scenario: High Skill Migration as a Resource for Development in Italy." *International Migration* 55(4):171–187.

7. Sbalchiero, Stefano, and Arjuna Tuzzi. 2017. "Italian Scientists Abroad in Europe's Scientific Research Scenario: High Skill Migration as a Resource for Development in Italy." *International Migration* 55(4):171–187.

8. Saint-Blancat, Chantal. 2017. "Making Sense of Scientific Mobility: How Italian Scientists Look Back on Their Trajectories of Mobility in the EU." *Higher Education Policy* 31(1):37–54.

9. Davis, Nancy J., and Robert V. Robinson. 2009. "Overcoming Movement Obstacles by the Religiously Orthodox: The Muslim Brotherhood in Egypt, Shas in Israel, Comunione e Liberazione in Italy, and the Salvation Army in the United States." *American Journal of Sociology* 114(5):1302–1349.

10. RASIC_ITA58, biology, female, research scientist, conducted 10/14/14

11. See pages 7 and 25 of Garelli, Franco. 2014. *Religion Italian Style: Continuities and Changes in a Catholic Country.* Farnham, UK: Ashgate Publishing.

12. See Damerow, Peter, Peter McLaughlin, Gideon Freudenthal, and Jurgen Renn. 1992. *Exploring the Limits of Preclassical Mechanics.* New York: Springer-Verlag; and Garelli, Franco. 2014. *Religion Italian Style: Continuities and Changes in a Catholic Country.* Farnham, UK: Ashgate Publishing.

13. See page 3 of Garelli, Franco. 2014. *Religion Italian Style: Continuities and Changes in a Catholic Country.* Farnham, UK: Ashgate Publishing.

14. In 1987, the Congregation for the Doctrine of the Faith, the Vatican body that oversees Church doctrine, issued a document declaring, "[I]t is immoral to produce human embryos destined to be exploited as disposable 'biological material.'" More explicitly, the doctrine argues against in vitro fertilization (IVF) stating, "such

fertilization is in itself illicit and in opposition to the dignity of procreation and of the conjugal union." See Congregation for the Doctrine of the Faith. 1987. "Instruction on Respect for Human Life in Its Origin and on the Dignity of Procreation." Retrieved April 18, 2018 (http://www.vatican.va/roman_curia/congregations/cfaith/documents/rc_con_cfaith_doc_19870222_respect-for-human-life_en.html).

15. Congregation for the Doctrine of the Faith. 2008. "Instruction *Dignitas Personae* on Certain Bioethical Questions." Retrieved April 18, 2018 (http://www.vatican.va/roman_curia/congregations/cfaith/documents/rc_con_cfaith_doc_20081208_dignitas-personae_en.html).

16. Fineschi, Vittorio, M. Neri, and E. Turillazzi. 2005. "The New Italian Law on Assisted Reproduction Technology (Law 40/2004)." *Journal of Medical Ethics* 31(9):536–539.

17. See Reuters. 2014. "Italian Court Overturns Divisive Ban on Donor Eggs, Sperm." Retrieved April 18, 2018 (https://www.reuters.com/article/us-italy-fertility/italian-court-overturns-divisive-ban-on-donor-eggs-sperm-idUSBREA381BG20140409?feedType=RSS&feedName=scienceNews); and Levi Setti, Paolo E., and Pasquale Patrizio. 2012. "The Italian Experience of a Restrictive IVF Law: A Review." *Journal of Fertilization: In-Vitro* 2(1):164–169. However, in a reflection of the Church's moral positions, the law still currently permits only married heterosexual couples to undergo treatment. In 2009, the Health and Welfare Department of Italy allocated 8 million euros (approximately $11 million USD) to stem cell research, but issued a decree restricting the funds to adult stem cells.

18. See PBS. 2001. "Roundtable: Science and Faith." Retrieved February 12, 2015 (http://www.pbs.org/wgbh/evolution/religion/faith/statement_01.html); Congregation for the Doctrine of the Faith. 1987. "Instruction on Respect for Human Life in Its Origin and on the Dignity of Procreation." Retrieved April 18, 2018 (http://www.vatican.va/roman_curia/congregations/cfaith/documents/rc_con_cfaith_doc_19870222_respect-for-human-life_en.html); National Center for Science Education. 2004. "Decision to Remove Evolution from Italian Schools Reversed." Retrieved February 10, 2015 (https://ncse.com/news/2004/04/decision-to-remove-evolution-from-italian-schools-reversed-00562); and Nature. 2006. "Anti-Evolutionists Raise Their Profile in Europe." Retrieved February 10, 2015 (https://www.nature.com/articles/444406a).

19. Goodstein, Laurie. 1996. "Pope Backs Acceptance of Evolution," *Washington Post*, October 25.

20. Withnall, Adam. 2014. "Pope Francis Declares Evolution and Big Bang Theory Are Real and God Is Not 'a Magician with a Magic Wand,'" *Independent*, October 28.

21. Lorenzi, Rossella. 2004. "Darwin Back in Italy's Schools," *The Scientist*, April 29.

22. RASIC_ITA31, biology, male, researcher, conducted 9/26/14

23. RASIC_ITA66, biology, male, postdoctoral fellow, conducted 11/26/14

24. RASIC_ITA13, physics, male, professor, conducted 9/2/14

25. RASIC_ITA61, biology, female, associate professor, conducted 10/22/14

26. RASIC_ITA08, biology, female, professor, conducted 8/24/14

27. Sbalchiero, Stefano. 2012. *Scienza e Spiritualità: Ruoli e Percezioni Della Ricerca Nel Mondo Contemporaneo*. Rome: Carocci; Sbalchiero, Stefano, and Arjuna Tuzzi.

2016. "Scientists' Spirituality in Scientists' Words. Assessing and Enriching the Results of a Qualitative Analysis of In-depth Interviews by Means of Quantitative Approaches." *Quality and Quantity* 50(3):1333–1348.

28. RASIC_ITA28, biology, female, associate professor, conducted 9/25/14

29. RASIC_ITA04, physics, male, researcher, conducted 7/10/14

30. $F = 5.50$, $p = .0192$.

31. $F = 8.94$, $p = .0028$.

32. $F = 5.11$, $p = .0239$.

33. See pages 14–15 of of Garelli, Franco. 2014. *Religion Italian Style: Continuities and Changes in a Catholic Country*. Farnham, UK: Ashgate Publishing.

34. $F = 7.63$, $p = .0058$.

35. $F = 8.55$, $p = .0035$.

36. RASIC_ITA02, physics, male, senior research associate, conducted 7/10/14

37. $F = 2.63$, $p = .1049$.

38. $F = .94$, $p = .3314$.

39. Independent of one another, as well as gender, career stage, marital status, immigrant status, religious affiliation, and disbelief in God, biologists had 127 percent higher odds than physicists of holding the collaboration view instead of the independence view, and scientists at elite institutions had 46 percent lower odds of the same.

40. Gould, Stephen Jay. 1997. "Nonoverlapping Magisteria." *Natural History* 106:16–22.

41. RASIC_ITA18, biology, male, professor, conducted 9/3/14

42. RASIC_ITA36, biology, male, professor, conducted 9/26/14

43. Gould, Stephen Jay. 1997. "Nonoverlapping Magisteria." *Natural History* 106:16–22.

44. RASIC_ITA38, biology, female, associate professor, conducted 9/27/14

45. RASIC_ITA33, biology, male, professor, conducted 9/26/14

46. RASIC_ITA64, physics, male, postdoctoral fellow, conducted 11/11/14

47. RASIC_ITA52, physics, male, graduate student, conducted 10/1/14

48. Similar themes of the fluidity of spirituality and its compatibility with science are found in Sbalchiero's (2012) research on Italian scientists. See Sbalchiero, Stefano. 2012. *Scienza e Spiritualità: Ruoli e Percezioni Della Ricerca Nel Mondo Contemporaneo*. Rome: Carocci.

49. RASIC_ITA52, physics, male, graduate student, conducted 10/1/14

50. RASIC_ITA16, biology, female, associate professor, conducted 9/3/14

51. RASIC_ITA39, physics, female, associate professor, conducted 9/27/14

52. Saint-Blancat, Chantal. 2014. "Italy." Pp. 265–310 in *The Oxford Handbook of European Islam*, edited by J. Cesari. Oxford, UK: Oxford University Press; Pace, Enzo. 2007. "A Peculiar Pluralism." *Journal of Modern Italian Studies* 12(1):86–100.

53. RASIC_ITA03, physics, male, research fellow, conducted 7/11/14

54. RASIC_ITA36, biology, male, professor, conducted 9/26/14

55. RASIC_ITA28, biology, female, associate professor, conducted 9/25/14

56. RASIC_ITA60, biology, female, research director, conducted 10/15/14

57. BBC News. 2008. "Papal Visit Scuppered by Scholars." Retrieved April 18, 2018 (http://news.bbc.co.uk/2/hi/7188860.stm).

58. See page 15 of Tropman, John E. 2002. *The Catholic Ethic and the Spirit of Community*. Washington, DC: Georgetown University Press.

59. RASIC_ITA33, biology, male, professor, conducted 9/26/14

60. RASIC_ITA38, biology, female, associate professor, conducted 9/27/14

61. On this theme, see also Sbalchiero, Stefano. 2012. *Scienza e Spiritualità: Ruoli e Percezioni Della Ricerca Nel Mondo Contemporaneo*. Rome: Carocci, pp. 53–59.

62. RASIC_ITA64, physics, male, postdoctoral fellow, conducted 11/11/14

63. RASIC_ITA03, physics, male, research fellow, conducted 7/11/14

64. RASIC_ITA11, biology, female, primo ricercatore, conducted 9/1/14

65. RASIC_ITA34, physics, male, professor, conducted 9/26/14

66. The term is from Martinotti, Guido, and Alberto Giasanti. 1977. "The Robed Baron: The Academic Profession in the Italian University." *Higher Education* 6(2):189–207. See also Woolf, Stuart. 2003. "On University Reform in Italy: Contradictions and Power Relations in Structure and Function." *Minerva* 41(4):347–363; Chronicles. 2009. "The University of Barons: This Is How It Works." Retrieved April 18, 2018 (http://www.corriere.it/cronache/09_febbraio_11/paese_baroni_universita_gori_6a989304-f879-11dd-9277-00144f02aabc.shtml); Rooster GNN. 2015. "The Italian University and Its Aristocracy." Retrieved April 18, 2018 (https://rgnn.org/2015/11/14/the-italian-university-its-aristocracy/); Pianigiani, Gaia. 2010. "In Italy, Education Protests Spread," *New York Times*, November 26; and Grove, Jack. 2016. "Anti-Corruption Boss to Target Italian Universities," *Times Higher Education*, October 11.

67. RASIC_ITA28, biology, female, associate professor, conducted 9/25/14

68. RASIC_ITA35, physics, female, professor, conducted 9/26/14

69. RASIC_ITA41, physics, male, researcher, conducted 9/27/14

70. RASIC_ITA19, physics, female, researcher, conducted 9/4/14

71. See Pace, Enzo. 2006. "Religion as Communication: The Changing Shape of Catholicism in Europe." Pp. 37–50 in *Everyday Religion: Observing Modern Religious Lives*, edited by N. T. Ammerman. New York: Oxford University Press.

72. RASIC_ITA77, physics, male, professor, conducted 10/26/12

Chapter 7

1. BBC. 2017. "Turkey Reverses Female Army Officers' Headscarf Ban." Retrieved May 3, 2018 (http://www.bbc.com/news/world-europe-39053064).

2. RASIC_TK06, biology, male, assistant professor, conducted 6/16/12

3. It is important to note that a large minority of the Turkish population are Alevi—a heterodox Islamic group. Some then differentiate official Sunni Islam, and all sorts of what they call unofficial, marginal, and/or persecuted "Islams." See, for example, Hallam, Mark. 2016. "Turkey Discriminates Against Alevi Faith, ECHR Rules," *Deutsche Welle*, April 26.

4. See Ecklund, Elaine Howard, David R. Johnson, and Kirstin R. W. Matthews. 2016. "Opinion: The Persecution of Turkey's Scientists," *The Scientist*, September 14. Unfortunately, this is a very complex issue. It is still not exactly clear who was behind this attempt, but the group most directly targeted as the perpetrator by the government is the Gulen movement, which is a *religious* movement. Among the targets of the postcoup purge were Gulenists. Many left-leaning academics, especially those that criticized the government's policies toward the Kurdish minority, may have been

fired as well, but at least officially, the purge's main targets were Gulenists. See Weise, Zia. 2017. "Long Arm of Turkey's Anti-Gulenist Purge," *Politico*, August 21.

5. RASIC_TK44, biology, female, professor, conducted 6/14/12

6. See Abbott, Alison. 2005. "Turkish Rectors Rally in Support of University Head Thrown in Jail." *Nature* 438:8–9; and Abbott, Alison. 2012. "Secularist Academic Jailed in Turkey," *Nature*, June 26.

7. See OECD. 2016. "Turkey." In *OECD Science, Technology and Innovation Outlook 2016*. OECD Publishing, http://dx.doi.org/10.1787/sti_in_outlook-2016-en.

8. See page 219 of Yalçinkaya, M. Alper. 2015. *Learned Patriots: Debating Science, State, and Society in the Nineteenth-Century Ottoman Empire*. Chicago, IL: University of Chicago Press.

9. See Tubitak. 2018. "National Science, Technology and Innovation Statistics of Turkey." Retrieved March 23, 2018 (https://www.tubitak.gov.tr/en/content-national-science-technology-and-innovation-statistics-of-turkey).

10. Basal, Tayfun, and Gamze Keskin. 2013. "Turkey's Scientific Research Output Is Booming—But What About the Quality?," *Elsevier Turkey*, April 15.

11. See National Science Board. 2018. "Science and Engineering Indicators 2018." Retrieved April 26, 2018 (https://www.nsf.gov/statistics/2018/nsb20181/).

12. See Mizikaci, Fatma. 2006. *Monographs on Higher Education: Higher Education in Turkey*. Bucharest: UNESCO European Centre for Higher Education.

13. Rabasa, Angel, and F. Stephen Larrabee. 2008. *The Rise of Political Islam in Turkey*. Santa Monica, CA: RAND Corporation.

14. A good analysis of the Turkish case is Davison, Andrew. 2003. "Turkey, A 'Secular' State? The Challenge of Description." *South Atlantic Quarterly* 102(2/3):333–350. It is important to note how Turkish laicism is different from the French model as well, as Davison argues.

15. See Karanfil, Nese. 2015. "Intelligence, Religious Affairs Set to Take Huge Share of Turkey's 2016 Budget," *Hurriyet Daily News*, October 13.

16. RASIC_TK47, biology, female, assistant professor, conducted 6/15/12

17. RASIC_TK23, biology, female, assistant professor, conducted 5/27/15

18. Butler, Daren. 2017. "With More Islamic Schooling, Erdogan Aims to Reshape Turkey," *Reuters*, January 25.

19. RASIC_TK21, physics, female, full professor, conducted 5/27/15

20. RASIC_TK18, biology, female, graduate student, conducted 5/25/15

21. RASIC_TK20, biology, female, graduate student, conducted 5/26/15

22. RASIC_TK25, physics, male, full professor, conducted 5/28/15

23. RASIC_TK09, biology, female, professor, conducted 5/20/15

24. RASIC_TK27, biology, male, postdoctoral fellow, conducted 5/29/15

25. $F = 6.24$, $p = .0128$.

26. Nineteen percent of biologists say either that they don't believe in God or that they don't know whether there is a God and don't believe there is any way to find out, compared to 11 percent of physicists ($F = 4.96$, $p = .0264$).

27. $F = 5.44$, $p = .0201$.

28. $F = 18.46$, $p = .0000$.

29. $F = .02$, $p = .8873$.

30. $F = .15$, $p = .6998$.

31. $F = 2.76$, $p = .0974$.

32. $F = 17.57$, $p = .0000$.

33. Survey questions are of course limited; one of our advisors mentioned that for Turkish scientists the question may not be so much about how scientific knowledge itself made them more religious, but more about becoming more religious during their education. One could suggest that the latter would be the case if they became affiliated with religious networks/Islamic orders while they were PhD students, which is not uncommon.

34. $F = 2.74$, $p = .0988$.

35. Miller, Jon D., Eugenie C. Scott, and Shinji Okamoto. 2006. "Public Acceptance of Evolution." *Science* 313(5788):765–766.

36. $F = 6.35$, $p = .0121$.

37. $F = 6.87$, $p = .0091$.

38. $F = 5.09$, $p = .0245$.

39. $F = 10.73$, $p = .0011$.

40. $F = 8.54$, $p = .0036$. There could be many interpretations for this. Several hypotheses may be: the government's lower ability to influence staffing decisions in elite universities, and the location of the university (a cosmopolitan, big city versus a smaller city, where professors could feel more pressure to conform).

41. $F = 11.44$, $p = .0008$.

42. $F = 2.79$, $p = .0954$.

43. $F = 7.69$, $p = .0058$.

44. RASIC_TK31, physics, male, associate professor, conducted 7/10/15

45. RASIC_TK29, biology, female, associate professor, conducted 6/6/15

46. RASIC_TK42, physics, female, graduate student, conducted 10/15/15

47. RASIC_TK18, biology, female, PhD student, conducted 5/25/15

48. RASIC_TK40, physics, male, assistant professor, conducted 10/8/15

49. RASIC_TK28, biology, female, assistant professor, conducted 6/2/15

50. RASIC_TK46, physics, male, associate professor, conducted 6/14/12

51. RASIC_TK32, biology, male, assistant professor, conducted 6/13/15

52. We did interviews with fifty survey respondents; of these fifty interview respondents, twenty-nine have a non-null response for rlgaffi. Of them, seventeen are Muslim, and twelve are nones.For those who are Muslim, only seven say they are part of a particular tradition of Islam. Of these, six were Sunni/Hanefi and one is Bektashi (Shia).

53. RASIC_TK25, physics, male, professor, conducted 5/28/15

54. RASIC_TK33, physics, male, assistant professor, conducted 7/20/15

55. RASIC_TK01, biology, female, professor, conducted 5/11/15

56. RASIC_TK18, biology, female, PhD student, conducted 5/25/15

57. RASIC_TK48, physics, male, postdoctoral fellow, conducted 6/15/12

58. RASIC_TK20, biology, female, PhD student, conducted 5/26/15

59. RASIC_TK26, biology, female, professor, conducted 5/28/15

60. RASIC_TK4, biology, female, assistant professor, conducted 6/14/12

61. RASIC_TK27, biology, male, postdoctoral fellow, conducted 5/29/15

62. RASIC_TK38, biology, male, postdoctoral fellow, conducted 10/7/15

63. RASIC_TK47, biology, female, assistant professor, conducted 15/6/12

64. Of course these kinds of fears did make us wonder whether scientists we interviewed in Turkey may have been reticent to talk with us honestly; in this case, in particular, it was extremely important to couple survey and interview data in analysis and to have both non-Turkish and Turkish interviewers.

65. RASIC_TK09, biology, female, professor, conducted 5/20/15

66. RASIC_TK12, physics, female, professor, conducted 5/21/15

67. RASIC_TK10, biology, female, specialist, conducted 5/20/15

68. RASIC_TK41, biology, male, professor, 10/13/15

69. RASIC_TK21, physics, female, professor, conducted 5/27/15

70. Accommodating the religious practices of colleagues or avoiding such topics can be a strategic move to be able to keep one's job as well.

71. Ahval. 2018. "Prayer Breaks Come to Turkish Universities." Retrieved May 4, 2018 (https://ahvalnews.com/education/prayer-breaks-come-turkish-universities).

72. Abbott, Alison. 2017. "The Turkish Paradox: Can Scientists Thrive in a State of Emergency?," *Nature*, February 15.

73. Sirkeci, Ibrahim, and Jeffrey H. Cohen. 2016. "Turkey's Purge Could Cause a Massive Brain Drain," *The New Republic*, August 26.

Chapter 8

1. Ram, Arun. 2013. "ISRO Chief Seeks Divine Help for Mars Mission," *The Times of India*, November 5.

2. NDTV. 2014. "Kerala: Prayers to Be Held in Temple for Success of Mangalyaan." Retrieved April 18, 2018 (http://www.ndtv.com/south/kerala-prayers-to-be-held-in-temple-for-success-of-mangalyaan-668490).

3. Jacob, Jijo. 2013. "India's Space Chief Offered Mini Rocket to Gods Before Mars Mission," *International Business Times*, November 5.

4. See page 202 of Subbarayappa, B. V. 2011. "Indic Religions." Pp. 195–209 in *Science and Religion Around the World*, edited by J. H. Brooke and R. L. Numbers. New York: Oxford University Press.

5. Burke, Jason. 2014. "India's Mars Mission Set for Attempt to Enter Orbit," *The Guardian*, September 23.

6. Firstpost. 2013. "Tirupati and Mars Mission: Rationalists Cry Foul Over Isro Chief's Temple Visit." Retrieved April 17, 2018 (https://www.firstpost.com/india/tirupati-and-mars-mission-rationalists-cry-foul-over-isro-chiefs-temple-visit-1216771.html).

7. RASIC_IND74, physics, male, professor, conducted 4/16/12

8. RASIC_IND60, physics, male, reader, conducted 5/28/14

9. Madan, Triloki N. 1989. "Religion in India." *Daedalus* 118(4):114–146.

10. Das Acevedo, Deepa. 2013. "Secularism in the Indian Context." *Law and Social Inquiry* 38(1):138–167.

11. Symonds, Richard. 1950. *The Making of Pakistan*. London: Faber and Faber Publishing.

12. See page 9 of Brooke, John Hedley, and Ronald L. Numbers, eds. 2011. *Science and Religion Around the World*. New York: Oxford University Press.

13. Madan, Triloki N. 1987. "Secularism in Its Place." *Journal of Asian Studies* 46(4):747–759.

14. Hart, Henry C. 1980. "The Indian Constitution: Political Development and Decay." *Asia Survey* 20(4):428–451.

15. Government of India Ministry of Human Resource Development. 2016. "Constitutional Provision." Retrieved April 18, 2018 (http://mhrd.gov.in/fundamental_duties_article-51A).

16. See page 86 of Prakash, Gyan. 1999. *Another Reason: Science and the Imagination of Modern India*. Princeton, NJ: Princeton University Press.

17. Gosling, David L. 2016. "India's Response to Darwin." Pp. 70–87 in *Science and Religion: East and West*, edited by Y. Fehige. New York: Routledge. Perhaps the most famous piece on this topic is Brown, C. Mackenzie. 2016. "Jagadish Chandra Bose and Vedantic Science." Pp. 104–122 in *Science and Religion: East and West*, edited by Y. Fehige. New York: Routledge. See also Brown, C. Mackenzie. 2012. *Hindu Perspectives on Evolution: Darwin, Dharma, and Design*. New York: Routledge.

18. See page 519 of Vivekananda, Swami. 1964. *The Complete Works of Swami Vivekananda—Mayavati Memorial Edition*. Almora: Advaita Ashram.

19. RASIC_IND13, physics, male, professor emeritus, conducted 4/30/14

20. Subbarayappa, B. V. 2011. "Indic Religions." Pp. 195–209 in *Science and Religion Around the World*, edited by J. H. Brooke and R. L. Numbers. New York: Oxford University Press.

21. Jayaraman, K. S. 2001. "Angry Researchers Pour Scorn on Astrology Classes." *Nature* 411:227.

22. BBC World Service. 2001. "India Astrology vs. Indian Science." Retrieved February 9, 2015 (http://www.bbc.co.uk/worldservice/sci_tech/highlights/010531_vedic.shtml#top); Narlikar, Jayant V. 2001. "Vedic Astrology or Jyotirvigyan: Neither Vedic nor Vigyan." *Economic and Political Weekly* 36(24):2113–2115.

23. Vyas, Hetal. 2011. "Astrology Is a Science: Bombay HC," *Times of India*, February 3; Ramachandran, R. 2004. "Astrology on a Pedestal." *Frontline* 21(12).

24. RASIC_IND05, biology, male, professor, conducted 3/16/14

25. RASIC_IND36, biology, female, assistant professor, conducted 5/23/14

26. RASIC_IND59, physics, male, graduate student, conducted 5/27/14

27. An important work on this topic is Thomas, Renny. 2016. "Being Religious, Being Scientific: Science, Religion and Atheism in Contemporary India." Pp. 140–157 in *Science and Religion: East and West*, edited by Y. Fehige. New York: Routledge.

28. Note that Hong Kong is similar to India in this respect, the only other region where affiliation of scientists and the public are similar.

29. The only nationally representative data on belief in God in India simply asks a "yes" or "no" question, limiting our ability to compare Indian scientists to the public in a more precise manner.

30. In a series of binary logistic regressions, we find that elite scientists are significantly less likely to believe in God ($p < .05$). This finding persists while controlling for factors such as gender, discipline, age, PhD status, marital status, religious tradition, religious practices, and religious exclusivity.

31. The sociologist Renny Thomas discusses atheism among Indian scientists in great detail. See Thomas, Renny. 2017. "Atheism and Unbelief Among Indian Scientists; Towards an Anthropology of Atheism(s)." *Society and Culture in South Asia* 3(1):45–67.

32. Mander, William. 2012. "Pantheism." In *The Stanford Encyclopedia of Philosophy* Summer 2013 edition, edited by E. N. Zalta. Stanford, CA: Metaphysics Research Lab, CSLI, Stanford University.

33. RASIC_IND18, biology, male, research scientist, conducted 5/20/14

34. Some of our respondents also express a panentheistic view, which maintains an ontological distinction between the divine and the universe, thus allowing for both immanence and transcendence.

35. RASIC_IND08, biology, female, professor, conducted 3/17/14

36. RASIC_IND58, physics, female, graduate student, conducted 5/27/14

37. RASIC_IND19, biology, male, research scientist, conducted 5/20/14

38. RASIC_IND13, physics, male, professor emeritus, conducted 4/30/14

39. RASIC_IND37, physics, male, associate professor, conducted 5/23/14

40. It is possible that some might read this section and say, in the words of Richard Dawkins, "Pantheism is sexed-up atheism." (See page 40 of Dawkins, Richard. 2008. *The God Delusion.* New York: Houghton Mifflin Company.) This is tied to one of the largest critiques of pantheism, that it is inappropriate to call the universe "god." See also Mander, William. 2012. "Pantheism." In *The Stanford Encyclopedia of Philosophy*, Fall 2015 edition, edited by E. N. Zalta. Santa Clara County, CA: Center for the Study of Language and Information, Stanford University.

41. RASIC_IND24, biology, male, graduate student, conducted 5/21/14

42. RASIC_IND59, male, physics, graduate student, conducted 5/27/14

43. RASIC_IND07, physics, male, assistant professor, conducted 3/17/14

44. RASIC_IND49, biology, male, principal scientist, conducted 5/25/14

45. $F = 12.4$, $p = .0004$. Net of discipline, elite status, career stage, marital status, immigrant status, religious affiliation, and disbelief in God, female scientists had 43 percent lower odds than male scientists of holding the conflict view rather than the independence view in India.

46. RASIC_IND13, physics, male, professor emeritus, conducted 4/30/14

47. RASIC_IND38, physics, male, professor emeritus, conducted 5/23/14

48. Thomas, Renny. 2018. "Beyond Conflict and Complementarity Science and Religion in Contemporary India." *Science, Technology and Society* 23(1):47–64.

49. Multinomial logistic regression predicting the collaboration view shows that Hindus ($p < .002$), Sikhs ($p < .026$), and Muslims ($p < .000$) are significantly more likely than the nonaffiliated to embrace collaboration over independence or conflict views. Controls in the analysis include gender, discipline, organizational context (elite or nonelite institution), doctoral status, religious beliefs, and religious practices.

50. RASIC_IND71, biology, male, professor, conducted 9/3/14

51. RASIC_IND31, biology, male, associate professor, conducted 5/22/14

52. RASIC_IND28, biology, male, associate professor, conducted 5/22/14

53. RASIC_IND07, physics, male, assistant professor, conducted 3/17/14

54. RASIC_IND54, physics, male, associate professor, conducted 5/27/14

55. RASIC_IND23, biology, male, graduate student, conducted 5/21/14

56. RASIC_IND19, biology, male, research scientist, conducted 5/20/14

57. RASIC_IND69, biology, female, assistant professor, conducted 8/23/14

58. RASIC_IND18, biology, male, research scientist, conducted 5/20/14

59. RASIC_IND06, biology, female, PhD student, conducted 3/17/14

60. RASIC_IND59, physics, male, graduate student, conducted 5/27/14

61. RASIC_IND01, biology, female, PhD student, conducted 3/13/14

62. RASIC_IND55, physics, female, professor, conducted 5/27/14

63. RASIC_IND56, physics, male, associate professor, conducted 5/27/14

64. RASIC_IND38, physics, male, professor emeritus, conducted 5/23/14

65. Thomas, Renny, and Robert M. Geraci. 2018. "Religious Rites and Scientific Communities: Ayudha Puja as 'Culture' at the Indian Institute of Science." *Zygon* 53(1):95–122.

66. RASIC_IND23, biology, male, graduate student, conducted 5/21/14

67. RASIC_IND18, biology, male, research scientist, conducted 5/20/14

68. RASIC_IND09, biology, female, professor, conducted 3/17/14

69. RASIC_IND60, physics, male, reader, conducted 5/28/14

70. RASIC_IND37, physics, male, associate professor, conducted 5/23/14

71. RASIC_IND36, biology, female, assistant professor, conducted 5/23/14

72. RASIC_IND46, biology, male, principal scientist, conducted 5/25/14

73. RASIC_IND71, biology, male, professor, conducted 9/3/14

74. RASIC_IND25, biology, female, graduate student, conducted 5/21/14

75. RASIC_IND22, biology, female, PhD student, conducted 5/21/14

76. Khan, Shehab, and Becca Meier. 2017. "Bangalore College Becomes First Indian University to Make Global Top 10," *Independent*, March 7.

77. Offord, Catherine. 2017. "Scientists to Protest Across India," *The Scientist*, August 7.

78. Prasannal, Laxmi. 2017. "Hundreds Join 'March for Science' in Thiruvananthapuram," *The Times of India*, August 9.

79. RASIC_IND36, biology, male, assistant professor, conducted 5/23/14

80. RASIC_IND28, biology, male, associate professor, conducted 5/22/14

81. RASIC_IND53, physics, male, senior professor, conducted 5/26/14

82. World Values Survey, India. 2014. V147–148.

83. Wallace, David Foster. 2009. *This Is Water*. New York: Little, Brown and Company.

Chapter 9

1. Weller, Robert P. 1999. *Alternative Civilities: Democracy and Culture in China and Taiwan*. New York: Routledge; and Zhao, Suisheng, ed. 1999. *Across the Taiwan Strait: Mainland China, Taiwan, and the 1995–1996 Crisis*. New York: Routledge.

2. Mathews, Gordon, Eric Kit-wai Ma, and Tai-lok Lui. 2008. *Hong Kong, China: Learning to Belong to a Nation*. New York: Routledge.

3. National Science Board. 2018. "Science and Engineering Indicators 2018." Retrieved April 26, 2018 (https://www.nsf.gov/statistics/2018/nsb20181/).

4. Government of the Hong Kong Special Administrative Region. 2017. "Science and Technology." Retrieved April 26, 2018 (https://www.censtatd.gov.hk/hkstat/sub/sp120.jsp?ID=0&productType=8&tableID=207).

5. RASIC_HK05, biology, female, associate professor, conducted 12/15/14

6. RASIC_HK08, physics, male, professor, conducted 12/16/14

7. Freedman, Maurice. 1974. "On the Sociological Study of Chinese Religion." Pp. 19–41 in *Religion and Ritual in Chinese Society*, edited by A. P. Wolf. Standford,

CA: Stanford University Press; and Hu, Anning, and Reid J. Leamaster. 2013. "Longitudinal Trends of Religious Groups in Deregulated Taiwan: 1990 to 2009." *Sociological Quarterly* 54(2):254–277.

8. Yang, C. K. 1961. *Religion in Chinese Society: A Study of Contemporary Social Functions of Religion and Some of Their Historical Factors*. Berkeley: University of California Press.

9. See page 310 of Overmyer, Daniel L. 2003. *Folk Buddhist Religion: Dissenting Sects in Late Traditional China*. Cambridge, MA: Harvard University Press.

10. See page 775 of Liu, Eric Y. 2009. "Beyond the West: Religiosity and the Sense of Mastery in Modern Taiwan." *Journal for the Scientific Study of Religion* 48(4):774–788. See also Sun, Anna. 2013. *Confucianism as a World Religion: Contested Histories and Contemporary Realities*. Princeton, NJ: Princeton University Press.

11. See page 556 of Voas, David. 2014. "Does Education Develop or Diminish Spirituality in Taiwan?" *Journal for the Scientific Study of Religion* 53(3):556–574. See also Yang, Fenggang, and Anning Hu. 2012. "Mapping Chinese Folk Religion in Mainland China and Taiwan." *Journal for the Scientific Study of Religion* 51(3):505–521; and Leamaster, Reid J., and Anning Hu. 2014. "Popular Buddhists: The Relationship Between Popular Religious Involvement and Buddhist Identity in Contemporary China." *Sociology of Religion* 75(2):234–259.

12. Yang, C. K. 1961. *Religion in Chinese Society: A Study of Contemporary Social Functions of Religion and Some of Their Historical Factors*. Berkeley: University of California Press.

13. See Hu, Anning, and Fenggang Yang. 2014. "Trajectories of Folk Religion in Deregulated Taiwan: An Age-Period-Cohort Analysis." *Chinese Sociological Review* 46(3):80–100.

14. See Cheng, May M., and Wong Siu-Lun. 1997. "Religious Convictions and Sentiments." Pp. 299–329 in *Indicators of Social Development: Hong Kong*, edited by L. Siu-Kai, L. Ming-Kwan, W. Po-San, and W. Siu-Lun. Hong Kong: Hong Kong Institute of Asia-Pacific Studies.

15. See Bouma, Gary D., and Andrew Singleton. 2004. "A Comparative Study of the Successful Management of Religious Diversity: Melbourne and Hong Kong." *International Sociology* 19(1):5–24.

16. See Bouma, Gary D., and Andrew Singleton. 2004. "A Comparative Study of the Successful Management of Religious Diversity: Melbourne and Hong Kong." *International Sociology* 19(1):5–24; and Yee, Pattie Luk Fong Yuk. 2005. "Managing Change in an Integrated School: A Hong Kong Hybrid Experience." *International Journal of Inclusive Education* 9(1):89–103.

17. See Lee, Joseph S. 2010. "Taiwan: Immigration to Taiwan." Pp. 335–351 in *Immigration Worldwide: Policies, Practices, and Trends*, edited by U. A. Segal, D. Elliott, and N. S. Mayadas. New York: Oxford University Press.

18. See Hu, Anning, and Reid J. Leamaster. 2013. "Longitudinal Trends of Religious Groups in Deregulated Taiwan: 1990 to 2009." *Sociological Quarterly* 54(2):254–277; and Lee, Chengpang, and Myungsahm Suh. 2017. "State Building and Religion: Explaining the Diverged Path of Religious Change in Taiwan and South Korea, 1950–1980." *American Journal of Sociology* 123(2):465–509.

19. Qu, Haiyuan. 2002. "New Religions in Taiwan (Taiwan Xin Xing Zong Jiao)." *Twenty-One Century* 73:103–113; and Weber, Max. 1951. *The Religion of China: Confucianism and Taoism*. Free Press.

20. Leamaster, Reid J., and Anning Hu. 2014. "Popular Buddhists: The Relationship Between Popular Religious Involvement and Buddhist Identity in Contemporary China." *Sociology of Religion* 75(2):234–259; and Wang, Shunmin. 1995. "The Studies on the Transition of Contemporary Taiwan Buddhism." *Hung-Hwa Buddhist Journal* 8:315–342.

21. Leamaster, Reid J., and Anning Hu. 2014. "Popular Buddhists: The Relationship Between Popular Religious Involvement and Buddhist Identity in Contemporary China." *Sociology of Religion* 75(2):234–259; and Yang, Fenggang, and Anning Hu. 2012. "Mapping Chinese Folk Religion in Mainland China and Taiwan." *Journal for the Scientific Study of Religion* 51(3):506–522.

22. See Heron, Liz. 2009. "Victory for Darwin," *South China Morning Post*, June 26. See Huang, Wenya, Guojia Weng, Xiangfei Chen, and Pinhao Qui. 2011. "We Will Not Let Our Teachers Down," *Tzu Chi*, September 16 for examples of public debate about science and religion in Hong Kong and Taiwan.

23. See Heron, Liz. 2009. "Victory for Darwin," *South China Morning Post*, June 26, for a report about the debate that centers on teaching evolution in schools in Hong Kong.

24. See Heron, Liz. 2009. "Victory for Darwin," *South China Morning Post*, June 26, for a description of "Victory of Darwin" in Hong Kong.

25. See Liang, Delun. 2014. "Cooperating with Religious Mawan Park, Science Festival Is Blamed to Be Pseudo-Science," *Apple Daily*, March 2.

26. See Huang, Wenya, Guojia Weng, Xiangfei Chen, and Pinhao Qui. 2011. "We Will Not Let Our Teachers Down," *Tzu Chi*, September 16.

27. See Life Conservationist Association. 2004. "Religious Welfare and Animal Protection: A Case of Live Animal Anatomy in High School." Retrieved May 7, 2018 (http://www.lca.org.tw/column/node/713).

28. RASIC_HK05, biology, female, associate professor, conducted 12/15/14

29. Forty-one percent of nonimmigrants are affiliated, and only 22 percent of immigrants are affiliated. F = 6.67, p = .0103. That said, the Hong Kong regional survey included a write-in question that allowed respondents to indicate the nation/region from which they migrated. These data should be interpreted with caution, as only 42 respondents of the 164 who were born outside of Hong Kong entered a response. But of these 42 respondents, 38 indicated they were from China or a province of China, and 31 of them were unaffiliated with a religious tradition. Compared to the 124 respondents from Hong Kong, among whom 42 percent were affiliated, significantly fewer of those from China—16 percent—were affiliated. F = 8.57, p = .0039.

30. Yang, Fenggang, and Anning Hu. 2012. "Mapping Chinese Folk Religion in Mainland China and Taiwan." *Journal for the Scientific Study of Religion* 51(3):506–522.

31. RASIC_TW44, biology, male, professor, conducted 5/4/15

32. RASIC_TW38, biology, female, research specialist, conducted 12/11/14

33. RASIC_HK01, biology, male, associate professor, conducted 12/11/14

34. RASIC_HK04, physics, male, associate professor, conducted 12/12/14

35. RASIC_TW25, physics, female, PhD student, conducted 11/13/14
36. RASIC_TW19, physics, male, professor, conducted 11/10/14
37. RASIC_TW50, biology, male, associate professor, conducted 11/9/12
38. RASIC_HK03, physics, male, postdoc, conducted 12/12/14
39. RASIC_HK04, physics, male, associate professor, conducted 12/12/14
40. RASIC_HK05, biology, female, associate professor, conducted 12/15/14
41. RASIC_HK29, biology, female, professor, conducted 12/11/12
42. RASIC_HK04, physics, male, associate professor, conducted 12/12/14
43. RASIC_TW13, biology, female, associate professor, conducted 11/6/14
44. RASIC_HK15, biology, male, associate professor, conducted 12/22/14
45. The International Social Survey Programme (2008), which we use to compare scientists' beliefs about God to the public in other regions discussed in this book, did not survey those in Hong Kong. And while it did include a sample of the Taiwanese public, the measure for belief in God was problematic because the response options would not be valid for many non-Christian or polytheistic traditions. We therefore created our own question with response options reflected in Table 9.2 that we could ask in both Hong Kong and Taiwan.
46. On Table 9.3 we can see that, among the 11.6 percent of Taiwanese scientists who attend religious services at least once a week, 3.8 percent of them attend religious services more than once a week.
47. Yang, Fenggang, and Anning Hu. 2012. "Mapping Chinese Folk Religion in Mainland China and Taiwan." *Journal for the Scientific Study of Religion* 51(3):506–522.
48. In Hong Kong, 60 percent of immigrant scientists identified as either atheist ("I don't believe in any God or gods") or agnostic (I don't know whether there is a God or gods, and I don't believe there is any way to find out), compared to only 29 percent of native-born scientists ($F = 15.81$, $p = .0001$). In Taiwan, about half of immigrant scientists were atheist or agnostic and about a quarter of nonimmigrant scientists were ($F = 9.66$, $p = .0019$).
49. In Hong Kong, 57 percent of immigrant scientists never or practically never attend religious services, compared to 32 percent of native-born scientists ($F = 10.76$, $p = .0012$). Among immigrants in Taiwan, 38 percent never or practically never attend religious services, compared to 21 percent of nonimmigrants ($F = 5.13$, $p = .0238$).
50. More than one in five (22 percent) of immigrant scientists in Hong Kong believe there is little truth in any religion, compared to less than one in ten (9 percent) of native-born scientists ($F = 6.23$, $p = .0131$). In Taiwan, 14 percent of immigrant scientists believe there is little truth in any religion while 6 percent of nonimmigrants do, though the difference is not statistically significant ($F = 2.27$, $p = .1326$).
51. RASIC_HK22, biology, male, professor, conducted 11/21/12
52. RASIC_HK29, biology, female, professor, conducted 12/11/12 (Citizenship: both British citizen and Hong Kong permanent resident)
53. RASIC_TW02, biology, male, research fellow, conducted 10/24/14
54. RASIC_HK04, physics, male, associate professor, conducted 12/12/14
55. $F = 6.70$, $p = .0101$.
56. RASIC_TW19, physics, male, professor, conducted 11/10/14
57. RASIC_TW14, physics, male, research fellow, conducted 11/7/14
58. RASIC_HK02, biology, male, clinical assistant professor, conducted 12/11/14

59. RASIC_HK01, biology, male, associate professor, conducted 12/11/14

60. RASIC_TW32, physics, female, research assistant, conducted 11/27/14

61. RASIC_TW48, physics, female, professor, conducted 11/8/12

62. RASIC_TW48, physics, female, professor, conducted 11/8/12

63. RASIC_TW17, biology, female, research assistant, conducted 11/10/14

64. RASIC_TW35, biology, female, assistant research fellow, conducted 12/5/14

65. RASIC_TW02, biology, male, research fellow, conducted 10/17/14

66. RASIC_ TW48, physics, female, professor, conducted 11/8/12

67. RASIC_HK21, physics, male, post-doctoral fellow, conducted 11/20/12

68. RASIC_TW51, physics, female, professor, conducted 11/9/12

69. RASIC_TW23, biology, female, professor, conducted 11/12/14

70. RASIC_TW03, biology, female, associate professor, conducted 10/23/14

71. RASIC_HK02, biology, male, clinical assistant professor, conducted 12/11/14

72. RASIC_TW15, physics, female, postdoc, conducted 11/7/14

73. RASIC_TW43, biology, female, professor, conducted 8/14/15

74. RASIC_TW01, physics, male, associate professor, conducted 10/16/14

75. RASIC_HK06, physics, male, associate professor, conducted 11/21/14 (Citizenship: both Australia and the United Kingdom)

76. See Di, Di, and Elaine Howard Ecklund. 2017. "Producing Sacredness and Defending Secularity: Faith in the Workplace of Taiwanese Scientists." *Socius: Sociological Research for a Dynamic World* 3:1–15.

77. RASIC_HK23, physics, male, professor, conducted 11/22/12

78. RASIC_HK04, physics, male, associate professor, conducted 12/12/14

79. RASIC_TW21, physics, male, professor, conducted 11/11/14

80. RASIC_TW43, biology, female, professor, conducted 8/14/15

81. See Fuller, Steve. 2007. *Science vs. Religion? Intelligent Design and the Problem of Evolution*. Malden, MA: Polity Press.

82. Yang, Fenggang, and Anning Hu. 2012. "Mapping Chinese Folk Religion in Mainland China and Taiwan." *Journal for the Scientific Study of Religion* 51(3):506–522.

Chapter 10

1. It may have also led to an anti-immigration backlash, including the passing of Brexit in 2016, which would remove the United Kingdom from the European Union.

2. The proportion of scientists holding the conflict view is greater than the proportion holding the collaboration views in France, Italy, the United Kingdom, and United States, while the proportion holding the collaboration view is greater than that holding the conflict view in Hong Kong, India, Taiwan, and Turkey.

3. See, for example, Ecklund, Elaine Howard, and Christopher P. Scheitle. 2017. *Religion vs. Science: What Religious People Really Think*. New York: Oxford University Press.

4. Emerson, Michael O., and David Hartman. 2006. "The Rise of Religious Fundamentalism." *Annual Review of Sociology* 32:127–144.

5. See, for example, Gieryn, Thomas F. 1983. "Boundary-Work and the Demarcation of Science from Non-Science: Strains and Interests in Professional Ideologies of Scientists." *American Sociological Review* 48(6):781–795.

6. See Ecklund, Elaine Howard. 2010. *Science vs. Religion: What Scientists Really Think*. New York: Oxford University Press.

7. Taylor, Charles. 2007. *A Secular Age*. Cambridge, MA: Harvard University Press.

8. See, Peterson, Gregory R. 2003. "Demarcation and the Scientistic Fallacy." *Zygon: Journal of Religion and Science* 38:751–761.

Appendix B

1. Ecklund, Elaine Howard, David R. Johnson, Christopher P. Scheitle, Kirstin R. W. Matthews, and Steven W. Lewis. 2016. "Religion Among Scientists in International Context: A New Study of Scientists in Eight Regions." *Socius* 2:1–9. Response rates based on the American Association for Public Opinion Research's definition Number 3 (See The American Association for Public Opinion Research. 2016. *Standard Definitions: Final Dispositions of Case Codes and Outcome Rates for Surveys. 9th edition.* Oakbrook Terrace, IL: AAPOR.)

2. Although we attempted to exclude these groups through the sampling process, some scientists who specialize or conduct research in these areas still made it into our survey and interview samples. For example, they might have been included if they were part of the broader department and their area of research was not clear.

3. Kaiman, Jonathan. 2014. "Hong Kong's Umbrella Revolution—The Guardian Briefing," *The Guardian*, September 30.

4. Chevaillier, Thierry. 2001. "French Academics: Between the Professions and the Civil Service." *Higher Education* 41:49–75.

5. Tattersall, Nick, and Seyhmus Cakan. 2015. "Eight Soldiers Killed, Istanbul Palace Attacked as Turkish Unrest Mounts," *Reuters*, August 19.

6. 620020002 survey respondent

Appendix C

1. Excluded from the UK survey. In France, the question asked "Are you currently affiliated with <Lab>?"

2. Text entry not recorded in India.

3. As worded on the US survey. Response categories varied by nation. In France, categories included 1 = "doctorant," 2 = "chercheur postdoctoral," 3 = "chargé de Recherche 2ème classe," 4 = "chargé de recherche 1ère classe," 5 = "directeur de recherche 2ème classe," 6 = "directeur de recherche 1ère classe," 7 = "directeur de recherche de classe exceptionnelle," 8 = "maitre de conférence," 9 = "professeur 2ème classe," 10 = "professeur 1ère classe," 11 = "professeur de classe exceptionnelle," and 12 = "other [specify]." In Hong Kong, responses included 1 = "graduate student," 2 = "postdoctoral researcher," 3 = "research associate," 4 = "assistant professor," 5 = "associate professor," 6 = "professor," and 7 = "other [specify]." In India, categories included 1 = "graduate/postgraduate student (MSc, PhD)," 2 = "postdoctoral fellow," 3 = "research fellow," 4 = "lecturer," 5 = "senior lecturer," 6 = "reader," 7 = "research associate," 8 = "scientist (B-D)," 9 = "scientist (E-G)," 10 = "scientific officer," 11 = "assistant professor," 12 = "associate professor," 13 = "professor," and 14 = "other [specify]." In Italy, categories included 1 = "dottorando di ricerca," 2 = "postdoctoral fellow," 3 = "ricercatore / research fellow / research scientist," 4 = "professore associato / di II fascia," 5 = "professore ordinario / di I fascia," and 6 = other [specify]." In Taiwan, categories included 1 = "graduate student," 2 = "postdoctoral researcher,"

3 = "assistant research fellow," 4 = "assistant professor," 5 = "associate research fellow," 6 = "associate professor," 7 = "research fellow," 8 = "professor," and 9 = other [specify]." In Turkey, categories included 1 = "graduate student," 2 = "postdoctoral fellow," 3 = "research assistant," 4 = "assistant professor," 5 = "associate professor," 6 = "professor," and 7 = "other [specify]." In the United Kingdom, categories included 1 = "postgraduate student," 2 = "postdoctoral fellow," 3 = "research fellow," 4 = "lecturer," 5 = "senior lecturer," 6 = "reader," 7 = "professor," and 8 = "other [specify]."

4. Excluded from India and UK surveys. In Hong Kong and Taiwan, response category 3 was worded "my position is not permanent, and I am not certain that I am moving towards a permanent position."

5. Text entry not recorded in India.

6. Only included on India survey.

7. In France, Hong Kong, Italy, Taiwan, and Turkey, response options were binary, with categories including only the region of study (e.g., "France") and "other."

8. Wording varied by region. In France, we asked, "Do you have a degree or specialization in medicine or surgery?" In Hong Kong, we asked, "Do you have a medical degree such as a Doctor of Medicine (MD) or an MBBS or MBChB (Bachelor of Medicine or Bachelor of Surgery)?" In India and the United Kingdom, we asked, "do you have an MBBS (that is, Bachelor of Medicine or Bachelor of Surgery)?" In Italy, we asked, "Do you have a degree or specialization in medicine or surgery?" In Taiwan, we asked, "Do you have a medical degree such as a Doctor of Medicine (MD) or an MBBS (Bachelor of Medicine, Bachelor of Surgery)?" In Turkey, we asked, "Do you have a degree or specialization in medicine or surgery?"

9. Excluded from the Hong Kong, India, Taiwan, and the UK surveys.

10. Excluded from France, Italy, Turkey, and the US surveys. In India, the question was worded "your regional or ethnic background."

11. Excluded from the UK survey. In India, the question was worded "your regional language or mother-tongue."

12. Included on the India survey only.

13. Excluded from the UK survey.

14. In France, Turkey, and the United States, the category was identified as "graduate instructional activities."

15. In France, Turkey, and the United States, the category was identified as "graduate instructional activities."

16. Text entry excluded from the India and UK surveys.

17. Items included only on the US survey.

18. Text entry excluded from the India and UK surveys.

19. Reads " . . . located outside of Hong Kong" and " . . . located outside of Taiwan" on the respective surveys.

20. Reads " . . . located outside of Hong Kong" and " . . . located outside of Taiwan" on the respective surveys.

21. Reads " . . . located outside of Hong Kong" and " . . . located outside of Taiwan" on the respective surveys.

22. Reads " . . . located outside of Hong Kong" and " . . . located outside of Taiwan" on the respective surveys.

23. Text entry not recorded in India.

24. Text entry not recorded in India.

25. Reads " . . . denomination or sect . . . " in India.

26. Text entry not recorded in India.

27. The Hong Kong survey omits the phrase " . . . these days," and the Taiwan survey replaces this phrase with "lately." In India, we asked, "Apart from weddings and funerals, about how often do you perform or participate in religious services and rituals these days (including household pujas, public religious services, etc.)?" In Turkey, we asked Muslim respondents, "Apart from funerals, about how often do you go to the mosque these days?" and we asked non-Muslim respondents, "Apart from funerals, weddings and baptisms, about how often do you go to the synagogue/church these days?" The Italy survey asked, "Apart from some religious rituals such as marriages, funerals, and baptisms, about how often do you attend religious functions?" with response categories including 1 = "more than once a week," 2 = "once a week," 3 = "two-three times a month," 4 = "once a month," 5 = "only on special holy days," 6 = "once a year," 7 = "less often," 8 = "never, practically never."

28. The Hong Kong, India, Taiwan, and the UK surveys omit the phrase "Now thinking about the present . . . ." On the Italy survey, we asked, "Think of your current situation. How often to you happen to pray?"

29. Reads "An atheist" on the France, Italy, and Turkey surveys.

30. Excluded from the Hong Kong and Taiwan surveys.

31. Included on the Hong Kong and Taiwan surveys only.

32. Included on the Turkey survey only.

33. Excluded from the France, Italy, UK, and US surveys. On the Turkey survey, the question is phrased, "How often have you read the Qur'an in the past 12 months?" and was asked only if respondent identified as Muslim (RLGAFF1 = 5).

34. Excluded from the Turkey survey.

35. Skip pattern excluded on the US survey. All US respondents were prompted to answer this question.

36. Excluded from the Turkey survey.

37. Included on the India survey only.

38. Included on the India survey only.

39. Included on the India survey only.

40. Included on the Hong Kong and Taiwan surveys only.

41. Included on the Hong Kong, India, and Taiwan surveys only.

42. Included on the Hong Kong, India, and Taiwan surveys only.

43. Text entry not recorded in India.

44. Excluded from the Hong Kong and Taiwan surveys.

45. Included on the Hong Kong and Taiwan surveys only.

46. Text entry not recorded in India.

47. Text entry not recorded in India.

48. Reads "An atheist" on the France, Italy, and Turkey surveys.

49. In France, Hong Kong, India, Taiwan, and Turkey, response options were binary, with categories including only the region of study (e.g., "France") and "other."

50. As worded on the US survey. Question wording and response categories varied by nation. In France, we asked, "What is the highest level of education your mother or

father (or the main person who took care of you during your childhood) has achieved?" with response categories including 1 = "never went to school," 2 = "primary school, with or without certificate," 3 = "junior high school (6th to 9th grade)," 4 = "professional/technical school after junior high school, without baccalaureate," 5 = "professional/technical school after junior high school, with baccalaureate," 6 = "high school (10th to 12th grade), without baccalaureate," 7 = "high school (10th to 12th grade), with baccalaureate," 8 = "university, first cycle (or equivalent to Bac +2)," and 9 = "university, second or third cycle (or equivalent to Bac +3 / graduate studies and beyond)." In Hong Kong, response categories included 1 = "no formal education / kindergarten," 2 = "primary schools," 3 = "lower secondary schools," 4 = "higher secondary schools," 5 = "matriculation," 6 = "technical institutes—craft courses," 7 = "commercial college / polytechnic—diploma and certificate courses," 8 = "tertiary—degree," and 9 = "postgraduate studies (masters and doctors)." In India, response categories included 1 = "nonliterate," 2 = "below primary: literate but did not complete primary school," 3 = "primary pass: completed class V but not class VIII," 4 = "middle pass: completed class VIII but not class X," 5 = "matric: completed class X / high school or equivalent," 6 = "intermediate / college no deg: class XI / PUC / post matric dpl," 7 = "graduate: BA, BSc, BCom, Polytech, Computer, BTC," 8 = "post graduate: MA, MSc, MCom, BEd, MEd, LlB, PG," and 9 = "professional degrees and higher research degrees (e.g., PhD)." In Italy, response categories included 1 = "no formal education," 2 = "incomplete primary school," 3 = "complete primary school," 4 = "incomplete secondary school: technical / vocational type," 5 = "complete secondary school: technical / vocational type," 6 = "incomplete secondary: university-preparatory type," 7 = "complete secondary: university-preparatory type," 8 = "some university-level education, without degree," 9 = "university-level education, with degree," and 10 = "PhD or equivalent." In Taiwan, response categories included 1 = "illiterate," 2 = "no school but can read / write," 3 = "some primary school," 4 = "primary school graduate," 5 = "some middle school," 6 = "middle school graduate," 7 = "some high school," 8 = "high school graduate," 9 = "some vocational high school," 10 = "vocational high school graduate," 11 = "technical school graduate," 12 = "college / university graduate," and 13 = "graduate school." In Turkey, response categories included 1 = "no formal education," 2 = "incomplete primary school," 3 = "complete primary school," 4 = "incomplete secondary school," 5 = "complete secondary school," 6 = "incomplete high school," 7 = "complete high school," 8 = "some university-level education, without degree," 9 = "university-level education, with degree," and 10 = "completed Masters' or PhD." In the United Kingdom, response categories included 1 = "no formal education," 2 = "incomplete primary school," 3 = "complete primary school," 4 = "incomplete secondary school: technical / vocational type," 5 = "complete secondary school: technical / vocational type," 6 = "incomplete secondary: university-preparatory type," 7 = "complete secondary: university-preparatory type," 8 = "some university-level education, without degree," 9 = "university-level education, with degree," and 10 = "PhD or equivalent."

51. Item included on the US survey only.

52. "Taiwanese" omitted from the Hong Kong survey.

53. Text entry not recorded for the India and UK surveys.

54. Text entry not recorded for the India and UK surveys.

55. The Hong Kong survey reads, "Apart from weddings, funerals and christenings, how often does your youngest child attend religious services?" The Taiwan survey reads " . . . youngest child participate in religious rituals and services these days." In Turkey, we asked Muslim respondents, "Apart from funerals, about how often does your youngest child go to the mosque these days?" and we asked non-Muslim respondents "Apart from funerals, weddings and baptisms, about how often does your youngest child go to the synagogue/church these days?" Response categories on the Italy survey included 1 = "more than once a week," 2 = "once a week," 3 = "two-three times a month," 4 = "once a month," 5 = "only on special holy days," 6 = "once a year," 7 = "less often," 8 = "never, practically never."

56. As worded on the US survey. Question wording and response categories varied by nation. In France and Italy, we asked, "Please specify your personal income before tax, counting all wages, salaries, pensions and benefits, and so on" with response categories including 1 = "less than €10,000," 2 = "€10,001–20,000," 3 = "€20,001–30,000," 4 = "€30,001–40,000," 5 = "€40,001–50,000," 6 = "€50,001–60,000," 7 = "€60,001–70,000," 8 = "€70,001–80,000," 9 = "€80,001–90,000, " 10 = "€90,001–100,000," 11 = "€100,001–125,000," 12 = "€125,001–150,000," 13 = "€150,001–200,000," 14 = "€200,001 or more," and 15 = "prefer not to say." In Hong Kong, we asked, "What is the approximate monthly income of your family (including all those living together)?" with response categories including 1 = "less than 5,000 dollars," 2 = "5,001–10,000 dollars," 3 = "10,001–15,000 dollars," 4 = "15,001–20,000 dollars," 5 = "20,001–25,000 dollars," 6 = "25,001–30,000 dollars," 7 = "30,001–50,000 dollars," 8 = "50,001–100,000 dollars," and 9 = "more than 100,000 dollars." In India, we asked, "Please specify your personal monthly income before tax; counting all wages, salaries, pensions and benefits and so on," with response categories including 1 = "less than Rupees 10,000," 2 = "Rupees 10,001–20,000," 3 = "Rupees 20,001–30,000," 4 = "Rupees 30,001–40,000," 5 = "Rupees 40,001–50,000," 6 = "Rupees 50,001–60,000," 7 = "Rupees 60,001–70,000," 8 = "Rupees 70,001–80,000," 9 = "Rupees 80,001–90,000," 10 = "Rupees 90,001–1,00,000," 11 = "Rupees 1,00,001–1,25,000," 12 = "Rupees 1,25,001–1,50,000," 13 = "Rupees 1,50,001–2,00,000," 14 = "Rupees 2,00,001 or more," and 15 = "prefer not to say." In Taiwan, we asked, "What is your average monthly income (including your salary from full- or part-time jobs, year-end bonus, commission, interest income, income from personal business or investments, government subsidies, rent, pension, etc.)?" with response categories including 1 = "no income," 2 = "NT$10,000 or less," 3 = "NT$10,001–NT$20,000," 4 = "NT$20,001–NT$30,000," 5 = "NT$30,001–NT$40,000," 6 = "NT$40,001–NT$50,000," 7 = "NT$50,001–NT$60,000," 8 = "NT$60,001–NT$70,000," 9 = "NT$70,001–NT$80,000," 10 = "NT$80,001–NT$90,000," 11 = "NT$90,001–NT$100,000," 12 = "NT$100,001–NT$110,000," 13 = "NT$110,001–NT$120,000," 14 = "NT$120,001–NT$130,000," 15 = "NT$130,001–NT$140,000," 16 = "NT$140,001–NT$150,000," 17 = "NT$150,001–NT$160,000," 18 = "NT$160,001–NT$170,000," 19 = "NT$170,001–NT$180,000," 20 = "NT$180,001–NT$190,000," 21 = "NT$190,001–NT$200,000,"

22 = "NT\$200,001–NT\$300,000," and 23 = "More than NT\$300,000." In Turkey, we first asked, "Could you indicate which category your family's average total monthly income falls into? Please include all sources such as salary, wages, profit, interest," which had an open entry response option {INCOME_OPEN_TR}. If respondents skipped the open entry response option, we then asked, "If you prefer not to report your exact income, could you at least indicate which category your family's total monthly income falls into?" {INCOME_TR}, which response categories including 1 = "0–499 TL," 2 = "500 TL–749 TL," 3 = "750 TL–999 TL," 4 = "1,000 TL–1,249 TL," 5 = "1,250 TL–1,499 TL," 6 = "1,500 TL–1,749 TL," 7 = "1,750 TL–1,999 TL," 8 = "2,000 TL–2,499 TL," and 10 = "3,000 TL +."

REFERENCES

Abbott, Alison. 2005. "Turkish Rectors Rally in Support of University Head Thrown in Jail." *Nature* 438:8–9.

Abbott, Alison. 2012. "Secularist Academic Jailed in Turkey." *Nature*, June 26.

Abbott, Alison. 2017. "The Turkish Paradox: Can Scientists Thrive in a State of Emergency?." *Nature*, February 15.

Adam, Charles, and Paul Tannery, eds. 1964–76. *Oeuvres de Descartes*. Paris: Vrin/ CNRS.

Ahval. 2018. "Prayer Breaks Come to Turkish Universities." Retrieved May 4, 2018 (https://ahvalnews.com/education/prayer-breaks-come-turkish-universities).

Alexander, Denis. 2014. *Creation or Evolution: Do We Have to Choose?* Oxford, UK: Monarch Books.

Alexander, Denis R., and Ronald L. Numbers, eds. 2010. *Biology and Ideology from Descartes to Dawkins*. Chicago, IL: University of Chicago Press.

Alister E. McGrath. "Brief Biography." Retrieved June 29, 2017 (http://alistermcgrath. weebly.com/biography.html).

American Association for Public Opinion Research. 2016. *Standard Definitions: Final Dispositions of Case Codes and Outcome Rates for Surveys. 9th edition*. Oakbrook Terrace, IL: AAPOR.

Anderson, Robert. 2006. *British Universities Past and Present*. London, UK: Bloomsbury Publishing.

Ash, Summer. 2016. "Guy Consolmangno, the Vatican's Chief Astronomer, on Balancing Church with the Cosmos." *Smithsonian*, May 31.

Basal, Tayfun, and Gamze Keskin. 2013. "Turkey's Scientific Research Output Is Booming—But What About the Quality?" *Elsevier Turkey*, April 15.

BBC. 2009. "Hijab." Retrieved April 13, 2018 (http://www.bbc.co.uk/religion/ religions/islam/beliefs/hijab_1.shtml).

BBC. 2017. "Turkey Reverses Female Army Officers' Headscarf Ban." Retrieved May 3, 2018 (http://www.bbc.com/news/world-europe-39053064).

BBC News. 2008. "Papal Visit Scuppered by Scholars." Retrieved April 18, 2018 (http://news.bbc.co.uk/2/hi/7188860.stm).

BBC World Service. 2001. "India Astrology vs. Indian Science." Retrieved February 9, 2015 (http://www.bbc.co.uk/worldservice/sci_tech/highlights/010531_vedic.shtml#top).

Beckford, Martin. 2010. "Atheists Are Wrong to Claim Science and Religion Are Incompatible, Church of England Says." *The Telegraph*, February 12.

Berger, Peter L., ed. 1999. *The Desecularization of the World: Resurgent Religion and World Politics*. Washington, DC: Ethics and Public Policy Center.

Berger, Peter L. 2014. *The Many Altars of Modernity: Toward a Paradigm for Religion in a Pluralist Age*. Berlin: Walter de Gruyter.

Bingham, John. 2013. "Christians Now a Minority in the UK as Half the Population Has No Religion." *Telegraph*, September 10.

BioLogos. n.d. "BioLogos." Retrieved May 3, 2018 (https://biologos.org/).

BioLogos. 2010. "France's Own Evolution Debate." Retrieved July 28, 2017 (http://biologos.org/blogs/archive/france%E2%80%99s-own-evolution-debate).

Blackwell, Richard J. 2002. "Galileo Galilei." Pp. 105–116 in *Science and Religion: A Historical Introduction*, edited by G. B. Ferngren. Baltimore, MD: Johns Hopkins University Press.

Bolger, Daniel, and Elaine Howard Ecklund. 2018. "Whose Authority? Perceptions of Science Education in Black and Latino Churches." *Review of Religious Research* 60:49–70.

Bouma, Gary D., and Andrew Singleton. 2004. "A Comparative Study of the Successful Management of Religious Diversity: Melbourne and Hong Kong." *International Sociology* 19(1):5–24.

Bourdieu, Pierre. 1988. *Homo Academicus*. Stanford, CA: Stanford University Press.

Bowler, Peter J. 2001. *Reconciling Science and Religion: The Debate in Early-Twentieth-Century Britain*. Chicago, IL: University of Chicago Press.

Branigan, Tania. 2002. "Top School's Creationists Preach Value of Biblical Story over Evolution." *The Guardian*, March 8.

Branigan, Tania. 2003. "Dawkins Attacks 'Educational Debauchery' of Creationist Schools." *The Guardian*, April 29.

Brinsden, Peter R. 1993. "Reproductive Health Care Policies Around the World: The Effect of the Human Fertilisation and Embryology Act 1990 upon the Practice of Assisted Reproduction Techniques in the United Kingdom." *Journal of Assisted Reproduction and Genetics* 10(8):493–499.

Brooke, John Hedley, and Ronald L. Numbers, eds. 2011. *Science and Religion Around the World*. New York: Oxford University Press.

Brown, C. Mackenzie. 2003. "The Conflict Between Religion and Science in Light of the Patterns of Religious Belief among Scientists." *Zygon: Journal of Religion and Science* 38(3):603–632.

Brown, C. Mackenzie. 2012. *Hindu Perspectives on Evolution: Darwin, Dharma, and Design*. New York: Routledge.

Brown, C. Mackenzie. 2016. "Jagadish Chandra Bose and Vedantic Science." Pp. 104–122 in *Science and Religion: East and West*, edited by Y. Fehige. New York: Routledge.

Burke, Jason. 2014. "India's Mars Mission Set for Attempt to Enter Orbit." *The Guardian*, September 23.

Butler, Daren. 2017. "With More Islamic Schooling, Erdogan Aims to Reshape Turkey." *Reuters*, January 25.

Casanova, José. 2008. "Public Religions Revisited." Pp. 101–119 in *Religion: Beyond a Concept*, edited by H. DeVries. New York: Fordham University Press.

Cheng, May M., and Wong Siu-Lun. 1997. "Religious Convictions and Sentiments." Pp. 299–329 in *Indicators of Social Development: Hong Kong*, edited by L. Siu-Kai, L. Ming-Kwan, W. Po-San, and W. Siu-Lun. Hong Kong: Hong Kong Institute of Asia-Pacific Studies.

Chevaillier, Thierry. 2001. "French Academics: Between the Professions and the Civil Service." *Higher Education* 41:49–75.

Chronicles. 2009. "The University of Barons: This Is How It Works." Retrieved April 18, 2018 (http://www.corriere.it/cronache/09_febbraio_11/paese_baroni_universita_gori_6a989304-f879-11dd-9277-00144f02aabc.shtml).

Clarke, Desmond. 2015. "Blaise Pascal." In *The Stanford Encyclopedia of Philosophy*, Fall 2015 edition, edited by E. N. Zalta. Santa Clara County, CA: Center for the Study of Language and Information, Stanford University (https://plato.stanford.edu/archives/fall2015/entries/pascal/).

Collins, Francis S. 2006. *The Language of God: A Scientist Presents Evidence for Belief.* New York: Free Press.

Congregation for the Doctrine of the Faith. 1987. "Instruction on Respect for Human Life in Its Origin and on the Dignity of Procreation." Retrieved April 18, 2018 (http://www.vatican.va/roman_curia/congregations/cfaith/documents/rc_con_cfaith_doc_19870222_respect-for-human-life_en.html).

Congregation for the Doctrine of the Faith. 2008. "Instruction *Dignitas Personae* on Certain Bioethical Questions." Retrieved April 18, 2018 (http://www.vatican.va/roman_curia/congregations/cfaith/documents/rc_con_cfaith_doc_20081208_dignitas-personae_en.html).

Cooley, Charles H. 1909. *Social Organization.* New York: Charles Scribner's Sons.

Copson, Andrew. 2012. "Free Schools Are Exploiting Loopholes to Teach Creationism." *The Guardian*, November 30.

Crockett, Alasdair, and David Voas. 2006. "Generations of Decline: Religious Change in 20th-Century Britain." *Journal for the Scientific Study of Religion* 45(4):567–584.

DailyMail.com. 2011. "Muslim Medical Students Boycotting Lectures on Evolution . . . Because It 'Clashes with the Koran.'" Retrieved April 17, 2015 (http://www.dailymail.co.uk/news/article-2066795/Muslim-students-walking-lectures-Darwinism-clashes-Koran.html).

Damerow, Peter, Peter McLaughlin, Gideon Freudenthal, and Jurgen Renn. 1992. *Exploring the Limits of Preclassical Mechanics.* New York: Springer-Verlag.

Das Acevedo, Deepa. 2013. "Secularism in the Indian Context." *Law and Social Inquiry* 38(1):138–167.

Davie, Grace. 1990. "Believing Without Belonging: Is This the Future of Religion in Britain?" *Social Compass* 37(4):455–469.

Davie, Grace. 1994. *Religion in Britain Since 1945: Believing Without Belonging.* Oxford, UK: Blackwell Publishers.

Davis, Nancy J., and Robert V. Robinson. 2009. "Overcoming Movement Obstacles by the Religiously Orthodox: The Muslim Brotherhood in Egypt, Shas in Israel,

Comunione e Liberazione in Italy, and the Salvation Army in the United States." *American Journal of Sociology* 114(5):1302–1349.

Davison, Andrew. 2003. "Turkey, A 'Secular' State? The Challenge of Description." *South Atlantic Quarterly* 102(2/3):333–350.

Dawkins, Richard. 2008. *The God Delusion.* New York: Houghton Mifflin Company.

Di, Di, and Elaine Howard Ecklund. 2017. "Producing Sacredness and Defending Secularity: Faith in the Workplace of Taiwanese Scientists." *Socius: Sociological Research for a Dynamic World* 3:1–15.

Dooley, James, and Helen Kerch. 2000. "Evolving Research Misconduct Policies and Their Significance for Physical Scientists." *Science and Engineering Ethics* 6(1):109–121.

Doward, Jamie. 2012. "Richard Dawkins Celebrates a Victory over Creationists." *The Guardian*, January 14.

Dubuisson, Daniel. 2003. *The Western Construction of Religion: Myths, Knowledge, and Ideology.* Baltimore, MD: John Hopkins University Press.

Durkheim, Emile. 1915. *The Elementary Forms of the Religious Life.* New York: Free Press.

Ecklund, Elaine Howard. 2010. *Science vs. Religion: What Scientists Really Think.* New York: Oxford University Press.

Ecklund, Elaine Howard, David R. Johnson, and Kirstin R. W. Matthews. 2016. "Opinion: Turkey's Scientists Under Pressure." *The Scientist*, September 14.

Ecklund, Elaine Howard, David R. Johnson, Christopher P. Scheitle, Kirstin R. W. Matthews, and Steven W. Lewis. 2016. "Religion Among Scientists in International Context: A New Study of Scientists in Eight Regions." *Socius* 2:1–9.

Ecklund, Elaine Howard, and Elizabeth Long. 2011. "Scientists and Spirituality." *Sociology of Religion* 72(3):253–274.

Ecklund, Elaine Howard, Jerry Park, and Katherine L. Sorrell. 2011. "Scientists Negotiate Boundaries Between Religion and Science." *Journal for the Scientific Study of Religion* 50(3):552–569.

Ecklund, Elaine Howard, Jerry Z. Park, and Phil Todd Veliz. 2008. "Secularization and Religious Change Among Elite Scientists." *Social Forces* 86(4):1805–1839.

Ecklund, Elaine Howard, and Christopher P. Scheitle. 2017. *Religion vs. Science: What Religious People Really Think.* New York: Oxford University Press.

The Economist. 2015. "How Secular France Is Giving Faith a Voice in the Planet's Future." Retrieved April 16, 2018 (https://www.economist.com/blogs/erasmus/2015/11/religion-and-climate-change).

The Economist. 2017. "The State and the Veil." Retrieved April 16, 2018 (https://www.economist.com/news/international/21715679-dispute-over-muslim-womens-attire-helping-nobody-state-and-veil).

Edemariam, Aida. 2008. "A Matter of Life and Death." *The Guardian*, March 27.

Elsdon-Baker, Fern. 2006. *The Selfish Genius: How Richard Dawkins Rewrote Darwin's Legacy.* London, UK: Icon Books.

Emerson, Michael O., and David Hartman. 2006. "The Rise of Religious Fundamentalism." *Annual Review of Sociology* 32:127–144.

Encylopedia Britannica. 2018. "United Kingdom." Retrieved April 27, 2018 (http://www.britannica.com/EBchecked/topic/615557/United-Kingdom/44685/Religion).

Evans, John H. 2002. *Playing God? Human Genetic Engineering and the Rationalization of Public Bioethical Debate*. Chicago: University of Chicago Press.

Evans, John H. 2010. *Contested Reproduction: Genetic Technologies, Religion, and Public Debate*. Chicago: University of Chicago Press.

Evans, John H. 2012. *The History and Future of Bioethics: A Sociological View*. New York: Oxford University Press.

Evans, John H. 2016. *What Is a Human? What the Answers Mean for Human Rights*. New York: Oxford University Press.

Evans, John H. 2018. *Morals Not Knowledge: Recasting the Contemporary U.S. Conflict Between Religion and Science*. Oakland: University of California Press.

Evans, John H., and Michael S. Evans. 2008. "Religion and Science: Beyond the Epistemological Conflict Narrative." *Annual Review of Sociology* 34:87–105.

Fanelli, Daniele. 2010. "Positive Results Increase down the Hierarchy of the Sciences." *PLoS ONE* 5(4):e10068.

Fath, Sebastien. 2007. "Putting God into the City: Protestants in France." Pp. 49–62 in *Politics and Religion in France and the United States*, edited by A. G. Hargreaves, J. Kelsay, and S. B. Twiss. Lanham, MD: Lexington Books.

Fineschi, Vittorio, M. Neri, and E. Turillazzi. 2005. "The New Italian Law on Assisted Reproduction Technology (Law 40/2004)." *Journal of Medical Ethics* 31(9):536–539.

Finocchiaro, Maurice A. 2009. "That Galileo Was Imprisoned and Tortured for Advocating Copernicanism." Pp. 68–78 in *Galileo Goes to Jail and Other Myths About Science and Religion*, edited by R. L. Numbers. Cambridge, MA: Harvard University Press.

Firstpost. 2013. "Tirupati and Mars Mission: Rationalists Cry Foul over ISRO Chief's Temple Visit." Retrieved April 17, 2018 (https://www.firstpost.com/india/tirupati-and-mars-mission-rationalists-cry-foul-over-isro-chiefs-temple-visit-1216771.html).

Fitzgerald, Timothy. 2003. *The Ideology of Religious Studies*. New York: Oxford University Press.

Forster, Siegfried. 2011. "Jef Aerosol Fait 'Chuuuttt!!!' Dans La Grande Symphonie Urbaine De Paris." *Les Voix Du Monde*, June 17.

France. Constitution, 1946. *Préambule de la Constitution du 27 octobre 1946*.

Freedman, Maurice. 1974. "On the Sociological Study of Chinese Religion." Pp. 19–41 in *Religion and Ritual in Chinese Society*, edited by A. P. Wolf. Standford, CA: Stanford University Press.

Fuller, Steve. 2007. *Science vs. Religion? Intelligent Design and the Problem of Evolution*. Malden, MA: Polity Press.

Gallup. 2017. "In U.S., Belief in Creationist View of Humans at New Low." Retrieved April 9, 2018 (http://news.gallup.com/poll/210956/belief-creationist-view-humans-new-low.aspx).

Garelli, Franco. 2014. *Religion Italian Style: Continuities and Changes in a Catholic Country*. Farnham, UK: Ashgate Publishing.

Giberson, Karl, and Mariano Artigas. 2007. *Oracles of Science: Celebrity Scientists Versus God and Religion*. New York: Oxford University Press.

Gieryn, Thomas F. 1983. "Boundary-Work and the Demarcation of Science from Non-Science: Strains and Interests in Professional Ideologies of Scientists." *American Sociological Review* 48(6):781–795.

Goodstein, Laurie. 1996. "Pope Backs Acceptance of Evolution." *Washington Post*, October 25.

Gosling, David L. 2016. "India's Response to Darwin." Pp. 70–87 in *Science and Religion: East and West*, edited by Y. Fehige. New York: Routledge.

Gould, Stephen Jay. 1997. "Nonoverlapping Magisteria." *Natural History* 106:16–22.

Government of the Hong Kong Special Administrative Region. 2017. "Science and Technology." Retrieved April 26, 2018 (https://www.censtatd.gov.hk/hkstat/sub/sp120.jsp?ID=0&productType=8&tableID=207).

Government of India Ministry of Human Resource Development. 2016. "Constitutional Provision." Retrieved April 18, 2018 (http://mhrd.gov.in/fundamental_duties_article-51A).

GOV.UK. "Free Schools." Retrieved July 17, 2017 (https://www.gov.uk/types-of-school/free-schools).

Greeley, Andrew M. 1967. "Religion and Academic Career Plans: A Note on Progress." *American Journal of Sociology* 72(6):668–672.

Greeley, Andrew M. 1973. *The New Agenda*. Doubleday.

Grimaux, Edouard. 1888. *Lavoisier 1743–1794*. Paris: Arno Press.

Grove, Jack. 2016. "Anti-Corruption Boss to Target Italian Universities." *Times Higher Education*, October 11.

Grove, Jack. 2016. "Catholic Priest Named as French University Head." *Times Higher Education*, December 20.

Gusterson, Hugh. 2001. "The Virtual Nuclear Weapons Laboratory in the New World Order." *American Ethnologist* 28(2):417–437.

Guth, Jessica, and Bryony Gill. 2008. "Motivations in East–West Doctoral Mobility: Revisiting the Question of Brain Drain." *Journal of Ethnic and Migration Studies* 34(5):825–841.

Habermas, Jurgen. 2010. *An Awareness of What Is Missing: Faith and Reason in a Post-Secular Age*. Cambridge, UK: Polity Press.

Hallam, Mark. 2016. "Turkey Discriminates Against Alevi Faith, ECHR Rules." *Deutsche Welle*, April 26.

Hargreaves, Alec G., John Kelsay, and Sumner B. Twiss, eds. 2007. *Politics and Religion in France and the US*. Lanham, MD: Lexington Books.

Hart, Henry C. 1980. "The Indian Constitution: Political Development and Decay." *Asia Survey* 20(4):428–451.

Heron, Liz. 2009. "Victory for Darwin." *South China Morning Post*, June 26.

Hill, Jonathan. 2014. "Rejecting Evolution: The Role of Religion, Education, and Social Networks." *Journal for the Scientific Study of Religion* 53(3):575–594.

Hill, Peter C., Kenneth I. Pargament, Ralph W. Hood, Michael E. McCullough Jr., James P. Swyers, David B. Larson, and Brian J. Zinnbauer. 2000. "Conceptualizing Religion and Spirituality: Points of Commonality, Points of Departure." *Journal for the Theory of Social Behaviour* 30(1):51–77.

Hu, Anning, and Reid J. Leamaster. 2013. "Longitudinal Trends of Religious Groups in Deregulated Taiwan: 1990 to 2009." *Sociological Quarterly* 54(2):254–277.

Hu, Anning, and Fenggang Yang. 2014. "Trajectories of Folk Religion in Deregulated Taiwan: An Age-Period-Cohort Analysis." *Chinese Sociological Review* 46(3):80–100.

Huang, Wenya, Guojia Weng, Xiangfei Chen, and Pinhao Qui. 2011. "We Will Not Let Our Teachers Down." *Tzu Chi*, September 16.

The Huffington Post. 2016. "Differentiating the Hijab from the Headscarf." Retrieved April 13, 2018 (http://www.huffingtonpost.com/rawan-abushaban/reducing-hijab-to-the-hea_b_9075126.html).

Inglehart, Ronald F., and Pippa Norris. 2004. *Sacred and Secular: Reexamining the Secularization Thesis.* Cambridge, UK: Cambridge University Press.

International Monetary Fund. 2012. "Italy 2012 Article IV Consultation." Retrieved April 18, 2018 (http://www.imf.org/external/pubs/ft/scr/2012/cr12167.pdf).

ISSP Research Group. 2012. International Social Survey Programme: Religion III - ISSP 2008. GESIS Data Archive, Cologne. ZA4950 Data file Version 2.2.0, doi:10.4232/1.11334.

Jacob, Jijo. 2013. "India's Space Chief Offered Mini Rocket to Gods Before Mars Mission." *International Business Times*, November 5.

Jayaraman, K. S. 2001. "Angry Researchers Pour Scorn on Astrology Classes." *Nature* 411:227.

Jeffries, Stuart. 2007. "Britain's New Cultural Divide Is Not Between Christian and Muslim, Hindu, and Jew. It Is Between Those Who Have Faith and Those Who Don't." *The Guardian*, February 26.

Johnson, David R. 2017. *A Fractured Profession: Commercialism and Conflict in Academic Science.* Baltimore, MD: Johns Hopkins University Press.

Johnson, David, Elaine Howard Ecklund, Di Di, and Kirstin Matthews. 2016. "Responding to Richard: Celebrity and (Mis)Representation of Science." *Public Understanding of Science* 27(5):535–549. doi: 10.1177/0963662516673501.

Johnson, David R., and Joseph C. Hermanowicz. 2017. "Peer Review: From 'Sacred Ideals' to 'Profane Realities.'" Pp. 485–527 in *Higher Education: Handbook of Theory and Research*, Vol. 32, edited by M. B. Paulsen. Springer.

Johnson, David R., and Jared L. Peifer. 2017. "How Public Confidence in Higher Education Varies by Social Context." *Journal of Higher Education* 88(4):619–644.

Johnson, David R., Christopher P. Scheitle, and Elaine Howard Ecklund. 2016. "Conservative Protestantism and Anti-Evolution Curricular Challenges Across States." *Social Science Quarterly* 97(5):1227–1244.

Kaden, Tom, Stephen H. Jones, Rebecca Catto, and Fern Elsdon-Baker. 2017. "Knowledge as Explanandum: Disentangling Lay and Professional Perspectives on Science and Religion." *Studies in Religion* 1–22. doi: 10.1177/0008429817741448.

Kaiman, Jonathan. 2014. "Hong Kong's Umbrella Revolution—The Guardian Briefing." *The Guardian*, September 30.

Karanfil, Nese. 2015. "Intelligence, Religious Affairs Set to Take Huge Share of Turkey's 2016 Budget." *Hurriyet Daily News*, October 13.

Keysar, Ariela, and Barry A. Kosmin, eds. 2008. *Secularism and Science in the 21st Century.* Hartford, CT: Institute for the Study of Secularism in Society and Culture.

Khan, Shehab, and Becca Meier. 2017. "Bangalore College Becomes First Indian University to Make Global Top 10." *Independent*, March 7.

Killian, Caitlin. 2007. "From a Community of Believers to an Islam of the Heart: 'Conspicuous' Symbols, Muslim Practices, and the Privatization of Religion in France." *Sociology of Religion* 68(30):305–320.

Kuru, Ahmet. 2009. *Secularism and State Policies Toward Religion: The United States, France, and Turkey*. Cambridge, UK: Cambridge University Press.

Lambert, Yves. 1994. "Un Paysage Religieux En Profonde Evolution." Pp. 123–162 in *Les Valeurs des Francais*, edited by H. Riffault. Paris: PUF.

Larson, Edward, and Edward Witham. 1997. "Scientists Are Still Keeping the Faith." *Nature* 386(3):435–436.

Leamaster, Reid J., and Anning Hu. 2014. "Popular Buddhists: The Relationship Between Popular Religious Involvement and Buddhist Identity in Contemporary China." *Sociology of Religion* 75(2):234–259.

Lee, Chengpang, and Myungsahm Suh. 2017. "State Building and Religion: Explaining the Diverged Path of Religious Change in Taiwan and South Korea, 1950–1980." *American Journal of Sociology* 123(2):465–509.

Lee, Joseph S. 2010. "Taiwan: Immigration to Taiwan." Pp. 335–351 in *Immigration Worldwide: Policies, Practices, and Trends*, edited by U. A. Segal, D. Elliott, and N. S. Mayadas. New York: Oxford University Press.

Le Parisien. 2015. "Réchauffement Climatique: Qu'en Disent Les Religions?" Retrieved July 31, 2017 (http://www.leparisien.fr/environnement/rechauffement-climatique-qu-en-disent-les-religions-28-11-2015-5321335.php#xtref=https%3A%2F%2Fwww.google.com%2F).

Leuba, James H. 1916. *The Belief in God and Immortality: A Psychological, Anthropological and Statistical Study*. Boston, MA: Sherman, French & Company.

Leuba, James H. 1934. *God or Man? A Study of the Value of God to Man*. London, UK: Kegan Paul, Trench & Trubner.

Levi Setti, Paolo E., and Pasquale Patrizio. 2012. "The Italian Experience of a Restrictive IVF Law: A Review." *Journal of Fertilization: In-Vitro* 2(1):164–169.

Liang, Delun. 2014. "Cooperating with Religious Mawan Park, Science Festival Is Blamed to Be Pseudo-Science." *Apple Daily*, March 2.

Life Conservationist Association. 2004. "Religious Welfare and Animal Protection: A Case of Live Animal Anatomy in High School." Retrieved May 7, 2018 (http://www.lca.org.tw/column/node/713).

Liu, Eric Y. 2009. "Beyond the West: Religiosity and the Sense of Mastery in Modern Taiwan." *Journal for the Scientific Study of Religion* 48(4):774–788.

Llana, Sara Miller. 2016. "As Demand for Secularism Grows in France, Believers Push Back at Work." *Christian Science Monitor*, November 7.

Lorenzi, Rossella. 2004. "Darwin Back in Italy's Schools." *The Scientist*, April 29.

Machamer, Peter, ed. 1998. *The Cambridge Companion to Galileo*. New York: Cambridge University Press.

Madan, Triloki N. 1987. "Secularism in Its Place." *Journal of Asian Studies* 46(4):747–759.

Madan, Triloki N. 1989. "Religion in India." *Daedalus* 118(4):114–146.

Mander, William. 2012. "Pantheism." In *The Stanford Encyclopedia of Philosophy*, Summer 2013 edition, edited by E. N. Zalta. Stanford, CA: Metaphysics Research

Lab, CSLI, Stanford University (https://plato.stanford.edu/archives/win2016/entries/pantheism/).

Martin, Daniel. 2012. "2030: The Year Britain Will Cease to Be a Christian Nation with the March of Secularism." *Daily Mail*, March 2.

Martinotti, Guido, and Alberto Giasanti. 1977. "The Robed Baron: The Academic Profession in the Italian University." *Higher Education* 6(2):189–207.

Mathews, Gordon, Eric Kit-wai Ma, and Tai-lok Lui. 2008. *Hong Kong, China: Learning to Belong to a Nation*. New York: Routledge.

McCutcheon, Russell T. 1997. *Manufacturing Religion: The Discourse on Sui Generis Religion and the Politics of Nostalgia*. New York: Oxford University Press.

McGrath, Alister, and Joanna Collicutt McGrath. 2010. *The Dawkins Delusion? Atheist Fundamentalism and the Denial of the Divine*. Downers Grove, IL: InterVarsity Press.

Mehta, Sharan, Elaine Howard Ecklund, and Bob Thomson. 2017. "The Intersection of Gender with Religion and Science." Paper Presented at the Annual Meeting of the Society for the Scientific Study of Religion, October 14, Washington, DC.

Merton, Robert. 1938. *Science, Technology and Society in Seventeenth-Century England*. Bruges: Saint Catherine Press.

Merton, Robert K. 1970. *Science, Technology, and Society in Seventeenth Century England*. New York: H. Fertig.

Miller, Jon D., Eugenie C. Scott, and Shinji Okamoto. 2006. "Public Acceptance of Evolution." *Science* 313(5788):765–766.

Mizikaci, Fatma. 2006. *Monographs on Higher Education: Higher Education in Turkey*. Bucharest: UNESCO European Centre for Higher Education.

Narlikar, Jayant V. 2001. "Vedic Astrology or Jyotirvigyan: Neither Vedic nor Vigyan." *Economic and Political Weekly* 36(24):2113–2115.

National Center for Science Education. 2004. "Decision to Remove Evolution from Italian Schools Reversed." Retrieved February 10, 2015 (https://ncse.com/news/2004/04/decision-to-remove-evolution-from-italian-schools-reversed-00562).

National Science Board. 2018. "Science and Engineering Indicators 2018." Retrieved April 26, 2018 (https://www.nsf.gov/statistics/2018/nsb20181/).

Nature. 2006. "Anti-Evolutionists Raise Their Profile in Europe." Retrieved February 10, 2015 (https://www.nature.com/articles/444406a).

Naughton, Barry, ed. 1997. *The China Circle: Economic and Technology in the PRC, Taiwan, and Hong Kong*. Washington, DC: Brookings Institute Press.

NDTV. 2014. "Kerala: Prayers to Be Held in Temple for Success of Mangalyaan." Retrieved April 18, 2018 (http://www.ndtv.com/south/kerala-prayers-to-be-held-in-temple-for-success-of-mangalyaan-668490).

Nolan, Mary Lee, and Sidney Nolan. 1989. *Christian Pilgrimage in Modern Western Europe*. Chapel Hill: University of North Carolina Press.

Numbers, Ronald. 1985. "Science and Religion." Pp. 59–80 in *Historical Writing on American Science: Perspectives and Prospects*, edited by S. G. Kohlstedt and M. W. Rossiter. Baltimore: Johns Hopkins University Press.

Numbers, Ronald L. 2006. *The Creationists: From Scientific Creationism to Intelligent Design*, expanded edition. Cambridge, MA: Harvard University Press.

Numbers, Ronald, ed. 2009. *Galileo Goes to Jail: And Other Myths About Science and Religion*. Cambridge, MA: Harvard University Press.

OECD. 2014. "Italy." In *OECD Science, Technology and Industry Outlook 2014*. OECD Publishing (http://dx.doi.org/10.1787/sti_outlook-2014-en).

OECD. 2016. "Turkey." In *OECD Science, Technology and Innovation Outlook 2016*. OECD Publishing (http://dx.doi.org/10.1787/sti_in_outlook-2016-en).

Office for National Statistics. 2013. "Full Story: What Does the Census Tell Us About Religion in 2011." Retrieved June 26, 2017 (http://webarchive.nationalarchives. gov.uk/20160105160709/http://www.ons.gov.uk/ons/dcp171776_310454.pdf).

Offord, Catherine. 2017. "Scientists to Protest Across India." *The Scientist*, August 7.

Organisation for Economic Co-operation and Development. 2016. "G20 Innovation Report 2016." Retrieved August 23, 2017 (https://www.oecd.org/sti/inno/G20-innovation-report-2016.pdf).

Overmyer, Daniel L. 2003. *Folk Buddhist Religion: Dissenting Sects in Late Traditional China*. Cambridge, MA: Harvard University Press.

Owen, David, and Tracy B. Strong, eds. 2004. *Max Weber, The Vocation Lectures: "Science as a Vocation," "Politics as a Vocation."* Indianapolis, IN: Hackett Publishing Company.

Pace, Enzo. 2006. "Religion as Communication: The Changing Shape of Catholicism in Europe." Pp. 37–50 in *Everyday Religion: Observing Modern Religious Lives*, edited by N. T. Ammerman. New York: Oxford University Press.

Pace, Enzo. 2007. "A Peculiar Pluralism." *Journal of Modern Italian Studies* 12(1):86–100.

Park, Alison, Caroline Bryson, Elizabeth Clery, John Curtice, and Miranda Philips. 2013. *British Social Attitudes: The 30th Report*. London, UK: NatCen Social Research.

PBS. 2001. "Roundtable: Science and Faith." Retrieved February 12, 2015 (http://www. pbs.org/wgbh/evolution/religion/faith/statement_01.html).

Peifer, Jared L., David R. Johnson, and Elaine Howard Ecklund. 2017. "The Moral Limits of the Market: Science Commercialization and Religious Traditions." *Journal of Business Ethics* 1–15.

Peterson, Gregory R. 2003. "Demarcation and the Scientistic Fallacy." *Zygon: Journal of Religion and Science* 38:751–761.

Pew Research Center. 2015. "Extremism Concerns Growing in West and Predominantly Muslim Countries." Retrieved May 1, 2018 (http://www.pewglobal.org/2015/07/ 16/extremism-concerns-growing-in-west-and-predominantly-muslim-countries/).

Pew Research Center. 2015. "U.S. Becoming Less Religious." Retrieved April 9, 2018 (http://www.pewforum.org/2015/11/03/u-s-public-becoming-less-religious/).

Phillips, Tom. 2015. "Hong Kong 'Umbrella Movement' Marks First Anniversary and Vows to Fight On." *The Guardian*, September 28.

Pianigiani, Gaia. 2010. "In Italy, Education Protests Spread." *New York Times*, November 26.

Polkinghorne, John C. 1998. *Science and Theology: An Introduction*. Minneapolis, MN: Fortress Press.

Prakash, Gyan. 1999. *Another Reason: Science and the Imagination of Modern India*. Princeton, NJ: Princeton University Press.

Prasannal, Laxmi. 2017. "Hundreds Join 'March for Science' in Thiruvananthapuram." *Times of India*, August 9.

Qu, Haiyuan. 2002. "New Religions in Taiwan (Taiwan Xin Xing Zong Jiao)." *Twenty-One Century* 73:103–113.

Rabasa, Angel, and F. Stephen Larrabee. 2008. *The Rise of Political Islam in Turkey.* Santa Monica, CA: RAND Corporation.

Ram, Arun. 2013. "ISRO Chief Seeks Divine Help for Mars Mission." *Times of India*, November 5.

Ramachandran, R. 2004. "Astrology on a Pedestal." *Frontline* 21(12).

Regnerus, Mark, David Sikkink, and Christian Smith. 1999. "Voting with the Christian Right: Contextual and Individual Patterns of Electoral Influence." *Social Forces* 77(4):1375–1401.

Religion News Service. 2016. "Catholic Priest's Appointment as University President Stuns French." Retrieved December 22, 2016 (http://religionnews.com/2016/12/22/catholic-priests-appointment-as-university-president-stuns-french/).

Reuters. 2011. "Muslim Creationists Tour France Denouncing Darwin." Retrieved July 28, 2017 (http://www.reuters.com/article/us-islam-creationism-france-idUSTRE74F3GC20110516).

Reuters. 2014. "Italian Court Overturns Divisive Ban on Donor Eggs, Sperm." Retrieved April 18, 2018 (https://www.reuters.com/article/us-italy-fertility/italian-court-overturns-divisive-ban-on-donor-eggs-sperm-idUSBREA381BG20140409?feedType=RSS&feedName=scienceNews).

Reuters. 2016. "Face au Terrorisme, Faire Changer la Peur de Cote, Dit Sarkozy." Retrieved July 26, 2017 (http://fr.reuters.com/article/topNews/idFRKCN10M0CX).

Rienzo, Cinzia, and Carlos Vargas-Silva. 2015. "Targeting Migration with Limited Control: The Case of the UK and the EU." *IZA Journal of European Labor Studies* 4(16):1–19.

Riesebrodt, Martin. 2010. *The Promise of Salvation: A Theory of Religion.* Chicago, IL: University of Chicago Press.

Rivers, Julian. 2010. *The Law of Organized Religions: Between Establishment and Secularism.* Oxford, UK: Oxford University Press.

Rooster GNN. 2015. "The Italian University and Its Aristocracy." Retrieved April 18, 2018 (https://rgnn.org/2015/11/14/the-italian-university-its-aristocracy/).

Ross, Edward A. 1901. *Social Control: A Survey of the Foundations of Order.* New York: Macmillan.

Saint-Blancat, Chantal. 2014. "Italy." Pp. 265–310 in *The Oxford Handbook of European Islam*, edited by J. Cesari. Oxford, UK: Oxford University Press.

Saint-Blancat, Chantal. 2017. "Making Sense of Scientific Mobility: How Italian Scientists Look Back on Their Trajectories of Mobility in the EU." *Higher Education Policy* 31(1):37–54.

Sbalchiero, Stefano. 2012. *Scienza e Spiritualità: Ruoli e Percezioni Della Ricerca Nel Mondo Contemporaneo.* Rome: Carocci.

Sbalchiero, Stefano, and Arjuna Tuzzi. 2016. "Scientists' Spirituality in Scientists' Words. Assessing and Enriching the Results of a Qualitative Analysis of In-depth Interviews by Means of Quantitative Approaches." *Quality and Quantity* 50(3):1333–1348.

Sbalchiero, Stefano, and Arjuna Tuzzi. 2017. "Italian Scientists Abroad in Europe's Scientific Research Scenario: High Skill Migration as a Resource for Development in Italy." *International Migration* 55(4):171–187.

Scheitle, Christopher P. 2011. "Religious and Spiritual Change in College: Assessing the Effect of a Science Education." *Sociology of Education* 84(2):122–136.

Scheitle, Christopher P., and Elaine Howard Ecklund. 2017. "Recommending a Child Enter a STEM Career: The Role of Religion." *Journal of Career Development* 44(3):251–265.

Scheitle, Christopher P., David R. Johnson, and Elaine Howard Ecklund. 2018. "Scientists and Religious Leaders Compete for Cultural Authority of Science." *Public Understanding of Science* 27(1):59–75.

Schilbrack, Kevin. 2010. "Religions: Are There Any?" *Journal of the American Academy of Religion* 78(4):1112–1138.

Science and Religion: Exploring the Spectrum. "About." Retrieved April 30, 2018 (http://sciencereligionspectrum.org/about-2/).

Scott, Eugenie C. 1997. "Antievolution and Creationism in the United States." *Annual Review of Anthropology* 26:263–289.

Sedghi, Ami. 2013. "UK Census: Religion by Age, Ethnicity and Country of Birth." *The Guardian*, May 16.

Sirkeci, Ibrahim, and Jeffrey H. Cohen. 2016. "Turkey's Purge Could Cause a Massive Brain Drain." *New Republic*, August 26.

Smith, Christian. 2017. *Religion: What It Is, How It Works, and Why It Matters.* Princeton, NJ: Princeton University Press.

Sorrell, Katherine, and Elaine Howard Ecklund. Unpublished Manuscript. "How UK Scientists Legitimize Religion Through Boundary Work."

Spencer, Herbert. 1904. *First Principles.* New York: J. A. Hill & Co.

Stark, Rodney. 2003. *On True God: Historical Consequences of Monotheism.* Princeton, NJ: Princeton University Press.

Stirrat, Michael, and R. Elisabeth Cornwell. 2013. "Eminent Scientists Reject the Supernatural: A Survey of the Fellows of the Royal Society." *Evolution, Education and Outreach* 6(33):1–5.

Stolz, Jorg, and Oliver Favre. 2005. "The Evangelical Milieu. Defining Criteria and Reproduction Across the Generations." *Social Compass* 52(2):169–183.

Subbarayappa, B. V. 2011. "Indic Religions." Pp. 195–209 in *Science and Religion around the World*, edited by J. H. Brooke and R. L. Numbers. New York: Oxford University Press.

Sun, Anna. 2013. *Confucianism as a World Religion: Contested Histories and Contemporary Realities.* Princeton, NJ: Princeton University Press.

Symonds, Richard. 1950. *The Making of Pakistan.* London: Faber and Faber Publishing.

Tattersall, Nick, and Seyhmus Cakan. 2015. "Eight Soldiers Killed, Istanbul Palace Attacked as Turkish Unrest Mounts." *Reuters*, August 19.

Taylor, Charles. 2007. *A Secular Age.* Cambridge, MA: Harvard University Press.

Thomas, Renny. 2016. "Being Religious, Being Scientific: Science, Religion and Atheism in Contemporary India." Pp. 140–157 in *Science and Religion: East and West*, edited by Y. Fehige. New York: Routledge.

Thomas, Renny. 2017. "Atheism and Unbelief Among Indian Scientists; Towards an Anthropology of Atheism(s)." *Society and Culture in South Asia* 3(1):45–67.

Thomas, Renny. 2018. "Beyond Conflict and Complementarity: Science and Religion in Contemporary India." *Science, Technology and Society* 23(1):47–64.

Thomas, Renny, and Robert M. Geraci. 2018. "Religious Rites and Scientific Communities: Ayudha Puja as 'Culture' at the Indian Institute of Science." *Zygon* 53(1):95–122.

Thompson, Evan. 2014. "Picking Holes in the Concept of Natural Selection." *BioScience* 64(4):355–358.

Tropman, John E. 2002. *The Catholic Ethic and the Spirit of Community*. Washington, DC: Georgetown University Press.

Tubitak. 2018. "National Science, Technology and Innovation Statistics of Turkey." Retrieved March 23, 2018 (https://www.tubitak.gov.tr/en/content-national-science-technology-and-innovation-statistics-of-turkey).

Tylor, Edward B. 1871. *Primitive Culture: Researches into the Development of Mythology, Philosophy, Religion, Art, and Custom*, Vol 1. London: John Murray.

Unsworth, Amy, and David Voas. 2018. "Attitudes to Evolution Among Christians, Muslims, and the Non-Religious in Britain: Differential Effects of Religious and Educational Factors." *Public Understanding of Science* 27(1):76–93.

Vaidyanathan, Brandon, David R. Johnson, Pamela Prickett, and Elaine Howard Ecklund. 2016. "Rejecting the Conflict Narrative: American Jewish and Muslim Views on Science and Religion." *Social Compass* 63(4):478–496.

Vatican Observatory. 2016. "Science, Religion, Society." Retrieved April 24, 2018 (http://www.vaticanobservatory.va/content/specolavaticana/en/science--religion--society.html).

Village, Andrew, and Leslie J. Francis. 2009. *The Mind of the Anglican Clergy: Assessing Attitudes and Beliefs in the Church of England*. Lewiston, NY: Edwin Mellen Press.

Vivekananda, Swami. 1964. *The Complete Works of Swami Vivekananda—Mayavati Memorial Edition*. Almora: Advaita Ashram.

Voas, David. 2014. "Does Education Develop or Diminish Spirituality in Taiwan?" *Journal for the Scientific Study of Religion* 53(3):556–574.

Voas, David. 2015. "Religious Involvement over the Life Course: Problems of Measurement and Classification." *Longitudinal and Life Course Studies* 6(2):212–227.

Voas, David, and Mark Chaves. 2016. "Is the United States a Counterexample to the Secularization Thesis?" *American Journal of Sociology* 121(5):1517–1556.

Vyas, Hetal. 2011. "Astrology Is a Science: Bombay HC." *Times of India*, February 3.

Wagner, Roger, and Andrew Briggs. 2016. *The Penultimate Curiosity: How Science Swims in the Slipstream of Ultimate Questions*. Oxford, UK: Oxford University Press.

Walker, Peter. 2012. "Free Schools Must Teach Evolution, Ministers Announce." *The Guardian*, November 30.

Wall, Mike. 2018. "Stephen Hawking to Be Interred in Westminster Abbey." *Scientific American*, March 21.

Wallace, David Foster. 2009. *This Is Water*. New York: Little, Brown and Company.

Wang, Shunmin. 1995. "The Studies on the Transition of Contemporary Taiwan Buddhism." *Hung-Hwa Buddhist Journal* 8:315–342.

Weber, Max. 1951. *The Religion of China: Confucianism and Taoism.* Glencoe, IL: Free Press.

Weber, Max. 2002. *The Protestant Ethic and the Spirit of Capitalism,* 3rd edition. Translated by Stephen Kalberg. New York: Roxbury Publishing Company.

Weise, Zia. 2017. "Long Arm of Turkey's Anti-Gulenist Purge." *Politico,* August 21.

Weller, Robert P. 1999. *Alternative Civilities: Democracy and Culture in China and Taiwan.* New York: Routledge.

White, John. 2004. "Should Religious Education Be a Compulsory School Subject?" *British Journal of Religious Education* 26(2):151–164.

Willaime, Jean-Paul. 1998. "Religious and Secular France Between Northern and Southern Europe." *Social Compass* 45(1):155–174.

Williams, James David. 2008. "Creationist Teaching in School Science: A UK Perspective." *Evolution: Education and Outreach* 1(1):87–95.

Withnall, Adam. 2014. "Pope Francis Declares Evolution and Big Bang Theory Are Real and God Is Not 'a Magician with a Magic Wand.'" *Independent,* October 28.

Woolf, Stuart. 2003. "On University Reform in Italy: Contradictions and Power Relations in Structure and Function." *Minerva* 41(4):347–363.

Wuthnow, Robert. 1985. "Science and the Sacred." Pp. 187–203 in *The Sacred in a Secular Age,* edited by P. E. Hammond. Berkeley, Los Angeles, and London: University of California Press.

Wuthnow, Robert. 2007. *America and the Challenges of Religious Diversity.* Princeton, NJ: Princeton University Press.

Yalçinkaya, M. Alper. 2015. *Learned Patriots: Debating Science, State, and Society in the Nineteenth-Century Ottoman Empire.* Chicago, IL: University of Chicago Press.

Yang, C. K. 1961. *Religion in Chinese Society: A Study of Contemporary Social Functions of Religion and Some of Their Historical Factors.* Berkeley: University of California Press.

Yang, Fenggang, and Anning Hu. 2012. "Mapping Chinese Folk Religion in Mainland China and Taiwan." *Journal for the Scientific Study of Religion* 51(3):505–521.

Yee, Pattie Luk Fong Yuk. 2005. "Managing Change in an Integrated School: A Hong Kong Hybrid Experience." *International Journal of Inclusive Education* 9(1):89–103.

Zhao, Suisheng, ed. 1999. *Across the Taiwan Strait: Mainland China, Taiwan, and the 1995–1996 Crisis.* New York: Routledge.

Zinnbauer, Brian J., Kenneth I. Pargament, Brenda Cole, Mark S. Rye, Eric M. Butter, Timothy G. Belavich, Kathleen M. Hipp, Allie B. Scott, and Jill L. Kadar. 1997. "Religion and Spirituality: Unfuzzying the Fuzzy." *Journal for the Scientific Study of Religion* 36(4):549–564.

Italic letters *f* and *t* after numbers indicate *figures* and *tables*, respectively

Abbott, Alison, 144
Académie des Sciences (France), 83
accommodation of religious
    beliefs, 21–22
  in France, 98–99, 100–1
  in Hong Kong, 183–86
  in India, 163–64, 166
  in Taiwan, 183–86
  in the US, 27–28
Aérosol, Jef (Jean-Francois Perroy), 79
agnosticism, 32
agnostic scientists, as opportunities
    for dialogue, 205. *See also* God:
    scientists' belief in)
Alexander, Denis, 68
American Association for the
    Advancement of Science, 26
Anglican Church. *See* Church of
    England
Anglican Communion, 19–20, 56–57,
    172. *See also* Church of England
Animal Protection Law (Taiwan), 173
animals, killing of, for research, 72, 95,
    173, 185, 189–90
Answers in Genesis, 67
assertive secularism. *See* France:
    assertive secularism in
astrology, Indian, 151, 159, 165

Ataturk, Mustafa Kemal, 125, 126,
    128–29, 138
atheists, religiously affiliated, 55
atheist scientists, 9, 10, 31–32, 33, 106,
    199, 205. *See also* God: scientists'
    belief in
Atlas of Creation (Oktar), 84

bai bai, 175–76, 186
belief in God. *See* God: belief in
Benedict XVI, 106, 119–20
Berlusconi government, 105
Biblical literalism, 35, 67, 90
big bang theory, 17, 19, 107
biology
  creationist views and, 17
  gender representation in, 16
  prestige of, 16
  public disputes and, 36
biotechnologies, moral opposition to, 17
Bose, J. C., 145–46
boundary pioneers, religious scientists
    as, 9–10, 204
Bourdieu, Pierre, 69
British Humanist Society, 59–60
Broun, Paul, 25
Brown, C. Mackenzie, 23–24
Buddhism, 68, 170, 172, 173, 181

cadaver experiments, 173
Cambridge University, 57
Casanova, José, 21–22
Catholic Church, 57
  biblical literalism and, 90–91
  climate change position of, 84–85
  evolution position of, 107, 115–16
  in France, 81–82
  Italian scientists and, 104–5, 106, 107,
    109, 116, 117
  in Italy, 106, 115–16
  opposing IVF and hESC research, 106
  support of, for science, 68–69, 104
Catholic social ethic, workplace morality
  and, 120–21
Centre National de la Recherche
  Scientifique (CNRS; France), 83,
  96, 98, 99, 100, 101, 297n84
Charlie Hebdo attacks, 95
China
  atheist teachings in, 173
  scientific establishment in, 170
Chinese circles, 18
Christianity
  American scientists' attitude
    toward, 2–3 (see also evangelicals;
    fundamentalists)
  influence of, in Hong Kong, 182–83, 193
Church of England, 19–20, 56–57, 68
Church of Scotland, 57
Chuuuttt! (Aérosol), 79, 80f
climate change, 2
  Catholic Church stance on, 84–85
  French activism and, 84–85
CNRS. See Centre National de la
  Recherche Scientifique
Cohen, Jeffrey, 144
collaboration perspective. See science–
  religion relationship: collaboration
  perspective of
Collins, Francis, 1–2
Comunione e Liberazione, 105, 122–23
conflict perspective. See science–religion
  relationship, conflict perspective on
Confucianism, 169
Cooley, Charles, 12

cosmos, as divinity, 152, 154
creation, debates over, 17, 100–1. See also
  evolution
  in France, 84
  in the UK, 59–60, 67–68
Creation or Evolution (Alexander), 68
cultural festivals, as religious
  events, 13–14

Daoism, 170
Darwin, Charles, 25, 150
data sample, construction of, 219–25
Davie, Grace, 57
Dawkins, Richard, 1–2, 55, 56, 59, 64,
  75–77, 153–54, 200
Deneken, Michel, 85
Dennett, Daniel, 55
Descartes, René, 81
Directorate for Religious Affairs
  (Diyanet; Turkey), 128–29
discrimination, religious, 53, 97–100,
  103, 142–43
disease-focused hRGTs, 26
dogma, as source of science–religion
  conflict, 91
Draper, John William, 28–29
Durkheim, Emile, 12

Ecklund, Elaine Howard, 1, 2–3, 23–24,
  29–30, 52–53
embryonic stem cell research, 2, 106
Emmanuel creation controversy (UK;
  2002), 59
Erdogan, Recep Tayyip, 125, 126, 129,
  141, 143–44
Europe, secularity of, 5–6
European Court of Human
  Rights, 126–27
European Union, opposition in, to
  scientific research, 2
evangelical Christians, 25, 26, 27, 36–
  37, 46, 59, 84
  Christian Right, 28
  scientists equating religion with, 37–
  38, 40, 44–45, 52–53, 200
Evans, John H., 17, 26

evolution, conflicts over, 17, 26
  Catholic Church's position on, 19,
    107, 115–16
  in France, 101
  in Hong Kong, 172, 183
  in India, 150, 160
  teaching of, 1, 2
  in Turkey, 126, 129, 134–35,
    136–37, 141
  in the UK, 58–59
  in the US, 26, 43–45

Faraday, Michael, 64
Federation of Indian Rationalist
    Associations, 145–46
Five Pillars of Islam, 130
folk religion (East Asian), 170, 171, 172,
    175, 182, 186–87, 192–93
France
  assertive secularism in, 6, 81–82,
    93–95, 102
  belief in God in, 87t
  Catholicism in, 81–82
  Charlie Hebdo attacks in, 95
  climate change activism in, 84–85
  creationism in, 84
  cultural context in, for science and
    religion, 81–83
  data collection in, 237–39, 238–39t
  foreign-born scientists in, 93
  intolerance in, for religious
    expression, 82–83
  Muslims in, 84, 96–101, 103
  Muslim scientists in, 82–83, 88
  public controversies in, relating to
    science, 89–90
  religion as private matter in, 93–95
  religiosity of, 19
  religious accommodation in,
    98–99, 100–1
  religious affiliation in, 86t
  religious attendance in, 87t, 111–12
  religious discrimination in, 97–100,
    103, 203
  religious dogma as concern in, 91
  religious scientists in, 101

religious symbolism in scientific
    workplaces, 97–100
science–religion conflict in, 84
science–religion dialogue in, 103
science's history in, 83
scientific community in, 6, 8–9, 196
scientific infrastructure in, 60–61,
    83, 146
scientific workplace in, 91–102, 184
scientists' belief in God in, 86
scientists' perspective in, on the
    science–religion relationship, 88–
    91, 89t, 196, 209, 209t
scientists' religiosity in, 85–87, 92, 109
scientists' religious affiliation in, 110–11
scientists' religious attendance in, 33
scientists' religious practice in, 86–87
scientists' religious views and beliefs
    in, 196
secularism of, 6, 19–20, 79–82,
    93 (see also France: assertive
    secularism of)
Francis (pope), 19, 107
French Council of the Muslim
    Faith, 84–85
fundamentalists, 59, 68, 69, 76, 78. See
    also evangelical Christians

Galileo, 104
Gandhi, Mahatma, 149
Garelli, Franco, 6–7, 106
gender
  religiosity and, 64
  and view of the science–religion
    conflict, 34, 36
genetically modified organisms, 40
Geraci, Robert, 162
Germany, scientific infrastructure
    in, 60–61
GMOs. See genetically modified
    organisms
God
  descriptions of, 32, 152, 154
  natural phenomena explained
    through, 67
  science's implications for, 26

God, belief in
  in France, 87t
  among France's scientists, 86
  in Hong Kong, 177t, 287n16
  among Hong Kong's scientists, 177–78
  in India, 153t, 287n16
  among India's scientists, 153–54
  in Italy, 111t
  among Italy's scientists, 111
  in Taiwan, 177t
  among Taiwan's scientists, 177–78
  in Turkey, 132t
  among Turkey's scientists, 132, 133
  in the UK, 63t
  among UK scientists, 62–63, 86
  in the US, 31t
  among US scientists, 86
God Delusion, The (Dawkins), 1–2, 75–76
Gould, Stephen Jay, 10, 20–21, 113–14
Gulen movement (Turkey), 301–2n4

Harris, Sam, 55
Harun Yahya. See Oktar, Adnan
Hawking, Stephen, 16
hESC research. See human embryonic
  stem cell research
Higher Education Council (YÖK;
  Turkey), 142–43, 144
higher power
  belief in, 32, 153, 154, 177
  perception of, 129–30
Hill, Jonathan, 52–53
Hill, Peter, 14
Hinduism
  festivals in, 161–63
  pantheism in, 158
  religion–science interface and, 1
  scientific knowledge within, 150
History of Hindu Chemistry (Ray), 150
Hitchens, Christopher, 153–54
Hollande, François, 84–85
Hong Kong
  belief in God or gods in, 177t, 287n16
  as Chinese society, 169
  Christian elite in, scientists'
    perception of, 170
  Christian history in, 170

Christianity's influence in, 175, 177,
  182–83, 193
data collection in, 232–34, 233–34t
evolution as issue in, 172, 183
immigration and, 171, 173–74, 179,
  309n29
monotheism in, 177
religion in, as resource for
  overcoming challenges, 187, 188
religiosity of, 19, 171, 192–93
religious affiliation in, 174t
religious attendance in, 177–79, 178t
religious context in, 171
religious freedom in, 171
research ethics in, 188, 189–90
science infrastructure in, 169
science–religion debates in, 172
scientific community in, 7–9, 18,
  169–70, 198
scientific infrastructure in, 146
scientific workplace in, 182–86,
  190–91, 193
scientists' belief about God in, 177–78
scientists' emigration from, 170
scientists' perspective in, on the
  science–religion relationship,
  156–57, 179–81, 180t, 192, 198, 215,
  215t, 216t
scientists' religiosity in, 23–24, 173
scientists' religious affiliation in,
  173–75, 177–78
scientists' religious views and beliefs
  in, 198
scientists' understanding of religion
  in, 175–76
spirituality in, 176
hRGTs. See human reproductive genetic
  technologies
Human Fertilisation and Embryology
  Act of 1990 (UK), 60
human reproductive genetic
  technologies, opposition to, 26
humans, specialness of, 17, 26

immigration, 203
  Hong Kong and, 171, 173–74, 179, 309n29
  religion and, 291n19, 309n29

science infrastructure's effect on, 20
  to Taiwan, 170, 179
  to the UK, 56, 58–59, 93
  to the US, 30–31, 52–53
independence perspective. *See* science–
    religion relationship, independence
    (separation) perspective on
India
  astrology in, 151, 159, 165
  belief in God in, 153t, 287n16
  cultural celebrations in, 13–14
  data collection in, 229–31, 229–30t
  evolution accepted in, 150, 160
  institutional sanctioning in, of
      science–religion overlap, 159–60
  pantheism in, 154
  religion in, 149, 167–68
  religious accommodation in,
      163–64, 166
  religious affiliation in, 152t
  religious attendance in, 156t, 156
  religious festivals in, 161–63
  religious rituals in, 145–48, 159–60
  science curriculum in, 2, 149
  science and religion intertwined in,
      145–48, 154, 167–68, 192–93
  science and religion as public issues
      in, 150–51, 166–67
  scientific community in, 7–9, 159–60,
      163–64, 166, 198
  scientific infrastructure in, 145,
      146, 166
  scientific workplace in, 160–61,
      163–64, 165
  scientists' belief in God in, 153–54
  scientists' compartmentalization
      in, 148
  scientists' family life in, 167
  scientists' perspective in, on the
      science–religion relationship, 146–
      47, 156–58, 157t, 164, 179, 180–81,
      198, 214–15t
  scientists' religion in, 152–56, 198,
      214, 214t
  scientists' religious affiliation in, 152–53
  scientists' religious participation
      in, 161–63
  scientists' religious practices
      in, 155–56
  scientists' spiritual identity in, 214, 214t
  secularism in, 149, 150, 163, 166
Indian Academy of Sciences, 159
Indian Empire, partition of, 149
Indian Institute of Science, 166
Indian Space Research Organization,
    145–46, 159
Indian University Grants
    Commission, 151
institutional sanctioning, of science–
    religion overlap, 159–60
Intergovernmental Panel on Climate
    Change (UN), 84–85
interview guides, 275–79
in vitro fertilization, 60, 106–7
Islam
  encouraging scientific education, 158
  in France, 82–83 (*see also* Muslims: in
      France)
  Golden Rule in, 138
  as motivator for learning, 137
  politicization of, 143–44
  rituals of, 130, 139
  in Turkey, 125–27, 128–29, 132,
      134–35, 140–44
  in the UK, 54, 72–73, 74–75, 77–78
Islamic Society (UK), 70
ISRO. *See* Indian Space Research
    Organization
Italy
  atheist scientists in, 106
  austerity measures in, 105
  beauty and science in, 121–22
  belief in God in, 111t
  Catholicism and science overlapping
      in, 104–5, 106
  Catholicism's presence in, 104–5, 106,
      107–8, 115–16
  cultural context in, for science and
      religion, 105–6
  data collection in, 231–32, 231–32t
  higher education in, 122–23
  religion in, for scientists,
      107–9, 116–18
  religiosity in, 19, 110t

Italy (*cont.*)
    religious affiliation in, 6–7, 110*t*
    religious modernity in, 106
    religious networks in, 122–23
    religious service attendance in, 112*t*
    research in, involving fertilized
        human eggs, 106–7
    scientific community in, 6–7, 8–9,
        20, 104–6, 115, 119*t*, 122–23, 196, 197
    scientific workplace in, 117–21
    scientists emigrating from, 105
    scientists in, and the Catholic Church,
        104–5, 106, 107, 109, 116, 117
    scientists' belief in God in, 111
    scientists' perspective in, on the
        science–religion relationship, 112–
        17, 113*t*, 119*t*, 123–24, 197, 211–12*t*
    scientists' religiosity in, 109–10,
        111–12, 116–18
    scientists' religious attendance
        in, 111–12
    scientists' religious and spiritual
        identity in, 210, 210*t*
    scientists' religious tradition in, 110–11
    scientists' religious views and beliefs
        in, 196
    scientists' spirituality in, 121
    spirituality in, for scientists,
        108–9, 116
    state-church relationship in, 19–20
    stem cell research in, 119
IVF. *See* in vitro fertilization

Jansenism, 81
John Paul II, 107
Journal des Sçavans, 83

Kaden, Tom, 55
Kuru, Ahmet, 6, 27–28, 81–82
Kuyper, Abraham, 36–37

laïcité, 6, 79–80, 81–82, 83, 85, 93–95,
    97–98, 102–3, 128–29
Language of God, The (Collins), 1–2
Larrabee, F. Stephen, 128–29
La Sapienza University (Rome), 119–20

Lavoisier, Antoine, 81
Leuba, James, 2–3, 23–24, 29
Liberty University, 48
Life Conservation Association
    (Taiwan), 173
Long, Elizabeth, 2
Louis XIV, 83

Macron, Emmanuel, 83
magisteria, nonoverlapping, 10, 20–21,
    35, 66, 113–15, 137
March for Science (India), 166
McGrath, Alister, 55
Meditations on First Philosophy
    (Descartes), 81
Merton, Robert K., 57
Moratti, Letizia, 107
Muslims, in France, 96–101, 103. *See
    also* Islam

Nair, Madhavan, 145–46
nations
    ideology of, and effect on
        science, 3–5
    religious character of, 3, 4–5
Nehru, Jawaharlal, 149
New Atheists, 55, 56, 59, 199, 200
Numbers, Ronald, 28–29

Oktar, Adnan (Harun Yahya), 84
On the Origin of Species (Darwin), 150
Orthodox Buddhist Movement, 170, 172
Ottoman Empire, 127
Oxford University, 57

pantheism, 154, 158
Pascal, Blaise, 81
passive secularism, 27–28
Pew Religious Landscape Study, 27
physics
    gender representation in, 16
    moral tensions with, 17
    prestige of, 16
    public disputes and, 36
    religion and, 17, 134–35
Playing God (Evans), 26

Polkinghorne, John, 55
population, religiosity of, 19
Positive Sciences of the Hindus, The
    (Seal), 150
Prakash, Gyan, 150
prayer
    frequency of, in Turkey, 125, 134, 134*t*
    in the scientific workplace, 72–73,
        74–75, 139, 142–43, 146, 159–60,
        161, 201
Protestant Federation of France, 84–85
Protestants, 25. *See also* evangelicals;
    fundamentalists
    conservative, 17, 26–27, 44–45
    in the United States, 27
Puritanism, 57

Quakerism, 68

Rabasa, Angel, 128–29
Radhakrishnan, Koppillil, 145–46
RASIC. *See* Religion Among Scientists
    in International Context
Ray, Prafulla Chandra, 150
religion
    classification struggle and, 69
    contradicting physical
        information, 67
    definitions and descriptions of, 11–12,
        13, 61, 108, 116–17, 129–31, 138, 139,
        148, 157, 167–68, 175–76, 181
    discarding of, 13
    ethical decisions and, 201–2
    flexible forms of, 68
    functional approaches to, 12–13
    ideas from, used to advance science's
        pedagogical objectives, 43–44
    nontheistic, 171
    overcoming challenges
        through, 186–88
    overgeneralization about, 203
    practice-centered definition of, 13
    research and, 42, 72, 74
    in the scientific workplace, 10, 21–22,
        101–2 (*see also individual nation
        listings*)

science's impact on, 3–5
spirituality and, 15, 108–9 (*see also*
    spirituality)
US scientists' negative attitude
    toward, 46–49, 52–53
Religion Among Scientists in
    International Context, 219
*Religion vs. Science: What Religious
    People Really Think* (Ecklund and
    Scheitle), 52–53, 200
religiosity
    changes in, 57–58
    in Chinese societies, 171
    in France, 19
    gender differences in, 16
    in Hong Kong, 19, 171, 192–93
    in Italy, 19, 110*t*
    science's influence on, 23–24
    in Taiwan, 19, 171, 192–93
    in Turkey, 19, 128
    in the UK, 19, 57–58
    in the US, 19, 27, 128
religiosity scale, 19
religiosity of scientists
    in France, 85–87, 92, 109
    in Hong Kong, 23–24, 173
    in Italy, 109–10, 111–12, 116–18
    in Taiwan, 23–24, 173
    in Turkey, 23–24, 131–32
    in the UK, 63, 64, 85
    in the US, 26–27, 85, 109
religious adherence, 24
religious affiliation, 19
    in France, 86*t*
    in Hong Kong, 174*t*
    in India, 152*t*
    in Taiwan, 174*t*
    in Turkey, 131*t*
    in the UK, 61*t*
    in the US, 30*t*
religious affiliation of scientists
    in France, 85–86
    in Hong Kong, 173–75, 177–78
    in India, 152–53
    in Taiwan, 174–75, 177–78
    in Turkey, 131–32

religious affiliation of scientists (*cont.*)
  in the UK, 56, 85
  in the US, 85
religious culture, normalization
  of, 202–3
religious discrimination, 203. *See also*
  discrimination: religious
religious doctrine, and conceptions of
  God, 32–33
religious ethics, influence of, 101–2
religious festivals, 161–63
religious fundamentalism, 200–1, *See*
  also fundamentalists
religious groups, mockery of (US),
  39, 46–47
religious identity, compartmentalization
  of, 21–22, 37–39, 94, 139–40,
  148, 156–57
religious networks, influence of, on
  Italian science, 122–23
religious pluralism, scientific
  workplaces and, 202–3
religious practices of scientists. *See*
  individual nations' listings
religious rituals, 24, 157–58, 159–60
religious scientists, 9–10, 21–22, 35
  as boundary pioneers, 204
  career decisions of, 49–52
  commitment of, to religious
    organizations, 51–52
  discrimination against, 46, 47–49, 53
  openness of, to science–faith
    discussions, 204–5
  separation by, 37–39, 66
  in the US, 37–39
religious service attendance
  in France, 87t, 111–12
  in Hong Kong, 177–79, 178t
  in India, 156t, 156
  in Taiwan, 177–79, 178t
  in Turkey, 133t
  in the UK, 61t, 111–12
  in the US, 33t, 111–12
religious service attendance, of
  scientists
  in France, 33

  in India, 156
  in Italy, 111–12
  in Turkey, 133
  in the UK, 33, 62, 64
  in the US, 33–34
religious symbols, in scientists'
  offices, 161
religious traditions, 19, 24
Religious Understandings of Science
  survey (US), 29–30
reproductive issues, in the UK, 60
research, religion affecting, 42, 72, 74,
  188–90. *See also* animals: killing
  of, for research; biotechnologies;
  cadaver experiments; embryonic
  stem cell research; genetically
  modified organisms; human
  reproductive genetic technologies;
  in vitro fertilization
Riesebrodt, Martin, 13–14
Ross, Edward, 11

Sarkozy, Nicolas, 83
Sbalchiero, Stefano, 109
Scheitle, Christopher P., 23–24, 41, 52–53
Schilbrack, Kevin, 13–14
science
  beauty in, 121–22
  Catholicism overlapping with, in Italy,
    104–5, 106
  ethical decisions about, religion and,
    166–67, 201–2
  globalization of, 4
  independent of religion, 9–10, 165
  influence of, on religiosity, 23–24
  organizational features of, 16
  religion conflicting with, 36–37, 90–
    91 (*see also* biblical literalism)
  religion's impact on, 3–5, 21–22
  religious groups as minority in, 46
  religious response to, 17
  secularization and, 2
  spirituality in, 9
  suspicion of, 37, 40, 42
science infrastructure. *See also*
  individual nations' listings

components of, 20
global, 30–31
immigration and, 20
science-consistent spirituality, 9
science–religion relationship
    debates in, context for, 19
    dialogue in, 41–42, 101
    East–West divide in perception of,
        199–201
    fostering of, 22–23, 124
    Hinduism and, 1
    incompatibility of, 55–56
    scientists' perceptions of, 16 (see also
        individual nations' listings)
    social scientific approach to,
        10, 205–6
science–religion relationship,
        collaboration perspective on, 9–10
    in France, 88
    in Hong Kong, 180–81
    in India, 180–81
    in Italy, 113–14
    possibilities for, 204–6
    in Taiwan, 180–81
    in Turkey, 135–36, 137, 156–57, 158
    in the US, 36
science–religion relationship, conflict
        perspective on
    East–West divide in, 199–201
    in France, 89–91
    in Hong Kong, 179–80
    in India, 156–58, 179
    in Italy, 112–13
    presumption of, 23–24
    statistical table for, 210t
    in Taiwan, 179–80
    in Turkey, 135–37
    in the UK, 65
    in the US, 28–29, 34–37
    as Western construct, 7–8, 9–10, 90
science–religion relationship,
        independence (separation)
        perspective on, 20–21
    in France, 88–89, 93–95
    in Hong Kong, 180, 190–91
    in India, 156–57, 165

in Italy, 104–14
    in Taiwan, 180, 190, 191–92
    in Turkey, 135–36, 137
    in the UK, 65–68
    in the US, 35–36, 37–39
scientific community. See also individual
        nations' listings
    pluralism of, 20
    religiosity of, 8–9
Scientific and Technological Research
        Council (Turkey; TÜBİTAK),
        126, 144
scientific workforce, religiosity of, 20
scientific workplace. See also individual
        nations' listings
    conflict in, 141
    religion entering, 10, 201
    religious pluralism and, 202–3
    religious symbolism in, 97–100
scientists
    compared with the general
        public, 22–24
    distrust of, 37, 41, 48–49
    helping ethic among, 120
    on public attitudes about science
        (US), 40–42
    public's perception of, Dawkins's
        influence on, 76–77
    religious language of, 201–2
    social contract of, 40
    soft secularism among, 5–6
    spirituality of, 2–3
    transnational community of, 22
Scopes trial (US), 28–29
Seal, Brajendranath, 150
secularism
    assertive (France), 6, 19–20, 79–82,
        93–95, 102
    in India, 149, 150, 163, 166
    soft, 5–6
    in Turkey, 19–20, 128–29
    in the UK, 54, 59, 70–71
secularization
    individual-level, 23, 24
    private religion and, 21–22
    science and, 2

selection-focused hRGTs, 26
separation perspective. *See* science–
    religion relationship, independence
    (separation) perspective on
Sheng Kung Hui Welfare Council
    (Hong Kong), 172
Singh, Manmohan, 159–60
Sirkeci, Ibrahim, 144
Smith, Christian, 13–14
soft secularism, 5–6
Spencer, Herbert, 11
spiritual atheists, 2–3
spiritual but not religious, 9, 50,
    106, 108–9
spirituality
    definitions and descriptions of, 14–15,
        61, 109, 130–31
    in Eastern regions, 176
    institutionalized, 15
    Italian scientists on, 108–9, 116
    religion and, 15, 108–9, 139
    in science, 9
    science-consistent, 205
state-church relationship, 19–20
students, religious accommodation
    for, 100–1
surveys
    English questionnaire, 243–74
    procedures and response rates for,
        219–41t

Tagore, Rabindranath, 146–47
Taiwan
    belief in God or gods in, 177t
    as Chinese society, 169
    Christian history in, 170
    data collection in, 234–35, 234–36t
    folk religion in, 175–76, 177–78,
        186–87, 192–93
    immigration to, 174, 179
    polytheism in, 177
    religion in, as resource for
        overcoming challenges, 186–88
    religions practiced in, 170, 171, 172
    religiosity of, 19, 171, 192–93
    religious affiliation in, 174t

religious attendance in, 177–79, 178t
religious context in, 171
religious freedom in, 171
research ethics in, 188–90
science infrastructure in, 169
science–religion debates in, 172, 173
scientific community in, 7–9, 18,
    169–70, 198
scientific workplace in, 183–86, 190,
    191–92, 193
scientists' belief about God in, 177–78
scientists' emigration from, 170
scientists' perspective in, on the
    science–religion relationship, 113,
    156–57, 179–81, 180t, 192, 198, 215,
    216t, 217t
scientists' religiosity in, 23–24, 173
scientists' religious affiliation in,
    174–75, 177–78
scientists' religious views and beliefs
    in, 198
scientists' understanding of religion
    in, 175–76
spirituality in, 176
Tata Institute of Fundamental Research
    (India), 159–60
Thomas, Renny, 157–58, 162
Tropman, John E., 120
TÜBİTAK. *See* Scientific and
    Technological Research Council
    (Turkey)
Turkey
    belief in God in, 132t
    brain drain from, 144
    data collection in, 239–41, 240–41t
    education system in, 126–28,
        129, 142–43
    evolution as issue in, 126, 129, 134–35,
        136–37, 141
    Islam in, 7, 125–27, 128–29, 132,
        134–35, 143–44
    prayer frequency in, 134t
    religiosity of, 19, 128
    religious affiliation in, 131t
    religious discrimination against
        scientists in, 46

religious influence in, rising, 19–20
religious service attendance in, 133*t*
scientific community in, 7, 8–9, 20,
126–27, 135*t*, 141*t*, 143–44, 197
scientific infrastructure in,
127–28, 144
scientific workplace in, 118,
138–44, 184
scientists' belief in God in, 132, 133
scientists' perceived impact of science
on religion, 212, 212*t*
scientists' perspective in, on the
science–religion relationship, 129,
134–37, 135*t*, 138–42, 141*t*, 156–57,
180–81, 197, 213*t*
scientists' prayer frequency in, 134
scientists' religion in, 129–34
scientists' religiosity in, 23–24, 131–32
scientists' religious affiliation
in, 131–32
scientists' religious attendance in, 133
scientists' religious views and beliefs
in, 197
secularity of, 19–20, 128–29
as secular Muslim nation, 125, 143–44
spirituality in, for scientists, 130–31
Turkish Academy of Sciences, 126–27
Tylor, Edward, 11
Tzu Chi University (Taiwan), 173

United Kingdom
belief in God in, 63*t*
biological research opposed in, 17
biologists in, 64
celebrity scientists in, 78
challenges in, to science, 2
Christianity's historical role in, 56–57
creationism debate in, 59–60, 67–68
data collection in, 225–29, 226–28*t*
Dawkins's effect in, 75–77
demographics in, changes in, 56
evolution debate in, 58–59
foreign-born scientists in, 56, 93
immigration in, 6, 58–59
Islam's challenge in, 77–78
Islam's influence on science in, 54

moderate religions' contribution
in, 69–70
Muslim scientists in, 74–75
Muslim students in, 72–73, 74
national curriculum in, 59–60
New Atheists in, 55, 56, 59
physicists in, 64
population growth in, 58–59
public view in, of the science–religion
relationship, 78
religion as private matter in, 70–71, 72
religiosity of, 19, 57–58
religious affiliation in, 61*t*
religious attendance in, 111–12
religious diversity in, 58
religious fundamentalists in, 59
religious hostility in, 74–75
religious landscape in, changes to, 54
religious minorities in, 4–5
religious participation in, 56–58
religious pluralism in, 20
religious service attendance in, 62*t*
reproductive issues in, 60
science–religion dialogue in, 34,
59–60, 70
science–religion perspectives in,
variety of, 55, 56
science–religion relationship in,
56–58, 59
science–religion separation in, 65–
68, 70–71, 72
scientific community in, 6, 8–9, 195
scientific infrastructure in, 60–61, 146
scientific work, religion's presence
in, 72–73
scientific workplace in, 70–75, 183
scientists' belief in God in, 62–63, 86
scientists' family life in, 64
scientists' friendliness of, to religious
values, 63
scientists' perspective in, on the
science–religion relationship, 65–
78, 65*t*, 164, 195–96, 208, 208–9*t*
scientists' religion and spirituality
in, 61
scientists' religiosity in, 63, 64, 85

United Kingdom (*cont.*)
  scientists' religious affiliation in, 56, 61, 62, 64, 110–11
  scientists' religious attendance in, 33, 62, 64
  scientists' religious participation in, 61, 64
  scientists' religious views and beliefs in, 195
  secularization in, 54, 59, 70–71
  state-church relationship in, 19–20
  (*see also* Church of England)
United States
  agnosticism in, 32
  atheist scientists in, 31–32, 33
  belief in God in, 31*t*
  biological research opposed in, 17
  Christian Right in, 28
  creationist views in, 52–53
  data collection in, 236–37, 236–37*t*
  evangelicals in, 26–27
  evolution debate in, 26, 52–53
  foreign-born scientists in, 30–31, 93
  opposition in, to hRGTs, 26
  passive secularism in, 27–28
  progressive religious groups in, 40
  public attitude toward science in, scientists' view of, 40–42
  religion–science debates in, 2
  religiosity of, 19, 27, 128
  religious affiliation in, 30*t*
  religious attendance in, 111–12
  religious discrimination in, 46, 47–49, 203
  religious groups' influence in, 28
  religious minorities in, 4–5
  religious population of, 5–6
  religious scientists separating religion and science in, 37–39
  religious service attendance in, 33*t*
  religious students in, 42–45
  religious switching in, 27
  science education in, 44, 45

science infrastructure in, 28
science–religion conflict in, 25, 28–30, 34–37
scientific community in, 5–6, 8–9, 20, 30–31, 194–95
scientific infrastructure in, 146
scientific workplace in, 39–53, 118, 184
scientists' belief in God in, 31–33, 86
scientists' negative attitude in, toward religion, 46–49, 52–53
scientists' perspective on the science–religion relationship, 34*t*, 164, 195, 207, 207–8*t*
scientists' religiosity in, 26–27, 85, 109
scientists' religious affiliation in, 30–31
scientists' religious attendance in, 33–34
scientists' religious views and beliefs in, 29, 195
state-church relationship in, 19–20
suspicion in, about science, 40, 41, 42
University of Strasbourg, 85

Valls, Manuel, 83
Vardy Foundation, 59
Vatican Observatory, 104
Vishwakarma Puja, festival of, 162
Vivekananda (swami), 146–47, 150
vocation, 36–37

Wallace, David Foster, 167–68
Warnock, Mary, 60
Warnock report (UK), 60
Weber, Max, 2
White, Andrew Dickson, 28–29
Willaime, Jean Paul, 79, 82
workplace morality, Catholic social ethic and, 120–21
Wuthnow, Robert, 27

Yalçinkaya, Alper, 127